Harry Houdini
A Magical Life

written by Elizabeth MacLeod

Kids Can Press

To John Venner, with best wishes for a magical life

Consultant: David Ben, magic consultant

Sources: In researching this book I found the following books helpful: *Spellbinder: The Life of Harry Houdini* by Tom Lalicki and *Houdini!!!* by Kenneth Silverman.

Acknowledgments: Special thanks to David Ben for reviewing my manuscript and sharing his incredible knowledge about magic and Harry. I so appreciate the time he took to read the book and answer my questions.

Chris McClymont is a terrific editor and friend. Many thanks for the care she put into this book and for the fun meetings. Thanks also to series editor Valerie Wyatt for her help.

It is always wonderful to work with designer Karen Powers and I'm grateful to her for her incredibly creative solutions. I'm always amazed by Patricia Buckley's diligence and imagination in suggesting and obtaining photos. I'm very lucky to have such a terrific team working on this series of books.

Thanks also to the entire Kids Can Press team, especially Sheila Barry, Karen Boersma, Valerie Hussey and everyone in the Technical Services Department.

Many thanks to Dad, John and Douglas for their continuing support. And very special thanks and love to Paul, who brings real magic into my life.

Kids Can Press acknowledges the financial support of the Government of Ontario, through the Ontario Media Development Corporation's Ontario Book Initiative; the Ontario Arts Council; the Canada Council for the Arts; and the Government of Canada, through the BPIDP, for our publishing activity.

Published in Canada by	Published in the U.S. by
Kids Can Press Ltd.	Kids Can Press Ltd.
29 Birch Avenue	2250 Military Road
Toronto, ON M4V 1E2	Tonawanda, NY 14150

www.kidscanpress.com

Series editor: Valerie Wyatt
Edited by Christine McClymont
Designed by Karen Powers
Printed and bound in China

The hardcover edition of this book is smyth sewn casebound.
The paperback edition of this book is limp sewn with a drawn-on cover.

CM 05 0 9 8 7 6 5 4 3 2 1
CM PA 05 0 9 8 7 6 5 4 3 2 1

Kids Can Press is a **Corus**™ Entertainment company

National Library of Canada Cataloguing in Publication Data

MacLeod, Elizabeth
    Harry Houdini : a magical life / written by Elizabeth MacLeod.

Includes index.

ISBN 1-55337-769-9 (bound).   ISBN 1-55337-770-2 (pbk.)

1. Houdini, Harry, 1874–1926 — Juvenile literature. 2. Magicians — United States — Biography — Juvenile literature. 3. Escape artists — United States — Biography — Juvenile literature. I. Title.

GV1545.H8M33 2005   j793.8'092   C2004-906026-0

Photo credits

Every reasonable effort has been made to trace ownership of, and give accurate credit to, copyrighted material. Information that would enable the publisher to correct any discrepancies in future editions would be appreciated.

Abbreviations
t = top; b = bottom; c = center; l = left; r = right

Bettmann/Corbis/Magma: 9 (tr), 11 (l); **Chicago Historical Society/ICH-22859:** (cl); **Library of Congress:** 1, 3 (all), 4 (l), 5 (cl, tl, br), 6, 7 (cl, tr, cr, br), 8, 9 (bl, br), 10, 11 (tr, cr), 12, 13 (tl, tr, br), 14, 15 (all), 16, 17 (bl, tl, r), 19 (tr), 20 (all), 21 (all), 22, 23 (b, tr, cr), 25 (all), 27 (bl, tl, tr, br), 28 (b), 29 (all); **National Oceanic and Atmospheric Administration:** 17 (cl); **Outagamie Historical Society/Appleton, WI:** 4 (r), 18, 19 (b), 23 (tl), 26, 28 (t); **Harry Ransom Humanities Center/ The University of Texas at Austin/Performing Arts Collection:** 19 (l); **State Library of Victoria, Australia, H88.50/5:** 7 (bl); **The Museum of the City of New York:** 19 (cr); **The Museum of the City of New York/ Bandit's Roost by Jacob A. Riis/ The Jacob A. Riis Collection:** 9 (tl).

Contents

Meet Harry Houdini

"Never try to fool children. They expect nothing and therefore see everything."
— Harry

One of Harry's most amazing stunts was the Milk Can Escape. He was handcuffed, chained and squished into a milk can full of water. Then he had to escape from this solid metal container before he drowned.

Have you ever been dazzled by a magic show? Most magicians get started on their careers after watching a magician perform. That's how the most famous magician ever, Harry Houdini, got hooked on magic.

Walking Through a Brick Wall, Water-Torture Cell Escape, Needle Swallowing — these are just a few of the magic tricks and escapes Harry performed to amaze audiences around the world. Some of his tricks were so difficult and dangerous that few of today's best-trained magicians dare attempt them.

Behind Harry's magic was a lot of hard work and training. He wasn't a big man, but he exercised and became very strong. He was always practicing and thinking of new escapes and tricks. Although Harry didn't have much education, he taught himself everything he needed to know to excel as a magician.

Harry thought he was a great magician and wasn't afraid to say so. He also loved a good story and sometimes even made up things so he'd sound more amazing. Harry's stories were so convincing that it can be difficult to know the truth about his life.

Read on to find out what *is* known about Harry's life. How did he become the world's best-known magician? Could he actually escape from handcuffs? Was he able to make an elephant disappear? What was Harry really like?

Harry Houdini

Harry was born Ehrich Weisz (later spelled Weiss), but he changed his name to Harry Houdini when he began performing.

There weren't many who knew the secrets behind my tricks. My wife, Bess, was one of the few people I trusted.

EUROPE'S ECLIPSING SENSATION
HOUDINI
THE WORLD'S HANDCUFF KING & PRISON BREAKER

NOTHING CAN HO... HOUDI... A PRISO...

Harry's success was amazing for his time. In the early 1900s, people had little money to spend on shows, and there were no TVs or national newspapers to help make people famous.

Standing less than 168 cm (5 ft., 6 in.) tall, Harry had blazing blue eyes and thick, curly black hair.

What an incredible performer and showman! Harry could create a sense of wonder around his tricks that dazzled audiences.

HOW DOES HOUDINI DO WHAT HOUDINI DOES?

HOUDINI---The name conjures up Jails, Prisons, Handcuffs, Bolts, and Bars, for he is the creator of that branch of work. A daring man, skillful, careful entertainer, and never having met with defeat, he is open to accept any challenge during his engagement at the Orpheum Theatre the coming week, that will interest the general public. When not accepting a challenge, during his regulation performance, he will introduce his original invention, "The Chinese Water Torture Cell." Houdini is the only legitimate jailbreaker in the world and was proclaimed by Theodore Roosevelt "The Most Stupendous Mystifier I Have Ever Seen." Let us hope he will receive some interesting challenges, and that our local carpenters, locksmiths and other craftsmen will construct something from which Houdini cannot extricate himself.

The Genius of Escape
HOUDINI
Who Will Startle and Amaze

Orpheum MAIN 4161
Orpheum Circuit Vaudeville
ONE WEEK ONLY
Starting Saturday Matinée
MAY 5th
SAME POPULAR PRICES—NEVER CHANGE
Daily Matinees, 15c to 50c   Every Night, 15c to $1.00

One of Harry's acts was escaping from heavy chains, tires and locks. He could do it in just 19 minutes.

Little Ehrich

"October 28, 1883, was the date of my first appearance before an audience. I appeared as a contortionist and trapeze performer ..."
— Harry

Here are Ehrich and his little brother Theo before they left Budapest. Ehrich later helped Theo become the magician known as "Hardeen."

Harry made up many stories about his life, especially about his childhood. For instance, he claimed he was born in the United States, though records prove he was born in Budapest, Hungary, in 1874. Maybe Harry thought his American audiences would like him more if they thought that he was American, too.

Ehrich Weisz was Harry's real name, but the family's last name was later changed to Weiss. His father, Mayer Samuel Weiss, worked as a rabbi (a leader of a Jewish congregation). When he couldn't get a job in Budapest, he left the family, sailed to the United States and became the rabbi of a congregation in Appleton, Wisconsin. Ehrich was only two at the time. Two years later, in 1878, Ehrich's father had saved enough money to bring his family to join him.

Ehrich's mother, Cecilia, had never seen a baby like him. He rarely cried and slept very little. He always seemed to be awake and staring. But Cecilia had other things to think about. She had seven children to look after and her husband's salary was small. It soon became smaller. In 1882, Ehrich's father's congregation in Appleton let him go. So the family moved to nearby Milwaukee, Wisconsin's largest city.

It was in Milwaukee that Ehrich saw his first magic show. His father took him to see Dr. Lynn, a magician whose gruesome act included a dismembering trick. He'd slash off the arms, legs and head of a man, then magically reassemble him. Ehrich was astounded.

In Milwaukee, the family moved five times, to smaller and smaller homes. There were no laws to make kids attend school, so Ehrich took whatever jobs he could to support his family. He once made money by standing motionless on a wintry sidewalk holding out his cap. As snow piled up, so did the coins in his hat. Ehrich hid the money in his clothes, headed home, then told his mother to shake him. Like magic, coins flew out! Ehrich was already performing, as he would for the rest of his life.

With his father working only occasionally, there was never enough money, despite Ehrich's efforts. How would the family survive?

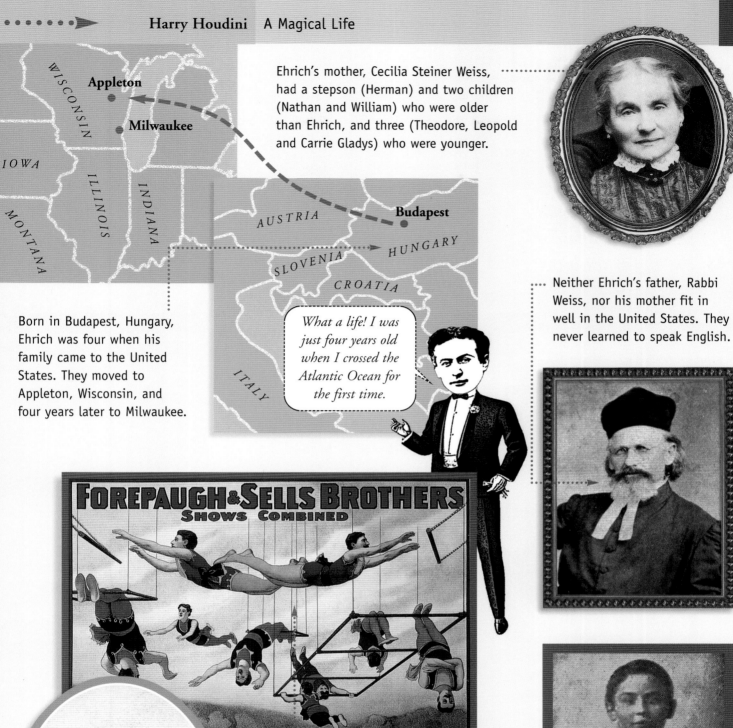

Ehrich's mother, Cecilia Steiner Weiss, had a stepson (Herman) and two children (Nathan and William) who were older than Ehrich, and three (Theodore, Leopold and Carrie Gladys) who were younger.

Born in Budapest, Hungary, Ehrich was four when his family came to the United States. They moved to Appleton, Wisconsin, and four years later to Milwaukee.

What a life! I was just four years old when I crossed the Atlantic Ocean for the first time.

Neither Ehrich's father, Rabbi Weiss, nor his mother fit in well in the United States. They never learned to speak English.

FOREPAUGH & SELLS BROTHERS
SHOWS COMBINED

...OUPE – IN THE MOST ASTONISHING MID-AIR ACHIEVEMENTS EVER ACCOMPLISHED.

Trapeze artists amazed Ehrich. At age nine, he was an agile acrobat, performing in his neighborhood and making money his family badly needed. He called himself "Ehrich, the Prince of the Air."

Dr. Lynn, the magician, inspired eight-year-old Ehrich. In Dr. Lynn's show, he seemed to cut people up and put them back together again!

By the time Ehrich was eight, he was earning money by selling newspapers, running errands, shining shoes and more.

Runaway!

"We lived there, I mean starved there, several years. The less said on the subject the better."
— Harry

One of Ehrie's jobs in New York was errand boy. He also helped make metal tools and may have worked for a printer.

As he grew older, Ehrich found his family's poverty harder to bear. There was never enough money for food or heat. He did his best to earn money for his family, but there weren't many jobs a young boy could do. Maybe, thought Ehrich, there was work for him somewhere else. So, at age 12, he ran away from home.

Ehrich had planned to go to Galveston, Texas, but by mistake he jumped on the wrong train and landed in Kansas City, Missouri. He eventually ended up in Delavan, Wisconsin, just 80 km (50 mi.) from Milwaukee.

Ehrich never found work, but a kindly couple took him in and fed and cared for him for the summer. Meanwhile, Ehrich's dad had given up trying to find work in Milwaukee. He thought he might have a better chance in a bigger city. In 1887, he went to New York, and Ehrich joined him there, followed shortly by the whole family.

Ehrie, as Ehrich liked to be called now, heard about a job cutting fabric for neckties. But when he arrived to apply for the position, there was already a long line of people ahead of him. Ehrie's family was depending on him to get this job. What could he do?

Boldly marching to the front of the line, Ehrie grabbed the job sign and told the crowd that the position was filled. Then he went into the building, applied for the job and got it. Or is that what really happened? No one knows for sure — but that's what Ehrie told people because it made a good story.

Cutting neckties was a miserable, dirty job. But at work, Ehrie made a friend named Jacob Hyman. Determined to find better jobs and fascinated by magic, the teenagers decided to create a magic act. But first they needed a good name.

One of Ehrie's favorite magicians was a famous French showman called Jean-Eugène Robert-Houdin. Ehrie had heard that magicians sometimes added an "i" to the end of another magician's name to suggest they were like that person. So, at age 17, he created the last name "Houdini" for himself. The name "Harry" came from his nickname, Ehrie. Soon Harry and Jacob were performing magic tricks as "The Brothers Houdini."

Ehrie and his family lived in rundown apartment buildings in New York City. When Ehrie became successful, he rarely spoke about the poverty he'd experienced.

The name Houdini came from Jean-Eugène Robert-Houdin. This French magician used the latest technology and was one of the first magicians to perform in theaters rather than on street corners.

Despite working hard, Ehrie found time for swimming, boxing and running. Some of the racing medals here are real but others are fakes that Ehrie added for the photo.

Ehrie's spelling was often wrong (see how he spells Galveston) and his handwriting was always hard to read.

Even though I ran away, I made sure I wrote home.

A new act

"Our act is the supreme cabinet mystery in the World. [It] has been featured at ... the Oxford London and has created a sensation in Europe, Australia, and America." — Harry

(This was one of Harry's stories. He and Bess hadn't yet performed in Europe or Australia.)

When Harry first met Bess Rahner, she was singing and dancing in an act called "The Floral Sisters."

Harry and Jacob left necktie cutting in 1891 to focus full-time on magic. Before Harry's father died in 1892, he made Harry promise to look after his mother. Harry loved her deeply, and no matter how little money he made, he always gave her some.

In 1893, the stock market fell, companies went bankrupt and thousands of people lost their jobs. People could barely afford food, let alone tickets for magic shows. Harry might have been tempted to go back to cutting neckties, but he stuck with his Brothers Houdini magic show.

The Brothers Houdini performed at the World's Fair in Chicago, but few people saw them. Their act was just one of a long line of shows and had to compete with many other attractions, including a huge Ferris wheel. Harry and Jacob also toured upstate New York and the American Midwest, performing in small theaters and with groups of low-paid performers including puppeteers, fire-eaters and giants.

One of Harry's most successful illusions or tricks was Needle Swallowing. He seemed to chew and swallow dozens of needles and a long piece of thread, then regurgitate the thread with the needles threaded on it. This illusion, which did not involve actually swallowing needles, amazed audiences throughout Harry's career. You can see Harry performing it on page 23.

Early in 1894, Jacob decided he wanted to perform on his own, so Jacob's brother Joe Hyman joined Harry. Then Joe was replaced by Harry's brother Theodore. But that spring, Harry met Bess Rahner, a singer and dancer. Three weeks later they were married. Bess became Harry's stage partner and the couple called themselves "The Houdinis."

Harry and Bess became famous for their illusion called Metamorphosis (it means transformation). It began with Harry stepping into a flannel bag, which was sealed shut. The bag was locked in a trunk, then the trunk was tied with thick ropes and wheeled into a curtained cabinet.

Standing at the open curtain, Bess announced, "Now then, I shall clap my hands three times, and at the third and last time I ask you to watch CLOSELY for — the — EFFECT!" Bess jerked the curtain closed and vanished, but instantly the curtain was reopened — by Harry! Bess was sealed in the bag in the still roped and padlocked trunk! Audiences applauded wildly. Was this the beginning of success for Harry?

Bess was Harry's best partner for Metamorphosis, the "cabinet mystery," because she was small, quick and willing to work hard.

In Harry's Color-Changing Handkerchief trick, a hankie switched color when he passed it through a seemingly empty tube.

The Brothers Houdini performed card tricks, pulled handkerchiefs out of candle flames and more.

My brother Theo and I appeared as The Brothers Houdini, but I was always the boss.

Tough times

"… any one in possession of my secret could laugh at locks just as heartily as I do."
— Harry

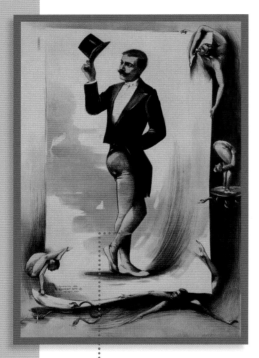

Contortionists (acrobats who can twist their bodies into almost impossible positions) fascinated Harry. He had to be a bit of a contortionist to escape from a straitjacket.

Harry and Bess dazzled audiences with Metamorphosis. But the crowd grew bored when Harry presented tricks that many other magicians could perform. Some people thought Harry spoke poorly with bad grammar and looked shabby in his old clothes. Harry knew to make it big he'd have to improve his act and present 20 minutes of mind-boggling magic.

In November 1895, Harry had the idea of being handcuffed before stepping into the Metamorphosis bag. When he emerged, the cuffs hung open from his wrists. But audiences weren't impressed — they assumed he'd used trick handcuffs. So Harry began showing up at police stations and unlocking their cuffs. Soon newspapers were running articles about his stunts and giving him the publicity he craved.

The Houdinis toured with various groups across North America, performing magic, comedy, music — anything that paid. While in eastern Canada, Harry visited a mental hospital and watched violent patients try to break free from their straitjackets (long-sleeved jackets that bound the patients' arms).

Of course, Harry had to try escaping from one. It took seven tries and left him bruised and bloody, but he managed to wriggle out. Straitjacket escapes would later become an important part of his act.

In 1898, Harry added a new kind of act — performing séances on stage. He made ghostly hands and faces appear and pretended to pass on messages from dead people to their grieving families. But Harry felt bad hoaxing people and taking advantage of their sorrow.

Despite some success, there were times when Harry and Bess had nothing to eat. At the end of the year, they were back in New York, out of work and living with Harry's mother. Ready to give up, Harry ran an ad in a newspaper offering to sell all of his magic tricks and secrets for $20. There were no buyers.

While Harry was deciding whether to quit magic, he had to perform a few shows that he'd promised to give. In early 1899, big-time theater manager Martin Beck caught Harry's act in St. Paul, Minnesota.

Beck gave Harry his big break. The manager agreed to book Harry and Bess into top theaters, but suggested they concentrate on escapes. Soon Harry was in demand at the best vaudeville houses, performing in variety shows along with singers, contortionists, dancing dogs and jugglers.

Harry presented card tricks using the nickname "King of Cards" or "Cardo." He also performed as the "Great Wizard," "Professor Murat" and "Projea the Wild Man." None of these acts succeeded.

At first, people thought I used trick handcuffs for my escapes. When I used police cuffs and still escaped, audiences were amazed by me.

There wasn't a pair of handcuffs Harry couldn't get out of — or so he claimed.

IN THE CIRCUS. THE HOUDINIS ARE AT THE RIGHT OF THE FRONT ROW. MRS. HOUDINI WEARS A LORD FAUNTLEROY SUIT.

Harry and Bess toured with many groups, including the Welsh Brothers Circus.

International star

Harry could now afford expensive suits for his show. But off stage, he was a sloppy dresser — he was always thinking about magic and escapes, not clothes.

Before he got into vaudeville, Harry had been paid just $25 a week, if he got paid at all. Now his salary quickly soared to $400 a week — about what most families lived on for a whole year! He could finally afford to wear elegant clothes to impress audiences.

But Harry wanted more spectators to dazzle. He also disliked working for someone else and having to pay Martin Beck a part of his salary. So Harry and Bess headed for Europe. They arrived in England with no shows lined up but lots of confidence — and high hopes that Harry's genius for publicity would open up new audiences to them.

Harry's amazing escape from the "Mirror Cuffs" on March 17, 1904, made him famous in England. These handcuffs got their name from the *London Daily Illustrated Mirror* newspaper. Staff with the paper found a special pair of "unpickable" handcuffs — which a blacksmith had taken five years to make — and challenged Harry to break out of them.

On stage, the Mirror Cuffs were snapped around Harry's wrists. Then Harry disappeared into his cabinet. In less than an hour, Harry appeared again. But the cuffs were still on — he was only asking to have them removed so he could take off his jacket. The newspaper's representative refused to do it — he was worried that Harry would learn how to escape from the cuffs if he watched them being unlocked.

So Harry, still handcuffed, wriggled a jackknife out of a pocket, opened the knife with his teeth and slashed at his jacket until it fell off. Then he headed back into the cabinet. In ten minutes he was out, with the cuffs hanging from his hands! It was an amazing show, especially because, for most of it, the spellbound audience was staring at a curtained cabinet.

Then Harry and Bess headed for Germany. Before Harry was allowed to perform there, his act had to be reviewed by the police. He was nervous because people were put in jail in Germany for trying to fool the public, and you might say that's what Harry planned to do. But the police approved his act, and audiences flocked to his shows.

In Paris, France, Harry hired seven bald-headed men for a publicity stunt. With one letter painted on top of each bald head, the men would sit in a row in sidewalk cafés wearing hats. Then they bowed their heads and took off their hats, one by one, until they spelled out "HOUDINI"!

By 1905, Harry was earning as much as $2150 a week. It was time for him and Bess to return to America and become big stars at home, too.

Harry performed in England, Scotland, Germany, France, Holland, Denmark and Russia.

SCOTLAND

DENMARK

RUSSIA

ENGLAND

HOLLAND

GERMANY

FRANCE

"Most of my success in Europe was due to the fact that I lost no time in stirring up local interest in every town I played. The first thing was to break out of jail."
— Harry

Bess and I smuggled our little dog, Charlie, across country borders.

In Germany, Harry had many nicknames, including "Escape King," the "Unexplained Riddle" and "King of Handcuffs."

CIRCUS BUSCH

Houdini

Sometimes Bess still assisted Harry on stage. Harry said they were "two young (?) people, roaming around trying to make an honest million."

Back in the USA

"The easiest way to attract a crowd is to let it be known that at a given time and a given place some one is going to attempt something that in the event of failure will mean sudden death."
— Harry

Harry rarely slept more than five hours a night. "I have tried through many a sleepless night to invent schemes to make an audience appreciate some worthy effort of mine," he said.

Harry and Bess came home in the summer of 1905. Harry had missed his mother and was glad to be back in the United States. During a visit from Europe in 1904, he had bought a house in New York for $25 000. (Today it would cost more than $2 000 000.) He and Bess hoped to raise a family there, but they never had children.

Their New York house became both a home and a lab where, for instance, Harry practiced holding his breath underwater in a huge tub. To prepare for an escape he had in mind, Harry also practiced enduring cold water until he could stand temperatures barely above freezing.

By now Harry spoke well and looked very polished on stage. As he toured the United States, performing from Boston to San Francisco, he complimented his audiences and seemed delighted to perform for them. But he knew he had to develop more amazing stunts to hold their interest.

While in Rochester, New York, in 1907, Harry performed his first Manacled Bridge Jump. ("Manacled" is another word for "handcuffed.") The scene was the Weighlock Bridge. Thousands began gathering hours beforehand to see Harry, shackled in handcuffs and chains, jump into the water far below. Harry waited till the crowd was silent, then took a deep breath … and leaped off the bridge.

The onlookers held their breath. Would Harry free himself or would he drown? Fifteen seconds after Harry hit the water, a bare arm thrust up above the surface, holding the open cuffs. He'd done it!

How did Harry perform his amazing escapes? Few people know for sure, but many have tried to guess. Before attempting an escape, Harry would often select people from the audience to test the locks and make sure there was no trickery. Then he shook hands with them all. Maybe the last person to shake hands with Harry was a friend who passed him a lock-opening pick.

Sometimes, just before he was locked up, Bess gave Harry a kiss. Could she have passed a pick from her mouth to his? Harry performed his escapes almost naked, which meant he couldn't hide anything in his clothes. Men carefully searched Harry's mouth and nose — but there are other places where he could have concealed a pick, including the thick skin on the soles of his feet.

If there was any trickery involved, no one could spot it. That was Harry's special skill.

When Harry performed a Manacled Bridge Jump, he had trouble finding a clear spot in the water because there were so many spectators in boats.

Harry was still taking good care of his mother. He and Bess lived in New York, along with his mother and sister.

> I could get out of anything — a coffin, a burglarproof safe and even a preserved giant squid!

In 1906 Harry began producing the *Conjurers' Monthly Magazine*. Over the years he also filled his New York home with more than 5000 books and posters about magic. His collection is now at the Library of Congress.

THE CONJURERS' MONTHLY MAGAZINE

READING
REVIEWING BOOKS AND THINGS
RUBBISH
49

FROM THE PRESS
WISE
AND
OTHERWISE

by Harry Handcuff Houdini.

The Right Bosco Wronged by Hilliar.

In the July number of the *Sphinx*, under the title of "Some of the Magicians I have Met," W. J. Hilliar, an old English friend of mine, writes very entertainingly, but he unknowingly makes a few misstatements.

He writes in 1886 he met the veteran Italian Bosco, "an old man near... &o mark, with flowing... most an exact...

ture have his likeness on his bills to protect himself and the public from imposition. Any one using bills without the likeness is not the genuine Bosco." Permanent address, Signor Bosco & Son, Paragon House, Hastings.

The oldest imitator is Alfred, then follows Signor, then Madame, then dame, then Madame trav... this Louis Bos...
To rl...

Milk can magic

"Ladies and Gentlemen, my latest invention — the Milk Can. I will be placed in this can and it will be filled with water … I will attempt to escape." — Harry

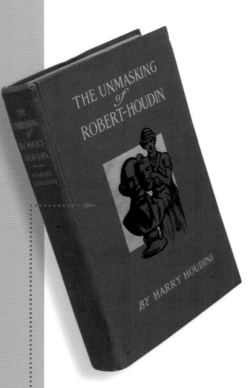

In 1908, Harry wrote *The Unmasking of Robert-Houdin*, which criticized the magician whose name he'd taken. Harry always wanted to be better than everyone else.

The Milk Can Escape was Harry's next famous escape. From the first time he performed it in 1908, it enchanted audiences.

Wearing just a bathing suit and handcuffs, Harry pointed to a large, old-fashioned milk can into which he was about to disappear and announced, "Should anything happen, and should I fail to appear within a certain time, my assistants will open the curtains, rush in, smash the Milk Can and do everything possible to save my life …"

Then Harry squeezed into the milk can, which was filled with water. The lid was locked down and a cabinet was slipped around the can. Harry had to escape from the inky darkness — or drown.

Harry's assistant stood by with an ax. Spectators tried to hold their breath for long as Harry held *his*. A band played as the seconds ticked by on a huge clock. After a minute, most people gave up and took a breath, but there was no sign of Harry. The audience became hysterical. After almost three grueling minutes, Harry breathlessly appeared.

Actually, Harry had escaped quickly from the milk can, but he waited to show himself just to get the audience more excited. How did Harry escape so fast? The collar of the can *seemed* to be tightly bolted in place by many heavy rivets. The can had been examined by members of the audience — but were the rivets real? Behind the cabinet, Harry kept his secrets to himself.

In 1908 and 1909, Harry and Bess were back in Europe, amazing audiences. While there, Harry became fascinated by airplanes. He'd always been intrigued by scientific breakthroughs and thought of himself as an inventor. While in Europe, he even bought his own biplane (a plane with two pairs of wings).

When Harry got a good offer to perform in Australia, he couldn't turn it down. During the many weeks it took to sail down under — planes couldn't fly very far then — he hoped to relax and recover from the strain of performing. Instead, Harry was seasick the whole way. But he was being paid for his travel time so he thought it was a great deal.

In January 1910, Harry, Bess and the biplane, also on the ship, arrived in Australia. Harry was determined to win the award for the first person to fly in Australia. Despite competition from rival pilots, blistering temperatures and engine troubles, on March 18, 1910, Harry soared into the sky and claimed the prize.

Harry's Milk Can Escape was advertised with the slogan, "Failure means a drowning death!"

See my name on the plane? I never missed a chance for publicity.

Harry always performed the Milk Can Escape successfully, but an imitator drowned trying it.

Harry performed terrifying escapes and flew airplanes but he rarely drove a car — it made him too nervous!

Much more magic

In 1914, Harry had his picture taken in a group that included former US President Theodore Roosevelt. Harry wanted people to think they were friends, so he airbrushed everyone else out of the photo below.

Despite suffering from seasickness, Harry spent the next three years crisscrossing the Atlantic Ocean, touring England, Europe and the United States. But he was forced to take a break in November 1911. During one of his escapes, he was strapped too tightly into a bag and received the first major injury of his long, daredevil career.

Harry ignored the pain for several weeks until he was forced to see a doctor. A ruptured blood vessel in one of his kidneys was the diagnosis. The doctor ordered Harry to rest for a few months and said if he kept performing such strenuous escapes, he'd be dead in a year. But Harry kept going, finishing the tour before he took a break. And, after only two weeks, he was back on stage. He just couldn't stop.

Always looking for sensational new acts, Harry combined two stunts to create the Underwater Box Escape. *Scientific American* magazine called it "one of the most remarkable tricks ever performed." On July 7, 1912, at New York Harbor, Harry was handcuffed and squeezed into a wooden crate. The box was dumped into the water, where it started to sink. But Harry quickly made his escape, leaving the box lid nailed shut and the cuffs inside.

Some people say Harry's next escape was his greatest ever. It was known as the Water-Torture Cell Escape, but Harry usually called it the "Upside Down" or "USD." This trick took more than three years to perfect before he began performing it in 1912.

In the USD, Harry dangled upside down in a slim glass case full of water, with heavy clamps holding his feet. In less than two minutes, Harry escaped, leaving the cuffs that had held his feet still locked. Audiences roared their approval.

July 1913 was supposed to be a great month for Harry. He legally changed his name to Harry Houdini, and he set sail for Europe, where he was to perform for the king of Sweden. But shortly after he started his show tour, he received a telegram that made him faint — his mother had died.

Harry and Bess caught the next ship back to New York. He insisted that his family not bury his mother immediately, as Jewish people usually do, but wait so that he could see her one last time. Harry got his wish, but he never got over his mother's death.

"I believe that [the Water-Torture Cell Escape] is the climax of all my studies and labors … Never will I be able to construct anything that will be more dangerous or difficult for me to do." — Harry

In a movie made about me, I drowned in this Water-Torture Cell. But in real life, I always escaped.

For the Underwater Box Escape, Harry was squished inside this thick pine box, which was tightly sealed with nails, heavy rope and metal bands.

Despite being married almost 20 years, Harry and Bess continued to leave love notes around their house for each other to find.

The disappearing elephant

"With due modesty, I recognize no one as my peer." — Harry

After his visit to New Brunswick, in eastern Canada, years earlier, Harry had tried to entertain audiences by struggling out of a straitjacket. At that time, people weren't impressed — they figured the jacket was fake. But Harry never gave up on a good escape. In 1915 he found a way to perform the Suspended Straitjacket Escape and attract his biggest crowds ever.

This new version began outside, in front of a skyscraper. First Harry was tightly strapped into the straitjacket. His ankles were tied together and a long rope attached. Slowly Harry was hauled up by the rope until he dangled upside down many stories above the crowd below. As people watched, he writhed and jerked, at times squirming so hard that he was almost standing up. Within minutes, he wriggled out of the straitjacket and triumphantly let it fall to the ground.

The Suspended Straitjacket Escape put an incredible strain on Harry's whole body, especially his ankles. If he wasn't pulled up smoothly, he could smash against the building — he once cut his head badly on a window ledge. The trick was so dangerous it killed some other performers who attempted it.

In 1917, the United States joined World War I and Harry volunteered to fight. But he was considered too old, so he made his contribution to the war effort by giving free performances for soldiers, raising money and getting other magicians involved. He even gave away some of his secrets to teach soldiers useful things such as how to escape from handcuffs, untie ropes and survive underwater.

All his life, Harry performed without charge for many groups, including seniors, orphans and children in hospitals. He even developed a show for blind people in which he did mind-reading tricks.

In 1918 Harry performed at the Hippodrome, a gigantic theater in New York. He knew he needed a magic trick as enormous as the stage, so he decided to perform the Disappearing Elephant Trick. After members of the audience examined a huge wooden box, Harry led Jenny the elephant into it. The door on the box was closed and when Harry reopened it, Jenny was gone!

Actually, Jenny was still in the box, hidden behind a huge, tilted mirror. It made the box's sides look straight, though one was angled enough to conceal an elephant. The "vanish" got lots of publicity. Harry stayed at the Hippodrome for 19 weeks, the longest he'd ever performed in one place.

Harry bragged that making Jenny the elephant disappear was "the biggest vanish the world has ever seen."

Harry first attempted the Suspended Straitjacket Escape in 1915. He performed it for the next three years in any city he visited that had skyscrapers.

In his Hippodrome show, Harry performed the Needle Swallowing Trick. Actually, he never swallowed the needles.

I always swallowed the needles "eye" first, so they could "see" where they were going. Get the joke?

This was Harry's view of the huge crowds below while he performed his Suspended Straitjacket Escape.

How did Harry get out of a straitjacket? Among other things, he expanded his chest and held his shoulders wide while the jacket was being tightened around him. This gave him some room to move when he started squirming out of it.

Hollywood star

"No illusion is good in a film, as we simply resort to camera trix, and the deed is did."
— Harry

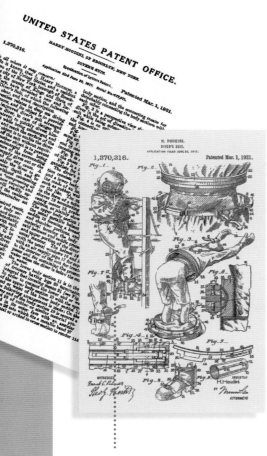

Harry was so interested in inventions and underwater escapes that he invented a diving suit.

The latest trends always caught Harry's interest. In the early 1900s he could see that movies were taking over from stage shows. In 1916 he started the Film Development Company to sell a fast, cheap process for developing movie film. Now he wanted to become a movie actor, too.

Harry's first movie was *The Master Mystery*, a 15-part series with a new adventure each week. This 1919 serial included impossible escapes and feats of great daring, such as Harry getting out of a collapsed cave and fighting a robot (probably one of the first robots ever seen in a movie). The film also featured a scene in which Harry showed how agile his toes were — he could use them almost like fingers. *The Master Mystery* became a major hit.

Later that year, Harry starred in *The Grim Game*. The climax showed Harry climbing from one biplane to another in mid-air, then surviving a terrifying crash. Harry had been willing to perform the stunt, but the director wouldn't risk it. A stuntman stood in for Harry in the plane, and the crash was accidental — luckily no one was hurt and it made for amazing action. However, Harry seemed to forget that a stand-in had actually done the stunt and began taking credit for it.

At the end of 1919, Harry sailed to Europe to perform the shows he'd had to postpone because of World War I. Audiences adored both his stage act and his movies, and he earned a fantastic $3750 or more each week.

Terror Island, Harry's third movie, was released in 1920. One year later he brought out *The Soul of Bronze*. In 1922 he starred in, wrote and produced *The Man from Beyond*. To make sure the film was a success, he added live magic performances to its showings. But each movie was less successful than the one before. Harry's sixth movie, *Haldane of the Secret Service*, was a flop and the last film he made.

It may have been a relief to Harry to get out of filmmaking. Movie audiences weren't impressed with his amazing stunts because they couldn't tell whether Harry was really performing them or just relying on camera trickery. As well, Harry broke bones and tore muscles while filming and was injured far more than he ever had been on stage.

You can still watch some of my great movies on video. Don't miss 'em!

Harry said this photo from *The Grim Game* was taken 1220 m (4000 ft.) up in the air. That made a good story, but the photo was actually shot on the ground.

Here's the French poster for Harry's film *The Master Mystery*. In France he was called "The Most Popular Man in the Entire World."

In the film *The Man from Beyond*, Harry played a man frozen in a wall of ice for 100 years before being thawed.

HOUDINI
LE MAÎTRE DU MYSTÈRE
GRAND ROMAN CINÉMA
Adapté par
Mr J. PETITHUGUENIN
ÉDITÉ PAR
PATHÉ
PUBLIÉ DANS
L'ORDRE PUBLIC
E.G.

houdinize: to release or extricate oneself from (confinement, bonds, or the like), as by wriggling out.

By now Harry was so famous that he got a word based on his name into the 1920 edition of Funk & Wagnall's dictionary.

In *The Man from Beyond*, Harry wrestled on a cliff, escaped after being tied up in a wet sheet, and rescued his sweetheart at the top of Niagara Falls.

Séance scandals

"It takes a flimflammer to catch a flimflammer."
— Harry

Recognize me? I'm in disguise to expose a fake medium. My magnifying lenses give me a close look at any sneaky tricks.

Ever since his mother had died, Harry had been looking into spiritualism, the belief that dead people can communicate with the living. Many people were interested in spiritualism at that time, especially if they'd lost loved ones in World War I or during the deadly flu epidemic of 1918.

Harry was against mediums (people who claimed to be able to contact the dead) because he felt they took advantage of people's grief just to get their money. He also knew about their tricks, such as making spirit faces appear or objects mysteriously move, because he'd once done the same things himself (see page 12).

In England, Harry had become friends with Sir Arthur Conan Doyle, the famous author of the Sherlock Holmes books, and his wife. The couple both believed in spiritulism, and Lady Jean Doyle offered to contact Harry's mother. Harry was eager to hear from his mother, despite not really believing that this was possible.

Harry had a séance with Lady Doyle back in the United States. Page after page of greetings flowed from her pen, all supposedly from Cecilia. Harry didn't believe a word of it — mostly because the words were all in English, a language his mother barely knew.

Harry began to lecture against spiritualism. He exposed many mediums as frauds and made lots of enemies, but audiences loved Harry's explanations of the trickery. In one case, Harry said, a medium sewed his own pant cuffs to the carpet to prove that he wasn't moving about in the dark during a séance. When the lights were suddenly turned on, everyone was shocked to see him sneaking around in his underwear!

In 1924, Harry joined a group from *Scientific American* magazine to investigate psychics, including Boston's famous medium Mina Crandon, known as Margery. She said she could communicate with spirits through her dead brother and his "spirit bat." Margery also seemed to lift objects without touching them and to exude ectoplasm, a slime that supposedly shows the presence of a ghost. If Margery could prove she was the real thing, she'd win $2500 from *Scientific American*.

For months Harry's committee attended Margery's séances and argued about them. Finally all but one of the members agreed with Harry that Margery was a fraud. Margery was furious that she hadn't won the money. But she later said, "I respect Houdini more than any of the bunch. He has both feet on the ground all the time."

Here's Harry in the wooden box he put Margery into during séances. He wanted to see if the "spirits" could still move objects while Margery was in the box.

Harry set up this photo to show how a medium might fool people. In the dark, many would believe this person was a real spirit.

PALACE
B.F. KEITH THEATRE

MOST MAGNIFICENT PLAYHOUSE IN THE WORLD. CLEVELAND'S GREATEST INSTITUTION OF AMUSEMENT
STARTING TODAY, TWICE DAILY, 2:15 AND 8:15

GO TODAY! Do Not Buy Seats From Speculators

2D BIG WEEK!
GREATEST SENSATION IN YEARS
THE ACTUAL EXPOSE OF A WORLD PROBLEM
METHODS OF FAKE MEDIUMS BROUGHT BEFORE YOUR EYES BY

HOUDINI

AFTER SEEING HIS EXHIBITION THIS WEEK YOU CAN HAVE A THOUSAND THRILLS AT HOME. BE YOUR OWN MEDIUM. IT IS POSITIVELY EASY AND SIMPLE.

OPEN FORUM OF FIVE MINUTES AFTER ACT.
MR. HOUDINI CANNOT GIVE A PRIVATE AUDIENCE WITHOUT APPOINTMENT

MARGERY GENUINE, SAYS CONAN DOYLE; HE SCORES HOUDINI

MEDIUM AND HER NEW CHAMPION

MINA CRANDON ... Is Storm Centre in ... ic Controversy

SIR ARTHUR ... Who Com...

MAKES COUNTER-CHARGES

Counter-charges against the members of the committee who opposed Bird's and Carrington's proposal of a favorable report and a sense of a favorable report and a sense of amazement at their stubborn incredulity, characterize Sir Arthur's message. He states that a cabal, headed by Houdini, was undoubtedly organized against Bird and finally resulted in his removal as secretary of the body.

He is particularly bitter in his criticism of Houdini and states that "he far as psychic research is concerned, left Boston a very discredited man so In conclusion he expresses his "amazement" that the committee, consisting of "honorable gentlemen" should permit the attack on the reputation of a ... and permitted a man "wit... different standards to ... geons attack, ... so they ...

Margery said spirits made ectoplasm pour from her nose, mouth and ears. The goo looked like bread dough.

Final curtain?

"I want my show to be the best of its kind whilst I am alive. When I am dead there will not be another like it."
— Harry

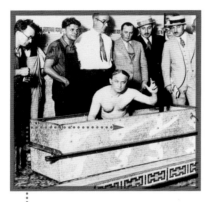

Harry tried to use his survival in the airless coffin to help others. He said people in collapsed mines might live longer if they stayed calm and breathed slowly.

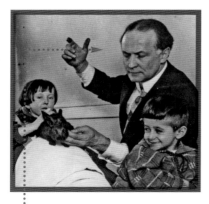

Harry was loved by many for his kindness to children. But he had enemies — did an angry medium hire the student who punched him?

At Christmastime in 1925, Harry opened a show called "HOUDINI" at a Broadway theater in New York. No longer a vaudeville act, it competed with the best theater shows and actors. He was very proud to have gained such fame and respectability.

What a show! It opened with magic tricks and illusions, including one like the Dismembering Trick Harry had seen Dr. Lynn perform long ago (see page 6). "HOUDINI" featured Harry's most famous escapes, including the Water-Torture Cell, and finished with him debunking spiritualism.

Harry could never ignore a challenge. When another magician in New York began to get good reviews for his Buried Alive Escape, Harry claimed that he could stay in an airtight casket longer. The other magician lasted without air for an hour, so Harry knew what he had to do — he immediately began three weeks of strenuous training.

On August 5, 1926, Harry climbed into a coffin that held only three or four minutes' worth of air. The coffin was lowered into a swimming pool. An hour and a half later, Harry emerged. He was confused and hallucinating, but he had beaten the other magician.

Harry went on tour in the fall of 1926, bringing along a bronze casket for publicity. In Montreal, Quebec, he entertained some university students in his dressing room. One student asked, "Is it true, Mr. Houdini, that you can resist the hardest blows struck to the abdomen?" Before Harry could prepare himself, the student began punching him in the stomach. After a few hits, the fellow stopped, but the damage was done.

Harry made it through the next show and headed for Detroit, Michigan, by train. But his pain was too severe. A doctor was summoned to meet him at the train station. It turned out that Harry already had appendicitis (swelling of the appendix) and the punches had made it worse.

Despite his suffering, Harry was determined to perform that night. He collapsed during the show but finished it, then had to be rushed to hospital to have his appendix removed. But it was too late. His appendix had ruptured and spread infection through his body.

Harry died on October 31, 1926. His body was taken back to New York and buried in the same coffin he'd brought along on his tour. But Harry Houdini's fame lives on. He was able to tap into people's desire to be amazed by things they couldn't understand. Through determination, hard work and incredible talent, Harry changed the world of magic forever.

Houdini's brother Hardeen went on performing many of Harry's tricks and escapes after Harry's death.

One reason Harry became so famous was because, for 16 years after his death, Bess hired a publicist to keep his legend alive.

Bess, seen here with Hardeen at Harry's grave, held séances every October 31. She hoped Harry would speak from the grave. After ten years, Bess gave up. But other people are still trying to contact Harry.

At first newspapers wrote that Houdini's secrets died with him. But he actually passed on his props and techniques to his brother Hardeen.

LONG BEACH PRESS-TELEGRAM

NOVEMBER 1, 1926

HOUDINI KEEPS HIS SECRETS
* * *
Tricks Go to Grave With Magician

DETROIT, Nov. 1. – (By Associated Press.) – Harry Houdini's mysterious feats of escape, which thrilled spectators throughout the world in his life, today were locked in the mystery of death. The magician, hailed by his fellow workers as the greatest of them all, died here last night, taking with him the secrets of how he escaped from manacles, chains, coffins, straight jackets and other contrivances, performances which no other man ever had duplicated under his challenge.

Although Houdini wrote __ly on magic, the fruit __entury experi- __manag-

"His stunts were his own, and not adapted from som__ thing some one else ha__ done," said B. M. L. En__ Vice President of the S__ American Magicia__ explanatio__

Harry's life at a glance

1874   March 24 — Ehrich Weisz is born in Budapest, Hungary

1876   Ehrich's father, Mayer Samuel Weisz, leaves for the United States to find a job

Wilhelmina Beatrice ("Bess") Rahner, Ehrich's future wife, is born

1878   September — Ehrich's mother, Cecilia Steiner Weisz, and children join Rabbi Weisz in Appleton, Wisconsin, where he has a small congregation. The family's name is changed to Weiss.

1883   Ehrich performs acrobatics at a backyard circus in Milwaukee, Wisconsin, and calls himself "Ehrich, the Prince of the Air"

1886   Ehrich runs away from home for a year

1887   Rabbi Weiss moves to New York City. Ehrich, and then the rest of the family, join him. Ehrich, now known as Ehrie, gets a job at a necktie cutting company.

1891   Ehrie teams up with his friend Jacob Hyman in a magic act called "The Brothers Houdini." Ehrie starts calling himself Harry Houdini.

1892   October 5 — Harry's father dies after surgery for cancer

1893   The Brothers Houdini perform at the World's Fair in Chicago, Illinois. Their tricks include Needle Swallowing.

1894   Jacob Hyman leaves the Brothers Houdini and is replaced for a short time by Harry's brother Theodore

June 22 — Harry marries performer Bess Rahner, after knowing her for only three weeks. Bess replaces Theo in the stage act, now known as "The Houdinis."

1895   The Houdinis become known for their trick, Metamorphosis. Harry also begins performing handcuff escapes.

1896   On tour in New Brunswick, in Canada, Harry tries on a straitjacket and gets the idea of trying to escape from it

1898   With no money, Harry and Bess are forced to live with his mother in New York. Harry thinks about leaving the magic business and offers to sell the secrets behind his tricks. No one buys them.

1899   Martin Beck, a theater manager, sees Harry's handcuff act in St. Paul, Minnesota, and hires him. Within months, Harry is performing at top vaudeville houses across the United States.

1900   Harry and Bess sail to Europe. He spends most of the next five years there, performing and becoming a star.

1904   Harry performs his legendary Mirror Cuff handcuff escape in London, England

Harry buys a house in New York, which becomes his home for the rest of his life

1905   Harry and Bess return to live in the United States

1907   January — Harry makes his first Manacled Bridge Jump in Rochester, New York

1908   January 27 — Harry begins performing the Milk Can Escape in St. Louis, Missouri

April 10 — Harry escapes after being tied up with tire chains, car tires and locks from the Weed Tire Chain Grip Company

Harry publishes *The Unmasking of Robert-Houdin*

1910   March 18 — Harry wins a prize for making the first airplane flight in Australia, staying in the air for three and a half minutes

1911 Harry is injured when strapped into a bag while performing in Detroit, Michigan. He's forced to rest for two weeks.

1912 July 7 — Harry performs his Underwater Box Escape in New York Harbor. He repeats the feat nightly in a huge tank in a theater in the city.

September 21 — Harry first performs the Water-Torture Cell Escape in Berlin

1913 Harry legally changes his name to Harry Houdini

July 16 — Harry's mother dies

1914 May — Harry sails home from Europe on board a ship with former US President Theodore Roosevelt

August — World War I begins

In New York, Harry presents the trick Walking Through a Brick Wall

1915 Harry introduces the Suspended Straitjacket Escape

1916 Harry begins organizing the Film Development Corporation to process film

1917 The United States enters World War I. Harry volunteers for the army but is turned down because of his age.

1918 During his show in New York, Harry makes an elephant disappear. He also teaches soldiers how to escape from handcuffs.

World War I ends

1919 Harry's first movie, *The Master Mystery*, opens. It is successful worldwide.

Harry stars in the movie *The Grim Game*

1920 The 1920 edition of Funk & Wagnall's dictionary includes the verb "houdinize"

Harry stars in the movie *Terror Island*

Harry becomes friends with the famous author Sir Arthur Conan Doyle

1921 Harry forms the Houdini Picture Corporation, his own movie production company

Harry stars in the movie *The Soul of Bronze*

Harry publishes his book *Miracle Mongers and Their Methods*, about people who eat fire, swallow poison and more

1922 The movie *The Man from Beyond* opens, written by, produced by and starring Harry

1923 Harry's sixth and last movie, *Haldane of the Secret Service*, opens

1924 Harry tours the United States lecturing against fraudulent mediums

Harry publishes *The Unmasking — A Magician Among the Spirits*

Harry joins the *Scientific American* magazine committee to investigate fake mediums

July — Harry has his first sittings with Mina Crandon, also known as Margery, a well-known medium from Boston, Massachusetts

1925 Harry begins his show "HOUDINI"

1926 Harry testifies before a Congress committee investigating fake mediums

August 5 — Harry survives in a sealed coffin, underwater, for an hour and a half

October 31 — Harry dies in Detroit of a ruptured appendix

Nobody had a life like mine!

Visit Harry

American Museum of Magic,
Marshall, Michigan

At this museum you can see a milk can from Harry's famous Milk Can Escape, as well as posters, books, magazines and equipment used by performers in magic shows around the world. (Call ahead to make an appointment.)

Houdini Historical Center,
Appleton, Wisconsin

Located in the Outagamie Museum, this center celebrates one of the most famous people to live in Appleton. Get a map and take a walking tour of places that were important in Harry's early years.

Houdini Museum,
Scranton, Pennsylvania

Harry performed in Scranton often on his vaudeville tours. You can enjoy a magic show at this museum, watch clips from Harry's movie *The Master Mystery*, and see locks, straitjackets and more. (Call for opening hours.)

Harry and Bess's townhouse,
278 West 113th Street,
New York, New York

You can't go into the house Harry lived in for so many years, but some people feel that Harry still haunts his home. Harry, of course, didn't believe in ghosts.

You can see plenty of photos of Bess and me at the Library of Congress Web site!

Index

A SHORT HISTORY OF THE MIDDLE AGES

A SHORT HISTORY OF THE MIDDLE AGES

BARBARA H. ROSENWEIN
SECOND EDITION

broadview press

National Library of Canada Cataloguing in Publication

Rosenwein, Barbara H.
    A short history of the Middle Ages / Barbara H. Rosenwein. — 2nd ed.

Includes bibliographical references and index.
ISBN 1-55111-616-2

1. Middle Ages — History.   2. Europe — History —476-1492.   I. Title.

D117.R67 2004   940.1   C2004-901640-7

Broadview Press Ltd. is an independent, international publishing house, incorporated in 1985. Broadview believes in shared ownership, both with its employees and with the general public; since the year 2000 Broadview shares have traded publicly on the Toronto Venture Exchange under the symbol BDP.

We welcome comments and suggestions regarding any aspect of our publications—please feel free to contact us at the addresses below or at broadview@broadviewpress.com

www.broadviewpress.com
North America:

PO Box 1243, Peterborough,
Ontario, Canada K9J 7H5

3576 California Road, Orchard Park,
NY, USA 14127

Tel: (705) 743-8990;
Fax: (705) 743-8353
E-mail: customerservice@
broadviewpress.com

UK, Ireland, and continental Europe:

NBN Plymbridge
Estover Road
Plymouth PL6 7PY UK

Tel: 44 (0) 1752 202301;
Fax: 44 (0) 1752 202331
Fax Order Line: 44 (0) 1752 202333
Customer Service:
cservs@nbnplymbridge.com
Orders: orders@nbnplymbridge.com

Australia and New Zealand:

UNIREPS,
University of New South Wales
Sydney, NSW, 2052

Tel: 61 2 9664 0999;
Fax: 61 2 9664 5420
E-mail: info.press@unsw.edu.au

Text design and composition by George Kirkpatrick

PRINTED IN CANADA

To the memory of my father, Norman Herstein (May 27, 1921–May 25, 2002).

The Medieval World Today

- • Capital cities
- ○ Other cities

Scale

0   500   1000   1500 km

0   500   1000 mi

Lambert Conformal Conic projection.

THE UNION of the Roman empire was dissolved; its genius was humbled in the dust; and armies of unknown barbarians, issuing from the frozen regions of the North, had established their victorious reign over the fairest provinces of Europe and Africa.

Edward Gibbon,
The Decline and Fall of the Roman Empire

IT MAY very well happen that what seems for one group a period of decline may seem to another the birth of a new advance.

Edward Hallett Carr,
What is History?

CONTENTS

MAPS

PLATES

GENEALOGIES

FIGURES

LISTS

ABBREVIATIONS, CONVENTIONS, WEBSITES

ABBREVIATIONS

c. circa. Used in dates to mean that they are approximate.

cent. century

d. date of death

emp. emperor

fl. flourished. This is given when even approximate birth and death dates are unknown.

pl. plural. The plural form of a noun.

r. rule. Indicates the dates of rule.

sing. singular. The singular form of a noun.

DATE CONVENTIONS

All dates are C.E./A.D. unless otherwise noted (the two systems are interchangeable). The dates of popes are not preceded by *r.* because they took their papal names upon accession to office, and the dates after those names apply only to their papacies.

WEBSITES

www.georgetown.edu/labyrinth/labyrinth-home.html = The Labyrinth: resources for medieval studies sponsored by Georgetown University.

www.fordham.edu/halsall/sbook.html = The International Medieval Sourcebook, which contains important sets of primary sources for the medieval period.

www.broadviewpress.com/shorthistory = The website for this book, which has searchable Genealogies, Key Events, Lists, and Maps.

PREFACE

At the beginning of the first volume of his long and learned trilogy *Suicide in the Middle Ages*, Alexander Murray remarks amiably, "Unconventionally long, the book remains, to the author's certain knowledge, 'a mere introduction.'" Well, if *that* is just an introduction (and it undoubtedly is), then what is *this* book?

It is meant to be an easy pass through a dense thicket. It has been written so that you, the reader, may know enough about the Middle Ages after reading it to move on afterwards with some confidence to meatier fare: to "secondary sources" (so called not because they are "second best" but because they are present-day interpretations of the past) and to "primary sources," the texts, pictures, artefacts, and other bits and pieces of their lives and thought that medieval people left behind.

Because most people read about medieval history in college courses, and because most college courses last at most fifteen weeks, a short textbook may be better than a long one because it can be supplemented without being unduly burdensome. For others — those who may be students no longer but want to pick up a book to learn about the Middle Ages — a short book may well be more pleasant than a long one. But why a survey at all? Because a general orientation is very useful. Without it, primary and secondary sources tend to get unmoored: Abelard becomes a contemporary of Augustine, Murray's suicidal men and women kill themselves everywhere and nowhere.

There are at least two ways to use *A Short History of the Middle Ages* in the classroom. In the first, you read it in one or two weeks — say, at the beginning of the semester — and then refer to it as needed. In the second, you read a chapter or two a week, alongside other readings. This book has lots of maps, genealogies, and plates to help you figure out the context of the other things that you will need or want to study. The index is a handy way to look up names (which are followed by dates where possible), events, and places. Some technical words are explained in a glossary. There are bibliographies after every chapter for further reading. In this way, this book may, if you wish, serve as a permanent reference tool for historical facts.

A Short History of the Middle Ages is meant to be an uncluttered narrative of the whole of the Middle Ages, from about 300 to about 1500 (there are no decisive "start" and "stop" dates, so an author can put them where they seem to make sense). It covers not just Europe (though the focus increasingly moves there) but also the Byzantine and Islamic worlds. I have tried to make "Europe" more than the history of France, England, and Germany, so often the focus of books like this. I have also tried to write not just political history but also social, economic, and cultural history. There is, however, a conscious emphasis on political history, deriving from my twofold conviction that (1) politics tells us a good deal about the uses and distribution of power, always important if we wish to consider general conditions of life; and (2) politics, with its decisive events, provides a nice, clear grid for everything else.

The organization of this book is chronological because everything in a period—culture, social life, political order—is interconnected. It is true that Abelard does not make sense without Augustine before him; theoretically, he could appear in a long chapter on the medieval intellectual tradition. But he makes even less sense outside the context of the rise of cities, a money economy, and new employment opportunities for university men—the world in which he lived, in short—so he comes in a chapter on all those things.

A word on bibliographies: they, like the book, are short. Although they contain only secondary sources, the notes to each chapter contain references to many important primary sources. The notes, then, are meant to serve as a rough and ready bibliography of primary sources.

While preparing this text I have incurred many debts, which I am happy to acknowledge. Anne Wingenter, my research assistant in Spring 2000, ably gathered books for my foray into the realm of the Seljuk Turks. Charles Brauner was kind enough to read and critique my sections on medieval music, Esther Cohen offered useful suggestions for the discussion of the later Middle Ages, and Walter Pohl's advice was invaluable on the "Germans." Via e-mail Monique Bourin advised and aided, while my sister, Naomi Honeth, dispensed sympathy and encouragement. My Loyola colleague Theresa Gross-Diaz shared her thoughts on things medieval (and renaissance) with exemplary generosity. Other colleagues, Blake Dutton and Allen Frantzen, allowed me to draw on their particular expertises in medieval philosophy and Anglo-Saxon respectively. I am grateful to Steven A. Epstein, Paul Freedman, Mayke de Jong, Maureen C. Miller, Julia M.H. Smith, and the anonymous readers solicited by Broadview Press for reading the entire book in manuscript and offering incisive and enormously helpful criticism. Broadview's Betsy Struthers was an able and indefatigable permissions editor, while Paul Heersink showed infinite patience in making the maps. Warm thanks are due as well to production editor Barbara Conolly, assistant production editor Judith Earnshaw, and designer George Kirkpatrick. I owe a different debt to Ian Wood, who once asked me if I might write a book like this; little did he imagine what his words might inspire! Thanks bound up with the very rhythms of daily life go to my family: my parents, Rosaline and Norman Herstein; my husband, Tom; and my children, Frank and Jess. Without them I could not have written even a "short" history. Finally, I am grateful to my students, who tried hard to teach me what needs to be in a book like this—and what does not. I hope they will be pleased with the result.

PREFACE TO THE SECOND EDITION

For the second edition, I have corrected some errors and added some materials, especially on political and economic history. I thank Giles Constable, Adam Kosto, Graham Loud, Michael Morony, Walter Pohl, and Carine van Rhijn for pointing out errors and suggesting changes. Monique Bourin, Riccardo Cristiani, Samuel Leturcq, Rosamond Mack, R. I. Moore, and Anders Winroth generously contributed their expertise to particular sections. Thomas Head shared photographs. Maureen Miller was, as always, a wonderful resource and sounding-board. I am indebted to my students in History 310; I wish to thank Jamie McGowan, Eric Nethercott, Susie Newman, and Suzette Vela in particular for their thoughtful suggestions. Paul Heersink prepared new maps with his customary professionalism; George Kirkpatrick worked his magic with the design, and Martin Boyne copyedited with a keen eye. Finally I am grateful to the people at Broadview Press—especially Barbara Conolly, Don LePan, Mical Moser, and Tammy Roberts—for their help and support.

ONE

PRELUDE: THE ROMAN WORLD TRANSFORMED (*c*.300-*c*.600)

IN THE THIRD CENTURY, the Roman empire wrapped around the Mediterranean Sea like a scarf. (See Map 1.1.) Thinner on the North African coast, it bulked large as it enveloped what is today Spain, England, Wales, France, and Belgium, then evened out along the southern coast of the Danube river, following that river eastward, taking in most of what is today the Balkans and Greece, crossing the Hellespont and engulfing in its sweep the territory of present-day Turkey, much of Syria, and all of modern Lebanon, Israel, and Egypt. All the regions but Italy comprised what the Romans called the "provinces."

This was the Roman empire whose "decline and fall" was famously proclaimed by the eighteenth-century historian Edward Gibbon. But in fact his verdict was misplaced. The empire was never livelier than at its reputed end. It is true that the old elites of the cities, especially of Rome itself, largely regretted the changes taking place around them *c*.250-350. They were witnessing the end of their political, military, religious, economic, and cultural leadership, which was passing to the provinces. But for the provincials (the Romans living outside of Italy) this was in many ways a heady period, a long-postponed coming of age. They did not regret the division of the Roman empire into two parts under the Emperor Diocletian (*r*.284-305); the partition was tacit recognition of the importance of the provinces. Some did, however, regret losing their place in the sun (as happened *c*.400-500) to people still farther afield, whom they called "barbarians." In turn, the barbarians were glad to be the heirs of the Roman empire even as they contributed to its transformation (*c*.450-600).

North Sea

Baltic Sea

Britain

FRANKS

Weser

Elbe

Vistula

BURGUNDIANS

Oder

V A N D A L S

Meuse

Trier •

Belgica

G e r m a n i a

Atlantic

Seine

Lugdunensis

Rhine

Ocean

Loire

Raetia

Noricum

G a u l

Pannonia

Sava

Aquitania

Alpes Poen
Alpes Graiae

Po

• Milan

Roman until 270

Garonne

Rhône

Alpes
Cottiae

Alpes
Maritimes

I

Adriatic

Dalmatia

Narbonensis

t

Tiber

Sea

a

Corsica

l

**Dacia
Ripensis**

• Sar

Duero

i

Hispania

Lusitania

a

Rome •

Macedonia

Tagus

Pompeii •

Baleares

Sardinia

Tyrrhenian

Baetica

Sea

Guadalquivir

Epirus

M e d i

Sicilia

Achaia

t

M a u r e t a n i a

Numidia

Carthage •

Africa proconsularis

e

r

r

a

n

e

a

n

Western and Eastern Roman Empire

Dividing line between

Cyr

Legend

VANDALS   Peoples

Scale

0   500 km

0   300 mi

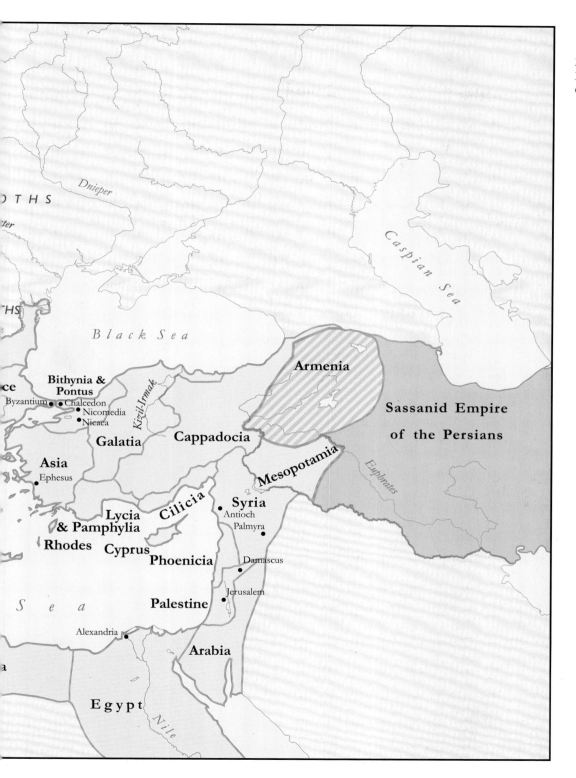

Map 1.1: The Roman Empire in the Third Century

THE PROVINCIALIZATION OF THE EMPIRE (*c.*250-*c.*350)

The Roman empire was too large to be ruled by one man in one place except in peacetime. This became clear during the "crisis of the third century," when two different groups from two different directions came pounding on the borders of the empire. From the north, beyond the Rhine and Danube rivers, came people the Romans called "barbarians"; from the east, the Persians. To contend with these attacks, the Roman government responded with wide-ranging reforms that brought new prominence to the provinces.

Above all, the government expanded the army. It set up new crack mobile forces as well as reinforcing the standing army. Soldier-workers threw up new fortifications, cities hedged themselves with walls, farms gained lookout towers and fences. It was not easy to find enough recruits to man this newly expanded defensive system. Before the crisis, the legions had been largely self-perpetuating. Their soldiers, drawn mainly from local provincial families, had settled permanently along the borders and raised the sons who would make up the next generation of recruits. Now, however, this supply was dwindling: the birthrate was declining, and around 257 an epidemic, perhaps of smallpox, ravaged the population further. Recruits would have to come from farther away, in Germania (beyond the northern borders of the empire) and elsewhere. In fact, long before this time, Germanic warriors had been regular members of Roman army units; they had done their stints and gone home. But in the third century the Roman government regularized the process. They settled Germanic and other barbarian groups within the empire, giving them land in return for military service.

The term "crisis of the third century" refers not only to the wars that the empire had to fight on its borders but also to a political succession crisis that saw more than twenty men claim, then lose (with their lives), the title of emperor between the years 235 and 284. (See list on p.328: Late Roman Emperors; but this names only the most important emperors!) Most of these men were the creatures of the army, chosen to rule by their troops. Often competing emperors wielded authority in different regions at the same time. They had little interest in the city of Rome, which, in any case, was too far from any of the fields of war to serve as military headquarters. For this reason Emperor Valerian (*r.*253-259) shifted the imperial residence and mint from Rome to Milan. Soon other favored imperial places—Trier, Sardica, Nicomedia, and, eventually, Constantinople—joined Milan in overshadowing Rome. The new army and the new imperial seats belonged to the provinces.

The primacy of the provinces was further enhanced by the need to feed and supply the army. To meet its demand for ready money, the Roman government debased the currency, increasing the proportion of base metals to silver. While helpful in the short term, this policy produced severe inflation. Strapped for cash, the state increased taxes and used its power to requisition goods and services. To clothe the troops it confiscated uniforms; to arm them it set up weapons factories staffed by artisans who were bound to produce a regular quota for the state. Food for the army had to be produced and delivered; here too the state depended on the labor of growers, bakers, and haulers. New taxes assessed on both land and individual "heads" were collected. The wealth and labor of the empire moved inexorably towards the provinces, to the hot spots where armies were clashing.

The whole empire, organized for war, became militarized. In about the middle of the third century, the senatorial aristocracy—the old Roman elite—was forbidden to lead the army; tougher men from the ranks were promoted to command positions instead. It was no wonder that those men also became the emperors. They brought new provincial tastes and sensibilities to the very heart of the empire, as we shall see.

Diocletian, a provincial from Dalmatia (today Croatia), brought the crisis under control, and Constantine (r.306–337), from Moesia (today Yugoslavia), brought it to an end. For administrative purposes, Diocletian divided the empire into two parts. Although the two emperors who ruled the halves were supposed to confer on all matters, the reform was a harbinger of things to come, when the Greek-speaking East and Latin-speaking West would go their separate ways. Meanwhile, the wars over imperial succession ceased with the establishment of Constantine's dynasty, and political stability put an end to the border wars.

A New Religion

The empire of Constantine was the Roman empire restored. Yet nothing could have been more different from the old Roman empire. It was the beginning of what historians call "Late Antiquity," a period transformed by the culture and religion of the provinces.

The province of Palestine—to the Romans of Italy a most dismal backwater—had been in fact a hotbed of creative religious and social ideas around the beginning of what we now call the first millennium. Chafing under Roman domination, experimenting with new notions of morality and new ethical life-styles, the Jews of Palestine gave birth to religious groups of breathtaking originality. One coalesced around Jesus. After his death, under the impetus of the Jew-turned-Christian Paul (d.c.65), a new and radical brand of monotheism under Jesus' name was actively preached to Gentiles (non-Jews) not only in Palestine but beyond. Its core belief was that men and women were saved—redeemed and accorded eternal life in heaven—by their faith in Jesus.

At first Christianity was of nearly perfect indifference to elite Romans, who were devoted to the gods who had served them so well over years of conquest and prosperity. Nor did it attract many of the lower classes, who were still firmly rooted in old local religious traditions. The Romans had never insisted that the provincials whom they conquered give up their beliefs; they simply added official Roman gods into local pantheons. For most people, both rich and poor, the rich texture of religious life at the local level was both comfortable and satisfying. In dreams they encountered their personal gods, who served them as guardians and friends. At home they found their household gods, evoking family ancestors. Outside, on the street, they visited temples and monuments to local gods, reminders of home-town pride. Here and there could be seen monuments to the "divine emperor," put up by rich town benefactors. Everyone engaged in the festivals of the public cults, whose ceremonies gave rhythm to the year. Paganism was thus at one and the same time personal, familial, local, and imperial.

Map 1.2:
Christian Churches
Founded Before the
Great Persecution of
Diocletian (A.D.304)

But Christianity had its attractions too. It was, in the first place, persuasive to Romans and other city-dwellers of the middle class, who could never hope to

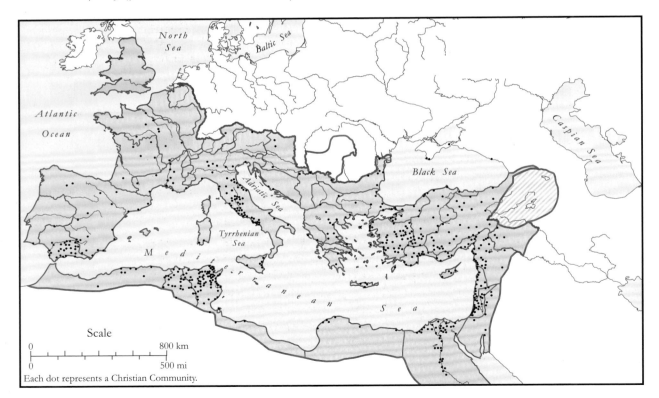

Scale

0   800 km

0   500 mi

Each dot represents a Christian Community.

become part of the educated upper crust. Christianity substituted "the elect" for the elite. Education, long and expensive, was the ticket into Roman high society. Christians had their own solid, less expensive knowledge. It was the key to an even "higher" society. Saint Perpetua (*d*.203), imprisoned, awaiting martyrdom, debated her father with the assurance of a Socrates:

> "Father, do you see this vase here...?" "Yes, I do," said he. And I told him: "Could it be called by any other name than what it is?" And he said: "No." "Well, so too I cannot be called anything other than what I am, a Christian."[1]

Christianity attracted as well those provincials who had never been given the chance to feel truly Roman. (Citizenship was not granted to all provincials until 212.) The new religion was confident, hopeful, and universal. As the empire settled into an era of peaceful complacency in the second century, its hinterlands opened to the influence of the center, and vice versa. Men and women whose horizons in earlier times would have stretched no farther than their village now took to the roads as traders—or confronted a new cosmopolitanism right at their doorsteps. Uprooted from old traditions, they found comfort in small assemblies—churches—where they were welcomed as equals and where God was the same, no matter what region the members of the church hailed from.

The Romans persecuted Christians—after besting her father in debate, Perpetua went off joyfully to her martyrdom—but at first only locally, sporadically, and above all in times of crisis. At such moments the Romans feared that the gods were venting their wrath on the empire because Christians would not carry out the proper sacrifices. True, the Jews also refused to honor the Roman gods, but the Romans could usually tolerate—just barely—Jewish practices as part of their particular cultural identity. Christians, however, among whom numbered even Romans, claimed God not only for themselves but for all. Major official government persecutions of Christians began in the 250s, with the third-century crisis.

Meanwhile the Christian community organized itself. By 304, on the eve of the last great persecution, when perhaps only 10 per cent of the population was Christian, numerous churches dotted the imperial landscape. (See Map 1.2.) Each church was two-tiered: at the bottom were the people (the "laity"), at the top the clergy (from *kleros*, or "Lord's portion"). In turn, the clergy were supervised by the bishop, assisted by his "presbyters" (the priests who served with the bishops), deacons, and lesser servitors. Some bishops—those of Alexandria, Antioch, Carthage, Jerusalem, and Rome (whose bishop was later called the "pope"),—were more important than others. No religion was better prepared for official recognition.

This it received in 313, in the so-called Edict of Milan. Emperor Constantine, attributing his imperial triumph to the God of the Christians, declared toleration for all religions. In fact, he converted to Christianity and favored it: he built and endowed church buildings, made sure that property was restored to churches which had been stripped during the persecutions, and gave priests special privileges. Under him, the ancient Greek city of Byzantium became a new Christian city, residence of emperors, and named for the emperor himself: Constantinople. The bishop of Constantinople became a patriarch, a "superbishop," equal to the bishops of Antioch and Alexandria although not as important as the pope. In one of the crowning measures of his career, Constantine called and then presided over the first ecumenical (universal) church council, the Council of Nicaea, in 325. There the assembled bishops hammered out some of the canon law and doctrines of the Christian church.

With Constantine's conversion and his privileging of Christianity, it was simply a matter of time before most people considered it both good and expedient to convert. Though after Constantine's time several emperors espoused "heretical"—unacceptable—forms of Christianity, and one (Julian, the "Apostate") professed paganism, the die had been cast. In 391 Emperor Theodosius (r.379-395) declared Christianity the official religion of the Roman empire. All the old public cults were outlawed, and pagan temples were smashed. Soon, at Carthage in 401, Saint Augustine (354-430), bishop of Hippo, and the most influential of the Church Fathers, was telling his congregation that "all superstition of pagans and heathens should be annihilated"; he may well have inspired the massacre of sixty people in a nearby city.[2] In this way—via law, coercion, and conviction—a fragile religion hailing from one of the most backward of the provinces triumphed everywhere in the Roman world.

But with triumph came competition and even strife. Who would control and direct this new religion with its all-powerful God? Who would determine what was holy? Who would know when the old gods, now reclassified as demons, might claim to be gods again? Vigilance was necessary. After Constantine, after the persecutions, Christians fought with each other over doctrine and over the location of the holy.

Doctrine

The men we call the "Church Fathers" were the victors in battles over doctrine. Already in Constantine's day, Saint Athanasius (c.295-373)—then secretary to the bishop of Alexandria, later bishop there himself—led the challenge against the beliefs of the Christians next door. He called them "Arians," rather than Christians, after the priest Arius (250-336), another Alexandrian and a competing focus of local loyalties. Athanasius promoted his views at the Council of Nicaea and won. It is because of this that he is the orthodox catholic "Father" and Arius the "heretic." For both

Athanasius and Arius, God was triune, that is, three persons in one: the Father, the Son, and the Holy Spirit. Their debate was about the nature of these persons. For the Arians, the Father was pure Godhead while the Son was created ("begotten"), flesh but not quite flesh, and thus neither purely human nor purely divine. To Athanasius and the assembled bishops at Nicaea, this was heresy — the wrong "choice" (the root meaning of the Greek term *hairesis*) — and a damnable faith. The Council of Nicaea wrote the party line: the Father and Son were co-eternal and equal in divinity. Arius was condemned and banished. His doctrine, however, persisted. It was the brand of Christianity that Wulfilas ("little Wolf")(*c.*311–383) preached to the Goths along the Danube, for example, when he and his followers translated the Bible into Gothic.

Arianism was only the tip of the iceberg. Indeed, the period 350–450 might be called the "era of competing doctrines." As church councils met — especially Ephesus (431) and Chalcedon (451) — to shave ever more closely the contours of right doctrine, dissent multiplied. Monophysites (a later, convenient term for those who opposed the rulings of Chalcedon) held that the "flesh" that God had assumed as Christ was nevertheless divine. Eventually this view, which tended to assimilate human flesh to Christ's and thus divinize humankind, became the doctrine of the Armenian, Coptic (Egyptian), and Ethiopian Christian churches. On the other hand, Pelagius (from Britain, *d.* after 418) was interested less in the nature of Christ than in that of humanity: for him conversion bleached out sins, and thereafter people could follow God by their own will. Entirely opposite to Pelagius was Saint Augustine, for whom human beings were capable of nothing good without God's grace working through them: "Come, Lord, act upon us and rouse us up and call us back! Fire us, clutch us, let your sweet fragrance grow upon us!"[3]

These debates were carried on everywhere, and with passion. Gregory of Nyssa reported that at Constantinople,

> if one asks anyone for change, he will discuss with you whether the Son is begotten or unbegotten. If you ask about the quality of bread you will receive the answer, "the Father is greater, the Son is less." If you suggest a bath is desirable, you will be told "there was nothing before the Son was created."[4]

Like commenting on sports figures today, this was more than small-talk: it identified people's loyalties. It also brought God down to earth. God had debased himself to take on human flesh. It was critical to know how he had done so and what that meant for the rest of humanity.

For these huge questions, Saint Augustine wrote most of the definitive answers, though they were certainly modified and reworked over the centuries. In the *City of*

God, a huge and sprawling work, he defined two cities: the earthly one in which our feet are planted, in which we are born, learn to read, marry, get old, and die; and the heavenly one, on which our eyes, heart, and mind are fixed. The first, the "City of Man," is impermanent, subject to fire, war, famine, and sickness; the second, the "City of God," is the opposite. Only there is true, eternal happiness. Yet the first, however imperfect, is where the institutions of society — local churches, schools, governments — make possible the attainment of the second. Thus, in Augustine's hands, the old traditions of the ancient world were reused and reoriented for a new Christian society.

THE SOURCES OF GOD'S GRACE

The City of Man was fortunate. There God had instituted his church. Christ had said to Peter, the foremost of his apostles (his "messengers"):

> Thou art Peter [*Petros*, or "rock" in Greek]; and upon this rock I will build my church, and the gates of hell shall not prevail against it. And I will give to thee the keys of the kingdom of heaven. And whatsoever thou shalt bind upon earth, it shall be bound also in heaven; and whatsoever thou shalt loose on earth, it shall be loosed also in heaven. (Matt. 16.18-19)

Although variously interpreted (above all by the popes at Rome, who took it to mean that the popes were the successors of Saint Peter, the first bishop of Rome), no one doubted that this declaration confirmed that the all-important powers of binding (imposing penance on) and loosing (forgiving) sinners were in the hands of Christ's earthly heirs, the priests and bishops. In the Mass, the central liturgy of the earthly church, the bread and wine on the altar became the body and blood of Christ, the "Eucharist." Through the Mass the faithful were joined to one another; to the souls of the dead, who were remembered in the liturgy; and to Christ himself.

The Eucharist was one potent source of God's grace. There were others. Above all, there were certain people so beloved by God, so infused with his grace, that they were both models of virtue and powerful wonder-workers. These were the saints. In the early church, the saints had largely been the martyrs, but martyrdom ended with Constantine. The new saints of the fourth and fifth centuries were "athletes" of God: like Saint Symeon Stylites (396-459), they climbed tall pillars and stood there for decades; or, like Saint Anthony (250-356), they entered tombs to fight, heroically and successfully, with the demons (whose reality was as little questioned as the existence of germs is today). These were neither flights of fancy nor the deeds of madmen. They were considered socially responsible acts by the surrounding community.

Purged of sin by their ascetic rigors—giving up their possessions, fasting, praying, not sleeping, not engaging in sex—and fearless in the face of the demons, holy men and women were intercessors with God on behalf of their neighbors and those who sought them out from afar. Saint Athanasius told the story of Saint Anthony: after years of solitude and asceticism the saint emerged

> as out of a shrine, as one initiated into sacred mysteries and filled with the spirit of God.... He was not embarrassed when he saw the crowd, nor was he elated at seeing so many there to receive him. No, he had himself completely under control—a man guided by reason and stable in his character. Through him the Lord cured many of those present who were afflicted with bodily ills, and freed others from impure spirits. He also gave Anthony charm in speaking; and so he comforted many in sorrow, and others who were quarreling he made friends.[5]

Healer of illnesses and of disputes, Anthony brought spiritual, physical, and civic peace. This was power indeed.

But who would control it? Bishop Athanasius of Alexandria laid claim to Anthony's legacy by writing about it. Yet writing was only one way to appropriate and harness the power of the saints (and also of making sure that demons were not craftily standing in for them). When holy men and women died, their power lived on in their relics (whatever they left behind: their bones, hair, clothes, sometimes even the dust from their tombs). In the fourth century, pious people knew this very well. They wanted access to these "special dead." Rich and influential Romans got their own holy monopolies by simply moving saintly bones home with them:

> [Pompeiana] obtained the body [of the martyr Maximilianus] from the magistrate and, after placing it in her own chamber, later brought it to Carthage. There she buried it at the foot of a hill near the governor's palace next to the body of [Saint] Cyprian. Thirteen days later [Pompeiana] herself passed away and was buried in the same spot.[6]

With enough ladies like Pompeiana, the saints were likely to be appropriated by the rich laity, buried on private estates, made the focal points of family burials. What place would the churches, the clergy, and the wider community have in this privatized system? Churchmen like Saint Ambrose (339-397), bishop of Milan, did not need to think twice. He had the newly discovered relics of Saints Gervasius and Protasius moved from their original resting place into his newly built cathedral and buried under the altar, the focus of communal worship. He allied himself, his successors, and the whole Christian community of Milan with the power of those saints. No single rich patron could thereafter control them. Ambrose set the pattern for other churchmen; henceforth bishops were in charge of the disposition of relics. (For an example of a reliquary, the container in which relics were generally placed, see Plate 6.1 on p.217.)

Art from the Provinces to the Center

Just as Christianity came from the periphery to transform the center, so too did provincial artistic traditions. Classical Roman art, nicely exemplified by the wall paintings of Pompeii (Plate 1.1 and Plate 1.2), was characterized by light and shadow, a sense of atmosphere—of earth, sky, air, light—and a feeling of movement, even in the midst of calm. Figures—sometimes lithe, sometimes stocky, always "plastic," suggesting volume and real weight on the ground—interacted, touching one another or talking, and caring little or nothing about the viewer. In Plate 1.1 the craggy mountains are the focus. A shepherd, painted with sketchy lines, pushes a goat toward a shrine, perhaps to sacrifice the animal. On the left, another goat frolics. Shadowy shepherds and goats appear in the distance. The scene is tranquil yet suggests both the grandeur of nature and the solemnity of the occasion. Plate 1.2 pictures a moment well known to Romans from their myths. A nude man—thus clearly an athlete—stands in quiet triumph while people kiss his hands and feet. Any Roman would know, from the "iconography"—the symbolic meaning of the elements—that the man is Theseus and that he has just slain the Minotaur (dying in the doorway on the left), who had demanded a tribute of Athenian youths each year in return for peace. The artist has chosen to depict the very instant that Theseus emerges from the Minotaur's lair, the intended victims crowding around him to express their gratitude. Even though the story is illustrated for the viewers' pleasure, the figures act as if no one is looking at them. They are self-absorbed, glimpsed as if through a window onto their private world.

The relief of Trajan's Column (Plate 1.3) shows that even in the medium of sculpture, classical artists were concerned with atmosphere and movement, figures turning and interacting with one another, and space created by "perspective," where some elements seem to recede while others come to the fore.

But even in the classical period there were other artistic conventions and traditions in the Roman empire. For many years these provincial artistic traditions had been tamped down by the juggernaut of Roman political and cultural hegemony. But in the third century, with the new importance of the provinces, these regional traditions re-emerged. As provincial military men became the new heroes and emperors, artistic

Plate 1.1: Landscape from Pompeii (*c*.79). The Roman artist of this painting created the illusion of space, air, and light directly on the flat surface of a wall (probably of a house).

Following pages:

Plate 1.2: Theseus the Minotaur Slayer, Pompeii (*c*.79). Theseus, hero of a Greek myth, and here portrayed both triumphant and adored, adorned the wall of a private house at Pompeii.

Plate 1.3: Trajan's Column (113). This is a small segment of a towering column built over Emperor Trajan's tomb in his forum at Rome. The entire tower is covered with sculpted reliefs narrating—in a continuous spiral—two of the emperor's military campaigns.

Plate 1.2

Plate L 3

Plate 1.4: Head from Palmyra (1st half of 1st cent.). Compare this fragment of a woman's head with the head of Theseus in **Plate 1.2** to see the very different notions of the human body and of beauty that co-existed in the Roman empire.

tastes changed as well. The center—Rome, Italy, Constantinople—now borrowed its artistic styles from the periphery.

To understand some of the old regional traditions, consider the sculpted head of a woman from Palmyra, Syria (Plate 1.4), a large stone coffer for holding the bones of the dead from Jerusalem (Plate 1.5), and a tombstone from the region of Carthage—Tunis, Tunisia today—(Plate 1.6). All of these were made in either the first or second century C.E., under the shadow of Roman imperial rule. Yet they are little like Roman works of art. Above all, the artists who made these pieces valued decorative elements. The Jerusalem coffer plays with formal and solemn patterns of light and shadow. The tombstone flattens its figures, varying them by cutting lines for folds, hands, and eyes. Any sense of movement here comes from the incised patterns, certainly not from the rigidly frontal figures. Although the head from Palmyra is more classical, it too is created by an artist in love with decoration. The lady's hair is a series of rings and lines; her pupils are spirals.

There may be something to the idea that such works of art were "inferior" to Roman—but not much. The artists who made them had their own values and were not much interested in classical notions of beauty. The Palmyra head is clearly the work of a sculptor who wanted to show the opposite of human interaction. His lady takes part in no familiar mythological story for viewers to enjoy. She has been

Plate 1.5: Decorated Coffer from Jerusalem (1st cent.?).
The human figure was of no interest to the carver of this stone chest, whose formal floral and architectural motives seemed more appropriate for its sober contents: the bones of the dead.

"abstracted" from any natural context. Her very head, eyebrows, and eyes are "abstract"—simplified until they have become shapes. All of this emphasizes her otherworldliness. Here is a woman who is deeply contemplative. Her eyes, the most prominent feature of her face, gaze outward beyond the viewer, transcending the here and now.

The same emphasis on transcendence explains the horizontal zones of the limestone tombstone. It may seem absurd to compare this piece with the Pompeian painting of mountains and shepherd (Plate 1.1). Yet it is crucial to realize that the subjects are largely the same: people and animals, in the context of a sacrifice. It is the approach that is different. On the provincial tombstone, the stress is on hierarchical order. In the center of the top zone is a god. In the middle zones are people busying themselves with proper religious ceremonies. At the bottom, the lowest rung, are three people praying. The proper order of the cosmos, not the natural order, is the focus. This tombstone is no window onto a private world; rather it teaches and preaches to those who look at it.

The extraordinary development of the fourth century was the center's appropriation of these artistic styles of the provinces. The trend is graphically illustrated by a

Plate 1.6 (facing page): Tombstone from near Carthage (2nd cent.?). The stiff, frontal figures on this relief show a delight in order, hierarchy, and decoration.

Plate 1.7: Base of the Hippodrome Obelisk (c.390). Nothing illustrates changing imperial artistic tastes so well as this carving, placed right in the middle of the most imperial part of Constantinople. It was inspired more by the style of **Plate 1.6** than by the older imperial style of **Plate 1.3**.

marble base made at Constantinople *c.*390 to support a gigantic ancient obelisk, transported at great cost from Egypt and set up with considerable difficulty at the Hippodrome, the great sports arena. The four-sided base depicts the games and races that took place in the stadium. The side shown in Plate 1.7 is decisively divided into two tiers: at the top is the imperial family and other dignitaries, formal, frontal, staring straight ahead. Directly in the center is the imperial group, higher than all others. Beneath, in the lower tier, are bearded, hairy-coated barbarians, bringing humble offerings to those on high. The two levels are divided by a decorative frame, a rough indication of the "sky boxes" inhabited by the emperor and his retinue. The folds of the drapery are graceful but stylized. The hair-do's are caps. The ensemble is meant to preach eternal truths: the highness of imperial power and its transcendence of time and place.

This style of art was not Christian in origin, but it was certainly adopted by Christians at the time. It was suited to a religion that saw only fleeting value in the City of Man, that sought to transcend the world, and that had a message to preach. We shall see the influence of this style throughout the Middle Ages. Nevertheless, at the end of the fourth and the beginning of the fifth century, around the same time that the emperor was ordering the Hippodrome base, other, more classical artistic styles were making a brief comeback. Sometimes called the "renaissance of the late fourth and early fifth century," this was the first of many recurring infusions of the classicizing spirit in medieval art. On a small ivory container made in the early fifth century (Plate 1.8), a young man with a book sits like a philosopher, gesturing with his free hand, teaching old and young alike. He moves and turns; his body has weight; his garment stretches exuberantly over knee and ankle. There is a sense of depth and interaction. The carving recalls Trajan's column. But it is Christian art: the teacher is Christ, and the container is a pyx, used to hold the wafers of the Eucharist.

Plate 1.8 (facing page): Ivory Pyx (5th cent.). The lively gestures of these figures and their high relief are reminiscent of the older style of Trajan's column (**Plate 1.3**), but the subject matter is entirely new: Christ teaching the elders.

THE BARBARIANS

The ivory pyx may have been carved just as the Visigoths were sacking Rome (410). The sack was a stunning blow. Like a married couple in a bitter divorce, both Romans and Goths had once wooed one another; they then became mutually and comfortably dependent; eventually they fell into betrayal and strife. Nor was the Visigothic experience unique. The Franks, too, had been recruited into the Roman army, some of their members settling peacefully within the imperial borders. The Burgundian experience was similar.

The Romans called all these peoples "barbarians." They called some of them

"Germani" — Germans — because they materialized from beyond the Rhine, in Germania. Historians today tend to differentiate these peoples linguistically: "Germanic peoples" are those who spoke Germanic languages. Whatever name we use (they certainly had no collective name for themselves), these peoples were long used to a settled existence. Archaeologists have found in northern Europe evidence of small hamlets built and continuously inhabited for centuries by Germanic groups before they entered the empire. At Wijster, one of their settlements near the North Sea, for example, about fifty or sixty families lived in a well-planned community, with hedged streets and carefully aligned houses. Elsewhere, smaller hamlets were the rule. Whether due to their contacts with the Romans or because of indigenous practices, Germanic society was not egalitarian: we can see the evidence of social inequalities in the different sorts of houses that archaeologists have uncovered: long wooden houses for the well-off, sunken cottages for lesser folk. Supporting themselves by herding and farming, Germanic traders bartered with Roman provincials along the empire's border.

There was no biological distinction between "Germanic" traders and "Roman" ones, nor was there any biological distinction between different Germanic tribesmen and –women. However, there were ethnic differences — differences created by preferences and customs surrounding food, language, clothing, hairstyle, customs, behaviors, and all the other elements that go into a sense of identity. But these ethnicities were in constant flux as tribes came together and broke apart.

The "ethnogenesis" of the Goths, for example — the ethnicities that came into being and changed over time — made them not one people but many. If it is true that a people called the "Goths" (Gutones) can be found in the first century C.E. in what is today northwestern Poland, that does not mean that they much resembled those "Goths" who, in the third century, organized and dominated a confederation of steppe peoples and forest dwellers of mixed origins north of the Black Sea (today Ukraine). The second set of Goths was a splinter of the first; by the time it got to the Black Sea, it had joined with many other groups. In short, the Goths were multiethnic.

Taking advantage — and soon becoming a part — of the crisis of the third century, the Black Sea Goths invaded and plundered the nearby provinces of the Roman empire. The Romans first responded with annual payments to buy peace, but then stopped, preferring confrontation. Around 250, Gothic and other raiders and pirates plundered in the Balkans and Anatolia (today Turkey). It took many years of bitter fighting for Roman armies, reinforced by Gothic and other mercenaries, to stop these raids. Afterwards, once again transformed, the Goths emerged as two different groups: eastern (later, Ostrogoths), again north of the Black Sea, and western (later, Visigoths), in what is today Romania. By the mid-330s the Visigoths were allies of the empire and fighting in their armies. Some rose to the position of army leaders.

By the end of the fourth century, many Roman army units were made up of whole tribes—Goths or Franks, for example—fighting as "federates" for the Roman government under their own chiefs.

This was the marriage. It fell apart under the pressure of the Huns, a nomadic people from the semi-arid, grass-covered plains (the "steppeland") of west-central Asia, who invaded the Black Sea region in 376, attacking and destroying its settlements like lightning and moving into Romania. The Visigoths, joined by other refugees driven from their settlements by the Huns, petitioned Emperor Valens (r.364-378) to be allowed into the Empire. He agreed; we have seen that barbarians had long been settled within the borders as army recruits. But in this case the numbers were unprecedented: tens of thousands, perhaps even up to 200,000. The Romans were overwhelmed, unprepared, and resentful. About two centuries later a humanitarian crisis was recalled by the Gothic historian Jordanes:

Map 1.3: The Former Western Empire, *c.*500

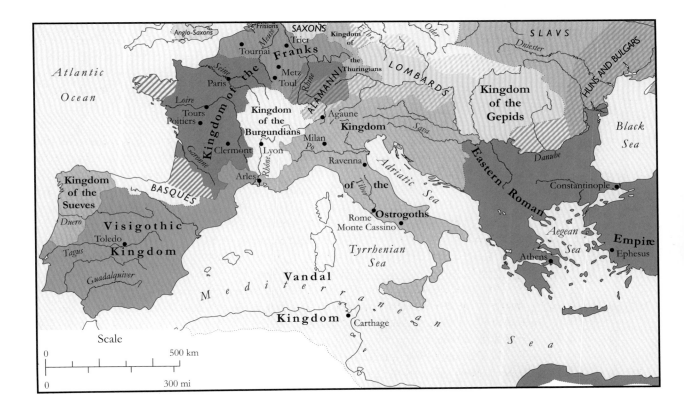

[The Goths] crossed the Danube and settled Dacia Ripensis, Moesia and Thrace by permission of the Emperor. Soon famine and want came upon them, as often happens to a people not yet well settled in a country. Their princes ... began to lament the plight of their army and begged Lupicinus and Maximus, the Roman commanders, to open a market. But to what will not the "cursed lust for gold" compel men to assent? The generals, swayed by avarice, sold them at a high price not only the flesh of sheep and oxen, but even the carcasses of dogs and unclean animals, so that a slave would be bartered for a loaf of bread or ten pounds of meat. When their goods and chattels failed, the greedy trader demanded their sons in return for the necessities of life. And the parents consented even to this.[7]

The parents did not consent for long. In 378 the Visigoths rebelled against the Romans, killing Emperor Valens at the battle of Adrianople. Thereafter, again bound as federates to serve the Romans, the Visigoths under Alaric began in about 397 to seek a place for permanent settlement. Moving first to Greece, then to Italy, taking Rome for a few days in 410, the Visigoths settled in Gaul, south of the Loire, in 416. By 484 they had taken most of Spain as well.

Meanwhile, beginning late in 406, perhaps also impelled by the Huns, other barbarian groups — Alans, Vandals, and Sueves — entered the Empire by crossing the Rhine River. They first moved into Gaul, then into Spain. The Vandals crossed into North Africa; the Sueves remained in Spain, but most of their kingdom was conquered by the Visigoths in the course of the sixth century. When, after Attila's death in 453, the empire that he had created along the Danubian frontier collapsed, still other groups moved into the Roman empire — Ostrogoths, Rugi, Gepids — each with a "deal" from the Roman government, each with the hope of working for Rome and reaping its rewards. In 476 the last Roman emperor in the West, Romulus Augustulus, was deposed by Odoacer, a barbarian (from one of the lesser tribes, the Sciri) leading Roman troops. Odoacer promptly had himself declared King of Italy and, in a bid to

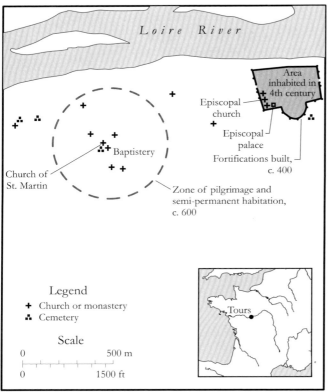

Map 1.4: Tours, *c.600*

"unite" the empire, sent Augustulus' imperial insignia to Emperor Zeno (*r*.474-491). But Zeno in his turn authorized Theodoric, king of the Ostrogoths, to attack Odoacer in about 490. Theodoric's conquest of Italy succeeded. Not much later the Franks, long used to fighting for the Romans, conquered Gaul under Clovis (*r*.481-511), a Roman official and king of the Franks, by defeating a provincial governor of Gaul and several barbarian rivals. Meanwhile other barbarian groups set up kingdoms of their own.

Around the year 500 the former Roman empire was no longer a scarf flung around the Mediterranean; it was a mosaic. (See Map 1.3.) Northwest Africa was now the Vandal Kingdom, Spain the Visigothic kingdom, Gaul the Kingdom of the Franks, and Italy the Kingdom of the Ostrogoths. The Anglo-Saxons occupied southeastern Britain; the Burgundians formed a kingdom centered in what is today Switzerland. Only the eastern half of the Empire—the long end of the scarf—remained intact.

THE NEW ORDER

What was new about the "new order" of the sixth century was less the rise of barbarian kingdoms than it was, in the West, the decay of the cities and corresponding liveliness of the countryside, the increased dominance of the rich, and the quiet domestication of Christianity. In the East, the Roman empire continued, made an ill-fated bid to expand, and finally retrenched as an autonomous entity: the Byzantine empire.

The Ruralization of the West

Where the barbarians settled, they did so with only tiny ripples of discontent from articulate Roman elites. It used to be thought that the Roman empire granted their invaders vast estates confiscated from Roman landowners. It now seems that the new tribal rulers were often content to live in cities or border forts, collecting land taxes rather than land.

For Romans, the chief objection to the new barbarian overlords was their Arian Christian beliefs. Clovis, king of the Franks, may have been the first Germanic king to overcome this problem. (If so, Sigismund, king of the Burgundians, was a close second.) Clovis flirted with Arianism early on, but he soon converted to the Catholic Christianity of his Gallic neighbors.

In other respects as well, the new rulers took over Roman institutions; they issued laws, for example. Under Alaric II (*r.*484–507) the Visigoths promulgated the *Breviary*, a compendium of Roman laws. Other barbarian law codes reflected more directly "tribal" customs, though in important ways these were indistinguishable from Roman provincial law. Sigismund, king of the Burgundians, issued a code of Burgundian laws in 517. A Frankish law code was compiled under King Clovis, fusing provincial Roman and Germanic procedures into a single whole.

Written in Latin, these laws revealed their Roman inspiration even in their language. Barbarian kings, some well educated themselves, often depended on Roman advisors to write up their letters and laws. In Italy, in particular, an outstanding group of Roman administrators, judges, and officers served Ostrogothic King Theodoric the Great (*r.*493–526). They included the encyclopedic Cassiodorus (490–583), author of the *Institutes of Christian Culture*, and the learned Boethius (480–524), who wrote the tranquil *Consolation of Philosophy* as he awaited execution for treason. Since the fourth century, Romans had become used to barbarian leaders; in the sixth, there was nothing very strange in having them as kings.

Far stranger was the disappearance of the urban middle class. The new taxes of the fourth century had much to do with this. The *curiales*—members of the town elites—had been used to collecting the taxes for their communities, making up any shortfalls, and reaping the rewards of prestige for doing so. In the fourth century, new land and head taxes impoverished the *curiales*, while very rich landowners, out in the countryside, surrounded by their bodyguards and slaves, simply did not bother to pay. Now the tax burdens fell on poorer people. Families pressed to pay taxes they could not afford escaped to the great estates of the rich, giving up their free status in return for land and protection. By the seventh century, the rich had won; the barbarian kings no longer bothered to collect general taxes.

The cities, most of them walled since the time of the crisis of the third century, were no longer thriving or populous, though they remained political and religious centers. For example, the episcopal complex at Tours (in Gaul) was within the walls of a fortification thrown up *c.*400. (See Map 1.4.) Although it still functioned as an institution of religion and government, almost no one lived there any longer. But outside the Roman city, in a cemetery that the Romans had carefully sited away from ordinary habitation, a new church rose over the relics of the local saint, Martin. This served as a magnet for the people of the surrounding countryside and even further away. A baptistery was constructed nearby, to baptize the infants of pilgrims and others who came to the tomb of Saint Martin hoping for a miracle. Sometimes people stayed for years. Gregory, bishop of Tours (*r.*573–594), our chief source for the history of Gaul in the sixth century, described Chainemund, a blind woman:

She was a very pious woman, and full of faith she went to the venerable church of the blessed bishop Martin. She was ... also covered with abrasions on her entire body. For a sickness had attacked all her limbs with sores, and her appearance was so horrible and so repulsive to look at that she was considered by the people as a leper. Every day she felt her way and went to the church of the glorious champion. After almost three years, while she was standing in front of his tomb, her eyes were opened and she saw everything clearly. All the weakness in her limbs disappeared ... and a healthy skin grew back.[8]

With people like Chainemund flocking to the tomb, no wonder that archaeologists have found evidence of semi-permanent habitations right at the cemetery.

War and plague no doubt reduced the overall population, but it is impossible to gauge the precise toll. More calculable were changes in styles of life. The shift from urban to rural settlements brought with it a new localism. The active long-distance trade of the Mediterranean slowed down, though it did not stop. But now this trade penetrated very little beyond the coast. This is nicely illustrated by the story of pottery, a cheap necessity of the ancient world. In the sixth century we find fine mass-produced African red pottery on even the most humble tables along the Mediterranean Sea coast; but inland, most people had to make do with local handmade wares as regional networks of exchange eroded long-distance connections.

For some—the rich—the new disconnection of the rural landscape with the wider world had its charms. When they were inclined, they could still take advantage of luxury goods. In some regions they could even enjoy a life of splendid isolation:

On the summit of the high rock a magnificent palace is built .... Marble columns hold up the imposing structure; from the top you can see boats gliding by on the surface of the river in summertime .... Water is channeled off along ducts following the contours of the mountain.... On these slopes, formerly sterile, Nicetius has planted juicy vines, and green vineshoots clothe the high rock that used to bear nothing but scrub. Orchards with fruit-trees growing here and there fill the air with the perfume of their flowers.[9]

The owner of this haven was Nicetius, bishop of Trier. He retreated to it when his pastoral cares gave him the chance. Bishops like Nicetius were among the rich; most rose to their episcopal status in their twilight years, after they had married and had sired children to inherit their estates. (Their wives continued to live with them but—or so it was hoped—not to sleep with them.) Great lay landlords, kings,

SCOTS

PICTS

ANGLES

SAXONS

BRITONS

North Sea

NORSE

SWEDES

DANES

FINNS

Baltic Sea

LITHUANIANS

PRUSSIANS

EASTERN SLAVS

Atlantic Ocean

FRISIANS

SAXONS

Elbe

THURINGIANS

WESTERN SLAVS

Oder

Vistula

Brittany
(Frankish Dependency)

Austrasia

Tertry

Soissons • Reims

Neustria

Cologne
Mainz

Seine

Metz •

Loire

Frankish Kingdoms

Tours •

Rhine

Bavarians
(Frankish Dependency)

Poitiers •

Burgundy

SLAVS

Suevian Kingdom
(Conquered by
Visigoths, 584)

BASQUES

Aquitaine

Garonne

Dnieper

Avar Khaganate

BULGARS

Rhône

Milan •

Visigothic Kingdom

Ebro

Toledo •

Lombard Kingdom

Adriatic Sea

SOUTHERN SLAVS

Danube

Black Sea

Córdoba •

Rome •

Mediterranean

Carthage •

Eastern

Roman

Constantinople •
• Chalcedon
Nicaea

Empire

Ephesus •

Antioc

BERBERS

terranean Sea

Alexandria •

Jerusalem

Dama

GARAMANTES

BERBERS

Scale

0   800 km

0   500 mi

Lambert Conformal Conic projection.

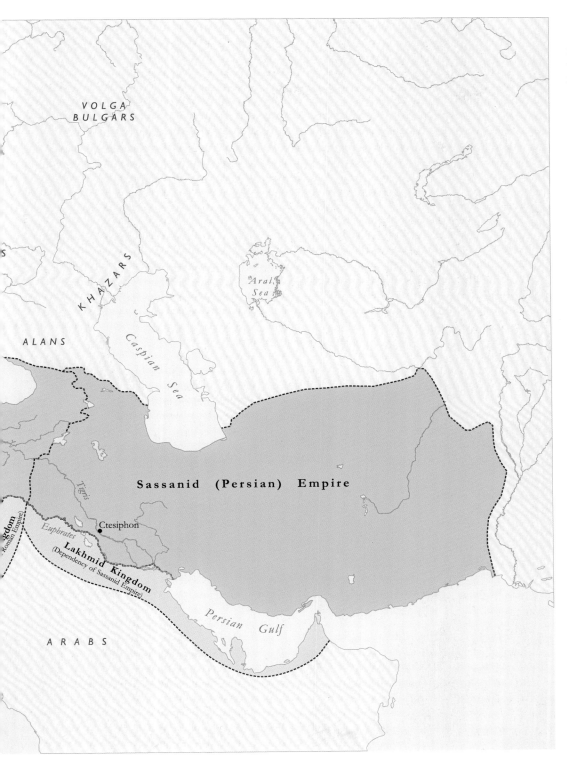

VOLGA
BULGARS

KHAZARS

*Aral
Sea*

ALANS

*Caspian
Sea*

Sassanid (Persian) Empire

Tigris

Euphrates

Ctesiphon

gdom
(Roman Empire)

Lakhmid Kingdom
(Dependency of Sassanid Empire)

ARABS

Persian Gulf

queens, warriors, and courtiers controlled and monopolized most of the rest of the wealth of the West, now based largely on land.

Monasteries, too, were beginning to become important corporate landowners. In the sixth century many monks lived in communities just far enough away from the centers of power to be holy, yet near enough to be important. Monks were not quite laity (since they devoted their entire life to religion) yet not quite clergy (since they were only rarely ordained) but something in between and increasingly admired. It is often said that Saint Anthony was the "first monk," and though this may not be strictly true, it is not far off the mark. Like Anthony, monks lived a life of daily martyrdom, giving up their wealth, family ties, and worldly offices. Like Anthony, who towards the end of his life came out of the tombs he had once retreated to in order to be with others, monks lived in communities. Some communities were of men only, some of women, some of both (in separate quarters). Whatever the sort, monks lived in obedience to a "rule" that gave them a stable and orderly way of life.

The rule might be unwritten, as it was at Saint-Maurice d'Agaune, a monastic community set up in 515 by Sigismund on the eve of his accession to the Burgundian throne. The monks at Agaune, divided into groups that went to the church in relay, carried out a grueling regime of non-stop prayer every day. Built outside the Burgundian capital of Geneva, high on a cliff that was held to be the site of the heroic martyrdom of a Christian Roman legion, this monastery tapped into a holy landscape and linked it to Sigismund and his episcopal advisors.

Other rules were written. Caesarius, bishop of Arles (r.502–542) wrote one for his sister, the "abbess" (head) of a monastery of women. He wrote another for his nephew, the "abbot" of a male monastery. In Italy, Saint Benedict (d.c.555) wrote the most famous of the monastic rules some time around 540. With its adoption, much later, by the Carolingian kings of the ninth century, it became the monastic norm in the West. Unlike the rule of Agaune, where prayer was paramount, Benedict's Rule divided the day into discrete periods of prayer, reading, and labor. Nevertheless, the core of its program, as at Agaune, was the "liturgy"—not just the Mass, but an elaborate round of formal worship that took place seven times a day and once at night. At these specific times, the monks chanted—that is sang—the "Offices," much of which consisted of the psalms, a group of 150 poems in the Old Testament:

> The Morning Office [Lauds] on Sunday shall begin with Psalm 66 recited straight through without an antiphon [antiphons were additional chants, normally added before and after each psalm verse]. After that let Psalm 50 be said with "Alleluia," then Psalms 117 and 62, the Canticle of Blessing [a text taken from St. Luke's Gospel] and the Psalms of praise [Psalms 148–150]; then a lesson from the Apocalypse to be recited by heart. [More chants follow.][10]

By the end of each week the monks were to have completed all 150 psalms.

Benedict's monastery, Monte Cassino, was in the shadow of Rome, far enough to be an "escape" but near enough to link it to the papacy. Pope Gregory the Great (590–604), arguably the man most responsible for making the papacy the greatest power in Italy, took the time to write a biography of Benedict and praise his Rule. Monasteries, by their ostentatious rejection of wealth and power, became partners of the powerful. The monks were seen as models of virtue, and their prayers were thought to reach God's ear. It was crucial to ally with them.

Little by little the Christian religion was domesticated to the needs of the new order, even as it shaped that order to fit its demands. Chainemund was not afraid to go to the cemetery outside of Tours. There were no demons there; they had been driven far away by the power of Saint Martin. The fame of Saint Benedict, Gregory reported, drew "pious noblemen from Rome," who "left their sons with him to be schooled in the service of God."[11] Benedict's monasteries had become the perfectly acceptable alternatives to the old avenues to prestige: armies and schools. Saint Radegund, founder of a convent at Poitiers (not far from Tours), obtained a fragment of the Holy Cross as a relic for her nuns. It would be hard to find anything more precious. Thus sacred things were dispersed and diffused into the countryside, into city convents, into the texture of everyday life.

The Retrenchment of the East

After 476 there was a "new order" in the East as well, but it was much less obvious. For one thing, there was still an emperor. His subjects called themselves "Romans" and thought that they spoke "Romaic" (though we call their language Greek).

The east Roman towns continued to thrive, and their middle classes even experienced renewed prosperity and influence. The best of the small-town educated elite went off to Constantinople, where they found good jobs as administrators, civil servants, and financial advisors. While barbarian kings were giving in to the rich and eliminating general taxes altogether, the eastern emperors were collecting state revenues more efficiently than ever. When Hagia Sophia ("Holy Wisdom"), the great church of Constantinople, burned to the ground, Emperor Justinian (r.527–565) dipped into the treasury to hire 10,000 workers to rebuild it. They covered its domed ceiling with gold and used 40,000 pounds of silver for its decoration.

Nevertheless, the eastern Roman empire was not the old Roman empire writ small. It was becoming a "Middle Eastern state," more akin to Persia than to Gaul. When the Visigoths sacked Rome, the eastern Emperor Theodosius II (r.408–450) did not send an army; he built walls around Constantinople instead. When the roads

MAXIMIANVS

Plate 1.9: Mosaic from San Vitale, Ravenna (*c.*540–548). Flanked on one side by churchmen (holding a cross and a Bible) and on the other by military men (holding spears and a shield inscribed with the sign of Christ), Emperor Justinian is here depicted in an offertory procession. He himself carries the paten, which contains the eucharistic bread. By both his position in the composition and his role in the mass, he is thus made the link between heavenly and earthly orders.

fell into disrepair, Justinian let them decay — except for the one that led to the border with Persia. When the Slavs pressed on the Roman frontier in the Balkans, Justinian let them enter. Borrowing the ceremony and pomp of the Persian King of Kings for himself, Justinian was pleased to be represented in the mosaics of San Vitale at Ravenna (Plate 1.9) in a crown and jewels, his head surrounded by a gleaming halo, his ministers — both secular and ecclesiastic — flanking him on both sides. At San Vitale, he is almost an icon, a simplified, radically "abstracted" image of a person suffused with divinity.

Icons, perhaps originally the creation of the Coptic Christians of Egypt, were another Middle Eastern product crucial to the culture of the east Romans. Without denigrating relics, eastern Christians found that icons — whether painted, woven, or carved — gave them more important access to the sacred. In the sixth-century Egyptian tapestry shown in Plate 1.10, the Virgin, dressed in the purple robes of an empress, sits on a gem-encrusted throne with the Christ Child in her lap. Like the Eucharist, icons concentrated and transmuted spiritual into material substance.

The fifth and sixth centuries brought retrenchment. For the first time emperors issued compendia of Roman laws. The *Theodosian Code*, which gathered together imperial "constitutions" (general laws) alongside "rescripts" (rulings on individual cases), was published in 438. The barbarian law codes of the sixth century attempted to match this achievement, but they were overshadowed by the great legal initiatives of Justinian, which included the *Codex Justinianus* (529), an imperial law code; an orderly compilation of Roman juridical thought called the *Digest* (533); and a textbook for lawyers known as the *Institutes* (534). From then on the laws of the eastern Roman empire were largely (though not wholly) fixed, though Justinian's books were soon eclipsed by short summaries in Greek, while in the West they had little impact until the twelfth century.

Under Justinian, this redefined Roman empire sought to recapture its past glory. It quickly took North Africa from the Vandals in 534. It added a strip of southeastern Spain in 552. Meanwhile Justinian's armies pressed on to wrench — but with great difficulty — Italy from the Ostrogoths. The first two enterprises were fairly successful; eastern Roman rule lasted in North Africa for another century. The last venture, however, was a disaster. The long war in Italy, which began in 535 and ended only in 552, devastated the country. Soon the Lombards, Germanic warriors employed by Justinian to help take Italy, returned to Italy on their own behalf. By 572 they were masters of part of northern Italy and, further south, of Spoleto and Benevento. (See Map 1.5.)

For the eastern Roman empire, the western undertaking was a sideshow. The empire's real focus was on the Sassanid empire of the Persians. The two "superpowers" confronted one another with wary forays throughout the sixth century. They thought that to the winner would come the spoils. Little did they imagine that

the real winner in the Middle East would be a new and unheard of group: the Muslims.

★　　★　　★　　★

The crisis of the third century demoted the old Roman elites, bringing new groups to the fore. Among these were the Christians, who insisted on one God and one way to understand and worship him. Declared the official religion of the empire in 391, Christianity redefined the location of the holy: no longer was it in private households or city temples but in the precious relics of the saints and the Eucharist, in those who ministered on behalf of the church on earth (the bishops), and in those who led lives of ascetic heroism (the monks).

Politically the empire, once a vast conglomeration of conquered provinces, was in turn largely conquered by its periphery. In spite of themselves, the Romans had tacitly to acknowledge and exploit the interdependence between the center and the hinterlands. They invited the barbarians in, and then declined to recognize the needs of their guests. The repudiation came too late. The barbarians were part of the empire, and in the western half they took it over. In the next century they would show how much they had learned from their former hosts.

CHAPTER ONE KEY EVENTS

212	Roman Citizenship granted to all free inhabitants of the provinces
235–284	Crisis of the Third Century
284–305	Reign of Diocletian
306–337	Reign of Constantine
313	Edict of Milan
325	Council of Nicaea
378	Emperor Valens killed by Visigoths
391	Emperor Theodosius declares Christianity the official religion of the Roman empire
410	Visigoths sack Rome
453	Death of Attila
476	Deposition of Romulus Augustulus
c.540	Benedictine (St. Benedict's) *Rule* written
527–565	Emperor Justinian
590–604	Pope Gregory the Great

NOTES

1. "The Passion of SS. Perpetua and Felicitas," in *Medieval Saints: A Reader,* ed. Mary-Ann Stouck, Readings in Medieval Civilizations and Cultures 4 (Peterborough, ON, 1999), p.22.
2. Quoted in Ramsay MacMullen, *Christianizing the Roman Empire (A.D. 100-400)* (New Haven, 1984), p.95.
3. *The Confessions of Saint Augustine* 8.4, trans. Rex Warner (New York, 1963), p.166.
4. Quoted in W.H.C. Frend, *The Rise of the Monophysite Movement: Chapters in the History of the Church in the Fifth and Sixth Centuries* (Cambridge, 1972), p.xii.
5. Saint Athanasius, *The Life of Saint Antony*, trans. Robert T. Meyer, Ancient Christian Writers 10 (New York, 1978), p.32, spelling slightly modified.
6. *Acta Maximiliani* 3,4, ed. and trans. H. Musurillo, *The Acts of the Christian Martyrs* (Oxford, 1972), p.248, quoted in Peter Brown, *The Cult of the Saints: Its Rise and Function in Latin Christianity* (Chicago, 1981), p.33.
7. Charles Christopher Mierow, trans., *The Gothic History of Jordanes* (Princeton, 1915), pp.88–89.
8. Gregory of Tours, *The Miracles of the Bishop Saint Martin*, trans. Raymond Van Dam in his *Saints and Their Miracles in Late Antique Gaul* (New Jersey, 1993), p.210.
9. Fortunatus, quoted in Georges Duby, *The Early Growth of the European Economy: Warriors and Peasants from the Seventh to the Twelfth Century* (Ithaca, 1974), p.58, spelling and punctuation slightly modified.
10. *St. Benedict's Rule for Monasteries*, trans. Leonard J. Doyle (Collegeville, 1948), p.33.
11. Gregory the Great, "The Life and Miracles of Saint Benedict," in Stouck, p.177.

FURTHER READING

Bowersock, G.W., Peter Brown, and Oleg Grabar, eds. *Late Antiquity: A Guide to the Postclassical World*. Cambridge, MA, 1999.

Brown, Peter. *The Cult of the Saints*. Chicago, 1981.

—. *The World of Late Antiquity*, 150-750. London, 1971.

Geary, Patrick J. *The Myth of Nations: The Medieval Origins of Europe*. Princeton, 2002.

Heinzelmann, Martin. *Gregory of Tours: History and Society in the Sixth Century*. Trans. Christopher Carroll. Cambridge, 2001.

Jones, A.H.M. *The Later Roman Empire, 284-602*, 2 vols. Baltimore, 1986.

Kitzinger, Ernst. *Early Medieval Art*. Rev. ed. Bloomington, 1983.

Knight, Jeremy K. *The End of Antiquity: Archaeology, Society and Religion AD 235-700*. Charleston, SC, 1999.

MacMullen, Ramsay. *Christianity and Paganism in the Fourth to Eighth Centuries*. New Haven, 1997.

Moorhead, John. *Justinian*. London, 1994.

Pohl, Walter, with Helmut Reimitz, eds. *Strategies of Distinction: The Construction of Ethnic Communities, 300-800*. Leiden, 1998.

Wolfram, Herwig. *The Roman Empire and Its Germanic Peoples*. Trans. Thomas J. Dunlap. Berkeley, 1997.

For searchable maps, genealogies, and other materials for this chapter, please visit the *Short History of the Middle Ages* website at www.broadviewpress.com/shorthistory.

PART I: THREE CULTURES FROM ONE

TWO

THE EMERGENCE OF SIBLING CULTURES (*c*.600-*c*.750)

THE RISE OF Islam in the Arabic world and its triumph over territories that had for centuries been dominated by either Rome or Persia is the first astonishing fact of the seventh and eighth centuries. The second is the persistence of the Roman empire both politically, in what historians call the "Byzantine empire," and culturally, in the Islamic world and Europe. By 750 there were three distinct and nearly separate worlds: the Greek-speaking Byzantines, the Latin-writing Europeans, and the Arabic-writing Muslims. They professed different values, struggled with different problems, adapted to different standards of living. Yet all three bore the marks of common parentage—or, at least, of common adoption. They were sibling heirs of Rome.

SAVING BYZANTIUM

In the seventh century, the eastern Roman empire was so transformed that historians by convention call it something new, the "Byzantine empire," from the old Greek name for Constantinople: Byzantium. (Often the word "Byzantium" alone is used to refer to this empire as well.) War, first with the Sassanid Persians, then with the Arabs, was the major transforming agent. Gone was the ambitious imperial reach of Justinian; by 700, Byzantium had lost all its rich territories in North Africa and its tiny Spanish outpost as well. (See Map 2.1.) True, it held tenuously to bits and pieces of

Italy and Greece. But in the main it had become a medium-size state, in the same location but about two-thirds the size of Turkey today. Yet, if small, it was also tough.

Sources of Resiliency

Byzantium survived the onslaughts of outsiders by preserving its capital city, which was well protected by huge, thick, and far-flung walls that embraced farmland and pasture as well as the city proper. Within, the emperor (still calling himself Roman) and his officials serenely continued to collect the traditional Roman land taxes from the provinces left to them. This allowed the state to pay regular salaries to its soldiers, sailors, and court officials. The navy, well supplied with ships and proud of its prestigious weapon—Greek Fire, an oil hurled over the water that exploded on impact with enemy ships—patrolled the Mediterranean Sea. The armies of the empire, formerly posted as frontier guards, were now pulled back and set up as regional units

Map 2.1:
The Byzantine Empire,
*c.*700

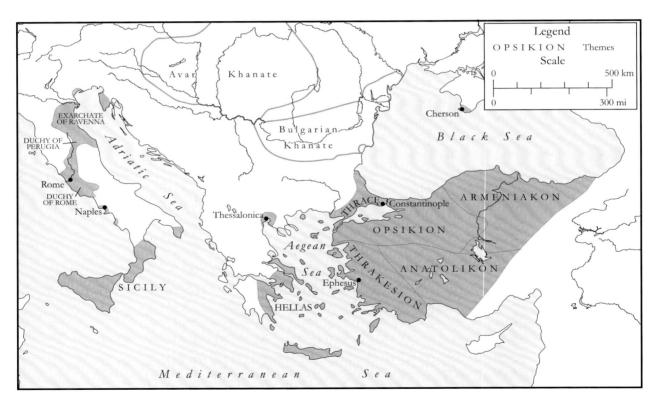

within the empire itself. These armies and their regions, both called "themes," were led by *strategoi* (*sing. strategos*), generals who were gradually given responsibility for both military and regional civil matters. They countered enemy raids while remaining close to sources of supplies and new recruits. Each soldier was given land in his theme to help him purchase his uniform and arms. In this way, the themes maintained the traditions of the imperial Roman army: well trained and equipped, Byzantium's troops served as reliable defenders of their newly compact state.

The Invaders and their Consequences

The Sassanid empire of Persia, its capital at Ctesiphon, its ruler styled "king of kings," was as venerable as the Roman empire—and as ambitious. (See Map 1.5 on pp.46-47.) King Chosroes II (r.591-628), not unlike Justinian a half-century before him, dreamed of recreating past glories. In his case the inspiration was the ancient empire of Xerxes and Darius, which had sprawled from a lick of land just west of Libya to a great swath of territory ending near the Indus River. Taking advantage of a dispute between two claimants to the imperial throne during the first decade of the seventh century, Chosroes marched into Byzantine territory in 607. By 613 he had taken Damascus, by 614 Jerusalem. The whole of Egypt fell to the Persians in 619. But Emperor Heraclius (r.610-641) rallied his troops and turned triumph into defeat; all territories taken by the Persians were back in Byzantine hands by 630. (For Heraclius and his successors, see list on p.330: Byzantine Emperors and Empresses.) On a map it would seem that nothing much had happened; in fact, the cities fought over were depopulated and ruined, and both Sassanid and Byzantine troops and revenues were exhausted.

Meanwhile, the Byzantines had to contend with Slavs and others north of the Danube. Again Map 1.5 makes the situation clear: Slavs—farmers and stock-breeders in the main—were pushing into the Balkans, sometimes accompanied by Avars, multiethnic horseback warriors and pastoralists. In 626, just before Heraclius wheeled around and bested the Persians on his frontiers, he was confronted with Avars and their Sassanid allies besieging—unsuccessfully, as it turned out—the very walls of Constantinople. It took another half-century for the Bulgars, a Turkic-speaking nomadic group, to become a threat, but in the 670s they began moving into what is today Bulgaria, defeating the Byzantine army in 681. By 700 the Balkan Peninsula was Byzantine territory no longer. (See Map 2.1 again.) The place where once the two halves of the Roman empire had met (see Map 1.1 on pp.20-21) was now a wedge that separated East from West.

An even more dramatic obliteration of the old geography took place further east, where attacks by Arab Muslims in the century after 630 ended in the conquest of Sassanid Persia and the further shrinking of Byzantium. We shall soon see how and why the Arabs poured out of Arabia. But we need first to know what the shrunken Byzantium was like.

Decline of Urban Centers

Figure 2.1 (facing page): The Changing Face of Ephesus

The city-based Greco-Roman culture on which the Byzantine empire was originally constructed had long been gradually giving way. Invasions and raids hastened this development. Urban centers, once bustling nodes of trade and administration, disappeared or reinvented themselves. Some became fortresses; others were abandoned; still others remained as skeletal administrative centers. The public activities of marketplaces, theaters, and town squares yielded to the pious pursuits of churchgoers or the private ones of the family. When warfare reduced cities to rubble, those that were rebuilt were remodeled along new lines.

The story of Ephesus is unique only in its details. (See Figure 2.1, noting the structures and labels in blue.) Ephesus had once been an opulent commercial and industrial center. Even after the turbulent centuries of the late Roman empire, Ephesus could still boast impressive vigor. Imagine it in about 600. Its vital center was the Embolos, a grand avenue paved with marble. (See Plate 2.1.) Extending the length of

Plate 2.1:
The Embolos, Ephesus. The center of Late Antique Ephesus was this grand avenue, the Embolos, paved with marble and lined with columns, statues, and shops colorfully decorated with frescoes. After the seventh century, however, the street was largely abandoned.

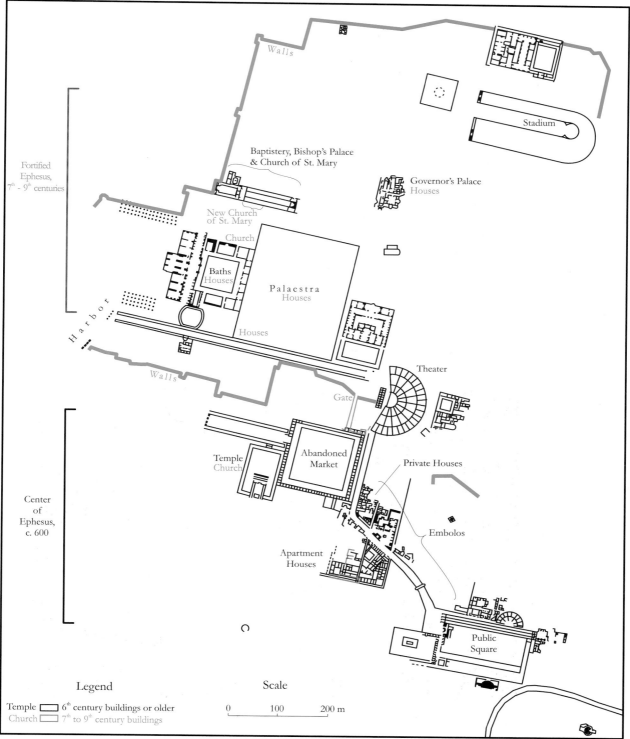

Walls

Stadium

Fortified
Ephesus,
7th - 9th centuries

Baptistery, Bishop's Palace
& Church of St. Mary

Governor's Palace
Houses

New Church
of St. Mary

Church

Harbor

Baths
Houses

P a l a e s t r a
Houses

Houses

Walls

Theater

Gate

Center
of
Ephesus,
c. 600

Temple
Church

Abandoned
Market

Private Houses

Embolos

Apartment
Houses

Public
Square

Legend

Temple ☐ 6th century buildings or older
Church ☐ 7th to 9th century buildings

Scale

0   100   200 m

more than three football fields, the Embolos began at its west end on an old (and no longer functioning) formal market square; it opened out at the east end onto another square; all along its length in between were statues, shops, and public buildings. Just behind the shops were private houses and apartments, evidence of a large and wealthy population.

There was no question of Ephesus's religious affiliation: the Embolos was well "Christianized" by numerous crosses carved as decorative motifs or scratched into the walls and paving stones. Although the church of Saint Mary, Ephesus's cathedral, was considerably north of the Embolos, there was at least one smaller church nearby, as well as a few chapels. The whole complex suggests a comfortable integration of old Roman institutions—baths, temples-turned-into-churches—with something new—an informal market jammed into the arcades of a street, itself fronting sprawling residential complexes.

By 700, little of this was left. The Persian wars disrupted Ephesus's trade and threatened its prosperity. Repeated visitations of bubonic plague began in the time of Justinian and recurred in virulent attacks until about 750. This was the first pandemic (widespread epidemic) in the historical record; Ephesus could not have been spared its grim demographic toll. An earthquake and fire in 614 struck decisive blows, destroying the Embolos and the luxurious houses built along its length. Arab attacks on Ephesus began in 654-655.

In the face of disaster, Ephesus was rebuilt, but not as before. The old vital center around the Embolos was abandoned. Walls, constructed around a much-reduced area to the north, enclosed the remaining population and a smaller cathedral. (See Figure 2.1 again, now noting the constructions and labels in green.) Old public baths were displaced by private houses, few of them elegant and many no more than huts. Exceptions to the decay were few: the bishop (housed just to the east of the new church of Saint Mary), his clergy, and local monasteries formed a rich and powerful upper stratum, as did imperial and military officials living in the vicinity.

Everywhere in Byzantium, cities became little more than fortresses in the course of the eighth century. Constantinople, with its walls, was only partially exceptional. As elsewhere, its population shrank, and formerly inhabited areas right within the city were abandoned or turned into farms. As the capital of church and state, however, Constantinople boasted an extraordinarily thriving imperial and ecclesiastical upper class. It also retained some trade and industry. Even in the darkest days of the seventh-century wars, it had taverns, brothels, merchants, and a money economy. Its factories continued to manufacture fine silk textiles. Even though Byzantium's economic life became increasingly rural in the seventh and eighth centuries, institutions vital to urban growth remained at Constantinople, ensuring a revival of commercial activity once the wars ended.

Ruralization

With the decline of cities came the rise of the countryside. Agriculture had all along been the backbone of the Byzantine economy. Apart from large landowners — the state, the church, and a few wealthy individuals — most Byzantines were free or semi-free peasant farmers. In the interior of Anatolia, on the great plateau that extends from the Mediterranean to the Black Sea, peasants must often have had to abandon their farms when Arab raiders came. Some may have joined the other pastoralists of the region, ready to drive their flocks to safety. Elsewhere (and, in times of peace, on the Anatolian plains as well), peasants worked small plots (sometimes rented, sometimes owned outright), herding animals, cultivating grains, and tending orchards.

The so-called Farmers' Law, which probably reflects rural conditions in at least some parts of the empire, paints a picture of autonomous village communities composed of small households. Since the *curiales* of the cities were gone, rural families now felt directly the impact of imperial rule, especially taxes. In turn, the state adopted an agenda of "family values," narrowing the grounds for divorce, setting new punishments for marital infidelity, and prohibiting abortions. New legislation gave mothers new power over their offspring and made widows the legal guardians of their minor children. These families no longer wanted their children to learn the classics — the Greek poets and philosophers — but rather the Bible. They used the psalms as a primer; from there their children might move on to hagiography (saints' lives), dogmatic treatises, and devotional works.

Iconoclasm

Such piety was partly a response to crisis. What had provoked God's anger, unleashing war, plague, earthquakes? What would appease him? The armies thought that they knew: they attributed Arab victories to the biblical injunction against graven images. Islam prohibited representations of the divine; Byzantine soldiers listened. They thought that icons revived pagan idolatry. As iconoclastic (anti-icon or, literally, icon breaking) feeling grew, some churchmen became outspoken in their opposition to icons, while others, especially monks, defended them.

Byzantine emperors, who were religious as well as political figures, sided with their troops. They had other reasons to oppose icons as well. As mediators between people and God, icons undermined the emperor's exclusive place in the divine and temporal order. In 726, in the wake of a terrifying volcanic eruption in the middle of the Aegean Sea, Emperor Leo III the Isaurian (r.717-741) had his officers tear down the great golden icon of Christ at the gateway of the imperial palace and replace it with a cross. A crowd of women protested in fury. Thus was launched the long iconoclastic period. Leo ordered all icons destroyed, and the ban lasted until 787. It was revived, in modified form, between 815 and 843.

Iconoclasm had a thousand intimate consequences. Anyone with a portable icon at home had to destroy or adore it in secret. The effects on the monasteries were dramatic: their treasuries were raided and properties confiscated. Most extreme was one zealous *strategos*, Michael Lachanodracon, who forced all the monks in his theme to marry or suffer blinding and exile. In this way, iconoclasm destroyed communities that might otherwise have served as centers of resistance to imperial power. That was perhaps incidental. The most important point was that it made the Byzantines, in the eyes of its defenders, the "people of God."

THE RISE OF THE "BEST COMMUNITY": ISLAM

The Muslims also considered themselves God's people. In the Qur'an, the "recitation" of God's words, Muslims are "the best community ever raised up for mankind ... having faith in God" (3:110). The community's common purpose is "submission to God," the literal meaning of "Islam." The Muslim (a word that derives from "Islam") is "one who submits." Beginning in Arabia under the leadership of Muhammad, within less than a century Islam had created a new world power.

Origins of Islam

"One community" was a revolutionary notion for the disparate peoples of Arabia (today Saudi Arabia), who first converted to this new religion in the course of the early seventh century. Pre-Islamic Arabia supported Bedouins: nomads (the word "arab" is derived from the most prestigious of these, the camel-herders) and semi-nomads. But by far the majority of the population was neither; it was sedentary. To the southwest, where rain was adequate, farmers worked the soil. Elsewhere people settled at oases, where they raised date palms (a highly prized food); some of these communities were prosperous enough to support merchants and artisans. Both the nomads and the settled population were organized as tribes — groups whose members thought themselves ultimately bound together by a common father.

Herding goats, sheep, or camels, the nomads and semi-nomads lived in small groups, largely making do with the products (leather, milk, meat) of their animals, and raiding one another for booty — including women. "Manliness" was the chief Bedouin virtue; it meant not sexual prowess (though polygyny — having more than one wife at a time—was practiced) but bravery, generosity, and a keen sense of honor. Lacking written literature, the nomads were proud of their oral culture of storytelling and poetry.

Islam began as a religion of the sedentary, but it soon found support and military strength among the nomads. It began at Mecca, a commercial center, the launching pad of caravans organized to sell Bedouin products—mainly leather goods and raisins—to the more urbanized areas at the Syrian border. (See Map 2.2.) Mecca was also a holy place. Its shrine, the Ka'ba, was rimmed with hundreds of idols. Within its sacred precincts, where war and violence were prohibited, pilgrims bartered and traded.

Within this commercial and religious center, Muhammad, the prophet of Islam, was born in about 570. Orphaned as a child, he came under the guardianship of his uncle, a leader of the Quraysh tribe, which dominated Mecca and controlled access to the Ka'ba. Muhammad became a trader, married, had children, and seemed comfortable and happy. But he sought something more: he would sometimes leave home, escaping to a nearby cave to pray.

Map 2.2: The Islamic World by 750

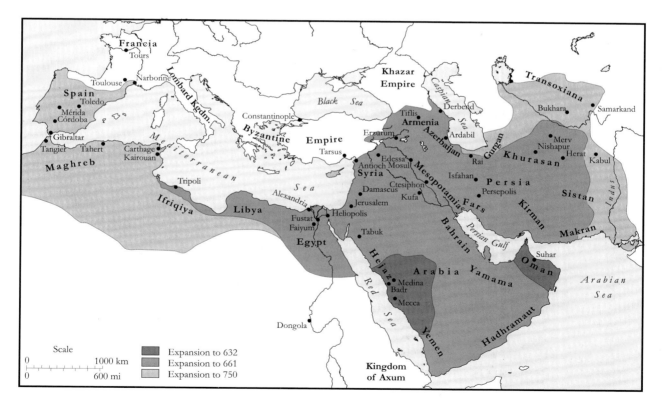

In about 610, on one such retreat, Muhammad heard a voice calling on him to worship God (the Arabic word for God is Allah). After he solemnly assented, the voice gave him further messages — they continued, intermittently, for the rest of his life. Later, when they had been written down and arranged — a process that was completed in the seventh century, but after Muhammad's death — these messages became the Qur'an, the holy book of Islam. The Qur'an is understood to be God's revelation as told to Muhammad by the angel Gabriel, then recited in turn by Muhammad to others. Its first chapter — or sura — is the Fatihah:

In the name of Allah, most benevolent, ever-merciful.
All praise be to Allah,
  1. Lord of all the worlds.
  2. Most beneficent, ever-merciful,
  3. King of the Day of Judgement.
  4. You alone we worship, and to You alone turn for help.
  5. Guide us (O Lord) to the path that is straight,
  6. The path of those You have blessed,
  7. Not of those who have earned Your anger, nor those who have gone astray.[1]

The Qur'an continues with a far longer sura, followed by others (114 in all) of gradually decreasing length. For Muslims the Qur'an covers the gamut of human experience — the sum total of history, prophecy, and the legal and moral code by which men and women should live — as well as the life to come.

Banning infanticide, Islam gave girls and women new dignity. It allowed for polygyny, but this was limited to four wives at one time, all to be treated equally. It mandated dowries and offered some female inheritance rights. At first women even prayed with men, though that practice ended in the eighth century.

It is striking that Islam emphasized the nuclear family at just about the same moment as the Byzantines did. In the Arab world this new emphasis worked to downgrade the tribe. In Islam there are three essential social facts: the individual, God, and the *ummah*, the community of the faithful. There are no intermediaries between the divine and human realms, no priests, Eucharist, relics, or icons.

Not all welcomed the new religion. Muhammad's insistence that paganism be abandoned threatened Quraysh tribal interests, so bound up with the Ka'ba. Its leaders tried to thwart his missionary efforts. When some of Muhammad's followers at Medina, an oasis about 200 miles to the northeast of Mecca, invited him to join them, he agreed. In 622 he made the *Hijra*, or flight from Mecca to Medina, where he was greeted not only as a religious but also as a secular leader. This joining of the political and religious spheres set the pattern for Islamic government thereafter. After Muhammad's death, the year of the *Hijra*, 622, became the year 1 of the Islamic calendar, marking the establishment of the Islamic era.

Muhammad consolidated his position as a religious and secular leader by asserting hegemony over three important groups. At Medina itself he took control by ousting and sometimes killing his main competitors, the Jewish clans of the city. With regard to the Meccans, to whom he was related, he fought a series of battles; the battle of Badr (624), waged against a Meccan caravan, marked the first Islamic military victory. After several other campaigns, Muhammad triumphed and took over Mecca in 630, offering leniency to most of its inhabitants, who in turn converted to Islam. Meanwhile, Muhammad allied himself with numerous nomadic groups, adding their contingents to his army. Warfare was thus integrated into the new religion as a part of the duty of Muslims to strive in the ways of God; *jihad*, often translated as "holy war," in fact means "striving." Through a combination of military might, conversion, and negotiation, Muhammad united many, though by no means all, Arabic tribes under his leadership by the time of his death in 632.

In time, new, defining practices for Muslims were instituted. There was the *zakat*, a tax to be used for charity; Ramadan, a month of fasting to mark the battle of Badr; the *hajj*, a yearly pilgrimage to Mecca; and the *salat*, formal worship at least three times a day (later increased to five), including the *shahadah*, or profession of faith: "there is no god but God, and Muhammad is His prophet." The place of worship was known as a "mosque." Breaking with Jewish practices, Muhammad had the Muslims turn their prayers away from Jerusalem, the center of Jewish worship, and towards Mecca instead. Detailed regulations for these practices, sometimes called the "five pillars of Islam," were worked out in the eighth and early ninth centuries.

Out of Arabia

"Strive, O Prophet," says the Qur'an, "against the unbelievers and the hypocrites, and deal with them firmly. Their final abode is Hell; And what a wretched destination." Cutting across tribal allegiances, Muhammad's *ummah* was itself a formidable "supertribe" dedicated to victory over the enemies of God. Led by caliphs, literally the "successors" of Muhammad, armies of Muslims moved into Sassanid and Byzantine territories, toppling or crippling the once great ancient empires. (See Map 2.2.) They captured the Persian capital, Ctesiphon, in 637 and continued eastward to take Persepolis in 648, Nishapur in 651, and then, beyond Persia, Kabul in 664, and Samarkand in 710. To the west, they picked off, one by one, the great cities of the Byzantine empire: Antioch and Damascus in 635, Alexandria in 642, Carthage

Plate 2.2:
The Great Mosque at Damascus (8th cent.). Mosaics such as these, symbolizing Umayyad rule over civilization (with its buildings and cities) and nature (with its rivers and vegetation) once covered most of the interior and exterior walls of the Great Mosque at Damascus. Very likely Byzantine mosaicists were imported to do the work; certainly the style is Byzantine. Thus the Islamic world under the Umayyads absorbed and made its own the traditions of Rome.

in 698. By the beginning of the eighth century, Islamic warriors held sway from Spain to India.

It was an astonishing triumph, but one not hard to understand with the benefit of hindsight. The Arabs were formidable fighters, and their enemies were relatively weak. The Persian and Byzantine empires were militarily exhausted from their years of fighting one another. Nor were their populations particularly loyal; some — Jews and Christians in Persia, Monophysites in Syria — even welcomed the invaders. In large measure they were proved right: the Muslims made no attempt to convert them. Setting up "garrison cities" to guard their conquests, the new Islamic rulers taxed their subjects but did not persecute them. The men and women of North Africa and Spain went back to work and play much as they had done before the invasions. Safe in his monastery near Jerusalem, Saint John of Damascus (c.657–c.749) thundered against iconoclasm. He would never have been able to do so in the Byzantine empire. Maps of the Islamic conquest divide the world into Muslims and Christians. But the "Islamic world" was only slightly Islamic; Muslims constituted a minority of the population. Even as their religion came to predominate, they were themselves absorbed, at least to some degree, into the cultures that they had conquered.

The Culture of the Umayyads

Dissension, triumph, and disappointment accompanied the naming of Muhammad's successors. The caliphs were not chosen from the old tribal elites but rather from a new inner circle of men close to Muhammad. The first two caliphs, Abu-Bakr and Umar, ruled without serious opposition. They were the fathers of two of Muhammad's wives. But the third caliph, Uthman, husband of two of Muhammad's daughters and great-grandson of the Quraysh leader Umayyah, aroused resentment. (See Genealogy 2.1: Muhammad's Relatives and Successors.) His family had come late to Islam, and some of its members had even once persecuted Muhammad. The Umayyad opponents supported Ali, the husband of Muhammad's daughter Fatimah. After a group of discontented soldiers murdered Uthman, civil war broke out between the Umayyads and Ali's faction. It ended when Ali was killed in 661 by one of his own erstwhile supporters. The caliphate remained thereafter in Umayyad hands until 750.

Yet the *Shi'ah*, the faction of Ali, did not forget their leader. They became the "Shi'ites," faithful to Ali's dynasty, mourning his martyrdom, shunning the "mainstream" caliphs of the other Muslims ("Sunni" Muslims, as they were later called), awaiting the arrival of the true leader — the *imam* — who would spring from the house of Ali.

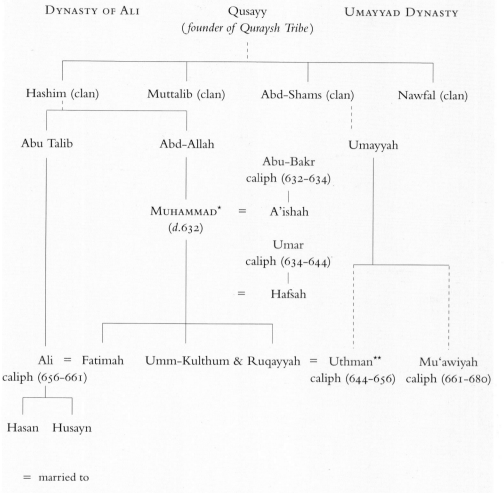

DYNASTY OF ALI

Qusayy
(*founder of Quraysh Tribe*)

UMAYYAD DYNASTY

Hashim (clan)   Muttalib (clan)   Abd-Shams (clan)   Nawfal (clan)

Abu Talib   Abd-Allah   Umayyah

Abu-Bakr
caliph (632–634)

MUHAMMAD*   =   A'ishah
(*d.*632)

Umar
caliph (634–644)

=   Hafsah

Ali = Fatimah   Umm-Kulthum & Ruqayyah = Uthman**   Mu'awiyah
caliph (656–661)   caliph (644–656)   caliph (661–680)

Hasan   Husayn

= married to

| direct descendant

⋮ indirect descendant

* Muhammad was married to both A'ishah and Hafsah as well as others
** Uthman was married to two of Muhammad's daughters, Umm-Kulthum and Ruqayyah

Genealogy 2.1:
Muhammad's Relatives
and Successors

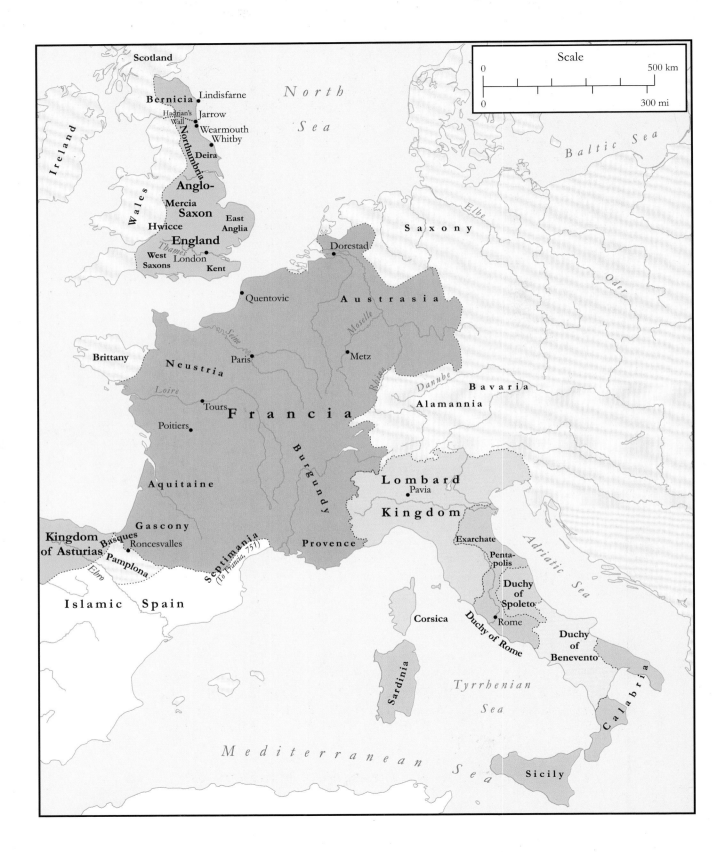

Scotland

North Sea

Bernicia • Lindisfarne
Hadrian's Wall • Jarrow
Northumbria • Wearmouth
• Whitby
Deira

Ireland

Wales

Anglo-
Saxon
Mercia
Hwicce
England
West
Saxons • London
Kent
East
Anglia
Thames

Baltic Sea

Elbe

Oder

Saxony

Dorestad

Quentovic

Austrasia

Seine

Moselle

Brittany

Neustria

Paris •

• Metz

Rhine

Loire

Danube

Bavaria

• Tours

F r a n c i a

Alamannia

Poitiers •

Burgundy

Aquitaine

L o m b a r d

• Pavia

K i n g d o m

Gascony
Kingdom
of Asturias
Basques
• Roncesvalles
Pamplona
Ebro

Septimania
(to Francia, 751)

Provence

Exarchate

Penta-
polis

Islamic Spain

Corsica

Duchy of Rome

Adriatic Sea

Duchy
of
Spoleto
• Rome

Duchy
of
Benevento

Sardinia

Tyrrhenian

Sea

Calabria

M e d i t e r r a n e a n S e a

Sicily

Scale
0   500 km
0   300 mi

Meanwhile, the Umayyads made Damascus, an important Syrian city, their capital. Here they adopted many of the institutions of the culture that they had conquered: they issued coins, employed former Byzantine officials as administrators, and hired artists trained in the Byzantine style and expert in the Byzantine medium of mosaic to decorate their new Great Mosque. (See Plate 2.2.) It is true that Arabic, the language of the Qur'an, eventually became the new official language. But into this language began to flow translations of Greek writings, bringing the new culture into contact with older traditions. At the same time, Muslim scholars determined the definitive form of the Qur'an and compiled pious narratives about the Prophet's sayings, or *hadith*. In the course of the seventh and eighth centuries, a new literate class—composed mainly of the old Persian and Syrian elite now converted to Islam and schooled in Arabic—created new forms of prose and poetry. A commercial revolution in China helped to vivify commerce in the Islamic world. At hand was a cultural flowering in a land of prosperity.

Map 2.3 (facing page): Western Europe, *c*.750

THE MAKING OF WESTERN EUROPE

No reasonable person in the year 750 would have predicted that, of the three heirs of the Roman empire, Western Europe would be the one eventually to dominate the world. While Byzantium cut back, reorganized, and forged ahead, while Islam spread its language and rule over territory that stretched nearly twice the length of the United States today, Western Europe remained an impoverished backwater. Fragmented politically and linguistically, its cities (left over from Roman antiquity) mere shells, its tools primitive, its infrastructure—what was left of Roman roads, schools, and bridges—collapsing, Europe lacked identity and cohesion. That these and other strengths did indeed eventually develop over a long period of time is a tribute in part to the survival of some Roman traditions and institutions and in part to the inventive ways in which people adapted those institutions and made up new ones to meet their needs and desires.

Impoverishment and Its Variations

Taking in the whole of Western Europe around this time means dwelling long on its variety. Dominating the scene was Francia. To its south were Spain (ruled first by the Visigoths, and then, after *c*.715, by the Muslims) and Italy (divided between the pope, the Byzantines, and the Lombards). To the north, joined to rather than separated from the Continent by the lick of water called the English Channel, the British Isles were home to a plethora of tiny kingdoms, about three quarters of which were native ("Celtic") and the last quarter Germanic ("Anglo-Saxons").

There were clear differences between the Romanized south—Spain, Italy, southern Francia—and the north. (See Map 2.3.) Travelers going from Anglo-Saxon England to Rome would have noticed them. There were many such travelers: some, like the churchman Benedict Biscop, were voluntary pilgrims; others were slaves on forced march. Making their way across England, voyagers such as these would pass fenced wooden farmsteads, each with a rectangular "hall" for eating and sleeping, a few outbuildings serving as sheds, and perhaps a sunken house, its floor below the level of the soil, its damp atmosphere suitable for weaving. (Even royal complexes were made of wood and looked much like humble farmsteads: see Figure 2.2.) Most farms were built in clusters of four to five, making up tiny hamlets. The farmstead, including its land, represented a family farm. Fields were planted with barley (used to make a thick and nourishing beer) as well as oats, wheat, and rye. The richest peasants had iron-coulter plows to turn the thick and heavy soils. There were many animals: sheep, goats, horses, cattle, pigs, and dogs. Little of this belonged outright to the men and women who farmed the soil and tended the animals. For the most part, great lords—under whose "protection" the workers toiled—owned the land and commanded a share of the produce. But all was not pastoral or agricultural in England: here and there, and especially towards the south, were commercial settlements—real emporia.

Crossing the Channel, travelers would enter northern Francia, also dotted with emporia (such as Quentovic and Dorestad) but also boasting old Roman cities, now mainly religious centers. Paris, for example, was to a large extent an agglomeration of churches: Montmartre, Saint-Laurent, Saint-Martin-des-Champs—perhaps 35 churches were jammed into an otherwise nearly abandoned city. Outside, the countryside was farmed by villagers who lived much like their Anglo-Saxon counterparts, though here and there stone was beginning to be used to construct farm buildings. Moving eastward, our voyagers would pass through thick forests and land more often used as pasture for animals than for cereal cultivation. Along the Moselle River they would find villages with fields, meadows, woods, and water courses, a few supplied with mills and churches. Some of the peasants in these villages would be tenants or slaves of a lord; others would be independent farmers who owned all or part of the land that they cultivated.

Southern Francia and much of Italy, by contrast, would have been home to vineyards and olive groves. Here the great hulks of Roman cities, with their amphitheaters, baths, and walls, dominated the landscape, though (as at Byzantium) their populations were much diminished. The countryside here had once been organized into great estates farmed by slave gangs. There were still a few of these, but for the most part slaves and other peasants were settled on their own plots of land, though, as elsewhere, most were not landowners but rather tenant farmers, owing a proportion of their produce to an aristocratic lord. Fewer animals roamed here; there was more emphasis on grain. The soil was lighter, easily worked with scratch plows—if any were to be had! Our travelers would normally have seen peasants using only hoes, spades, and weeders.

By 700, there was little left of the old long-distance Mediterranean commerce of the ancient Roman world. But, although this was an impoverished society, it was not without wealth or lively patterns of exchange. In the first place, money was still minted, but increasingly in silver rather than gold. The change of metal was due in part to a shortage of gold in Europe. But it was also a

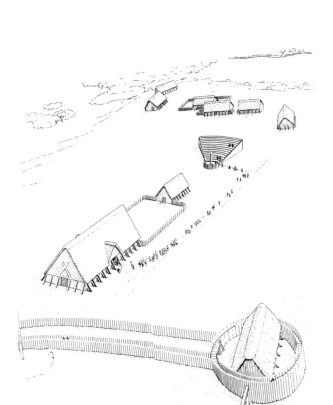

Figure 2.2: Yeavering, Northumberland. In this artist's reconstruction of an early seventh-century Anglo-Saxon royal complex in the north of England, the use of one-story rectangular halls reflects the architecture of the previous Roman-British settlers in the region.

nod to the importance of small-scale commercial transactions—sales of surplus wine from a vineyard, say, for which small coins were the most practical. In the second place, North Sea merchant-sailors—carrying, for example, ceramic plates and glass vessels—had begun to link northern Francia, the east coast of England, Scandinavia, and the Baltic Sea. Brisk trade gave rise to new emporia and revivified older Roman cities along the coasts. In the third place, a gift economy, that is, an economy of give and take, was flourishing. Booty was taken, tribute demanded, harvests hoarded, and coins struck, all to be redistributed to friends, followers, dependents, and the church. Kings and other rich and powerful men and women amassed gold, silver, ornaments, and jewelry in their treasuries and grain in their storehouses to give out in ceremonies that marked their power and added to their prestige. Even the rents that peasants paid to their lords, mainly in kind, were often couched as "gifts."

Politics and Culture

If variations were plentiful in even so basic a matter as material and farming conditions, the differences were magnified by political and cultural conditions. We need now to take Europe kingdom by kingdom.

FRANCIA

Francia comes first because it was the major player, a real political entity that dominated what is today France, Belgium, the Netherlands, Luxembourg, and much of Germany. In the seventh century, it was divided into three related kingdoms — Neustria, Austrasia, Burgundy — each of which included parts of a fourth, southern region, Aquitaine. By 700, however, the political distinctions between them were melting, and Francia was becoming one kingdom.

The line of Clovis — the Merovingians — ruled these kingdoms. (See Genealogy 2.2: The Merovingians.) The dynasty owed its longevity to biological good fortune and excellent political sense: it allied itself with the major lay aristocrats and ecclesiastical authorities of Gaul — men and women of high status, enormous wealth, and marked local power. To that alliance, the kings brought their own sources of power: a skeletal Roman administrative apparatus, family properties, appropriated lands once belonging to the Roman state, and the profits and prestige of leadership in war.

The royal court — which moved with the kings as they traveled from one palace to another, as they had no capital city — was the focus of political life. Here gathered talented young men, clerics-on-the-rise, aristocratic scions. The most important courtiers had official positions: there was, for example, the referendary and the cup-bearer. Highest of all was the "mayor of the palace," who controlled access to the king and brokered deals with aristocratic factions.

Queens were an important part of the court as well. One of them, Balthild (*d*.680), had once been among the unwilling travelers from England. Purchased there as a slave by the mayor of the palace of Neustria, she parlayed her beauty into marriage with the king himself. (Merovingian kings often married slaves or women captured in war. By avoiding wives with powerful kindred, they staved off challenges to their royal authority.) Balthild's biographer described how kindly she cared for the young men at court: "to the princes she showed herself a mother, to the priests as a daughter, and to the young and the adolescents as the best possible nurse." When her husband, King Clovis II, died, Balthild served as regent for her minor sons, acting, in effect, as king during this time. She arranged, "through the advice of the great magnates," (as her biographer put it) that one of her sons become king of Austrasia, and she maintained the prestige of the royal line through her extraordinary generosity:

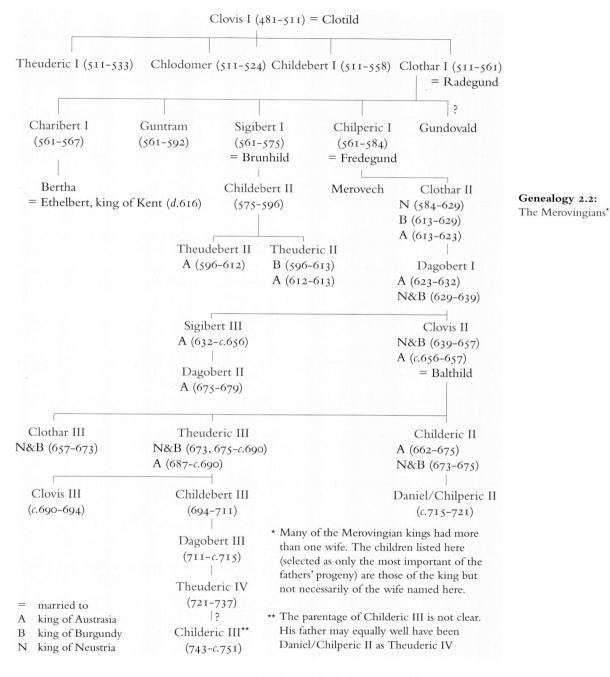

Clovis I (481–511) = Clotild

Theuderic I (511–533) Chlodomer (511–524) Childebert I (511–558) Clothar I (511–561)
= Radegund

Charibert I   Guntram   Sigibert I   Chilperic I   Gundovald
(561–567)   (561–592)   (561–575)   (561–584)
= Brunhild   = Fredegund

Bertha   Childebert II   Merovech   Clothar II
= Ethelbert, king of Kent (d.616)   (575–596)   N (584–629)
                                                                                   B (613–629)
                                                                                   A (613–623)

Theudebert II   Theuderic II   Dagobert I
A (596–612)   B (596–613)   A (623–632)
                 A (612–613)   N&B (629–639)

Sigibert III   Clovis II
A (632–c.656)   N&B (639–657)
                                                A (c.656–657)
Dagobert II   = Balthild
A (675–679)

Clothar III   Theuderic III   Childeric II
N&B (657–673)   N&B (673, 675–c.690)   A (662–675)
                          A (687–c.690)   N&B (673–675)

Clovis III   Childebert III   Daniel/Chilperic II
(c.690–694)   (694–711)   (c.715–721)

                          Dagobert III
                          (711–c.715)

                          Theuderic IV
                          (721–737)
                          | ?
                          Childeric III**
                          (743–c.751)

= married to
A king of Austrasia
B king of Burgundy
N king of Neustria

Genealogy 2.2:
The Merovingians*

* Many of the Merovingian kings had more
than one wife. The children listed here
(selected as only the most important of the
fathers' progeny) are those of the king but
not necessarily of the wife named here.

** The parentage of Childeric III is not clear.
His father may equally well have been
Daniel/Chilperic II as Theuderic IV

"Who, then, is able to say how many and how great were the sources of income, the entire farms and the large forests she gave up by donating them to the establishments of religious men ...?"[2] By the end of her life, she was counted a saint.

Important as the court was as a focus of power, aristocrats usually stayed at "home," though in fact they might (like kings) have many homes, scattered in many regions. Tending to their estates, honing their skills in the hunt, aristocratic men regularly led armed retinues to war. They proved their worth in the regular taking of booty and rewarded their faithful followers afterwards at generous banquets.

Or they bedded down. The bed — or rather the production of children — was the focus of marriage, the key to the survival of aristocratic families and the transmission of their property and power. Though churchmen had many ideas about the value of marriage, they had nothing to do with the ceremony; no one married in church. Rather, marriage was a family affair, and a very expensive one. There was more than one form of marriage: in the most formal, the husband-to-be gave to his future bride a handsome dowry of clothes, bedding, livestock, and land. Then, after the marriage was consummated, he gave his wife a morning gift of furniture and perhaps the keys to the house. Very rich men often had, in addition to their wife, one or more "concubines" at the same time. These enjoyed a less formal type of marriage, receiving a morning gift but no dowry.

The wife's role was above all to maintain the family. We have already seen how important the metaphor of motherhood was for Balthild, even in connection with unrelated men at court. A woman passed from one family (that of her birth) to the next (that of her marriage) by parental fiat. When they married, women left the legal protection of their father for that of their husband. Did women have any freedom of action? Yes. For one thing, they had considerable control over their dowries. Some participated in family land transactions: sales, donations, exchanges. Upon the death of their husbands, widows received a portion of the household property. Although inheritances generally went from fathers to sons, many fathers left bequests to their daughters, who could then dispose of their property more or less as they liked. In 632, for example, the nun Burgundofara, who had never married, drew up a will giving to her monastery the land, slaves, vineyards, pastures, and forests that she had received from her two brothers and her father. In the same will, she gave other property near Paris to her brothers and sister.

Burgundofara's generous piety was extraordinary only in degree. The world of kings, queens, and aristocrats intersected with that of the church. The arrival (*c.*590) on the Continent of the fierce Irish monastic reformer Saint Columbanus (543–615) marked a new level of association between the two. Columbanus's brand of monasticism, which stressed exile, devotion, and discipline, made a powerful impact on Merovingian aristocrats. They flocked to the monasteries that he established in both

Francia and Italy, and they founded new ones themselves on their own lands in the countryside. In Francia alone there was an explosion of monasteries: between the years 600 and 700, an astonishing 320 new houses were established, most of them outside of the cities. Some of the new monks and nuns were grown men and women, others were young children, given to a monastery by their parents. This latter practice, called oblation, was not only accepted but even considered essential for the spiritual well-being of both children and their families.

Irish monasticism introduced aristocrats on the Continent to a deepened religious devotion. Those who did not actively join or patronize a monastery still read, or listened to others read, books preaching penance, and they chanted the Psalms. The Merovingian laity developed a culture of domestic piety at about the same time as the Byzantines did.

Deepened piety did not, in this case, lead to the persecution of others—something that (as we shall see) happened in later centuries. In particular, where Jews were settled in Western Europe—along the Mediterranean coast and inland, in Burgundy, for example—they remained integrated into every aspect of secular life. They used Hebrew in worship, but otherwise they spoke the same languages as Christians and used Latin in their legal documents. Their children were often given the same names as Christians (and Christians often took Biblical names, such as Solomon); they dressed as everyone else dressed; and they engaged in the same occupations. Many Jews planted and tended vineyards, in part because of the importance of wine in synagogue services, in part because the surplus could easily be sold. Some were rich landowners, with slaves and dependent peasants working for them; others were independent peasants of modest means. While there certainly were urban Jews, most, like their Christian neighbors, lived on the land.

THE BRITISH ISLES

Roman Britain had been as habituated to barbarian defenders—in this case Saxons—as the rest of the empire. When all the Roman garrisons left England in 410 for service elsewhere, the Saxons gradually took over in the southeast, helped by massive invasions of their brethren from the Continent. The old and new tribes together are called "Anglo-Saxons"; where they conquered—in the southeastern lowlands of the British Isles—most Christians were absorbed as slaves into the pagan culture of the invaders. Elsewhere—in what is today the north and west of England, Scotland, and Ireland—Celtic kingdoms survived. Wales was already Christian when, in the course of the fifth century, Ireland and Scotland were converted by missionaries. (Saint Patrick, apostle to the Irish, is only the most famous of these.) These Celtic kingdoms supported relatively non-hierarchical church organizations. Rural monasteries often served as the seats of bishoprics as well as centers of population and settlement. Abbots and abbesses, often members of powerful families, enjoyed considerable power and prestige.

The Anglo-Saxon quadrant was reintroduced to Christianity from two different directions: the Celtic north and the Roman south. The Anglo-Saxon king of Northumbria Oswald (r.633–641), a convert to Christianity during his period of exile in Ireland, called for missionaries to come to his kingdom to preach. Monks and a bishop arrived from Ireland, setting up a monastery at Lindisfarne, just off the coast of Northumbria, and, as the historian and monk Bede (673?–735) put it about a century later,

Plate 2.3
(facing page):
Belt Buckle from Sutton Hoo (early 7th cent.). Beginning in 1939 and continuing through the 1980s, archaeologists excavated seventeen curious mounds at Sutton Hoo, a barren stretch of land in southeast England. Their finds included numerous Anglo-Saxon cremations and burials, the bones of horses, spears, shields, helmets, large open boats, jewelry, silver bowls, and many other objects, including this heavy buckle made of gold.

from that time, as the days went by, many came from the country of the Irish into Britain and to those English kingdoms over which Oswald reigned, preaching the word of faith with great devotion …. Churches were built in various places and the people flocked together with joy to hear the Word.[3]

In the south, Christianity arrived from the Continent, most spectacularly in 597 when missionaries sent from Rome by Pope Gregory the Great came to the court of King Ethelbert of Kent (d.616). Under their leader, Augustine (not the fifth-century bishop of Hippo!), the missionaries converted the king. He was primed for the change, having long before married a Christian Merovingian princess, who arrived in Kent with a bishop in her entourage.

Augustine had in mind more than the conversion of a king: he wanted to set up an English church on the Roman model, with ties to the pope and a clear hierarchy. He divided England into territorial units (dioceses) headed by an archbishop and bishops. Augustine himself became archbishop of Canterbury. There he set up the model English ecclesiastical complex: a cathedral, a monastery, and a school to train young clerics.

There was nothing easy or quick about the conversion of England. Everywhere paganism maintained its attractive hold. And once converted, as we have seen, the Christians of the north and south differed in their interpretation of the religious life and in the organization of the church. Above all, they clashed in their calculations of the date of Easter. Everyone agreed that they could not be saved unless they observed the day of Christ's Resurrection properly and on the right date. But what was the right date? Each side was wedded to its own view. A turning point came at the Synod of Whitby, organized in 664 by the Northumbrian King Oswy to decide between the Roman and Irish dates. When Oswy became convinced that Rome spoke with the very voice of Saint Peter, the heavenly doorkeeper, he opted for the Roman calculation of the date and embraced the Roman church as a whole.

As Christianization proceeded in Anglo-Saxon England, a particularly learned and eclectic clerical culture emerged there. The pull of Rome—symbol, in these clerics' view, of the Christian religion itself—was palpable. Benedict Biscop (*c.*630–690), a Northumbrian aristocrat-turned-abbot and founder of two important English monasteries, Wearmouth and Jarrow, made numerous arduous trips to Rome. He brought back saints' relics, liturgical vestments, and even a cantor to teach his monks the proper melodies in a time before written musical notation existed. Above all, he went to Rome to fetch books. In Anglo-Saxon England, as in Ireland, both of which lacked a strong classical foundation, books were precious and exotic objects.

From this fact came a flowering of manuscript illumination. The Anglo-Saxons, like other barbarian (and, indeed, Celtic) tribes, had artistic traditions particularly well suited to decorating flat surfaces. Belt-buckles, helmet nose-pieces, brooches and other sorts of jewelry of the rich were adorned with semi-precious stones and enlivened with decorative patterns, often made up of intertwining snake-like animals. A particularly fine example is a buckle from Sutton Hoo (see Plate 2.3), perhaps the greatest archaeological find for the Anglo-Saxon period. The style was quickly adapted to Christian needs.

Books, which were artefacts of Roman origin, inspired Anglo-Saxon artists to combine their decorative traditions with the classical pictorial style. The resulting illumination was perfectly suited to flat pages. Consider the Lindisfarne Gospels, probably made at the monastery of Lindisfarne in the first third of the eighth century. (The Gospels are the four canonical accounts of Christ's life and death in the New Testament.) The artist of this sumptuous book was clearly uniting Germanic, Irish, and Roman artistic traditions when he introduced each Gospel with three full-page illustrations: first, a portrait of the "author" (the evangelist); then an entirely ornamental "carpet" page; finally, the beginning words of the Gospel text. Plates 2.4 to 2.6 illustrate the sequence for the Gospel of Luke. The figure of Luke (see Plate 2.4), though clearly human, floats in space. His "throne" is a square of ribbons, his drapery a series of loopy lines. The artist captures the essence of an otherworldly saint without the distraction of three-dimensionality. The carpet page (see Plate 2.5), with its interlace panels, has some of the features of the Sutton Hoo brooch as well as Irish interlace patterns. It is more than decorative,

imago ui tuli

ACICES

LUCAS

Plate 24

Plate 2.5

Incipit euangelium   secundum lucam··

QUO
NIAM
QUIDEM
MULTI CONA
TI SUNT ORDINA
RENARRATIONEM

however: the design clearly evokes a cross. The next page (see Plate 2.6) begins with a great letter, Q (for the first word, "quoniam"), as richly decorated as the cross of the carpet page; gradually, in the course of the next few words, the ornamentation diminishes. In this way, after the fanfare of author and carpet pages, the reader is ushered into the Gospel text itself.

The amalgamation of traditions in England is perhaps most clearly illustrated by the so-called Franks Casket, probably made in Northumbria around the same time as—or a bit later than—the Lindisfarne Gospels. Carved out of whale bone, this box is decorated with scenes from Roman, Jewish, Christian, and Germanic tales. On the left side of the front panel (Plate 2.7), the princess Beadohild is tricked by Weyland the Smith into bearing his son, the hero Widia. Weyland, an otherworldly figure of incredible skill at the forge, was celebrated in the Anglo-Saxon poems *Beowulf* and *Deor*. On the right side of the same panel, the Magi bring gifts to Christ, seated on Mary's lap. That, of course, was a story from the Gospels. The two scenes thus pull together two traditions, playing on the theme of mothers who bear the son of an otherworldly father.

Just as the Anglo-Saxons held on to their legends after they were Christianized, so they retained their language. In England, the vernacular—the language of the people, as opposed to Latin—was quickly turned into a written language and used in every aspect of English life, from government to entertainment. But much the same was true in Ireland; the uniqueness of Anglo-Saxon culture should not be exaggerated. The model for the Franks Casket probably came from a similar one carved earlier in Francia or Italy, and certainly a similar cultural creativity and fusion of diverse elements was equally characteristic of early medieval Ireland and Scotland.

THE SOUTH: SPAIN AND ITALY

It is just possible that the exemplar for the Franks Casket came from Spain, which boasted an equally lively mix of cultures. Here, especially in the south and east, some Roman cities had continued to flourish after the Visigothic invasions. Merchants from Byzantium regularly visited Mérida, for example (see Map 2.2), and the sixth-century bishops there constructed lavish churches and set up a system of regular food distribution. Under King Leovigild (r.569-586) all of Spain came under Visigothic control. Under his son Reccared (r.586-601), the monarchy converted from Arian to Catholic Christianity. This event (587) cemented the ties between the king and the Hispano-Roman population, which included the great landowners and leading bishops. Two years later, at the Third Council of Toledo, most of the Arian bishops followed their king by announcing their conversion to Catholicism, and the assembled churchmen enacted decrees for a united church in Spain.

Preceding pages:

Plate 2.4: Saint Luke, Lindisfarne Gospels (1st third of 8th cent.?). Inspired by Late Roman traditions, the artist—who was also the scribe of this book—introduced the Gospel of Luke with an author's portrait. The winged calf perched on Luke's halo is his symbol.

Plate 2.5: Carpet Page, Lindisfarne Gospels (1st third of 8th cent.?). Anglo-Saxon and Celtic artistic ornamental traditions lie behind this elaborate cross, which follows Luke's portrait in **Plate 2.4** and faces the first text page depicted in **Plate 2.6**.

Plate 2.6 (facing page): First Text Page, Gospel of Saint Luke, Lindisfarne Gospels (1st third of 8th cent.?). The third page in the Luke Gospel sequence begins the text itself: "Quoniam quidem multi conati sunt ordinare narrationem," "Since many have undertaken to put in narrative order..."

Plate 2.7: Franks Casket (1st half of 8th cent.).
Made up of panels of carved whalebone, the Franks
Casket combines not only various literary traditions
but also some artistic ones. The whole idea of having figural scenes on a casket was classical, but the
style here is Anglo-Saxon. Compare the style of
cloaks and figures on the left (the Weyland scene)
with Luke in **Plate 2.4**.

Thereafter, the bishops and kings of Spain cooperated to a degree unprecedented in other regions. While the king gave the churchmen free rein to set up their own hierarchy (with the bishop of Toledo at the top) and to meet regularly at synods to regulate and reform the church, the bishops in turn supported the king. They even anointed him, daubing him with holy oil in a ritual that paralleled the ordination of priests and echoed the anointment of kings in the Old Testament. While the bishops in this way made the king's cause their own, their lay counterparts, the great landowners, helped supply the king with troops.

Unlike the Merovingians, the Visigothic kings were not able to establish a stable dynasty. The minority of a king's son almost always sparked revolts by rival families, and the child's deposition was often accompanied by wholesale slaughter of his father's followers and confiscation of their lands. This may help to explain why Visigothic courtiers painted a particularly lustrous picture of their kings, resplendent and dazzling, their throne "radiant with shining gold," and why royal laws punished treason by death or blinding.[4]

It was precisely the centralization of the Visigothic kingdom that proved its undoing. In 711, a small raiding party of Arabs killed the Visigothic king and thereby dealt the whole state a decisive blow. Between 712 and 715, armies led by Arabs took over the peninsula.

But this was less an Arab or Islamic conquest than a Berber one. The generals who led the invasion of Spain were Arab, to be sure; but their fighters were Berbers from North Africa. Perhaps a million people settled in Spain in the wake of the invasions, the Arabs generally taking the better lands in the south, the Berbers getting less rich properties in the center and north. Few Berbers were Muslims, while most of the conquered population consisted of Christians (and some Jews). The Islamic presence, then, was minuscule. The history of Spain would for many centuries thereafter be one of conversion, acculturation, and war.

Unlike Visigothic Spain, Lombard Italy presented no united front. In the center of the peninsula was the papacy, always hostile to the Lombard kings of the north. (See Map 2.3.) To Rome's east and south were the dukes of Benevento and Spoleto. Although theoretically the Lombard king's officers, in fact they were virtually independent rulers. Although many Lombards were Catholics, others, including important kings and dukes, were Arian. The "official" religion varied with the ruler in power. Rather than signal a major political event, then, the conversion of the Lombards to Catholic Christianity occurred gradually, ending only in the late seventh century. Partly as a result of this slow development, the Lombard kings, unlike the Visigoths, Franks, or even Anglo-Saxons, never enlisted the wholehearted support of any particular group of churchmen.

Yet the Lombard kings did not lack advantages. They controlled extensive estates, and they made use of the Roman institutions that survived in Italy. The Lombard kings made the cities their administrative bases, assigning dukes to rule from them and setting up one, Pavia, as their capital. Recalling emperors like Constantine and Justinian, the kings built churches and monasteries at Pavia, maintained city walls, and minted coins. Revenues from tolls, sales taxes, port duties, and court fines filled their coffers.

Emboldened by their attainments in the north, the Lombard kings tried to make some headway against the independent dukes of southern Italy. But that threatened to surround Rome with a unified Lombard kingdom. The pope, fearing for his own position, called on the Franks for help.

THE POPE: MAN IN THE MIDDLE

By the end of the sixth century, the pope's position was ambiguous. Bishop of Rome, he wielded real secular power within the city as well as a measure of spiritual leadership farther afield. Yet in other ways he was just a subordinate of Byzantium. Pope Gregory the Great (590-604), whom we have already met a number of times, laid the foundations for the papacy's later spiritual and temporal ascendancy. (See Popes and Antipopes to 1500 on pp.332-35.) During Gregory's tenure, the pope became the greatest landowner in Italy; he organized Rome's defense and paid for its army; he heard court cases, made treaties, and provided welfare services. The missionary expedition he sent to England was only a small part of his involvement in the rest of Europe. A prolific author of spiritual works and Biblical exegesis, Gregory digested and simplified the ideas of Church Fathers such as Saint Augustine, making them accessible to a wider audience. His practical handbook for clerics, *Pastoral Care*, went hand-in-hand with his practical church reforms in Italy, where he tried to impose regular episcopal elections and enforce clerical celibacy.

On the other hand, even Gregory was only one of many bishops in the former Roman empire, now ruled from Constantinople. For a long time the emperor's views on dogma, discipline, and church administration prevailed at Rome. However, this authority began to unravel in the seventh century. In 692, Emperor Justinian II convened a council that determined 102 rules for the church. When he sent the rules to Rome for papal endorsement, Pope Sergius I (687-701) found most of them acceptable, but he was unwilling to agree to the whole because it permitted priestly marriages (which the Roman church did not want to allow), and it prohibited fasting on Saturdays in Lent (which the Roman church required). Outraged by Sergius's refusal, Justinian tried to arrest the pope, but Italian armies (theoretically under the emperor's command) came to the pontiff's aid instead. Justinian's arresting officer was reduced to cowering under the pope's bed. Clearly Constantinople's influence and authority over Rome had become tenuous. Sheer distance as well as diminishing imperial power in Italy meant that the popes had in effect become the leaders of non-Lombard Italy.

The gap between Byzantium and the papacy widened in the early eighth century when Emperor Leo III tried to increase the taxes on papal property to pay for his wars against the Arabs. The pope responded by leading a general tax revolt. Meanwhile, Leo's fierce policy of iconoclasm collided with the pope's tolerance of images. For the pope, holy images could and should be venerated, though not worshiped.

Increasing friction with Byzantium meant that when the pope felt threatened by the Lombard kings, as he did in the mid-eighth century, he looked elsewhere for support. Pope Stephen II (752-757)

> besought the pestilential king of the Lombards for the flocks God had entrusted to him and for the lost sheep —[in short,] for the entire exarchate of Ravenna and for the people of the whole of this province of Italy, whom that impious king had deceived with devilish trickery and was now occupying. He was getting nowhere with him; and in particular he saw that no help would come his way from the imperial power [at Byzantium].... He sent word incessantly to the king of the Franks [Pippin III]: the king must dispatch his envoys here to Rome; he must have them summon [the pope] to come to [the king].[5]

Pippin listened to the pope's entreaties and marched into Italy with an army to fight the Lombards. The new Frankish/ papal alliance would change the map of Europe in the coming decades.

★　　　★　　　★　　　★

The "fall" of the Roman empire meant the rise of its children. In the east the Muslims swept out of Arabia—and promptly set up a Roman-style government where they conquered. The bit in the east that they did not take—the part ruled from Constantinople—still considered itself the Roman empire. In the west, impoverished kingdoms looked to the city of Rome for religion, culture, and inspiration. However much East and West, Christian and Muslim, would come to deviate from and hate one another, they could not change the fact of shared parentage.

NOTES

1. *Al-Qur'an: A Contemporary Translation*, trans. Ahmed Ali (Princeton, 1993), p.11.

2. *Late Merovingian France: History and Hagiography 640–720,* ed. and trans. Paul Fouracre and Richard A. Gerberding (Manchester, 1996), quotations on pp.121–23.

3. Bede, *The Ecclesiastical History of the English People*, ed. Judith McClure and Roger Collins (Oxford, 1994), p.114.

4. The "radiant throne" is from Eugenius of Toledo, quoted in Geneviève Bührer-Thierry, "'Just Anger' or 'Vengeful Anger'? The Punishment of Blinding in the Early Medieval West," in *Anger's Past: The Social Uses of an Emotion in the Middle Ages*, ed. Barbara H. Rosenwein (Ithaca, NY, 1998), p.79.

5. *The Lives of the Eighth-Century Popes (Liber Pontificalis): The Ancient Biographies of Nine Popes from AD 715 to AD 817*, trans. Raymond Davis, Translated Texts for Historians, 13 (Liverpool, 1992), pp.58–59.

FURTHER READING

For searchable maps, genealogies, and other materials for this chapter, please visit the *Short History of the Middle Ages* website at www.broadviewpress.com/shorthistory.

Barford, P.M. *The Early Slavs: Culture and Society in Early Medieval Eastern Europe.* Ithaca, 2001.

Charles-Edwards, T.M. *Early Christian Ireland.* Cambridge, 2001.

Donner, Fred McGraw. *The Early Islamic Conquests.* Princeton, 1981.

Foss, Clive. *Ephesus after Antiquity: A Late Antique, Byzantine and Turkish City.* Cambridge, 1979.

Foster, Sally M. *Picts, Gaels and Scots: Early Historic Scotland.* London, 1996.

Haldon, J.F. *Byzantium in the Seventh Century: The Transformation of a Culture.* Cambridge, 1990.

Hodgson, Marshall G.S. *The Venture of Islam: Conscience and History in a World Civilization*, 1: *The Classical Age of Islam.* Chicago, 1974.

Mayr-Harting, Henry. *The Coming of Christianity to Anglo-Saxon England.* University Park, PA, 1991.

Noble, Thomas F.X. *The Republic of St. Peter: The Birth of the Papal State, 680-825.* Philadelphia, 1984.

Peters, F.E. *Muhammad and the Origins of Islam.* Albany, 1994.

Whittow, Mark. *The Making of Byzantium, 600-1025.* Berkeley, 1996.

Wood, Ian. *The Merovingian Kingdoms, 450-751.* London, 1994.

THREE

CREATING NEW IDENTITIES
(*c.750-c.900*)

IN THE SECOND half of the eighth century the periodic outbreaks of plague that had devastated half of the globe for two centuries came to an end. In its wake came a gradual but undeniable upswing in population, land cultivation, and general prosperity. At Byzantium an empress took the throne, in the Islamic world the Abbasids displaced the Umayyads, in Francia the Carolingians deposed the Merovingians. New institutions of war and peace, learning, and culture developed, giving each state — Byzantium, the Islamic caliphate, Francia — its own characteristic identity (though with some telling similarities).

BYZANTIUM:
FROM TURNING WITHIN TO CAUTIOUS EXPANSION

In 750 Byzantium was a state with its back to the world. Its iconoclasm isolated it from other Christians, its theme structure focused its military operations on internal defense, its abandonment of classical learning set it apart from its past. By 900, all this had changed. Byzantium was iconophile (icon-loving), aggressive, and cultured.

New Icons, New Armies, New Territories

Within Byzantium, iconoclasm sowed dissension. In the face of persecution and humiliation, men and women continued to venerate icons, even in the very bedrooms of the imperial palace. The impasse was ended by a woman. In 780, upon the death of Leo IV, his widow, Irene, in effect became head of the Byzantine state as regent for her son Constantine VI. Long a secret iconophile, Irene immediately moved to replace important iconoclast bishops. Then she called a council at Nicaea (787), the first there since the famous one of 325. The meeting went as planned, and the assembled bishops condemned iconoclasm. Few Byzantines lamented its passing. A later revival of iconoclasm (815–843), though long, was half-hearted; with some exceptions, icons and their venerators were tolerated. After 843, Byzantium would henceforth be confidently iconophile.

At first the end of iconoclasm displeased the old guard in the army, but a canny ruler like Irene knew how to appoint loyal generals and defuse opposition. By her day, the army had been reformed and the theme organization supplemented by an even more responsive force. In the mid-eighth century, Emperor Constantine V (r.741–775) had created new crack regiments, the *tagmata* (*sing. tagma*). These were mobile troops, not tied to any theme. Many were composed of cavalry, the elite of fighting men; others—infantry, muleteers—provided necessary backup. At first deployed largely around Constantinople itself to shore up the emperors, the *tagmata* were eventually used in cautious frontier battles. Under the ninth- and tenth-century emperors, they helped Byzantium to expand.

To the west, in the Balkans, Emperor Nicephorus I (r.802–811) remodeled the old thematic territories and added new ones. Leading his army against the Slavs, he took the region around Serdica (today Sofia, Bulgaria). His successes prompted the Bulgarians to attack. To secure the area, Nicephorus uprooted thousands of families from Anatolia and sent them to settle in the Balkans. Reshaping old themes and adding new ones, Nicephorus created fortified centers to anchor the settlers. Although he intended to recreate an earlier Byzantium, his policies in fact ensured the future fission into Greek- and Slavic-speaking Balkan states.

Nicephorus's later foray into Bulgarian territory further north in the Balkans proved disastrous. Marshaling a huge army and escorted by the luminaries of his court, the emperor plundered the Bulgarian capital, Pliska, then coolly made his way west. But the Bulgarians blockaded his army as it passed through a narrow river valley, fell on the imperial party, and killed the emperor. The toll on the fleeing soldiers and courtiers was immense, but even more memorable was the imperial humiliation. Krum, the Bulgarian khan (ruler), lined Nicephorus's skull with silver and used it as a ceremonial drinking cup. Further defeats in the region in the late ninth century led to yet more shuffling of themes. The end result may be seen in Map 3.1, to which Map 2.1 on p.60 (Byzantium at its smallest) should be compared.

Another glance at the two maps reveals a second region of modest expansion, this time on Byzantium's eastern front. In the course of the ninth century the Byzantines had worked out a strategy of skirmish warfare in Anatolia. When Arab raiding parties attacked, the *strategoi* evacuated the population, burned the crops, and, while sending out a few troops to harass the invaders, largely waited out the raid within their local fortifications. But by 860, the threat of Arab invading armies—apart from raiding parties—was largely over (though the threat of Muslim navies—on Sicily and in southern Italy, for example—remained very real). In 900, Emperor Leo VI (*r.*886-912) was confident enough to go on the offensive, sending the *tagmata* in the direction of Tarsus. The raid was a success, and in its wake at least one princely family of Armenia, which was allied with the Arabs, was persuaded to enter imperial service and cede its principality to Byzantium. Reorganized as the theme of Mesopotamia, it was the first of a series of new themes that Leo created in an area that had been largely a no-man's-land between the Islamic and Byzantine worlds.

Map 3.1: The Byzantine Empire, *c.*917

But the rise of the *tagmata* eventually had the unanticipated consequence of downgrading the themes. The soldiers of the themes got the "grunt work"—the inglorious job of skirmish warfare with the Arabs, for example—without the honor and (probably) extra pay. The *tagmata* were the professionals, gradually taking over most of the fighting, especially as the need to defend the interior of Anatolia receded. By the same token, the troops of the themes became increasingly inactive.

Educating Without and Within

No longer turned in on itself, the Byzantine empire first brought most of the Slavic regions into its orbit, not with troops but via missionaries. The whole of the eastern and northern Balkans was ripe for conversion. Here Byzantium's competitors were the Roman church and the Franks, who preached the Catholic brand of Christianity. The Slavic principalities tried to manipulate the two sides—the Catholics and the Orthodox Byzantines—to their own advantage, but in the end they were pulled into one world or the other.

The prince of Moravia (a new Slavic state bounded by Francia to the west and the Bulgarian khanate to the east) made a bid for autonomy from Frankish hegemony by calling on Byzantium for missionaries. The imperial court was ready. Two brothers, Constantine (later called Cyril) and Methodius, set out in 863, armed with translations of the Gospels and liturgical texts. Born in Thessalonica, they well knew about the Slavic languages, which had been purely oral. Constantine devised an alphabet using Greek letters to represent the sounds of one Slavic dialect (the "Glagolitic" alphabet), and then added Greek words and grammar where the Slavic lacked Christian vocabulary and suitable expression. The resulting language, later called Old Church Slavonic, was an effective tool for conversion. Its use shows that Byzantium, relentlessly centralizing as it was in most matters, was willing in a few others to work with regional traditions. The Catholic church, by contrast, was more rigid: it insisted that the Gospels and liturgy be in Latin. Despite this, Moravia ended in the Catholic camp, but the Byzantine brand of Christianity prevailed in Bulgaria, Serbia, and later (see Chapter 4) Russia.

The creation of an alphabet in the mid-ninth century was part of a pattern of scholarly and educational initiatives. Constantinople had always had private schools, books, and teachers to train its civil servants. But in the eighth century the number of bureaucrats was steadily dwindling, the schools were decaying, and the books, painstakingly written out on papyrus, were disintegrating. Education had lost its prestige—except for the religious education of the Psalms.

Ninth-century confidence reversed the trend; fiscal stability and surplus wealth in

Plate 3.1 (facing page): Byzantine Book Cover (886-912). After the end of iconoclasm in 843, two distinct artistic styles flourished at Byzantium, easily seen by comparing this plate to **Plate 3.2**. The frontal, formal, hierarchical, and decorative style represented by this enameled book cover harks back to late imperial work, such as that of the Hippodrome obelisk base in **Plate 1.7** on p.37.

the treasury greased the wheels. Emperor Theophilus (r.829-842) opened a public school in the palace, headed by Leo the Mathematician, a master of geometry, mechanics, medicine, and philosophy. Controversies over iconoclasm sent churchmen scurrying to the writings of the Church Fathers to find passages that supported their cause. With the end of iconoclasm, the monasteries, staunch defenders of icons, garnered renewed prestige and gained new recruits. Because their abbots insisted that they read Christian texts, the monks had to get new manuscripts in a hurry. Practical need gave impetus to the creation of a new kind of script: minuscule. This was made up of lower case letters, written in cursive, the letters strung together. It was faster and easier to write than the formal capital uncial letters that had previously been used. Separating words by spaces, as they had not been before, made them easier to read. Papyrus was no longer easily available from Egypt, so the new manuscripts were made out of parchment—animal skins scraped and treated to create a good writing surface. Far more expensive than papyrus, parchment was nevertheless much more durable, making possible their preservation over the long haul.

A general cultural revival was clearly underway by the middle of the century. As a young man, Photius, the patriarch of Constantinople (r.858-867, 877-886), dictated summaries of hundreds of books he had read, including works of history, literature, and philosophy. As patriarch he gathered a circle of scholars around him; wrote sermons, homilies, and theological treatises; and tutored Emperor Leo VI. For his own part, Constantine-Cyril, the future missionary to the Slavs, was reportedly such a brilliant student in Thessalonica that an imperial official invited him to the capital:

> When he arrived at Constantinople, he was placed in the charge of masters to teach him. In three months he learned all the grammar and applied himself to other studies. He studied Homer and geometry and with Leo [the Mathematician] and Photius dialectic and all the teachings of philosophy, and in addition [he learned] rhetoric, arithmetic, astronomy, music, and all the other "Hellenic" [i.e., pagan Greek] teachings.[1]

The resurrection of "Hellenic" books helped inspire an artistic revival. Sometimes called the Macedonian Renaissance, after the ninth- and tenth-century imperial dynasty that fostered it, the new movement found its models in both the abstract, transcendental style of the pre-iconoclastic period and the natural, plastic style of classical art.

Even during the somber years of iconoclasm, artistic activity did not entirely end at Byzantium. But the new exuberance and sheer numbers of mosaics, manuscript illuminations, ivories, and enamels after 870 suggest a new era. Plate 3.1 illustrates the

Plate 3.2 (facing page): Ezechiel in the Valley of Dry Bones, Homilies of Gregory Nazianzen (880-886). The style of this miniature is inspired by classical art. However, depicting Ezechiel talking to an archangel is new. It reflects iconophile delight in the post-843 permission to portray the human vision of divinity.

return to the abstract style: Christ and the saints and archangels who surround him on this book cover have no weight or volume. Like Justinian and his ministers in Plate 1.9 (p.50-51), they stare out beyond their viewers to another, otherworldly reality. At about the same time, however, classical styles were also making a comeback. On the left of Plate 3.2 the prophet Ezekiel stands in a landscape of bones, the hand of God reaching toward him to tell him that the bones will rise and live again (Ezek. 37:1-11). On the right the prophet stands next to an angel. The figures have depth and weight; they turn and interact. It is true that their drapery flutters and loops unnaturally, giving the scene a nonclassical excitement; and it is true that the angel "floats," one foot in front of the prophet, one arm a bit behind him. But it is in just this way that the Byzantines adapted classical traditions to their overriding need to represent transcendence.

Not surprisingly, the same period saw the revival of monumental architecture. Already Emperor Theophilus was known for the splendid palace that he built on the outskirts of Constantinople, and Basil I (r.867-886) was famous as a builder of churches. Rich men from the court and church imitated imperial tastes, constructing palaces, churches, and monasteries of their own.

THE SHIFT TO THE EAST IN THE ISLAMIC WORLD

Just as at Byzantium the imperial court determined both culture and policies, so too the Islamic world of the ninth century was centered on the caliph and his court. The Abbasids, who ousted the Umayyad caliphs in 750, moved their center of power to Iraq (part of the former Persia) and stepped into the shoes of the Sassanid king of kings, the "shadow of God on earth." Yet in fact much of their time was spent less in imposing their will than in conciliating different interest groups.

The Abbasid Reconfiguration

Years of Roman rule had made Byzantium relatively homogeneous. Nothing was less true of the Islamic world, made up of regions wildly diverse in geography, language, and political, religious, and social traditions. Each tribe, family, and region had its own expectations and desires for a place in the sun. The Umayyads paid little heed. Their power base was Syria, formerly a part of Byzantium. There they rewarded their hard-core followers and took the lion's share of conquered land for themselves. They expected every other region to send its taxes to their coffers at Damascus. This annoyed regional leaders, even though they probably managed to keep most of the taxes that they raised. Moreover, with no claims to the religious functions of an *imam*, the Umayyads could never gain the adherence of the followers of Ali. Soon still other groups began to complain. Where was the equality of believers preached in the Qur'an? The Umayyads privileged an elite; Arabs who had expected a fair division of the spoils were disappointed. So too were non-Arabs who converted to Islam: they discovered that they had still to pay the old taxes of their non-believing days.

The discontents festered, and two main centers of resistance emerged: Khurasan (today eastern Iran) and Iraq. (See Map 3.2.) Both had been part of the Persian empire; the rebellion was largely a coming together of old Persian and newly "Persianized" Arab factions. In the 740s this defiant coalition at Khurasan decided to support the Abbasid family. This was an extended kin group with deep-rooted claims to the caliphate, tracing its lineage back to the very uncle who had cared for the orphaned Muhammad. With militant supporters, considerable money, and the backing of a powerful propaganda organization, the Abbasids organized an army in Khurasan and, marching it undefeated into Iraq, picked up more support there. In

Map 3.2: The Islamic World, *c.*800

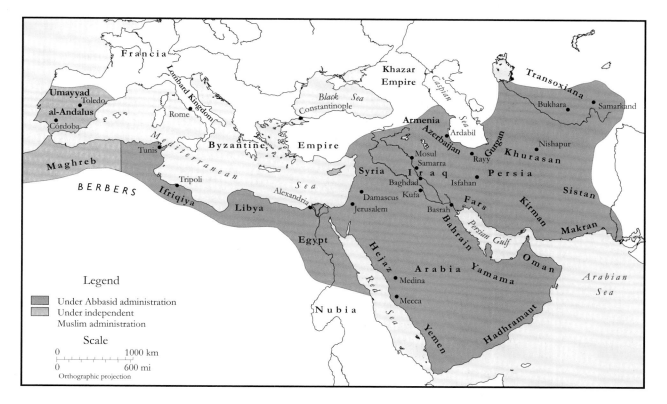

749 they defeated the Umayyad governor at Kufa, and al-Saffah was solemnly named the first Abbasid caliph. Less than a year later the last Umayyad caliph, abandoned by almost everyone and on the run in Egypt, was killed in a short battle.

The new dynasty seemed to signal a revolution. (See list of Islamic Rulers on p.336.) Most importantly, the Abbasids recognized the crucial centrality of Iraq and built their capital cities there: Baghdad was begun in 762, Samarra in the 830s, in the aftermath of a bitter civil war. The Abbasids had to recognize the quasi-independence of various regions—Syria, Egypt, and (at times) Khurasan—allowing some provincial governorships to become hereditary. They took the title of *imam* and even, at one point, wore the green color of the Shi'ites.

Yet as the Abbasids became entrenched, they in turn created their own elite, under whom other groups chafed. In the eighth century most of their provincial governors, for example, came from the Abbasid family itself. When building Baghdad, Caliph al-Mansur (r.754–775) allotted important tracts of real estate to his Khurasani military leaders. In the course of time, as Baghdad prospered and land prices inflated, the Khurasanis came to constitute a new, exclusive, and jealous elite. At the same time as they favored these groups, the Abbasids succeeded in centralizing their control even more fully than the Umayyads had done. This is clearest in the area of taxation. The Umayyads had demanded in vain that all taxes come to them. But the Abbasid al-Mu'tasim (r.833–842) was able to control and direct provincial revenues to his court in Iraq.

Control, however, was uneven. Until the beginning of the tenth century, the Abbasid caliphs generally could count on ruling Iraq (their "headquarters"), Syria, Khurasan, and Egypt. But they never had the Iberian peninsula; they lost Ifriqiya (today Tunisia) by about 800; and they never controlled the Berbers in the soft underbelly of North Africa. In the course of the tenth century, they would lose effective control even in their heartlands. That, however, was in the future (see Chapter 4).

Whatever control the Abbasids had depended largely on their armies. Unlike the Byzantines, the Abbasids did not need soldiers to stave off external enemies or to expand outwards. (The Byzantine strategy of skirmish warfare worked largely because the caliphs led raids to display their prowess, not to take territory. The serious naval wars that took Sicily from Byzantium were launched from Ifriqiya, independent of the caliphs.) Rather, the Abbasids needed troops to collect taxes in areas already conquered but weakly controlled.

Well into the ninth century the caliphs' troops were paid, but not mustered, by them. Generals recruited their own troops from their home districts, tribes, families, and clients. When the generals were loyal to the caliphs, this military system worked well. In the dark days of civil war, however, when two brothers fought over the caliphate (811–819), no one controlled the armies. After al-Ma'mun (r.813–833) won this civil war, he had no reliable army to back him up. His brother and successor, al-Mu'tasim, found the solution in a new-style, private army. He bought and trained his own slaves, many of them Turks and thus unrelated to other tribal groups. These men were given governorships as well as military posts. They were the reason that al-Mu'tasim was able to collect provincial taxes so effectively. He could not foresee that in time the Turks would come to constitute a new elite, one that would eventually help to overpower the caliphate itself.

With the Abbasid transformation came wealth. The Mediterranean region had always been a great trade corridor. In the ninth century, Baghdad, at the crossroad of east and west, drew that trade into a wider network. All of Iraq partook in the commercial buoyancy:

> From India are imported tigers, panthers, elephants, panther skins, rubies, white sandal, ebony, and coconuts. From China are imported silk stuffs, silk, chinaware, paper, ink, peacocks, racing horses, saddles, felts, cinnamon, Greek unblended rhubarb … racing horses, female slaves, knicknacks with human figures … hydraulic engineers, expert agronomists, marble workers, and eunuchs. From Arabia: Arab horses, ostriches, pedigreed she-camels … From Egypt: trotting donkeys, suits of fine cloth, papyrus, balsam, and—from its mines—topazes of superior quality. From the land of the Khazars [on the lower Volga River]: slaves of both sexes, coats of mail, [and] helmets.[2]

The porcelains from China inspired Islamic artisans to add tin to their own glazes to achieve a bright white color, over which they added decorative effects, from simple

Plate 3.3 (facing page): Dish from Iraq (9th cent.). Boasting an elaborate, multi-colored floral design that contrasts with its plain white background, this plate reflects the luxurious tastes of the Abbasid elite.

designs that used just one color to elaborate patterns created with metallic luster. (See Plate 3.3.) Dining off of such finely decorated plates and bowls was part of the elites' newly luxurious lifestyle: their clothes were made of richly woven fabrics, their homes were furnished with fine rugs (on both floors and walls) and perfumed with elaborately carved censers.

With revenues from commerce and (above all) taxes from agriculture in their coffers, the caliphs paid their armies, salaried their officials (drawn from the many talented men—but, in this relentlessly male-dominated society, not women—in the Persian, Arab, Christian, and Jewish population), and presided over a cultural revival even more impressive than the one at Constantinople.

New Cultural Forms

Plate 3.4 (facing page): Córdoba, Great Mosque (late 10th cent.). The Great Mosque of Córdoba was built in several phases. The view here is of an area added in 987. Note the two tiers of arches—the first set on pre-Islamic columns, the second on long piers—giving the building a sense of both height and liveliness.

Under the Abbasids (most spectacularly, under Harun al-Rashid [*r.*786-809] of *Arabian Nights* fame), science, law, and literature flourished. The caliphs launched scientific studies via a massive translation effort that brought the philosophical, medical, mathematical, and astrological treatises of the Indian and Greek worlds into Islamic culture. They encouraged new literary forms—the refined and learned prose and poetry of *adab* literature—as part of the education of gentlemen at court. Books of all sorts were relatively cheap (and therefore accessible) in the Islamic world because they were written on paper.

Shoring up the regime with astrological predictions; winning theological debates with the pointed weapons of Aristotle's logical and scientific works; understanding the theories of bridge-building, irrigation, and land-surveying with Euclid's geometry—these were just some of the motives behind the translations and original scientific work of the period. The movement had general support. Patrons of scientific writing included the caliphs, their wives, courtiers, generals, and ordinary people with practical interests. Al–Khwârazmî (*d.*850), author of a book on algebra (the word itself is from the Arab *al-jabr*), explained the many sensible uses of his topic:

> people constantly require [it] in cases of inheritance, legacies, partition, lawsuits, and trade, and in all their dealings with one another where surveying, the digging of canals, [and] geometrical computation ... are concerned.[3]

The same scholar also wrote the first Arabic treatise on the Indian method of calculation (Indian numerals are what *we* call Arabic numerals) and the use of the zero, essential for distinguishing 100 from 1, for example.

Similarly practical were the treatises on law (*fiqh*) that began to appear in the Abbasid period. They included commentaries on religious obligations, rules of war, and forms of taxation. Eminent jurists founded schools to perpetuate their ideas.

By contrast, *adab* literature was impractical, though "political" in the sense that it paved a man's way at court. It strove after an ideal of beauty and elegance. Knowledge was important, but only in the service of wit and style. The highest form of *adab* was poetry. When performed, it was sung, and thus was closely tied to music. *Adab* poets wrote verses of praise, satire, nostalgia, suffering, deep religious feeling, worldly loves and hates, and wry comments on the human condition:

Map 3.3 (facing page):
Europe, *c.* 814

> She said, "I love you"; "you're a liar," I said,
> "cheat someone else who cannot scrutinize
> these words which I can't accept!
> For truly I say, no one loves an old man!
> It's like saying, 'We have tethered the wind',
> or like saying, 'Fire is cold' or 'water is aflame'."[4]

Al-Andalus: A Society in the Middle

The poet who wrote those lines was al-Ghazal (775-864), a great practitioner of *adab*—in Spain! In the eighth and ninth centuries, Islamic Spain was a miniature caliphate minus the caliph. In the mid-eighth century Abd al-Rahman I, an Umayyad prince on the run from the Abbasids, managed to gather an army, make his way to Iberia, defeat the provincial governor at Córdoba, and (in 756) proclaim himself "emir" (commander) of al-Andalus. His dynasty would govern Islamic Spain for two and a half centuries, and one of his descendants, Abd al-Rahman III (r.912-961) would even take the title caliph. Nevertheless, like the Abbasid caliphs, the Umayyad rulers of Spain headed a state poised to break into its regional constituents.

Al-Andalus under the emirs was hardly Muslim and even less Arab. As the caliphs came to rely on Turks, so the emirs relied on a professional standing army of non-Arabs, the *al-khurs*, the "silent ones"—men who could not speak Arabic. They lived among a largely Christian—and partly Jewish—population; even by 900, only about 25 per cent of the people in al-Andalus were Muslims. This had its benefits for the regime, which taxed Christians and Jews heavily. Although, like Western European rulers, they did not have the land tax that the Byzantine emperors and caliphs could impose, the emirs did draw some of their revenue from Muslims, especially around their capital at Córdoba. (See Map 3.3.)

Money allowed the emirs to pay salaries to their civil servants and to sponsor a culture of science and literature of their own. Al-Ghazal was only one of the poets

Norway

Sweden

North Sea

Baltic Sea

Ireland

Denmark

Haithabu

OBODRITES

Scotland

York

Anglo-Saxon England

London

English Channel

Frisia

Elbe

Saxony

St. Amand
Meerssen
Cologne
Aachen
Hersfeld

Austrasia

Herstal

Fulda

CZECHS

Atlantic Ocean

Quierzy
Laon
Soissons
Attigny

Paris

Würzburg

Regensburg

Moravian Empire

Brittany

Neustria

Verdun

Sens

Rhine

Danube

Passau

Seine

Oder

Vistula

Dniester

Orléans

Tours

F r a n c i a

Poitiers

Loire

Aquitaine

Garonne

Lyon

Vienne

B u r g u n d y

Rhône

Kingdom

of

Italy

Milan
Pavia
Verona

Genoa

Po

Venice

CROATS

Drava

Sava

Theiss

Prut

B u l g a r i a n   E m p i r e

Danube

Kingdom of Asturias

Oviedo

León

Duero

Ebro

Barcelona

al-Andalus

Tagus

Guadiana

Córdoba

Guadalquivir

Ravenna

Spoleto

Rome

Naples

Duchy of Benevento

Benevento

Adriatic Sea

B y z a n t i n e   E m p i r e

M e d i t e r r a n e a n

M a g h r e b

Sea

I f r i q i y a

L i b y a

Legend

Carolingian Kingdom 768
Conquests of Charles the Great

Scale

0   500 km

0   300 mi

and musicians patronized by the court. Like the others, his poems—blunt and to the point—were not quite what a poet from, say, Baghdad would write. The culture of al-Andalus reflected its unique ethnic and religious mix. The Great Mosque in Córdoba is a good example. Begun under Abd al-Rahman I and expanded by his successors, it drew on the design of the Roman aqueduct at Mérida for its rows of columns connected by double arches. (See Plate 3.4.) For the shape of the arches, however, it borrowed a form—the "Visigothic" horseshoe arch—from the Christians. For the decorative motif of alternating light and dark stones, it looked to the Great Mosque of Damascus.

The cultural "mix" went beyond buildings and poems. Some Christians and Muslims intermarried; Muslim men were allowed to take Christian wives. Even religious practices may have melded a bit. The Christians who lived in al-Andalus were called "Mozarabs"—"would-be Arabs"—by Christians elsewhere. It used to be thought that the martyrdom of 48 Christians at Córdoba between 850 and 859 was proof of implacable hostility between Christians and Muslims there. But recent research suggests that the story of the martyrs was hugely exaggerated by its idiosyncratic author, Eulogius. It is likely that Christians and Muslims on the whole got along fairly well. Christians dressed like Muslims, worked side-by-side with them in government posts, and used Arabic in many aspects of their life. At the time of the supposed martyrdoms, there were in the region of Córdoba alone at least four churches and nine monasteries.

Still, some Andalusian Christians were not content—Eulogius was one—and they were glad to have contact with the north. For to the north of al-Andalus, beyond the Duero River, were tiny Christian principalities. Partaking in the general demographic and economic growth of the period, they had begun to prosper a little. One, Asturias, became a kingdom. There Alfonso II (r.791–842) and his successors established a capital city—first at Oviedo, then, at the beginning of the tenth century, at León. They built churches, encouraged monastic foundations, collected relics, patronized literary efforts, and welcomed Mozarabs from the south. The kings themselves looked to models still further north—to Francia, where Charlemagne and his heirs ruled as kings "by grace of God."

Between Byzantium and the Islamic world was Francia. While the other two were both politically centralized, subject to sophisticated tax systems, and served by salaried armies and officials, Francia inherited the centralizing traditions of the Roman empire without its order and efficiency. Francia's kings could not collect a land tax, the backbone of the old Roman and the more recent Byzantine and Islamic fiscal systems. There were no salaried officials or soldiers in Francia. Yet the new dynasty of kings there, the Carolingians, managed to muster armies, expand their kingdom, encourage a revival of scholarship and learning, command the respect of emperors and caliphs, and forge an identity for themselves as leaders of the Christian people (by which they meant Roman Catholics). Their successes bore striking resemblance to contemporary achievements at Constantinople and Baghdad. How was this possible? The answer is at least threefold. They took advantage of the same gentle economic upturn that seems to have taken place generally; they exploited to the full the institutions of Roman culture and political life that remained to them; at the same time, they were willing to experiment with new institutions and take advantage of unexpected opportunities.

The Making of the Carolingians

The Carolingian take-over was a "palace coup." After a battle (at Tertry, 687) between Neustrian and Austrasian noble factions, one powerful family with vast estates in Austrasia came to monopolize the high office of mayor in both places. In the first half of the eighth century these mayors took over much of the power and most of the responsibilities of the kings.

Charles Martel (mayor 714-741) gave the name Carolingian (from *Carolus*, Latin for Charles) to the dynasty. In 732 he won a battle near Poitiers against an army led by the Muslim governor of al-Andalus:

> He utterly destroyed their armies, scattering them like stubble before the fury of his onslaught; and in the power of Christ he utterly destroyed them. So did he triumph over all his enemies in this his glorious day of victory![5]

Thus did a contemporary chronicler laud the event with phrases borrowed from the Bible and the Church Fathers. The battle ended plundering raids from al-Andalus. But, as the chronicler said, Charles had other enemies: he spent most of his time fighting vigorously against regional Frankish aristocrats intent on carving out independent lordships for themselves. Playing powerful factions against one another, rewarding supporters, defeating enemies, and dominating whole regions by controlling monasteries and bishoprics that served as focal points for both religious piety and land donations, the Carolingians created a tight network of supporters.

Moreover, they chose their allies well, reaching beyond Francia to the popes and to Anglo-Saxon churchmen, who (as we have seen) were closely tied to Rome. When the Anglo-Saxon missionary Boniface (d.754) wanted to preach in Frisia (today the Netherlands) and Germany, the Carolingians readily supported the move as a prelude to their own conquest. Many of the areas Boniface missionized had long been Christian but their practices were local rather than tied to Rome. Boniface came from England as a papal ambassador: he set up a hierarchical church organization and founded monasteries dedicated to the "Roman" *Rule* of Saint Benedict (see p.48) rather than to the Columbanian or other traditions. His newly appointed bishops were loyal to Rome and the Carolingians, not to regional aristocracies. They knew that their power came from papal and royal fiat rather than from local power centers.

Men like Boniface opened the way to a more direct alliance between the Carolingians and the pope. Charles Martel's son Pippin III (d.768) and his supporters made it a reality. In 751 they petitioned a willing Pope Zachary to legitimize their deposition of the last Merovingian king. The Carolingians returned the favor a few years later when the pope asked for their help against the encircling Lombards. This marked a signal moment: before 754 the papacy had been part of the Byzantine Empire; afterward, it was part of the West. In that year the papacy and the Frankish king formed a close alliance based on "a bond of love and devotion and peace."[6] Two years later, in the so-called Donation of Pippin, the new king forced the Lombards to give some cities back to the pope. The arrangement recognized that the papacy was now ruler in central Italy of a territory that had once belonged to Byzantium. It was probably around this time that members of the papal chancery (writing office) forged a document, the "Donation of Constantine," that declared the pope the recipient of Constantine's crown, cloak, and military rank, along with "all provinces, palaces, and districts of the city of Rome and Italy and of the regions of the West."

The chronicler of Charles Martel had already tied his hero's victories to Christ. The Carolingian partnership with Rome and Romanizing churchmen added to the dynasty's Christian aura. Anointment provided the finishing touch. Churchmen daubed the Carolingian kings with holy oil, reminding contemporaries of David, king of the Israelites: "Then Samuel took the horn of oil and anointed him in the midst of his brethren; and the spirit of the Lord came upon David from that day forward" (1 Sam [or Vulgate 1 Kings] 16:13)

Charlemagne

The most famous Carolingian king was Charles (*r.*768–814), called "the Great" ("le Magne" in Old French). Large, tough, wily, and devout, he was almost everyone's model king. Einhard, his courtier and scholar, saw him as a Roman emperor: he patterned his *Life of Charlemagne* on the *Lives of the Caesars*, written in the second century by Suetonius. Alcuin, the king's courtier and an even more famous scholar, emphasized Charlemagne's religious side, nicknaming him "David." Empress Irene at Constantinople saw Charlemagne as a suitable husband for herself (though the arrangement eventually fell through). An anonymous Italian poet emphasized Charlemagne's achievements: "noble in wit, intrepid in the midst of war, the bearer of two diadems [the crowns of Francia and Lombardy]."[7]

War indeed was the key to both Charlemagne's image and real success. While the Byzantine and Islamic rulers clung tightly to what they had, Charlemagne expanded, waging wars of plunder and conquest. He invaded Italy, seizing the Lombard crown and annexing northern Italy in 774. He moved his armies northward, fighting the Saxons for more than thirty years, forcibly converting them to Christianity, and annexing their territory. To the southeast, in a series of campaigns against the Avars, Charlemagne captured their strongholds, forced them to submit to his overlordship, and made off with cartloads of plunder. (Once they were defeated, around 800, the Bulgars and Moravians moved in.) His expedition to al-Andalus gained him a band of territory north of the Ebro River, a buffer between Francia and the Islamic world. Even his failures were the stuff of myth: a Basque attack on Charlemagne's army as it returned from Spain became the core of the epic poem *Song of Roland*.

Conquests like these depended on a good army. Charlemagne's was led by his *fideles*, faithful aristocrats, and manned by free men, many the "vassals" (clients) of the aristocrats. The king had the *bannum*, the right to call his subjects to arms (and, more generally, to command, prohibit, punish, and collect fines when his ban was not obeyed). Soldiers provided their own equipment; the richest went to war on horseback, the poorest had to have at least a lance, shield, and bow. There was no standing army; men had to be mobilized for each expedition. No *tagmata*, themes, or Turkish slaves were to be found here! Yet, while the empire was expanding, it was a very successful system; men were glad to go off to war when they could expect to return enriched with booty.

By 800, Charlemagne's kingdom stretched 800 miles east to west, even more north to south when Italy is counted. (See Map 3.3.) On its eastern edge was a strip of "buffer regions" extending from the Baltic to the Adriatic; they were under Carolingian overlordship. Such hegemony was reminiscent of an empire, and Charlemagne began to act according to the model of Roman emperors, sponsoring building programs to symbolize his authority, standardizing weights and measures, and acting as a patron of intellectual and artistic efforts. He built a capital "city"—a palace complex, in fact—at Aachen, complete with a chapel patterned on San Vitale, the church built by Justinian at Ravenna (see p.52). So keen was he on his Byzantine models that he had columns, mosaics, and marbles from Rome and Ravenna carted up north to use in his own buildings.

Further drawing on imperial traditions, Charlemagne issued laws in the form of "capitularies," summaries of decisions made at assemblies held with the chief men of the realm. He appointed regional governors, called "counts," to carry out his laws, muster his armies, and collect his taxes. Chosen from Charlemagne's aristocratic supporters, they were compensated for their work by temporary grants of land rather than with salaries. This was not Roman; but Charlemagne lacked the fiscal apparatus of the Roman emperors (and of his contemporary Byzantine emperors and Islamic caliphs), so he made land substitute for money. To discourage corruption, he appointed officials called *missi dominici* ("those sent out by the lord king") to oversee the counts on the king's behalf. The *missi*, chosen from the same aristocratic class as bishops and counts, traveled in pairs across Francia, making "diligent investigation whenever any man claims that an injustice has been done to him by anyone."[8]

Thus Charlemagne set up institutions meant to echo those of the Roman empire. It was a brilliant move on the part of Pope Leo III (795–816) to harness the king's imperial pretensions to papal ambitions. In 799, accused of adultery and perjury by a hostile faction at Rome, Leo narrowly escaped blinding and having his tongue cut out. Fleeing northward to seek Charlemagne's protection, he returned home under escort, the king close behind. Charlemagne arrived in late November 800 to an imperial welcome orchestrated by Leo. On Christmas Day of that year, Leo put an imperial crown on Charlemagne's head, and the clergy and nobles who were present acclaimed the king "Augustus," the title of the first Roman emperor. In one stroke the pope managed to exalt the king of the Franks, downgrade Irene at Byzantium, and enjoy the role of "emperor maker" himself.

About twenty years later, when Einhard wrote about this coronation, he said that the imperial titles at first so displeased Charlemagne "that he declared that he would not have set foot in the church the day that they were conferred, although it was a great feast-day, had he foreseen the plan of the pope."[9] In fact, Charlemagne continued to use the title "king" for about a year; then he adopted a new one that was both long and revealing: "Charles, the most serene Augustus, crowned by God, great and peaceful emperor who governs the Roman empire and who is, by the mercy of God, king of the Franks and the Lombards." According to this title, Charlemagne was not the Roman emperor crowned by the pope but rather God's emperor, who governed the Roman empire along with his many other duties.

Charlemagne's Heirs

When Charlemagne died, only one of his sons remained alive: Louis, nicknamed "the Pious." (See Genealogy 3.1: The Carolingians.) Emperor he was (from 814 to 840), but over an empire that was a conglomeration of territories, not a unit. He had to contend with the revolts of his sons, the depredations of outside invaders, the regional interests of counts and bishops, and above all an enormous variety of languages, laws, customs, and traditions, all of which tended to pull his empire apart. He contended with gusto, his chief unifying tool being Christianity. Calling on the help of the monastic reformer Benedict of Aniane, Louis imposed the *Rule* of Saint Benedict on all the monasteries in Francia. Monks and abbots served as his chief advisors. Louis's imperial model was Theodosius I, who had made Christianity the official religion of the Roman empire. Organizing inquests by the *missi*, he looked into allegations of exploitation of the poor, standardized the procedures of his chancery, and put all Frankish bishops and monasteries under his control.

Charlemagne had used his sons as "sub-kings." Louis politicized his family still more. Early in his reign he had his wife crowned empress, named his firstborn son, Lothar, emperor and co-ruler, and had his other sons, Pippin and Louis (later called "the German"), agree to be sub-kings under their older brother. It was neatly planned. But when Louis's first wife died he married Judith, daughter of one of the most powerful kindreds (the Welfs) in the kingdom. In 823 she and Louis had a son, Charles (later "Charles the Bald"), and this (plus the death of Pippin in 838) upset the earlier arrangement. A family feud became bitter civil war as brothers fought one another and their father for titles and kingdoms. After Louis's death a peace was hammered out in the Treaty of Verdun (843). (See Map 3.4a.) The empire was divided into three parts, an arrangement that would roughly define the future political contours of Western Europe. The western third, bequeathed to Charles the Bald (r.840–877), would eventually become France, and the eastern third, given to Louis the German (r.840–876), would become Germany. The "Middle Kingdom," which became Lothar's portion (r.817–855) along with the imperial title, had a different fate: parts of it were absorbed by France and Germany, while the rest eventually coalesced into the modern states of Belgium, the Netherlands, Luxembourg, Switzerland, and Italy. All this was far in the future. As the brothers had their own children, new divisions were tried: one in 870 (the Treaty of Meerssen), for example, and another in 880. (See Map 3.4b and Map 3.4c.) After the deposition of Emperor Charles the Fat (888), as one chronicler put it,

> the kingdoms which had obeyed his will, as if devoid of a legitimate heir,
> were loosened from their bodily structure into parts and now awaited no

Genealogy 3.1
(facing page):
The Carolingians★

Below left to right:

Map 3.4a: Partition of
843 (Treaty of Verdun)

Map 3.4b: Partition of
870 (Treaty of Meerssen)

Map 3.4c: Partition
of 880

lord of hereditary descent, but each set out to create a king for itself from
its own inner parts.[10]

Dynastic problems were not the primary cause of the breakup of the Carolingian
empire, however. Nor were the invasions by outsiders — Vikings, Muslims, and, starting in 899, Hungarians — which harassed the Frankish Kingdom throughout the
ninth century. These certainly weakened the kings: without a standing army, they
were unable to respond to the lightning raids, and what defense there was fell into the
hands of local leaders, such as counts. The Carolingians lost prestige and money as
they paid out tribute to stave off further attacks. But the invasions were not all bad; to
some degree they even helped fortify the king. The Carolingian empire atomized
because linguistic and other differences between regions — and familial and other ties
within regions — were simply too strong to be overcome by directives from a central
court. Only today is a unified Europe more than a distant ideal. Anyway, as we shall
see, fragmentation had its own strengths and possibilities.

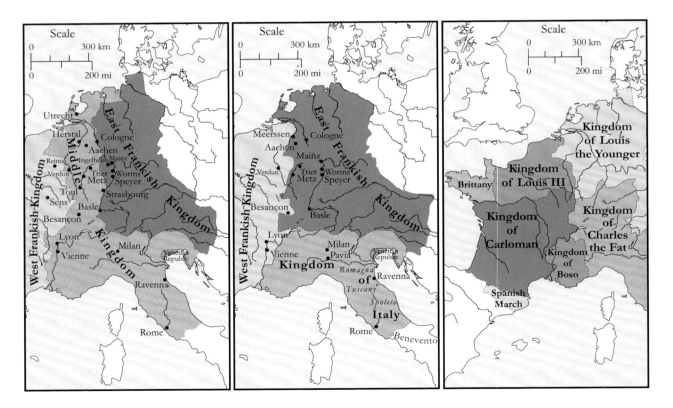

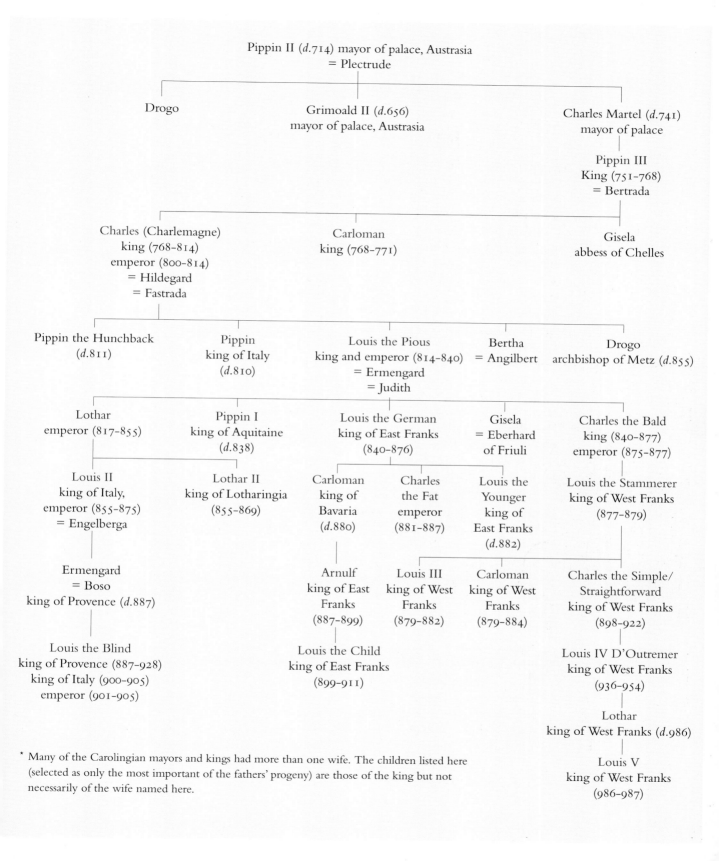

Pippin II (*d.*714) mayor of palace, Austrasia
= Plectrude

Drogo

Grimoald II (*d.*656) mayor of palace, Austrasia

Charles Martel (*d.*741) mayor of palace

Pippin III King (751–768) = Bertrada

Charles (Charlemagne) king (768–814) emperor (800–814) = Hildegard = Fastrada

Carloman king (768–771)

Gisela abbess of Chelles

Pippin the Hunchback (*d.*811)

Pippin king of Italy (*d.*810)

Louis the Pious king and emperor (814–840) = Ermengard = Judith

Bertha = Angilbert

Drogo archbishop of Metz (*d.*855)

Lothar emperor (817–855)

Pippin I king of Aquitaine (*d.*838)

Louis the German king of East Franks (840–876)

Gisela = Eberhard of Friuli

Charles the Bald king (840–877) emperor (875–877)

Louis II king of Italy, emperor (855–875) = Engelberga

Lothar II king of Lotharingia (855–869)

Carloman king of Bavaria (*d.*880)

Charles the Fat emperor (881–887)

Louis the Younger king of East Franks (*d.*882)

Louis the Stammerer king of West Franks (877–879)

Ermengard = Boso king of Provence (*d.*887)

Arnulf king of East Franks (887–899)

Louis III king of West Franks (879–882)

Carloman king of West Franks (879–884)

Charles the Simple/ Straightforward king of West Franks (898–922)

Louis the Blind king of Provence (887–928) king of Italy (900–905) emperor (901–905)

Louis the Child king of East Franks (899–911)

Louis IV D'Outremer king of West Franks (936–954)

Lothar king of West Franks (*d.*986)

Louis V king of West Franks (986–987)

* Many of the Carolingian mayors and kings had more than one wife. The children listed here (selected as only the most important of the fathers' progeny) are those of the king but not necessarily of the wife named here.

The Wealth of a Local Economy

The Carolingian economy was based on plunder, trade, and agriculture. After the Carolingians could push no further, and the booty raids of Charlemagne's day came to an end, trade and land became the chief resources of the kingdom. To the north, in Viking trading stations such as Haithabu (see Map 3.3), archaeologists have found Carolingian glass and pots alongside Islamic coins and cloth, showing that the Carolingian economy meshed with that of the Abbasid caliphate. Silver from the Islamic world probably came north from the Caspian Sea, up the Volga River (through what is today Russia) to the Baltic Sea. (You can figure out the likely route on the map at the front of this book.) There the coins were melted down, the silver traded to the Carolingians in return for wine, jugs, glasses, and other manufactured goods. The Carolingians turned the silver into coins of their own, to be used throughout the empire for small-scale local trade. Baltic sea emporia such as Haithabu supplemented those—Quentovic and Dorestad, for example (see Map 2.3 on p.74)—that served the North Sea trade.

Nevertheless, the backbone of the Carolingian economy was land. A few written records, called *polyptychs*, document the output of the Carolingian great estates—"villae," as they were called in Latin, "manors," as we term them. On the far-flung and widely scattered manors of rich landowners—churches, monasteries, kings, and aristocrats—a major reorganization and rationalization was taking place. The most enterprising landlords instituted a three-field rather than a two-field cultivation system. It meant that two-thirds of the land rather than one-half was sown with crops each year, yielding a tidy surplus.

Consider Villeneuve-Saint-Georges, one of the many manors belonging to the monastery of Saint-Germain-des-Prés (today right in the heart of Paris). This "new villa" was no compact farm but rather a conglomeration of essential parts: its lands, woods, meadows, and vineyards dotted the countryside. All were worked by peasant families, some legally free, some unfree, each settled on its own *mansus*, or "manse," including a house, a garden, small bits of several fields, and so on. The peasants farmed the land that belonged to them, and they also worked the *demesne*, the very large manse of their lord (in this case the monastery of Saint-Germain):

> Actard, villein *(colonus)*, and his wife, also a villein *(colona)*, named Eligilde, "men" of Saint-Germain, have with them six children …. They hold a free *manse* containing five *bonniers* of arable land and two *ansanges*, four *arpents* of vineyard, 4½ *arpents* of meadow. They provide four silver sous for military service and the other year two sous for the livery of meat, and the third year, for the livery of fodder, a ewe with a lamb. Two *muids* of

wine for the right of pannage, four deniers for the right of wood; for cartage a measure of wood, and 50 shingles. They plough four perches for the winter grain, and two perches for the spring. Manual and animal services, as much as is required of them....[11]

Actard and his family were "free peasants," with a fairly large "free" manse that included arable, vineyard, and meadow. They owed Saint-Germain many dues— some in money (sous), some in kind (like the ewe and lamb)—and labor services such as plowing Saint-Germain's *demesne*. Nearby lived other peasants, some with the status of slaves. They too had manses, but smaller ones, and they owed more dues and labor. Some of the women were required to feed the chickens or busy themselves in the *gynecaeum*, the women's workshop, where they made and dyed cloth and sewed garments.

Clearly the labor was onerous and the accounting system complex and unwieldy; but manors organized on the model of Saint-Germain made a profit. Like Saint-Germain and other lords, the Carolingian kings benefitted from their own extensive manors. Nevertheless, farming was still too primitive to return great surpluses, and as the lands belonging to the king were divided up in the wake of the partitioning of the empire, Carolingian dependence on manors scattered throughout their kingdom proved to be a source of weakness.

The Carolingian Renaissance

With profits from its manors, Saint-Germain-des-Prés put together a fine library of manuscripts. Some were copied right at the monastic scribal workshop (the *scriptorium*); others came from as near by as Saint-Amand (about 150 miles to the north) and as far away as Italy. Saint-Germain's library had books of liturgy (one book that came from Saint-Amand was a Sacramentary, a set of texts for the Mass), Latin grammars, and medical manuscripts. It had monk-scholars who used the books (sometimes writing in the margins) and expounded on them to their young pupils.

Saint-Germain was not unusual. The monastery of Saint-Amand, for example, was an even more important center of manuscript production. It produced Gospels, works of the Church Fathers, and grammars. Above all, the *scriptorium* of Saint-Amand made beautifully illustrated liturgical books, tailor-made for various other churches. Such liturgical manuscripts required particular expertise, for they were becoming books of music as well as text. The development of written music was a response to royal policy. Before Charlemagne's day, the melodies used for the Mass and the Divine Office were not at all uniform. Various churches in different places

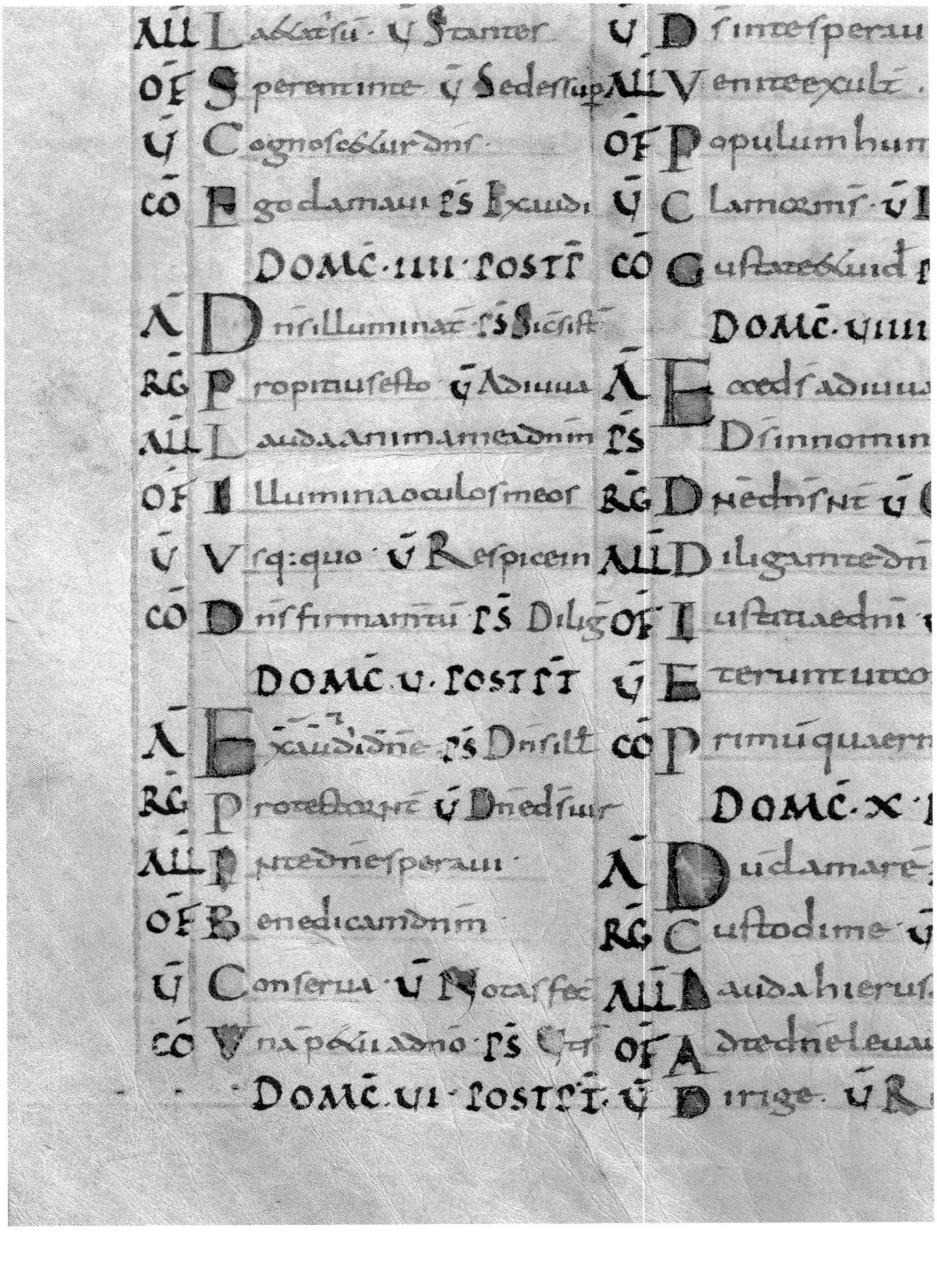

Plate 3.5: Sacramentary of Saint-Germain-des-Prés (early 9th cent.). The scribe of this list of *incipits* (the "first words") of mass chants provided a musical reminder of one (seven lines from the bottom, on the left) by adding neumes above the first words, "Exaudi Domine," "Hear, O Lord."

sang the tunes as they had learned them; music was part of local oral traditions. But since Charlemagne's time the melodies used for the Mass and the Divine Office were required to be "Roman," not Frankish. This reform—the imposition of the so-called "Gregorian chant"—posed great practical difficulties. It meant that every monk and priest had to learn a year's worth of Roman music; but how? A few cantors were imported from Rome; but without a system of musical notation, it was easy to forget new tunes. The monks of Saint-Amand were part of a musical revolution: they invented one of the first systems of musical notation. In the Sacramentary that they made for Saint-Germain they added "neumes," precursors of "notes," above some lines of text to indicate a melodic pattern. On the manuscript leaf shown in Plate 3.5, the neumes hover over a few words in the first column, 7 lines from the bottom of the page.

The same Sacramentary reveals another key development: the use of minuscule writing. As at Byzantium, and at about the same time, the Carolingians experiment-ed with letter forms that were quicker to write and easier to read. "Caroline minus-cule" lasted into the eleventh century, when it gave way to a more angular script called "Gothic." But the Carolingian letter forms were rediscovered in the fifteenth century—by scholars who thought that they represented ancient Roman writing!—and they became the model for modern lower-case printed fonts.

Like monasteries, cathedrals too were centers of cultural production in the Car-olingian period. Würzburg, for example, had a *scriptorium*, library, and school for young clerics. As enterprising about its books as Saint-Germain was about its manors, Würzburg made lists of its library's holdings. By the mid-ninth century these were substantial: Gospels, writings of the Church Fathers, liturgical manuscripts, grammars, biblical commentaries, and even books of canon (church) law. The bishops of Würzburg were avid collectors. When one of them wanted Hraban Maur's Bible commentaries, he sent his request for a copy along with a pile of blank parchment (there was no paper or papyrus in the West) to the monastery of Fulda, where Hra-ban was abbot. Meanwhile, Würzburg helped Fulda and other places build their own libraries, lending Fulda, for example, a manuscript of Gregory the Great's *Homilies* so that the monks there could copy it.

The Carolingian court was behind much of this activity. Most of the centers of learning, scholarship, and book production began under men and women who at one time or another had been part of the royal court. Alcuin (*c*.732-804), perhaps the most famous of the Carolingian intellectuals, was "imported" by Charlemagne from England—where, as we have seen, monastic scholarship flourished—to head up his palace school. Chief advisor to the king and tutor to the entire royal family, Alcuin eventually became abbot of Saint-Martin of Tours, grooming a new generation of teachers, including Hraban Maur (780-856). More unusual but equally telling was the

Plate 3.6

INCIPIT
ANGELIVM SECVN
DVM MARCVM
NITIVM
EVANGELII
IHVXPIFILII DI
SICVT SCRIP
TVM EST INE
SAIA PROPHE
TA ECCEMIT
TO ANGELVM MEVM

Plate 3-7

experience of Gisela, Charlemagne's sister. She too was a key royal advisor, the one who alerted the others at home about Charlemagne's imperial coronation at Rome in 800. She was also abbess of Chelles, a center of manuscript production in its own right. Chelles had a library, and its nuns were well educated. They wrote learned letters and composed a history (the "Prior Metz Annals") that treated the rise of the Carolingians as a tale of struggle between brothers, sons, and fathers eased by the wise counsel of mothers, aunts, and sisters.

Women and the poor make up the largely invisible half of the Carolingian Renaissance. But without doubt some were part of it. One of Charlemagne's capitularies ordered that the cathedrals and monasteries of his kingdom should teach reading and writing to all who could learn. There were enough complaints (by rich people) about peasants who had "made it" that we may be sure that some talented sons of the poor were getting an education. A few churchmen expressed the hope that schools for "children" would be established even in small villages and hamlets. Were they thinking of girls as well as boys? Certainly one woman—admittedly noble—in the mid-ninth century in the south of France proves that education was available to some women. We would never know about Dhuoda had she not worried enough about her absent son to write him a *Handbook* of advice. Only incidentally does it become clear in the course of her deeply felt moral text that Dhuoda was drawing on an excellent education: she clearly knew the Bible, writings of the Church Fathers, Gregory the Great, and "moderns," like Alcuin. Her Latin was fluent and sophisticated. And she understood the value of books:

> I, Dhuoda, am far away from you, my son William. For this reason I am anxious and filled with longing to do something for you. So I send you this little work written down in my name, that you may read it for your education, as a kind of mirror.[12]

The original manuscript of Dhuoda's text is not extant. Had it survived, it would no doubt have looked like other "practical texts" of the time: the "folios" (pages) would have been written in Caroline minuscule, each carefully planned to set off the poetry—Dhuoda's own and quotes from others—from the prose; the titles of each chapter (there are nearly a hundred, each very short) would have been enlivened with delicately colored capital letters. The manuscript would probably not have been illuminated; fancy books were generally made for royalty, for prestigious ceremonial occasions, or for books that were especially esteemed, such as the Gospels.

There were many such lavish productions. In fact, Carolingian art and architecture mark a turning point. For all its richness, Merovingian culture had not stressed artistic expression, though some of the monasteries inspired by Saint Columbanus produced a few illuminated manuscripts. By contrast, the Carolingians, admirers and

Preceding pages:

Plate 3.6: Saint Mark, Soissons Gospels (800-810). Compare this "author portrait" of St. Mark with that of St. Luke in **Plate 2.4** on p.84. Consider the different elements that each artist has used to render the portraits both figural and decorative.

Plate 3.7: First Text Page, Soissons Gospels (800-810). Compare this Carolingian first text page of the Gospel of Mark with the first text page of the Anglo-Saxon Gospel of Luke in **Plate 2.6** on p.86. In the Carolingian text, the letter forms are resolutely Roman looking, as if cut in stone. This classical allusion is reinforced by the artist's lavish use of purple (the Roman imperial color) and gold leaf. This is a manuscript meant for an emperor—Charlemagne.

Plate 3.8: Saint Mark, Coronation Gospels (*c.*800). Two portraits of St. Mark (this and the one in **Plate 3.6**), done at about the same time, and in about the same place, could hardly be in more disparate styles. They attest to the eclectic and wide-ranging artistic endeavors of the Carolingians.

imitators of Christian Rome, vigorously promoted a vast, eclectic, and ideologically motivated program of artistic work. They were reviving the Roman empire. We have already seen how Charlemagne brought the very marble of Rome and Ravenna home to Aachen to build his new palace complex. A similar impulse inspired Carolingian art.

As with texts, so with pictures: the Carolingians revered and imitated the past while building on and changing it. Their manuscript illuminations were inspired by a vast repertory of models: from the British Isles (where, as we have seen, a rich synthesis of decorative and representational styles had a long tradition), from late-antique Italy (which yielded its models in old manuscripts), and from Byzantium (which may have inadvertently provided some artists, fleeing iconoclasm, as well as manuscripts).

Plate 3.9 (facing page): Utrecht Psalter (*c*.820-835). Never completed, the Utrecht Psalter was commissioned by Archbishop Ebbo of Reims and executed at a nearby monastery. Providing a visual "running commentary" on every psalm, it may have been meant for Emperor Louis the Pious and his wife Queen Judith.

In Plate 3.6 and Plate 3.7, facing pages from a Carolingian manuscript made in the early ninth century, the artist has borrowed from the Anglo-Saxons by pairing his evangelist portrait of Mark with the beginning of Mark's Gospel text. The interlace motif of the large I in Plate 3.7 is also insular. But insofar as the figure of Saint Mark is sturdy, with clothes clinging to a body of convincing roundness, the artist has used a Byzantine model (compare Plate 3.2). And yet the real inspiration for this Mark is neither English nor Byzantine but entirely original. The evangelist's lively twist—his attention caught by the lion (Mark's symbol) about to give him the Word—and the bright, exuberant colors and designs that frame him are pure Carolingian invention. Like the artist of the Lindisfarne Gospels, the anonymous Mark artist has synthesized figural and decorative elements to suit the flat pages of a book; but the two syntheses are nothing alike.

Quite different, yet equally characteristic of Carolingian art, is the Saint Mark of Plate 3.8, made in the late eighth century. Here is a somber, utterly corporeal evangelist. He sits between mountains, with tinted sky above, light playing on his face. Were it not for his halo, he would be simply a man with a scroll. The colors are soft; the drapery subdued. No one was producing art like this outside of Francia. Its closest comparison is with Pompeiian wall paintings (see Plates 1.1 and 1.2 on pp. 31 and 32).

Both of these styles, the first richly decorative, the second subtly naturalistic, would have long lives in the West. It may even be said that they were the direct ancestors of the entire Western artistic tradition. One more model with a long life must be added: the Utrecht Psalter (Plate 3.9), a book containing all 150 Psalms and 16 other songs known as canticles. Fleeting precedents for this extraordinary manuscript of narrative art exist. For example, Plate 3.7 has lithe figures in the top corners to illustrate Bible stories: on the left is the baptism of Christ, on the right angels minister to Christ after the Temptation. The Utrecht Psalter, produced *c*.820-835, takes this impulse to its logical conclusion. It precedes each poem with drawings that depict its important elements in unified composition. In Plate 3.9, the illustration for Psalm 8, the artist

CIRCUMDABITTE
ETPROPTERHANCINALTU
REGREDERE DNSIUDI
CATPOPULOS
IUDICAMEDNESECUN
DUIUSTITIAMMEA ET
SECUNDUMINNOCEN
TIAMMEAMSUPERME
CONSUMMETURNEQUITI
APECCATORUETDIRI
GESIUSTUM ETSCRUTANS
CORDAETRENESDS
IUSTUMADIUTORIUM
MEUMADNO QUISAL
VIII INFINEM

UOSFACITRECTOSCORDE
DSIUDEXIUSTUSETFORTIS
ETPATIENS NUMQUIDI
RASCETURPERSINGU
LOSDIES
NISICONUERSIFUERITIS
GLADIUMSUUMUIBRA
BITARCUMSUUMTE
TENDITETPARAUITILLU
ETINEOPARAUITUASA
MORTIS SAGITTASSU
ASARDENTIBUSEFFECIT
ECCEPARTURITINIUS
TITIAM CONCEPITDO
PROTORCOLARIBUS

LOREMETPEPERITINIQUI
TATEM
LACUMAPERUITETEFFODIT
EUM ETINCIDITINFOUE
AMQUAMFECIT
CONUERTETURDOLOR
EIUSINCAPUTEIUS ET
INUERTICEMIPSIUSINI
QUITASEIUSDESCENDET
CONFITEBORDNOSECUN
DUMIUSTITIAMEIUS
ETPSALLAMNOMINI
DNIALTISSIMI;

PSALMUSDAUID

QUAMADMIRABILE
ESTNOMENTUUM
INUNIUERSATERRA
QNMELEUATAESTMAG
NIFICENTIATUA SU
PERCAELOS
EXOREINFANTIUMETLAC

TANTIUM PERFECISTI
LAUDEMPROPTERINI
MICOSTUOS UTDESTRU
ASINIMICUMETULTORE
QNMUIDEBOCAELOSTU
OSOPERADIGITORU
TUORUM LUNAMEIS
TELLASQUAETUFUNDASTI

QUIDESTHOMOQUOD
MEMORESHIUS AUT
FILIUSHOMINISQUO
NIAMUISITASEUM
MINUISTIEUMPAULOMI
NUSABANGELIS GLO
RIAETHONORECORO
NASTIEUM ETCONS

has, for example, sketched sheep and oxen on the bottom left, birds flying and fish swimming on the bottom right, to render literally verses 8 and 9:

> Thou hast subjected all things under his feet, all sheep and oxen: moreover the beasts also of the fields. / The birds of the air, and the fishes of the sea, that pass through the paths of the sea.

The ambition, style, wit, and narrative thrust of the Utrecht Psalter inspired much art in the Middle Ages and beyond.

★   ★   ★   ★

In the course of the eighth and ninth centuries, the three heirs of Rome established clearly separate identities, each largely bound up with its religious affiliation. Byzantium saw itself as the radiating center of Orthodox faith; the Caliphate was the guarantor of Islam; Francia was "the assembly of Christian people." From this perspective, there were few commonalities. Yet today we are struck more by the similarities than the differences. All were centralizing monarchies shored up by military might. All had a bit of wealth, though the East certainly had more than the West. All had pretensions to God-given power. And all used culture and scholarship to give luster and expression to their political regimes. All may also have known, without explicitly admitting it, how strong were the forces of dissolution.

NOTES

1. Quoted in *Byzantium: Church, Society, and Civilization Seen through Contemporary Eyes*, ed. Deno John Geanakoplos (Chicago, 1984), p.409.

2. "Imports of Iraq" in *Medieval Trade in the Mediterranean World: Illustrative Documents,* trans. Robert S. Lopez and Irving W. Raymond (New York, 1997), p.28.

3. *Algebra of Mohammed ben Musa* as quoted in Dimitri Gutas, *Greek Thought, Arabic Culture: The Graeco-Arabic Translation Movement in Baghdad and Early 'Abbasid Society (2nd-4th/8th-10th Centuries)* (London, 1998), p.113.

4. Quoted in Salma Khadra Jayyusi, "Andalusi Poetry: The Golden Period," in *The Legacy of Muslim Spain* (Leiden, 1994), 1:327.

5. *The Fourth Book of the Chronicle of Fredegar with its Continuations*, trans. J.M. Wallace-Hadrill (London, 1960), p.91.

6. Quoted in Thomas F.X. Noble, *The Republic of St. Peter: The Birth of the Papal State, 680-825* (Philadelphia, 1984), p.263.

7. "Epitaph for Adalhaid," in *Carolingian Civilization: A Reader*, ed. Paul Dutton (Peterborough, 1993), p.46.

8. "The General Capitulary for the Missi from 802," in *Carolingian Civilization*, p.61.

9. "Einhard's *Life of Charlemagne*," in *Carolingian Civilization*, p.38.

10. "Regino's Reasons for the End of the Carolingian Line," in *Carolingian Civilization*, p.507.

11. "Polyptyque of Saint-Germain-des-Prés," quoted in Georges Duby, *Rural Economy and Country Life in the Medieval West*, trans. Cynthia Postan (Philadelphia, 1998), p.368.

12. *Handbook for William: A Carolingian Woman's Counsel for Her Son by Dhuoda*, trans. Carol Neel (2nd ed., Washington, 1991), p.2.

FURTHER READING

For searchable maps, genealogies, and other materials for this chapter, please visit the *Short History of the Middle Ages* website at www.broadviewpress.com/shorthistory.

Beckwith, John. *The Art of Constantinople: An Introduction to Byzantine Art, 330-1453*. London, 1968.

Chazelle, Celia. *The Crucified God in the Carolingian Era: Theology and Art of Christ's Passion*. Cambridge, 2001.

Collins, Roger. *Charlemagne*. Toronto, 1998.

Fine, John V.A. *The Early Medieval Balkans. A Critical Survey from the Sixth to the Late Twelfth Century*. Ann Arbor, 1991.

Fouracre, Paul. *The Age of Charles Martel*. Harlow, Essex, 2000.

Ganshof, François Louis. *Frankish Institutions under Charlemagne*. Trans. Bryce and Mary Lyon. New York, 1970.

Herrin, Judith. *Women in Purple: Rulers of Medieval Byzantium*. Princeton, 2002.

James, Edward. *Britain in the First Millennium*. London, 2001.

Kennedy, Hugh. *The Abbasid Caliphate: A Political History*. London, 1981.

—. *Muslim Spain and Portugal: A Political History of al-Andalus*. London, 1996.

—. *The Prophet and the Age of the Caliphates: The Islamic Near East from the Sixth to the Eleventh Century*. 2d. ed. London, 2004.

McCormick, Michael. *Origins of the European Economy: Communications and Commerce, AD 300-900*. Cambridge, 2001.

McKitterick, Rosamond, ed. *Carolingian Culture: Emulation and Innovation*. Cambridge, 1994.

—. *The Carolingians and the Written Word*. Cambridge, 1989.

Nelson, Janet L. *Charles the Bald*. London, 1992.

—. *The Frankish World, 750-900*. London, 1996.

Treadgold, Warren. *The Byzantine Revival, 780-842*. Stanford, 1988.

Verhulst, Adriaan. *The Carolingian Economy*. Cambridge, 2002.

Whittow, Mark. *The Making of Byzantium, 600-1025*. Berkeley, 1996.

FOUR

POLITICAL COMMUNITIES
REORDERED (*c*.900-*c*.1050)

THE LARGE-SCALE CENTRALIZED governments of the ninth century dissolved in the tenth. The fission was least noticeable at Byzantium, where, although important landowning families emerged as brokers of patronage and power, the primacy of the emperor was never effectively challenged. Quite the opposite happened in the Islamic world, where new dynastic groups quickly established themselves as regional rulers. In Western Europe, Carolingian kings ceased to control land and men, while new political entities—some extremely local and weak, others quite strong and unified—emerged in their wake. Everywhere political reordering brought new military elites to the fore.

BYZANTIUM: THE STRENGTHS AND LIMITS OF CENTRALIZATION

By 1025 the Byzantine empire once again shadowed the Danube and touched the Euphrates. To the north it had a new and restless neighbor: Kievan Rus. The emperors at Constantinople maintained the traditional cultural importance of the capital city by carefully orchestrating the radiating power of the imperial court. Nevertheless, the centralized model of the Byzantine state was challenged by powerful men in the countryside, who gobbled up land and dominated the peasantry.

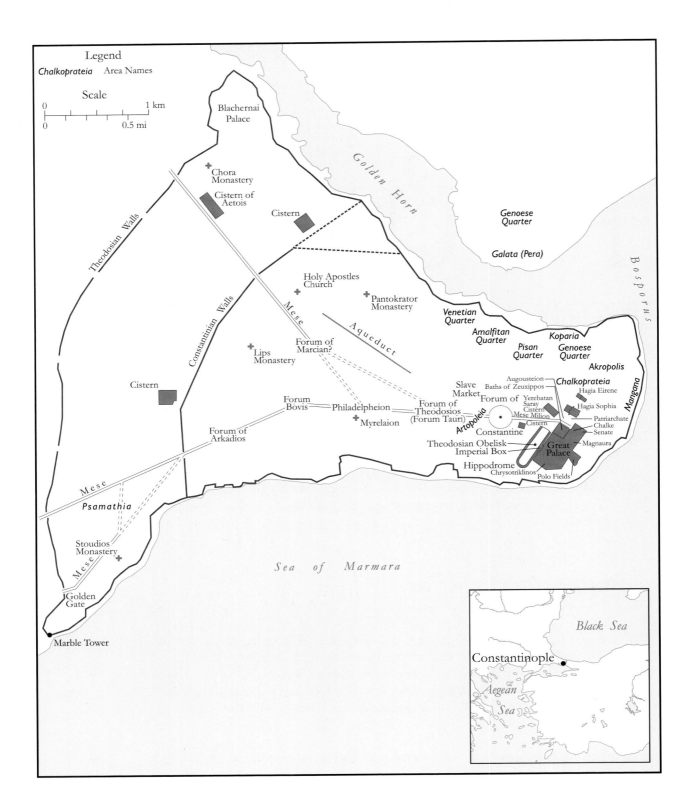

Legend

Chalkoprateia Area Names

Scale

0   1 km

0   0.5 mi

Blachernai Palace

Chora Monastery

Cistern of Aetois

Cistern

Golden Horn

Genoese Quarter

Galata (Pera)

B o s p o r u s

Theodosian Walls

Constantinian Walls

Holy Apostles Church

Pantokrator Monastery

Mese

Aqueduct

Venetian Quarter

Amalfitan Quarter

Pisan Quarter

Koparia

Genoese Quarter

Akropolis

Lips Monastery

Forum of Marcian?

Cistern

Slave Market

Augousteion

Baths of Zeuxippos

Chalkoprateia

Hagia Eirene

Hagia Sophia

Mangana

Forum Bovis

Philadelpheion

Myrelaion

Forum of Theodosios (Forum Tauri)

Artopoleio

Forum of Constantine

Yerebatan Saray Cistern

Mese Milion

Cistern

Patriarchate

Chalke

Senate

Theodosian Obelisk

Imperial Box

Great Palace

Magnaura

Forum of Arkadios

Hippodrome

Chrysotriklinos

Polo Fields

Mese

Psamathia

Stoudios Monastery

Mese

Golden Gate

Sea of Marmara

Marble Tower

Black Sea

Constantinople

Aegean Sea

The Imperial Court

The Great Palace of Constantinople, a sprawling building complex begun under Constantine, was expanded, redecorated, and fortified under his successors. (See Map 4.1.) It was more than the symbolic emplacement of imperial power; it was the central command post of the empire. Servants, slaves, and grooms; top courtiers and learned clergymen; cousins, siblings, and hangers-on of the emperor and empress lived within its walls. Other courtiers—civil servants, officials, scholars, military men, advisers, and other dependents—lived as nearby as they could manage. They were "on call" at every hour. The emperor had only to give short notice and all were to be at the Palace for impromptu but nevertheless highly choreographed ceremonies. These were in themselves instruments of power; the emperors manipulated courtly formalities to indicate new favorites or to signal displeasure.

Map 4.1 (facing page): Constantinople *c.*1100

Highly visible at the Great Palace were corps of eunuchs, castrated men who acted as advisers, guards, and go-betweens for the empress and her female entourage. There were important empresses in the tenth and eleventh centuries, women like Zoë, the niece of Basil II (*r.*963-1025), who orchestrated the downfall of one emperor and the rise of another. Nevertheless, she did so only because she was the wife of the first and the lover of the second; hers was the power of the bedroom. The eunuchs at court reminded everyone that *real* power was not a matter of fecundity. It was a matter of proximity to the emperor. Eunuchs, who could not have children and therefore could not pass possessions and power to their heirs, were close to the emperor precisely because they could be trusted to be innocently near the empress, bearer of the emperor's children. No wonder that in the tenth century, Basil the Nothos, the castrated bastard son of one emperor, rose to become grand chamberlain (responsible for internal affairs) at the court of another.

About a century later, the grand chamberlain was not a eunuch but rather a professor, Michael Psellos. The Macedonian Renaissance, which had begun in the ninth century, continued apace in the tenth and eleventh, bringing people like Psellos to the fore. Under his direction a new school of philosophy at Constantinople, founded by Constantine IX (*r.*1042-1055), began to flourish. Beyond his philosophical interests, Psellos was a moralist, keen to explore the character and emotional life of powerful men and women. In his hands, a new sort of historical writing was born: not a universal chronicle covering Creation to the present, as had been the style, but rather opinionated accounts of recent events, personalities, and well-oiled political networks:

> Basil [II] surrounded himself with favorites who were neither remarkable
> for brilliance of intellect, nor of noble lineage, nor too learned. To them

were entrusted the imperial rescripts [orders], and with them he was accustomed to share the secrets of State.[1]

The impression that Psellos gives of a self-indulgent emperor presiding over a frivolous court is only part of the story, however. As Psellos himself recognized, Basil was a successful centralizer, amassing enormous wealth through taxes, confiscations, and tribute. Above all—something that Psellos only hinted at—he was a tough military man whose rule reshaped the geography of Byzantium.

A Wide Embrace and Its Tensions

Map 4.2:
The Byzantine Empire, *c.*1025

The expansion of the Byzantine Empire, so cautiously begun in the ninth century, quickened under the tenth-century soldier-emperors Nicephorus Phocas and John Tzimisces. (See Map 4.2.) Crete, lost to the Muslims in the ninth century, was retaken in 961; Cyprus was reconquered in 965; Antioch, portal to Syria, in 969. Most

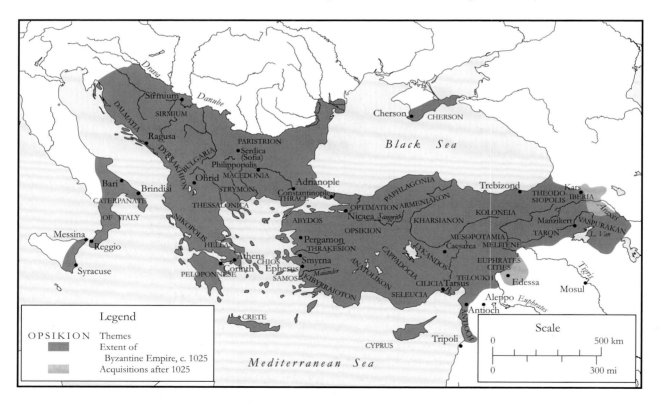

importantly, under Basil II, Bulgaria, a thorn in Byzantium's side since the seventh century, was at last definitively defeated (1018). The entire region was put under Byzantine rule, its territory divided into themes.

Certainly Basil's nickname, the "Bulgar Slayer," was apt. Nevertheless, it hid the fact that the same emperor was also busy setting up protectorates against the Muslims on his eastern front and that at the end of his life he was preparing an expedition to Sicily. By 1025 the Byzantine army was no longer focused on the interior but was rather mobilized at the peripheries of the empire.

This empire was no longer the tight fist centered on Anatolia that it had been in the dark days of the eighth century. On the contrary, it was an open hand: sprawling, multi-ethnic, and multilingual. To the east it embraced Armenians, Syrians, and Arabs; to the north it included Bulgarians and other Slavs as well as Pechenegs, a Turkic group that had served as allies of Bulgaria; to the west, in the Byzantine toe of Italy, it contained Lombards, Italians, and Greeks. There must have been Muslims right in the middle of Constantinople: a mosque was built for them there in 1027. Russian soldiers from the region of Kiev formed the backbone of Basil's "Varangian Guard," his elite troops; by mid-century, Byzantine mercenaries included "Franks" (mainly from Normandy), Arabs, and Bulgarians as well. In spite of ingrained prejudices, Byzantine princesses had occasionally been married to foreigners before the tenth century, but only in Basil's reign did this happen to a sister of the emperor himself.

All this openness went only so far, however. In the tenth century, the emperors expelled Jews from Constantinople, severely curtailing their participation in the silk trade (their traditional profession), and forcing them into the degrading labor of tanners. Some of these restrictions were lifted in the course of the eleventh century, but Jews were never integrated into Byzantine society. Similarly, the annexation of Armenia did not lead to the assimilation of Armenians, who kept their Monophysite beliefs, heretical to many Orthodox Byzantines.

Ethnic diversity was in part responsible for new regional political movements that threatened centralized imperial control. More generally, however, regional revolts were the result of the rise of a new class of wealthy provincial landowners, the *dynatoi* (*sing. dynatos*), "powerful men." Benefitting from a general quickening in the economy and the rise of new urban centers, they took advantage of unaccustomed wealth, buying land from still impoverished peasants as yet untouched by the economic upswing. The *dynatoi* made military men their clients (even if they were not themselves military men) and often held positions in government. The Dalasseni family was fairly typical of this group. The founder of the family was an army leader and governor of Antioch at the end of the tenth century. One of his sons, Theophylact, became governor of "Iberia"—not Spain but rather a theme on the very eastern edge of the empire. Another, Constantine, inherited his father's position at Antioch. With estates scattered throughout Anatolia and a network of connections to other powerful families, the Dalasseni at times could defy the emperor and even coordinate rebellions against him. From the end of the tenth century, imperial control had to contend with the decentralizing forces of provincial *dynatoi* such as these. But the emperors were not dethroned, and a man like Basil II could triumph over the families that challenged his reign to emerge even stronger than before.

The rise of the provincial aristocracy and the prestige of the soldier emperors worked a change in Byzantine culture: from civilian to military ideals. The emperor had long ceased to be "declared" by his troops; but in the eleventh century artists insisted on portraying the emperor hoisted on a shield, symbol of military power. An epic poem, *Digenis Akritas*, begun in the tenth century and probably put into its final form in the eleventh or twelfth, depicts the hero, Digenis, winning battles, wooing beautiful women, and (most important from the aristocratic point of view) giving advice to a respectful emperor. Military saints, such as George, became increasingly popular, while even non-military saints were now sometimes depicted as "knights" on horseback.

Map 4.3 (facing page):
Kievan Rus, *c.*1050

The Formation of Kievan Rus

During the eighth and ninth centuries, a fledgling principality had taken shape above the Black Sea, along the Dnieper River. (See Map 4.3.) At first the "Rus" were itinerant raiders and traders from Scandinavia, the eastern counterpart to the Viking invaders of the West. Gradually they imposed their rule over the Slavs inhabiting the broad river valleys connecting the Baltic with the Black Sea, adopting the language of their subjects. At the end of the ninth century, one Dnieper valley chief, Oleg, established control over most of the tribes in southwestern Russia and turned more distant groups into tributaries. The tribal association that he created formed the nucleus of Kievan Rus, named for the city that had become the commercial center of the region and is today the capital of Ukraine.

Rus and Byzantium began their relationship in war, developed it through trade agreements, and sustained it with religion. Around 905, Oleg launched a military expedition to Constantinople, forcing the Byzantines to pay a large indemnity and open their doors to Russian traders in exchange for peace. At the time, only a few Christians lived in Rus, along with Jews and probably some Muslims. The conversion of the Rus to Christianity was spearheaded by Grand Prince Vladimir (*d.*1015). In 988, he adopted the Byzantine form of Christianity, took the name "Basil" in honor of Emperor Basil II, and married Anna, the emperor's sister. Then he reportedly had all of the people of his state baptized in the Dnieper River.

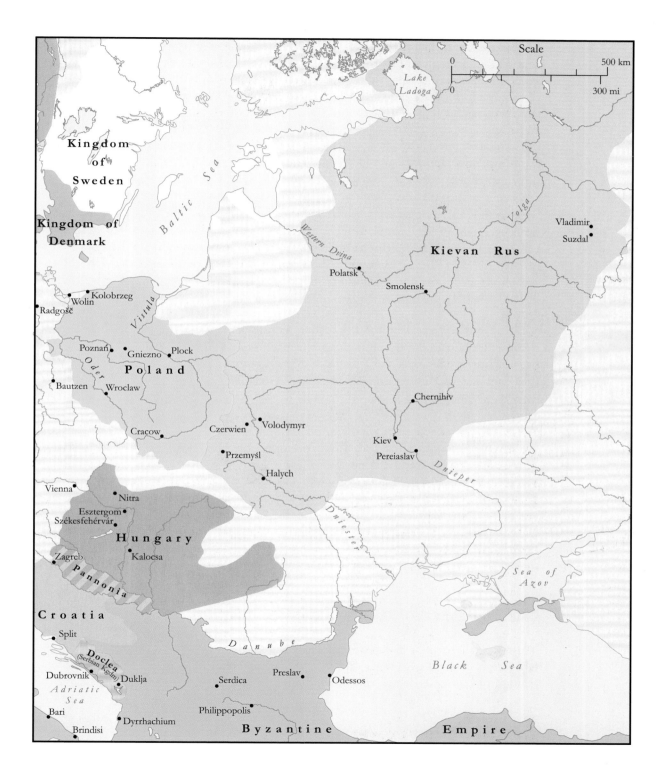

Scale

0   500 km

0   300 mi

Lake Ladoga

Kingdom of Sweden

Baltic Sea

Western Dvina

Volga

Vladimir

Suzdal

Kingdom of Denmark

Kievan Rus

Polatsk

Kolobrzeg

Wolin

Radgošč

Vistula

Smolensk

Poznań

Gniezno

Plock

Poland

Oder

Bautzen

Wroclaw

Chernihiv

Cracow

Czerwien

Volodymyr

Przemyśl

Kiev

Pereiaslav

Halych

Dnieper

Vienna

Nitra

Dniester

Esztergom

Székesfehérvár

Hungary

Zagreb

Kalocsa

Pannonia

Sea of Azov

Croatia

Split

Danube

Doclea
(Serbian Kgdm)

Black Sea

Dubrovnik

Duklja

Adriatic Sea

Serdica

Preslav

Odessos

Bari

Philippopolis

Brindisi

Dyrrhachium

B y z a n t i n e   **E m p i r e**

Vladimir's conversion was part of a larger movement of the tenth and eleventh centuries in which most of the remaining non-monotheistic peoples of the western Eurasian land mass adopted one of the four dominant monotheisms: Islam, Roman Catholicism, Byzantine Orthodoxy, or Judaism. Given its geographic location, it was anyone's guess which way Rus would go. On its western flank was Poland, where in 966, Mieszko I (r.963-992), leader of the tribe known as the Polanians, accepted baptism into the Roman Catholic faith. Eventually (in 991) he placed his realm under the protection of the pope. The experience of Hungary, just south of Poland, was similar: there Géza (r. c. 972-997) converted to Roman Catholicism and, according to a potent legend, his son, Stephen I (r.997-1038), accepted a royal crown from the pope in the year 1000 or 1001. Further north the ancestors of the Rus, the Scandinavians, were also turning to Catholic Christianity: the king of the Danes, for example, was baptized around 960. But to the east of Rus were other models: the Khazars were Jewish; the Volga Bulgars converted to Islam in the early tenth century. Why, then, did Vladimir choose the Byzantine form of Christianity? Perhaps because he could drive the hardest bargain with Basil, who badly needed Rus troops for his Varangian Guard.

That momentary decision left lasting consequences. Rus, ancestor of Russia, became the heir of the Byzantine church, customs, art, and political ideology. Adopting Christianity linked Russia to the West, but choosing the Byzantine form meant that Russia would always stand apart from Western Europe.

DIVISION AND DEVELOPMENT IN THE ISLAMIC WORLD

While at Byzantium the forces of decentralization were feeble, they carried the day in the Islamic world. Where once the caliph at Baghdad or Samarra could boast collecting taxes from Kabul (today in Afghanistan) to Benghazi (today in Libya), in the eleventh century a bewildering profusion of regional groups and dynasties divided the Islamic world. Yet this was in general a period of prosperity and intellectual blossoming.

The Emergence of Regional Powers

The Muslim conquest had never eliminated all local powers or regional affiliations. It had simply papered over them. While the Umayyad and Abbasid caliphates remained strong, they imposed their rule through their governors and army. But when the caliphate became weak, as it did in the tenth and eleventh centuries, old and new regional interests came to the fore.

A glance at a map of the Islamic world *c.*1000 (Map 4.4) shows, from east to west, the main new groups that emerged: the Samanids, Buyids, Hamdanids, Fatimids, and Zirids. But the map hides the many territories dominated by petty independent rulers. North of the Fatimid Caliphate, al-Andalus had a parallel history. Its Umayyad ruler took the title of caliph in 929, but in the eleventh century, he too was unable to stave off political fragmentation.

The key cause of the weakness of the Abbasid caliphate was lack of revenue. When landowners, governors, or recalcitrant military leaders in the various regions of the Islamic world refused to pay taxes into the treasury, the caliphs had to rely on the rich farmland of Iraq, long a stable source of income. But in the tenth century, Iraq was attacked by the Qaramita (sometimes called the "Carmathians"), a sect of Shi'ites based in Arabia. In the wake of this war, Iraq's agriculture was both sabotaged and neglected. The result was decisive: the caliphs could not pay their troops. New

Map 4.4: Fragmentation of the Islamic World

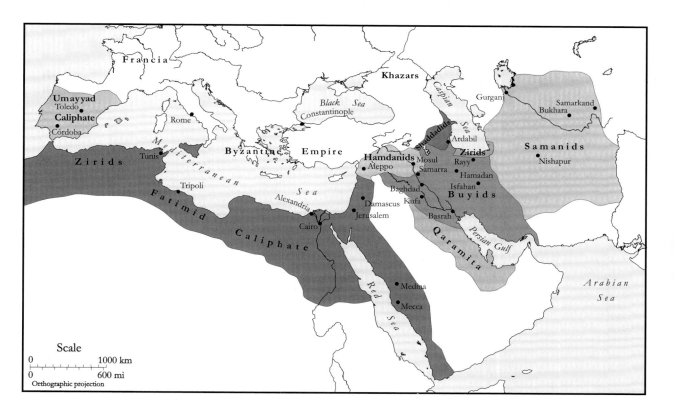

men—military men with their own armies and titles like "commander of commanders"—took the reins of power. They did not wipe out the Abbasid line, but they reduced the caliph's political authority to nothing.

The new leaders represented groups that had awaited their day in the sun. The Buyids, for example, belonged to ancient warrior tribes from the mountains of Iran. Even in the tenth century, most were relatively new converts to Islam. Bolstered by long-festering local discontent, one of them became "commander of commanders" in 945. Thereafter, the Buyids, with the help from their own Turkish mercenaries, dominated the region south of the Caspian Sea, including Baghdad (once again the home of the caliphs) itself. Yet already by the end of the tenth century, their own power was challenged by still more local men, in a political process—the progressive regionalization and fragmentation of power—echoed elsewhere in the Islamic world and in parts of Western Europe as well.

The most important of the new regional rulers were the Fatimids. They, like the Qaramita (and, increasingly in the course of time, the Buyids), were Shi'ites, taking their name from Muhammad's daughter Fatimah, wife of Ali. The Fatimid leader claimed to be not only the true *imam*, descendant of Ali, but also the *mahdi*, the "divinely guided" messiah, come to bring justice on earth. Because of this, the Fatimids were proclaimed "caliphs" by their followers—the true "successors" of the Prophet. Allying with the Berbers in North Africa, the Fatimids established themselves as rulers by 909 in what is today Tunisia and Libya. Within a half-century they had moved eastward (largely abandoning the Maghreb to the Zirids), to rule Egypt, southern Syria, and the western edge of the Arabian Peninsula.

The Fatimids looked east rather than west because the east was rich and because the west was dominated by Sunnis, hostile to Shi'ite rule. The most important of the Sunni rulers were the Umayyads at Córdoba. Abd al-Rahman III (r.912–961) took the title caliph in 929 as a counterweight to the Fatimids, although he claimed to rule only all of al-Andalus, not the whole Islamic world. An active military man backed by an army made up mainly of Slavic slaves, Abd al-Rahman defeated his rivals and imposed his rule not only on southern Iberia (as his predecessors had done) but also in northern regions (near the Christian kingdoms) and in the Maghreb. Under Abd al-Rahman and his immediate successors, al-Andalus became a powerful centralized state. But regional Islamic rulers there worked to undermine the authority of the Umayyads, so that between 1009 and 1031 bitter civil war undid the dynasty's power. After 1031, al-Andalus was split into small "kingdoms," called *taifas*, ruled by local strongmen.

Thus in the Islamic world, far more decisively than at Byzantium, newly powerful men came to the fore. They were less tied to private estates than the *dynatoi* of Byzantium, and their dependence on slaves and mercenaries—foreigners without any roots at all in local soil—was also different. At Byzantium the ascendency of the military classes led poets and artists to praise warriors in general. In the Islamic world as well, a few writers proudly portrayed old Persian and Bedouin heroes as model fighting men. In the *Shahnama* (*Book of Kings*) by the poet Firdawsi (*c*.935–*c*.1020), the hero slays demons and saves kings. But on the whole, poets and writers continued to laud "civilian" life and to embroider the old themes of *adab* literature.

Cultural Unity, Religious Polarization

In fact, the emergence of local strongmen meant not the end of Arab court culture but a multiplicity of courts, each attempting to out-do one another in brilliant artistic, scientific, theological, and literary productions. Consider Cairo, for example, which was founded by the Fatimids. Already by 1000 it was a huge urban complex. Imitating the Abbasids, the Fatimid caliphs built mosques and palaces, fostered court ceremonials, and turned Cairo into a center of intellectual life. One of the Fatimid caliphs, al-Hakim, founded the *dar al-ilm*, a sort of theological college plus public library.

Even more impressive was the Umayyad court at Córdoba, the wealthiest and showiest city of the west. It boasted 70 public libraries in addition to the caliphs' private library of perhaps 400,000 books. The Córdoban Great Mosque was a center for scholars from the rest of the Islamic world (the caliph paid their salaries), while nearly 30 free schools were set up throughout the city. A later chronicler boasted, "Córdoba held more books than any other city in al-Andalus, and its inhabitants were the most enthusiastic in caring for their libraries; such collections were regarded as symbols of status and social leadership."[2]

Córdoba was noteworthy not only because of the brilliance of its intellectual life but also because of the role women played in it. Elsewhere in the Islamic world there were certainly a few unusual women associated with cultural and scholarly life. But at Córdoba this was a general phenomenon: women not only were doctors, teachers, and librarians but also worked as copyists for the many books so widely in demand.

Male scholars were, however, everywhere the norm, and they moved easily from court to court. Ibn Sina (980–1037), known to the West as Avicenna, began his career serving the ruler at Bukhara, and then moved to Gurganj, Rayy, and Hamadan before ending up for thirteen years at the court of Isfahan. Sometimes in favor and sometimes decidedly not so (he was even briefly imprisoned), he nevertheless managed to study and practice medicine and write numerous books on the natural sciences and philosophy. His pioneering systematization of Aristotle laid the foundations of future philosophical thought.

Despite its political disunity, then, the Islamic world of the tenth and eleventh centuries remained in many ways an integrated culture. This was partly due to the model of intellectual life fostered by the Abbasids, which even in decline was copied by the new rulers, as we have just seen. It was also due to the common Arabic language, the glue that bound the astronomer at Córdoba to the philosopher at Cairo. Finally, integration was the result of open trade networks. With no national barriers to commerce and few regulations, merchants regularly dealt in far-flung, various, and sometimes exotic goods. From England came tin, while salt and gold were imported from Timbuktu in west-central Africa; from Russia came amber, gold, and copper; slaves were wrested from sub-Saharan Africa, the Eurasian steppes, and Slavic regions.

Although Muslims dominated these trade networks, other groups were involved in commerce as well. We happen to know a good deal about one Jewish community living at Fustat, about two miles south of Cairo. It observed the then-common custom of depositing for eventual ritual burial all writing containing the name of God. For good measure, the Jews in this community privileged everything written in Hebrew: letters, business transactions, shopping lists. By chance, the materials that they left in their *geniza* (depository) at Fustat were preserved rather than burned. These sources reveal a cosmopolitan, middle-class society. Many were traders, for Fustat was the center of a vast and predominately Jewish trade network that stretched from al-Andalus to India. Consider the Tustari brothers, Jewish merchants from southern Iran. By the early eleventh century, the brothers had established a flourishing business in Egypt. Informal family networks offered them many of the same advantages as branch offices: friends and family in Iran shipped the Tustaris fine textiles to sell in Egypt, while they exported Egyptian fabrics back to Iran.

Only Islam, ironically, pulled Islamic culture apart. In the tenth century the split between the Sunnis and Shi'ites widened to a chasm. At Baghdad, al-Mufid (*d.*1022) and others turned Shi'ism into a partisan ideology that insisted on publicly cursing the first two caliphs, turning the tombs of Ali and his family into objects of veneration, and creating an Alid caliph by force. Small wonder that the Abbasid caliphs soon became ardent spokesmen for Sunni Islam, which developed in turn its own public symbols. But many of the new dynasties—the Fatimids and the Qaramita especially—took advantage of the newly polarized faith to bolster their power.

THE WEST: FRAGMENTATION AND RESILIENCE

Fragmentation was the watchword in Western Europe in many parts of the shattered Carolingian Empire. Historians speak of "France," "Germany," and "Italy" in this period as a shorthand for designating broad geographical areas. But there were no national states, only regions with more or less clear borders and rulers with more or less authority. In some places—in parts of "France," for example—regions as small as a few square miles were under the control of different lords who acted, in effect, as independent rulers. Yet this same period saw both England and Scotland become unified kingdoms. And to the east, in Saxony, a powerful royal dynasty, the Ottonians, emerged to rule an empire stretching from the North Sea to Rome.

The Last Invaders of the West

Three groups invaded Western Europe during the ninth and tenth centuries: the Vikings, the Muslims, and the Hungarians. (See Map 4.5.) In the short run, they wreaked havoc on land and people. In the long run, they were absorbed into the European population and became constituents of a newly prosperous and aggressive European civilization.

THE VIKINGS

At the same time as they made their forays into Russia, the Vikings were raiding the coasts of France, England, Scotland, and Ireland. In their longships—often traveling as families with husbands, wives, children, and slaves—they crossed the Atlantic, making themselves at home in Iceland and Greenland and, in about 1000, touching on North America. They settled as well in Ireland, Scotland, England, and Normandy (giving their name to the region: Norman = Northman, or Viking).

In Ireland, where the Vikings settled in the east and south, the newcomers added their own claims to rule an island already fragmented among four or five competing dynasties. In Scotland, however, in the face of Norse settlements in the north and west, the natives drew together under kings who—in a process we have seen elsewhere—allied themselves with churchmen and other powerful local leaders. Cináed mac Ailpín (Kenneth I MacAlpin) (d.858) established a hereditary dynasty of kings that ruled over two hitherto separate native peoples. By c.900, the separate identities were gone, and most people in *Alba*, the nucleus of the future Scotland, had a common sense of their identity as Scots.

England underwent a similar process of unification. Initially divided into small competing kingdoms, it was weak prey in the face of invasion. By the end of the ninth century, the Vikings were plowing fields in eastern England and living in accordance with their own laws. In Wessex, the southernmost kingdom, King Alfred the Great (r.871–899) bought time and peace, paying a tribute with the income from a new tax, later called the Danegeld (it eventually became the basis of a relatively lucrative taxation system in England). Even more importantly, in 878 he mustered an army and, as his biographer, Asser, put it,

> gained the victory through God's will. He destroyed the Vikings with great slaughter, and pursued those who fled as far as the stronghold, hacking them down; he seized everything which he found outside the stronghold—men (whom he killed immediately), horses, and cattle—and boldly made camp in front of the gates of the Viking stronghold with all his army. When he had been there for fourteen days the Vikings, thoroughly terrified by hunger, cold and fear, and in the end by despair, sought peace.[3]

Thereafter the pressure of invasion eased as Alfred reorganized his army, set up strongholds of his own (called *burhs*), and created a fleet of ships—a real navy. An uneasy stability was achieved, with the Vikings dominating the east of England and Alfred and his successors gaining control over most of the rest.

On the Continent, too, the invaders came to stay, above all in Normandy. The new inhabitants of the region were integrated into the political system when, in 911, their leader Rollo converted to Christianity and received Normandy as a duchy from the Frankish king Charles the Simple (or Straightforward). Although many of the Normans adopted sedentary ways, some of their descendants in the early eleventh century ventured to the Mediterranean, where they established themselves as rulers of petty principalities in southern Italy; by mid-century they had their eyes on Sicily.

MUSLIMS

Sicily, once Byzantine, was the rich and fertile plum of the conquests achieved by the Muslim invaders of the ninth and tenth centuries. That they took the island attests to the power of a new Muslim navy developed by the dynasty that preceded the Fatimids in Ifriqiya. After 909, Sicily came under Fatimid rule, but by mid-century it was controlled by independent Islamic princes, and Muslim immigrants were swelling the population.

Elsewhere the new Muslim presence in western Europe was more ephemeral. In the first half of the tenth century, Muslim raiders pillaged southern France, northern

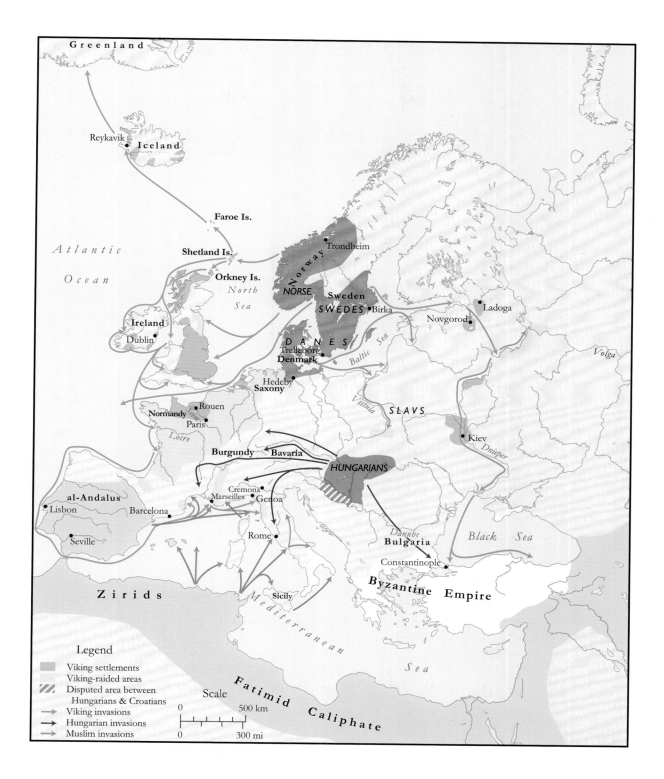

Greenland

Reykavik • **Iceland**

Atlantic

Ocean

Faroe Is.

Shetland Is.

Orkney Is.

North Sea

N o r w a y

NORSE

Trondheim •

Sweden

SWEDES

• Birka

Novgorod •

Ladoga •

Volga

Ireland

Dublin •

D A N E S

Trelleborg •

Denmark

Hedeby •

Saxony

Baltic Sea

Vistula

S L A V S

Kiev •

Dnieper

Normandy

Rouen •

Paris •

Loire

Burgundy

Bavaria

HUNGARIANS

al-Andalus

Lisbon •

Barcelona •

Cremona •

Marseilles •

Genoa •

Rome •

Danube

Bulgaria

Seville •

Black Sea

Constantinople •

Byzantine   **Empire**

Sicily •

Z i r i d s

Mediterranean

Sea

F a t i m i d   C a l i p h a t e

Legend

Viking settlements

Viking-raided areas

Disputed area between Hungarians & Croatians

→ Viking invasions

→ Hungarian invasions

→ Muslim invasions

Scale

0   500 km

0   300 mi

Italy, and the Alpine passes. But these were quick expeditions, largely attacks on churches and monasteries. Some of these Muslims did establish themselves at la Garde-Freinet, in Provence, becoming landowners in the region and lords of Christian serfs. They even hired themselves out as occasional fighters for the wars that local Christian aristocrats were waging against one another. But they made the mistake of capturing for ransom the holiest man of his era, Abbot Majolus of Cluny. Outraged, the local aristocracy finally came together and ousted the Muslims from their midst.

HUNGARIANS

By contrast, a new kingdom was created by the Hungarians. ("Magyar" was and remains their name for themselves, but the rest of Europe called them "Hungarians," from the Slavonic for "Onogurs," a people already settled in the Danube basin in the eighth and ninth centuries.) The Hungarians who invaded Europe came from the Black Sea region. Living as nomads who raised (and rode) horses, they spoke a language unrelated to any other in Europe (except Finnish). Known as effective warriors, they were employed by Arnulf, king of the East Franks (887-899), during his war against the Moravians and by the Byzantine emperor Leo VI (886-912) during his struggle against the Bulgars. In 894, taking advantage of their position, the Hungarians conquered much of the Danube basin for themselves.

From there, for over fifty years, the Hungarians raided into Germany, Italy, and even southern France. At the same time, however, they worked for various western rulers. Until 937 they spared Bavaria, for example, because they were allies of its duke. Gradually they made the transition from nomads to farmers and coalesced into the Kingdom of Hungary. This is no doubt a major reason for the end of their attacks. At the time, however, the cessation of their raids was widely credited to the German king Otto I (r.936-973), who won a major victory over a Hungarian marauding party at the battle of Lechfeld in 955.

Polytheists at the time of their entry into the West, the majority of the Hungarians were peasants, initially specializing in herding but soon busy cultivating vineyards, orchards, and grains. Above them was a warrior class, and above the warriors were the elites, whose richly furnished graves reveal the importance of weapons, jewelry, and horses to this society. Originally organized into tribes led by dukes, the Hungarians coalesced by the mid-tenth century under one ruling house—that of Géza. Determined to put his power on a new footing, Géza accepted baptism, probably by a bishop from Germany, and pledged to convert all his subjects. His son, Stephen I, consolidated the change to Christianity: he built churches and monasteries, and required everyone to attend church on Sundays. Establishing his authority as sole ruler, Stephen had himself crowned "king" in the year 1000 (or possibly 1001).

Public Power and Private Relationships

The invasions left new political configurations as they receded. Unlike the Byzantines and Muslims, Western rulers had no mercenaries and no salaried officials. They commanded others by ensuring personal loyalty. The Carolingian kings had had their *fideles*—their faithful men. Tenth-century rulers were even more dependent on ties of dependency: they needed their "men" (*homines*), their "vassals" (*vassalli*). Whatever the term, all were armed retainers who fought for a lord. Sometimes these subordinates held land from that lord, either as a reward for their military service or as an inheritance for which services were due. The term for such an estate, fief (*feodum*), gave historians the word "feudalism" to describe the social and economic system created by the relationships among lords, vassals, and fiefs. Some recent historians argue that the word "feudalism" has been used in too many different and contradictory ways to mean anything at all: is it a mode of exploiting the land that involves lords and serfs? A state of anarchy and lawlessness? Or a state of ordered gradations of power, from the king on down? All of these definitions have been given. Ordinarily we may dispense with the word feudalism, though it can be very useful as a "fuzzy category" when contrasting, for example, the political, social, and economic organization of Antiquity with that of the Middle Ages.

LORDS AND VASSALS

The key to tenth- and eleventh-century society was personal dependency. This took many forms. Of the three traditional "orders" recognized by writers in the ninth through eleventh centuries—those who pray (the *oratores*), those who fight (the *bellatores*), and those who work (the *laboratores*)—the top two were free. The pray-ers (the monks) and the fighters (the nobles and their lower-class cousins, the knights) participated in prestigious kinds of subordination, whether as vassals, lords, or both. Indeed, they were usually both: a typical warrior was lord of several vassals and the vassal of another lord. Monasteries normally had vassals to fight for them, while their abbots in turn were vassals of a king or other lord. At the low end of the social scale, poor vassals looked to their lords to feed, clothe, house, and arm them. At the upper end, vassals looked to their lords to enrich them with still more fiefs.

Some women were vassals, and some were lords (or, rather, "ladies," the female counterpart). Many upper-class laywomen participated in the society of warriors and monks as wives and mothers of vassals and lords and as landowners in their own right. Others entered convents and became *oratores* themselves. Through its abbess or a man standing in for her, a convent was itself often the "lord" of vassals.

Vassalage was voluntary and public. In some areas, it was marked by a ceremony:

the vassal-to-be knelt and, placing his hands between the hands of his lord, said, "I promise to be your man." This act, known as "homage," was followed by the promise of "fealty"—fidelity, trust, and service—which the vassal swore with his hand on relics or a Bible. Then the vassal and the lord kissed. In an age when many people could not read, a public moment such as this represented a visual and verbal contract, binding the vassal and lord together with mutual obligations to help one another.

LORDS AND PEASANTS

At the lowest end of the social scale were those who worked: the peasants. In many regions of Europe, as power fell into the hands of local rulers, the distinction between "free" and "unfree" peasants began to blur; many peasants simply became "serfs," dependents of lords. This was a heavy dependency, without prestige or honor. It was hereditary rather than voluntary: no serf did homage or fealty; no serf kissed his lord as an equal.

Indeed, peasants were barely noticed by the upper classes, except as sources of revenue. In the tenth century, the three-field system became more prevalent; heavy iron-coulter plows which could turn the heavy northern soils came into wider use; and horses (more efficient than oxen) were sometimes used to pull the plows. The result was surplus food and a better standard of living for nearly everyone.

In search of still greater profits, some lords lightened the dues and services of peasants temporarily to allow them to open up new lands by draining marshes and cutting down forests. Other lords converted dues and labor services into money payments, providing themselves with ready cash. Peasants benefitted from these rents as well because their payments were fixed despite inflation. As the prices of agricultural products went up, peasants became small-scale entrepreneurs, selling their chickens and eggs at local markets and reaping a profit.

In the eleventh century, and increasingly so in the twelfth, peasant settlements gained boundaries and focus: they became real villages. (For the example of Toury, see Map 7.5 on p.279.) The parish church often formed the center, around which was the cemetery. Then, normally crowded right onto the cemetery itself, were the houses, barns, animals, and tools of the living peasants. Boundary markers—sometimes simple stones, at other times real fortifications—announced not only the physical limit of the village but also its sense of community. This derived from very practical concerns: peasants needed to share oxen or horses to pull their plows; they were all dependent on the village craftsmen to fix their wheels or shoe their horses.

Variety was the hallmark of peasant society for this period of history across the regions of Europe. In Saxony and other parts of Germany free peasants prevailed. In

France and England most were serfs. In Italy peasants ranged from small independent landowners to leaseholders; most were both, owning a parcel in one place and leasing another nearby.

Where the power of kings was weak, peasant obligations became part of a larger system of local rule. As landlords consolidated their power over their manors, they collected not only dues and services but also fees for the use of their flour mills, bake houses, and breweries. In some regions—parts of France, for example—some lords built castles and exercised the power of the "ban": the right to collect taxes, hear court cases, levy fines, and muster men for defense. These lords were "castellans."

WARRIORS AND BISHOPS

Although the developments described here did not occur everywhere simultaneously (and in some places hardly at all), in the end the social, political, and cultural life of the West came to be dominated by landowners who saw themselves as both military men and regional leaders. These men and their armed retainers shared a common lifestyle, living together, eating in the lord's great hall, listening to bards sing of military exploits, hunting for recreation, competing with one another in military games. They fought in a group as well—as cavalry, riding on horses. In the month of May, when the grasses were high enough for their mounts to forage, the war season began. To be sure, there were powerful vassals who lived on their own fiefs and hardly ever saw their lord—except for perhaps forty days out of the year, when they owed him military duty. But they themselves were lords of knightly vassals who were not married and who lived and ate and hunted with them.

The marriage bed, so important to the medieval aristocracy from the start, now took on new meaning. Long before, in the seventh and eighth centuries, aristocratic families had been large, diffuse, loosely organized kin groups. (Historians often use the German word *Sippe*—clan—to refer to them.) These families were not tied to any particular estate, for they had numerous estates, scattered all about. With wealth enough to go around, the rich practiced partible inheritance, giving land (though not in equal amounts) to all of their sons and daughters. The Carolingians "politicized" these family relations. As some men were elevated to positions of dazzling power, they took the opportunity to pick and choose their "family members," narrowing the family circle. They also became more conscious of their male line, favoring sons over daughters. In the eleventh century, family definitions tightened even further. The claims of one son, often the eldest, overrode all else; to him went the family inheritance. (This is called "primogeniture"; but there were regions in which the youngest son was privileged, and there were also areas in which more equitable inheritance practices continued in place.) The heir in the new system traced his lineage only through the male line, backward through his father and forward through his own eldest son.

What happened to the other sons? Some of them became knights, others monks. Nor should we forget that some became bishops. In many ways the interests of bishops and lay nobles were similar: they were men of property, lords of vassals, and faithful men of patrons, such as kings, who appointed them to their posts. In some cities, bishops wielded the powers of a count or duke. Nevertheless, they were also "pastors," spiritual leaders charged with shepherding their flock. The "flock" included the priests and monks in the diocese, a district that gained clear definition in the eleventh century. And the flock included the laity, among them the very warriors from whose class the bishops came.

As episcopal power expanded and was clarified in the course of the eleventh century, some bishops in the south of France sought to control the behavior of the knightly class through a movement called the "Peace of God," which developed apace from 989 onwards. Their forum was the regional church council, where the bishops galvanized popular opinion, attracting both lords and peasants to their gatherings. There, drawing upon bits and pieces of defunct Carolingian legislation, the bishops declared the Peace: "If anyone takes as booty sheep, oxen, asses, cows, female goats, male goats, or pigs from peasants … or from other poor people … let him be anathema [excommunicated]."[4] In the Truce of God, which soon supplemented the Peace, warfare between armed men was prohibited from Lent to Easter, while at other times of the year it was forbidden on Sunday (because that was the Lord's Day), on Saturday (because that was a reminder of Holy Saturday), on Friday (because it symbolized Good Friday), and on Thursday (because it stood for Holy Thursday). Enforcement of the Truce fell to local knights and nobles, who swore over saints' relics to uphold it. The bishops who promulgated the Peace were ambivalent about warriors. There were the bad ones who broke the peace, but there were also others who were righteous upholders of church law. Soon the Peace and Truce were taken up by powerful lay rulers, eager to sanctify their own warfare and control that of others.

The new importance of the fighting man in the West gave rise to a military ethos mirrored in art and literature. It is no accident that the only extant manuscript of *Beowulf* was written *c.*1000:

> Then Halfdan's son presented Beowulf
> with a gold standard as a victory gift,
> an embroidered banner; also breast-mail
> and a helmet; and a sword carried high,
> that was both precious object and token of honour.[5]

The parallels with developments in the Byzantine and Islamic worlds are striking: everywhere a military class, more or less local, rose to power.

Equally important, however, are the differences: in no place but Europe were overlapping lordships the rule. Nowhere else was fealty so important. Nowhere else were rural enclaves the normal centers of power.

CITIES AND MERCHANTS

Though ruralism was the norm in the West, it was not invariable. In Italy the power structure reflected, if feebly, the political organization of ancient Rome. Whereas in France great landlords built their castles in the countryside, in Italy they often constructed their family seats within the walls of cities. From these perches the nobles, both lay and religious, dominated the *contado*, the rural area around the city.

In Italy, most peasants were renters, paying cash to urban landowners. Peasants depended on city markets to sell their surplus goods; their customers were not only bishops and nobles but also middle-class shopkeepers, artisans, and merchants. At Milan, for example, the merchants were prosperous enough to own houses in both the city center and the *contado*.

Rome, although exceptional in size, was in some ways a typical Italian city. Large and powerful families built their castles within its walls and controlled the churches and monasteries in the vicinity. The population depended on local producers for their food, and merchants brought their wares to sell within its walls. Yet Rome was special apart from its size: it was the "see"—the seat—of the pope, the most important bishop in the West. The papacy did not control the church, but it had great prestige, and powerful families at Rome fought to place one of their sons at its head.

Outside of Italy cities were less prevalent in the West. Yet even so we can see the rise of a new mercantile class. This was true less in the heartland of the old Carolingian empire than on its fringes. In the north, England, northern Germany, Denmark, and the Low Countries bathed in a sea of silver coins; commercial centers such as Haithabu reached their grandest extent in the mid-tenth century. Here merchants bought and sold slaves, honey, furs, wax, and pirates' plunder. Haithabu was a city of wood, but a very rich one indeed.

In the south of Europe, beyond the Pyrenees, Catalonia was equally commercialized, but in a different way. It imitated the Islamic world of al-Andalus (which was, in effect, in its backyard). The counts of Barcelona minted gold coins just like those at Córdoba. The villagers around Barcelona soon got used to selling their wares for money, and some of them became prosperous. They married into the aristocracy, moved to Barcelona to become city leaders, and lent money to ransom prisoners of the many wars waged to their south.

New-style Kingships

In such a world, what did kings do? At the least, they stood for tradition; they served as symbols of legitimacy. At the most, they united kingdoms and maintained a measure of law and order. (See Map 4.6.)

ENGLAND

Map 4.6 (facing page):
Europe, *c.*1050

Alfred was a king of the second sort. In the face of the Viking invasions, he developed new mechanisms of royal government, creating institutions that became the foundation of strong English kingship. We have already seen his military reforms: the system of burhs and the creation of a navy. Alfred was interested in religious and intellectual reforms as well. These were closely linked in his mind: the causes of England's troubles (in his view) were the sins — many due to ignorance — of its people. Alfred intended to educate "all free-born men." He brought scholars to his court and embarked on an ambitious program to translate key religious works from Latin into Anglo-Saxon (or Old English). This was the vernacular, the spoken language of the people. As Alfred wrote in his prose preface to the Anglo-Saxon translation of *The Pastoral Care* of Gregory the Great,

> I recalled how the Law was first composed in the Hebrew language, and thereafter, when the Greeks learned it, they translated it all into their own language, and all other books as well. And so too the Romans, after they had mastered them, translated them all through learned interpreters into their own language.... Therefore it seems better to me ... that we too should turn into the language that we can all understand certain books which are the most necessary for all men to know.[6]

Those "certain books" included writings by the Church Fathers — Gregory the Great, Saint Augustine, Boethius — and the Psalms as well. Soon Anglo-Saxon was used in England not only for literature but for official administrative purposes as well, in royal "writs" that kings and queens directed to their officials. England was not alone in its esteem for the vernacular: in Ireland, too, the vernacular language was also a written one. But the British Isles *were* unusual by the standards of Continental Europe, where Latin alone was the language of scholarship and writing.

As Alfred harried the Danes who were pushing south and westward, he gained recognition as king of all the English not under Viking rule. His law code, issued in the late 880s or early 890s, was the first by an English king since 695. Unlike earlier codes, which had been drawn up for each separate kingdom, Alfred's contained laws

Scale

0   500 km

0   300 mi

North Sea

Atlantic Ocean

Baltic Sea

Norway

Sweden

Denmark

Haithabu

Scotland

Ireland

England

Wales

London

Frisia

Saxony

Magdeburg

Hildesheim

Poland

Lower Lotharingia

Cologne

G e r m a n

Montreuil
Ponthieu

Flanders
Picardy

Vermandois

Franconia

Bohemia

Moravia

Beauvais

Trier

Normandy

Vexin

Upper
Lotharingia

Worms

K i n g d o m

Dreux

Paris

Île-de-France

Troyes

Alsace

Brittany

Maine

Blois

Gatinais

Swabia

Bavaria

Hungary

Amboise

Anjou

Touraine

Nevers

Bourges

Burgundy

Carinthia

Châteauroux

Aquitaine

Kingdom
of
Burgundy

Italy

Venice

Venice

Croatia

Byzantine Empire

Gevaudan

León

Gascony

Languedoc

Toulouse

Marseilles

Pisa

Patrimony of St. Peter

Spoleto

Adriatic Sea

Doclea

Navarre

Aragon

Barcelona

Barcelona

Rome

South Italian
principalities

Castile

I s l a m i c

T a i f a s

Córdoba

Corsica
(Pisan
c. 1020)

Sardinia
(Pisan
c. 1050)

M e d i t e r r a n e a n

S e a

from and for all the English kingdoms in common. The king's inspiration was the Mosaic law of the Bible. Alfred believed that God had made a new covenant with the victors over the Vikings; as leader of his people, Alfred, like the Old Testament patriarch Moses, should issue a law for all.

His successors, beneficiaries of that covenant, rolled back the Viking rule in England. (See Genealogy 4.1: Alfred and His Progeny.) "Then the Norsemen departed in their nailed ships, bloodstained survivors of spears," wrote one poet about a battle lost by the Vikings in 937.[7] But, as we have seen, many Vikings remained. Converted to Christianity, their great men joined Anglo-Saxons to attend the English king at court. The whole kingdom was divided into districts called "shires" and "hundreds," and in each shire, the king's reeve—the sheriff—oversaw royal administration.

Genealogy 4.1:
Alfred and His Progeny

Alfred's great-grandson Edgar (r.c.959-975) commanded all the possibilities early medieval kingship offered. The sworn lord of all the great men of the kingdom, he

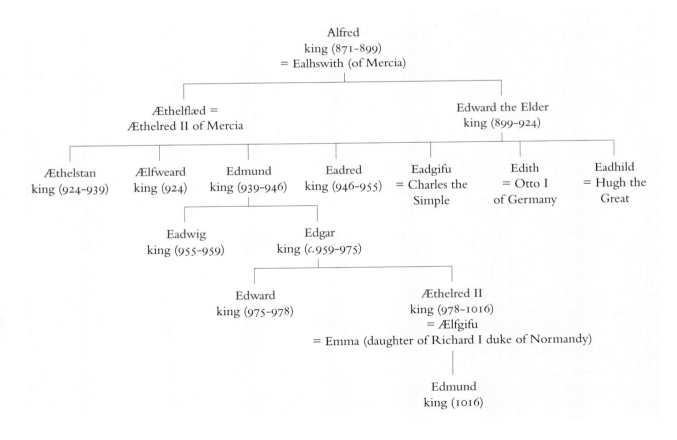

also controlled appointments to the English church and sponsored monastic reform. In 973, following the Continental fashion, he was anointed. Master of burhs and army, Edgar asserted hegemony over many of the non-Anglo-Saxon rulers in Britain. He extended Alfred's legal reforms by proclaiming certain crimes—arson and theft—to be under royal jurisdiction.

From the point of view of control, however, Edgar had nowhere near the power over England that, say, Basil II had over Byzantium at about the same time. The *dynatoi* might sometimes chafe at the emperor's directives and rebel, but the emperor had his Varangian guard to put them down and an experienced, professional civil service to do his bidding. The king of England depended less on force and bureaucracy than on consensus. The great landowners adhered to the king because they found it in their interest to do so. When they did not, the kingdom easily fragmented, becoming prey to civil war. Disunity was exacerbated by new attacks from the Danes. One Danish king, Cnut (or Canute), even became king of England for a time (r.1016–

Genealogy 4.2:
The Ottonians

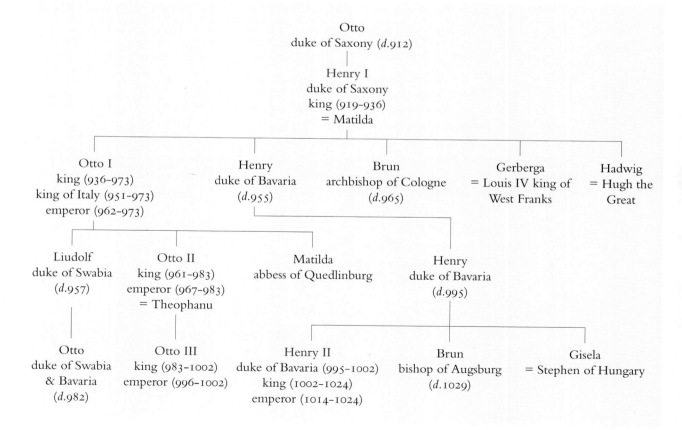

THE WEST: FRAGMENTATION AND RESILIENCE 155

1035). Yet under Cnut, English kingship did not change much. He kept intact much of the administrative, ecclesiastical, and military apparatus already established. By Cnut's time, Scandinavia had been Christianized and its traditions had largely merged with those of the rest of Europe. The Vikings were no longer an alien culture.

GERMANY

The king of Germany was as effective as the English king—and additionally worked with a much wider palette of territories, institutions, and possibilities. It is true that at first Germany seemed ready to disintegrate into duchies: five emerged in the late Carolingian period, each held by a military leader who exercised quasi-royal powers. But, in the face of their own quarrels and the threats of outside invaders, the dukes needed and wanted a strong king. With the death in 911 of the last Carolingian king in Germany, Louis the Child, they crowned one of themselves. Then, as Magyar attacks increased, the dukes gave the royal title to their most powerful member, the duke of Saxony, Henry I (r.919-936), who proceeded to set up fortifications and reorganize his army, crowning his efforts with a major defeat of the Hungarians in 933.

Henry's son Otto I (r.936-973) defeated rival family members, rebellious dukes, and Slavic and Hungarian armies soon after coming to the throne. Through astute marriage alliances and appointments, he was eventually able to get his family members to head up all of the duchies. In 951, Otto marched into Italy and took the Lombard crown. He was thus king of Germany and Italy, and soon (in 962) he received the imperial crown that recognized his far-flung power. Both to himself and to contemporaries he recalled the greatness of Charlemagne. Meanwhile, Otto's victory at Lechfeld in 955 (see p.146) ended the Hungarian threat. In the same year, Otto defeated a Slavic incursion, and for about a half-century the Slavs of central and eastern Europe came under German hegemony.

Victories such as these brought tribute, plum positions to disburse, and lands to give away, ensuring Otto a following among the great men of the realm. His successors, Otto II, Otto III—hence the dynastic name "Ottonians"—and Henry II, built on his achievements. (See Genealogy 4.2: The Ottonians.) Granted power by the magnates, they gave back in turn: they gave away lands and appointed their aristocratic supporters to duchies, counties, and bishoprics. Always, however, their decisions were tempered by hereditary claims and plenty of lobbying by influential men at court and at the great assemblies that met with the king to hammer out policies. The role of kings in appointing bishops and archbishops was particularly important because, unlike counties and duchies, these positions could not be inherited. Otto I created a ribbon of new bishoprics in newly converted regions along his eastern border, endowing them with extensive lands and subjecting the local peasantry to episcopal overlordship. Throughout Germany bishops gained the power of the ban, with the right to collect revenues and call men to arms. Once the king chose the bishop (usually with at least the consent of the clergy of the cathedral over which he was to preside), he "invested" the new prelate in his post by participating in the ceremony that installed him into office. Bishop Thietmar of Merseburg, for example, reported on his own experience:

> The archbishop [Tagino of Magdeburg, Thietmar's sponsor] led me to Bishop Bruno's chapel [Bruno was the king's brother], where the king [Henry II] awaited him. After preparing for the celebration of the mass, he commended me into the hands of the king. I was elected by those who were present and the king committed the pastoral office to me with the staff.[8]

With wealth coming in from their eastern tributaries, Italy, and the silver mines of Saxony (discovered in the time of Otto I), the Ottonians presided over a brilliant intellectual and artistic efflorescence. As in the Islamic world, much of this was dispersed; in Germany the centers of culture included the royal court, the great cathe-

Plate 4.1: Christ and the Centurion, Egbert Codex (977-993). Like Ebbo, the patron of the artists of the Utrecht Psalter (**Plate 3.9** on p.127), Egbert was an archbishop with keen interests in the arts. The Egbert Codex contains 51 gospel illustrations, the most extensive cycle up to his day.

Plate 4.2: Christ Asleep, Hitda Gospels (*c.*1000–1020). In this manuscript painting, the moral of the story is right in the picture. As the apostles look anxiously to the mast to save them from the stormy sea, one (in the exact center) turns to rouse the sleeping Christ, the real Savior.

Plate 4.3 (facing page): Saint Luke, Gospel Book of Otto III (998–1001). Compare this author portrait to the Saint Luke of the Lindisfarne Gospels (**Plate 2.4** on p.84). The artist working for Otto created a figure of great complexity, with his feet on earth, his seat on a rainbow, and his hands holding up the "cloud of witnesses" mentioned in the New Testament Epistle to the Hebrews 12:1.

FONT PATRŪ DUCTAS BOS AGNIS ELICIT UNDAS

dral schools, and women's convents. The most talented young men crowded the schools at episcopal courts such as those at Trier, Cologne, Magdeburg, Worms, and Hildesheim. Honing their Latin, they studied classical authors such as Cicero and Horace as well as Scripture, while their episcopal teachers wrote histories, saints' lives, and works on canon law, such as the *Decretum* (*c*.1020) by Burchard, bishop of Worms, a widely influential work. The men at the cathedral schools were largely in training to become courtiers, administrators, and bishops themselves. But bishops appreciated art as well as scholarship, and some, such as Egbert, archbishop of Trier (*r*.977-993), not only opened schools but also patronized artists and fine craftswork-ers. Plate 4.1, an illustration of Christ and the Centurion from the *Egbert Codex* (named, of course, for its patron) is a good example of what is called the "Ottonian style" at the end of the tenth century. Drawing freely on Carolingian work such as that illustrated in Plate 3.6 and Plate 3.7 (see pp.122 and 123), nevertheless, the *Egbert Codex* artist achieves a very different effect. Most importantly, he is utterly unafraid of open space. The figures, while recognizably human, float in a near void of pastel col-ors. The focus is on their gestures, their hands and fingers exaggerated to convey the amazement of Christ's followers, the centurion's petition, and Christ's gracious con-sent. (For the story, see Matt. 8:5-13.)

At around the same time, in convents that provided them with comfortable private apartments, noblewomen were writing books and (in the case of Hrotsvitha of Gan-dersheim) Roman-style plays. Ottonian noblewomen also supported other artists and scholars. Plate 4.2, from a manuscript made at Cologne between *c*.1000 and *c*.1020 for Abbess Hitda of Meschede, shows a more eclectic sensibility than the *Egbert Codex*. The artist draws from Byzantine as well as Carolingian traditions to produce a calm Christ, asleep during a wild storm on the Sea of Galilee that ruffles the sails of the ship and seems to toss it into sheer air. The marriage of Otto II to a Byzantine princess, Theophanu, helps account for the Byzantine influences.

Among the most active patrons of the arts were the Ottonian kings themselves. In a Gospel book made for Otto III, the full achievement of Ottonian culture is made clear in a work both artistically compelling and theologically sophisticated. In Plate 4.3, Saint Luke, in a gesture of ecstacy, holds his glory in his hands. Above him is his symbol, the ox; radiating outwards in fiery orbs are five crowned Old Testament prophets, each holding a scroll, each accompanied by an angel (the one at the top has two), while at the bottom lambs drink from the rivers of Paradise. Artistically, it is an emotional, glowing piece in reds, oranges, and gold. Theologically it is a statement about the unity of the Old Testament (the prophets) and the New (Luke himself).

FRANCE

By contrast with the English and German kings, those in France had a harder time coping with invasions. Unlike the English kings, who started small and built slowly, the French kings had half an empire to defend. Unlike the Ottonians, who asserted their military prowess in decisive battles such as the one at Lechfeld, the French kings generally had to let local men both take the brunt of the attacks and reap the prestige and authority that came with military leadership. Nor did the French kings have the advantage of Germany's tributaries, silver mines, or Italian connections. Much like the Abbasid caliphs at Baghdad, the kings of France saw their power wane. During most of the tenth century, Carolingian kings alternated on the throne with kings from a family that would later be called the "Capetians." At the end of that century the most powerful men of the realm, seeking to stave off civil war, elected Hugh Capet (r.987–996) as their king. The Carolingians were displaced, and the Capetians continued on the throne until the fourteenth century. (See Genealogy 5.3: The Capetian Kings of France, p.189.)

The Capetians' scattered but substantial estates lay in the north of France, in the region around Paris. Here the kings had their vassals and their castles. This "Ile-de-France" (which was all there was to "France" in the period; see Map 4.6) was indeed an "island," surrounded by independent castellans. In the sense that he, too, had little more military power than a castellan, Hugh and his eleventh-century successors were similar to local strongmen. But the Capetian kings had the prestige of their office. Anointed with holy oil, they represented the idea of unity and God-given rule inherited from Charlemagne. Most of the counts and dukes — at least those in the north of France — swore homage and fealty to the king, a gesture, however weak, of personal support. Unlike the German kings, the French could rely on vassalage to bind the great men of the realm to them.

★ ★ ★ ★

Political fragmentation did not mean chaos. It simply betokened a new order. At Byzantium, in any event, even the most centrifugal forces were focused on the center: the real trouble for Basil II, for example, came from *dynatoi* who wanted to be emperors, not from people who wanted to be independent rulers. In the Islamic world fragmentation largely meant replication, as courts patterned on or competitive with the Abbasid model were set up by Fatimid caliphs and other rulers. In the West, the rise of regional rulers was accompanied by the widespread adoption of forms of personal dependency — vassalage, serfdom — which could be (and were) manipulated even by kings—such as the Capetians—who seemed to have lost the most from the dispersal of power.

The *real* fragmentation was between the former heirs of the Roman Empire. They did not speak the same language, they were increasingly estranged by their religions, and they knew almost nothing about one another. In the next century, Christian Europeans, newly prosperous and self-confident, would go on the offensive. Henceforth, without forgetting about the Byzantine and Islamic worlds, we shall focus on this aggressive and dynamic new society.

CHAPTER FOUR KEY EVENTS

*c.*790–*c.*950	Invasions into Europe by Vikings, Muslims, and Hungarians
871–899	Reign of King Alfred the Great of England
c. 909	Fatimids (in North Africa) establish themselves as caliphs
929	Abd al-Rahman III (at Córdoba in al-Andalus) takes title of caliph
955	Victory of Otto I over Hungarians at Lechfeld
962	Otto I crowned emperor
980–1037	Ibn Sina (Avicenna)
988	Conversion of Vladimir, Rus Grand Prince, to Byzantine Christianity
989	Beginning of "Peace of God" movement
991	Mieszko I puts Poland under papal protection
1000 (or 1001)	Stephen I crowned king of Hungary
1025	Death of Basil II the Bulgar Slayer
c. 1031	Al-Andalus splits into *taifas*

NOTES

1. Michael Psellus, *Fourteen Byzantine Rulers: The "Chronographia" of Michael Psellus*, trans. E.R.A. Sewter (Harmondsworth, 1966), p.44, spelling slightly altered.
2. Ibn Sa'id, quoted in Robert Hillenbrand, "Medieval Córdoba as a Cultural Centre," in *The Legacy of Muslim Spain*, ed. Salma Khadra Jayyusi (Leiden, 1994), I:120.
3. "Asser's Life of King Alfred," in *Alfred the Great: Asser's "Life of King Alfred" and Other Contemporary Sources*, trans. Simon Keynes and Michael Lapidge (Harmondsworth, 1983), pp.84–85.
4. "The Acts of the Council of Charroux (989)," trans. Thomas Head in *The Peace of God: Social Violence and Religious Response in France around the Year 1000*, ed. Thomas Head and Richard Landes (Ithaca, NY, 1992), p.327.
5. *Beowulf: A New Verse Translation*, ll. 1019-1023, trans. Seamus Heaney (New York, 2000), p.69.
6. "From the Translations of Gregory's Pastoral Care," in *Alfred the Great*, pp.125-26.
7. Quoted in Gwyn Jones, *A History of the Vikings* (rev. ed., Oxford, 1984), p.238.
8. *Ottonian Germany: The Chronicon of Thietmar of Merseburg*, trans. David A. Warner (Manchester, 2001), p.265.

FURTHER READING

Abels, Richard. *Alfred the Great: War, Kingship and Culture in Anglo-Saxon England*. Harlow, Essex, 1998.

Angold, Michael. *The Byzantine Empire, 1025-1204: A Political History*. 2nd ed. London, 1997.

Berkey, Jonathan P. *The Formation of Islam: Religion and Society in the Near East, 600-1800*. Cambridge, 2003.

Engel, Pál. *The Realm of St. Stephen: A History of Medieval Hungary, 895-1526*. Trans. Tamás Pálosfalvi. London, 2001.

Fine, John V.A., Jr. *The Early Medieval Balkans: A Critical Survey from the Sixth to the Late Twelfth Century*. Ann Arbor, 1991.

Franklin, Simon, and Jonathan Shepard. *The Emergence of Rus, 750-1200*. London, 1996.

Frantzen, Allen. *King Alfred*. Boston, 1986.

Garland, Lynda. *Byzantine Empresses: Women and Power in Byzantium, AD 527-1204*. London, 1999.

Goitein, S.D. *A Mediterranean Society: The Jewish Communities of the Arab World as Portrayed in the Documents of the Cairo Geniza*. 6 vols. Berkeley, 1967-1993.

Jayyusi, Salma Khadra, ed. *The Legacy of Muslim Spain*. 2 vols. Leiden, 1994.

Kazhdan, A.P., and Ann Wharton Epstein. *Change in Byzantine Culture in the Eleventh and Twelfth Centuries*. Berkeley, 1985.

Lev, Yaacov. *State and Society in Fatimid Egypt*. Leiden, 1991.

Maguire, Henry, ed. *Byzantine Court Culture from 829 to 1204*. Washington, 1997.

Moore, R.I. *The First European Revolution, c. 970-1215*. Oxford, 2000.

For searchable maps, genealogies, and other materials for this chapter, please visit the *Short History of the Middle Ages* website at www.broadviewpress.com/shorthistory.

Reuter, Timothy. *Germany in the Early Middle Ages, c.800-1056*. London, 1991.

Reynolds, Susan. *Fiefs and Vassals: The Medieval Evidence Reinterpreted*. Oxford, 1994.

Stafford, Pauline. *Unification and Conquest: A Political and Social History of England in the Tenth and Eleventh Centuries*. London, 1989.

PART II: THE EUROPEAN TAKE-OFF

FIVE

THE EXPANSION OF EUROPE
(*c.*1050-*c.*1150)

EUROPEANS GAINED MUSCLE in the second half of the eleventh century. They built cities, reorganized the church, created new varieties of religious life, expanded their intellectual horizons, pushed aggressively at their frontiers, and even waged war over 1400 miles away, in what they called the Holy Land. Expanding population and a vigorous new commercial economy lay behind all this. So too did the weakness, disunity, and beckoning wealth of their neighbors, the Byzantines and Muslims.

THE SELJUKS AND THEIR AFTERMATH

In the eleventh century the Seljuk Turks, a new group from outside the Islamic world, entered and took over its eastern half. Eventually penetrating deep into Anatolia, they took a great bite out of Byzantium. Soon, however, the Seljuks themselves split apart, and the Islamic world fragmented anew under the rule of dozens of emirs.

From the Sultans to the Emirs

Pastoralists on horseback, the Turkish peoples called the "Seljuks" (after the name of their most enterprising leader) crossed from the region east of the Caspian Sea into Iran in about the year 1000. Within a little over fifty years, they had allied themselves with the caliphs as upholders of Sunni orthodoxy, defeated the Buyids, taken over the cities, and started collecting taxes. Between 1055 and 1092, a succession of formidable Seljuk leaders—Toghril Beg, Alp Arslan, and Malikshah—proclaimed themselves rulers, "sultans," of a new state. Bands of herdsmen followed in their wake, moving their sheep into the very farmland of Iran (disrupting agriculture there), then continuing westward, into Armenia, which had been recently annexed by Byzantium. Meanwhile, under Alp Arslan (r.1063–1072), the Seljuk army (composed precisely of such herdsmen but also, increasingly, of other Turkish tribesmen recruited as slaves or freemen) harried Syria. This was Muslim territory, but it was equally the back door to Byzantium. Thus the Byzantines got involved, and throughout the 1050s and 1060s they fought numerous indecisive battles with the Seljuks. Then in 1071 a huge Byzantine force met an equally large Seljuk army at Manzikert (today Malazgirt, in Turkey). The battle ended with the Byzantines defeated and Anatolia open to a flood of militant sheepherders. (See Map 5.1.)

Map 5.1:
The Seljuk World, *c.*1090

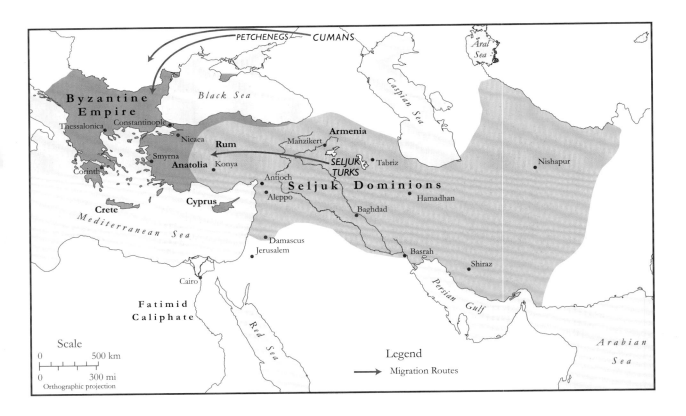

Though "Seljuk" in name, the new inhabitants of Anatolia were effectively independent. They did not so much declare themselves rulers of the region as simply take it over; for them it was Rum, "Rome." Meanwhile, other Seljuks took off on their own, hiring themselves out (as Turks long had done) as military leaders. Atsiz ibn Uwaq is a good example. For a while he worked for Alp Arslan, but in 1070 he was called in by the Fatimid caliph at Egypt to help shore up the crumbling rule of the Fatimids against their own military leaders. Seizing his chance, Atsiz turned the tables to become emir himself of a region that stretched from Jerusalem to Damascus.

Atsiz was the harbinger of a new order. After 1092, the Seljuks could no longer maintain any sort of centralized rule, even though they still were "wanted," if only to confer titles like "emir" on local rulers who craved legitimacy. Nor could the Fatimids prevent their own territories from splintering into tiny emirates, each centered on one or a few cities. Some emirs were from the Seljuk family; others were military men who originally served under them. We shall see that the tiny states set up by the crusaders who conquered the Levant in 1099 were, in size, not so very different from their neighboring Islamic emirates.

In the western part of North Africa, the Maghreb, Berber tribesmen (camel breeders rather than sheep herders) forged a state similar to that of the Seljuks. Fired (as the Seljuks had been) with religious fervor on behalf of Sunni orthodoxy, the Berber Almoravids took over north-west Africa in the 1070s and 1080s. In 1086, invited by the ruler of Seville to help fight Christian armies from the north, they sent troops into al-Andalus. This military "aid" soon turned into conquest. By 1094 all of al-Andalus not yet conquered by the Christians was under Almoravid control. Their hegemony over the western Islamic world ended only in 1147, with the triumph of the Almohads, a rival Berber group.

Together the Seljuks and Almoravids rolled back the Shi'ite wave. They kept it back through a system of schools, the "madrasas." Attached to mosques, these centers of higher learning were where young men came for lessons in religion, law, and literature. Sometimes visiting scholars came to debate in lively public displays of intellectual brilliance. More regularly, teachers and students carried on a quiet regimen of classes on the Qur'an and other texts. Established by the Sunni Seljuks to counter similar colleges in Shi'ite lands, madrasas were soon set up throughout the Islamic world. The fractured Islamic community remained united in the twelfth century by commerce and language, but not by schooling.

Byzantium: Bloodied but Unbowed

What had happened to the triumphant Byzantium of Basil II? It was unable to sustain its successes in the face of Turks on two fronts: in Anatolia, as we have seen, and also in the Balkans, where Pechenegs raided with ease. There was no longer much of a citizen army; many of the themes had lost their defenders; and the emperor's troops—made up largely of Turks, Normans, Franks, and Slavs—were unreliable. When emperor Constantine IX Monomachos (*r*.1042-1055) was unable to prevent the Pechenegs from entering the Balkans, he shifted policy, welcoming them, administering baptism, conferring titles, and settling them in depopulated regions. Much the same process took place in Anatolia, where the emperors at times welcomed the Turks to help them fight rival *dynatoi* and where even some Christians, especially the Monophysites of Armenia and Syria (see p.135), were glad to have new Turkish overlords. The Byzantine grip on its territories loosened and its frontiers became nebulous, but Byzantium still stood.

There were changes at the imperial court as well. The model of the "public" emperor ruling alone for his people gave way to a less costly, more "familial" model of government. To be sure, for a time competing *dynatoi* families swapped the imperial throne. But Alexius I Comnenus (*r*.1081-1118), a Dalassenus on his mother's side, managed to bring most of the major families together through a series of marriage alliances. (The Comneni remained on the throne for about a century; see Genealogy 5.1: The Dynasty of Comnenus.) Until her death *c*.1102, Anna Dalassena, Alexius's mother (rather than a civil servant) held the reins of government while Alexius occupied himself with military matters. At his revamped court, it was his relatives who held the highest positions. Many of them received *pronoiai* (*sing. pronoia*), temporary

Genealogy 5.1:
The Dynasty of
Comnenus

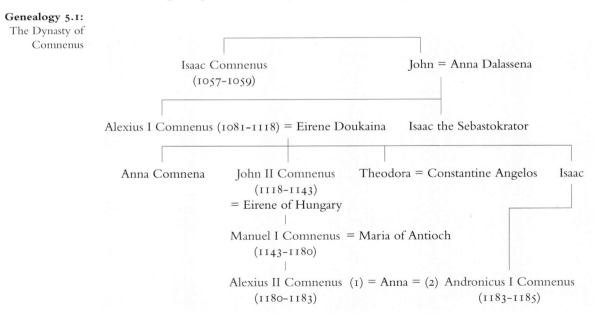

grants of imperial lands that they administered and profited from.

Altogether, Byzantine rulers were becoming more like European ones, holding a relatively small amount of territory, handing some of it out in grants that worked a bit like fiefs, spending most of their time in battle to secure a stronghold here, a city there. Sometimes their hostilities were with westerners themselves. Already before Alexius's time, the Normans—adventurous warriors from Normandy, in France— had taken southern Italy and Sicily; early in his reign he confronted (and defeated) their armies when they tried to conquer Byzantium itself. Clearly Europeans were on the move.

THE TAKE-OFF OF THE EUROPEAN ECONOMY

Behind the new European expansion was a new economy. Draining marshes, felling trees, setting up dikes: this was the backbreaking work that brought new land into cultivation. With their heavy, horse-drawn plows, peasants were able to reap greater harvests; using the three-field system, they raised more varieties of crops. Great landowners, the same "oppressors" against whom the Peace of God fulminated, could also be efficient economic organizers. They set up mills to grind grain, forced their tenants to use them, then charged a fee for the service. It was in their interest that the peasants produced as much grain as possible.

As the countryside became more productive, people became healthier, their fertility increased, and there were more mouths to feed. Even so, surprising surpluses made possible the growth of old and the development of new urban centers. Within a generation or two, city dwellers, intensely conscious of their common goals, elaborated new instruments of commerce, self-regulating organizations, and forms of self-government.

Towns and Cities

Around castles and monasteries in the countryside or at the walls of crumbling ancient towns, merchants came with their wares and artisans set up shop. At Bruges (today in Belgium), it was the local lord's castle that served as a magnet. As one late medieval chronicler put it,

> To satisfy the needs of the people in the castle at Bruges, first merchants
> with luxury articles began to surge around the gate; then the wine-sellers
> came; finally the inn-keepers arrived to feed and lodge the people who

had business with the prince…. So many houses were built that soon a great city was created.[1]

Churches and monasteries were the other centers of town growth. Recall Tours as it was in the early seventh century (Map 1.4 on p.42), with its semi-permanent settlements around the church of Saint-Martin, out in the cemetery, and its lonely cathedral nestling against one of the ancient walls. By the twelfth century (Map 5.2), Saint-Martin was a monastery, the hub of a small town dense enough to boast eleven parish churches, merchant and artisan shops, private houses, and two markets. To the east, the episcopal complex was no longer alone: a market had sprung up outside the old western wall, and private houses lined the street leading to the bridge. Smaller than the town around Saint-Martin, the one at the foot of the old city had only two parish churches, but it was big enough to warrant the construction of a new set of walls to protect it.

Early cities developed without prior planning, but some later ones were "chartered," that is, declared, surveyed, and plotted out. A marketplace and merchant settlement were already in place at Freiburg im Breisgau when the duke of Zähringen chartered it, promising each new settler there a house lot of 5000 square feet for a very small yearly rent. The duke had fair hopes that commerce would flourish right at his back door and yield him rich revenues.

The look and feel of medieval cities varied immensely from place to place. Nearly all included a marketplace, a castle, and several churches. All had rings of walls; by 1100, Speyer had three of them. (See Map 7.4, p.258, for the walls of Bruges.) Within the walls lay a network of streets—narrow, dirty, dark, smelly, and winding—made of packed

Map 5.2: Tours in the Eleventh and Twelfth Centuries

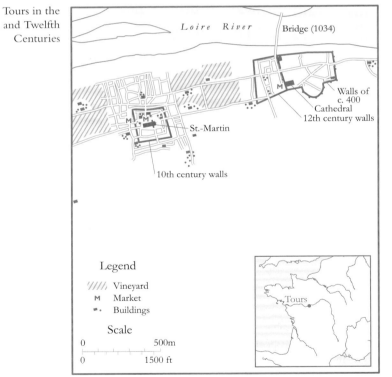

Loire River
Bridge (1034)
Walls of c. 400
Cathedral
12th century walls
St.-Martin
10th century walls

Legend

///// Vineyard
M Market
■· Buildings

Scale

0   500m
0   1500 ft

Tours

clay or gravel. Most cities were situated near waterways and had bridges; the one at Tours was built in the 1030s. And most had to adapt to increasingly crowded conditions. At the end of the eleventh century in Winchester, England, city plots were still large enough to accommodate houses parallel to the street; but soon those houses had to be torn down to make way for narrow ones, built at right angles to the street. The houses at Winchester were made of wattle and daub—twigs woven together and covered with clay. If they were like the stone houses built in the late twelfth century (about which we know a good deal), they had two stories: a shop or warehouse on

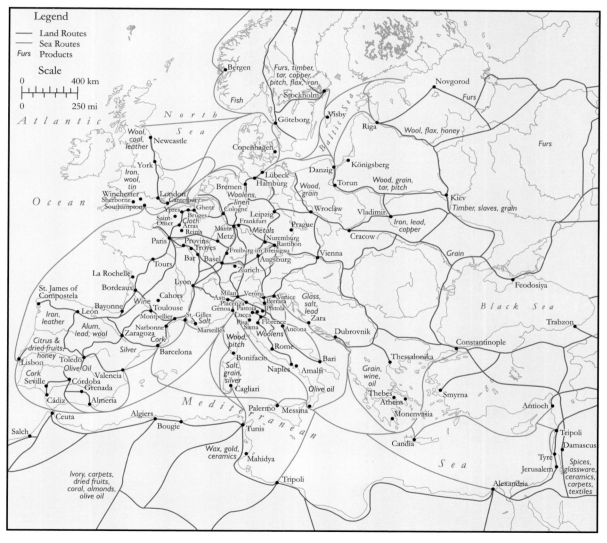

the lower floor and living quarters above. Behind this main building were the kitchen, enclosures for livestock, and a garden. Even city dwellers clung to rural pursuits, raising much of their food themselves.

Although commercial centers developed throughout western Europe, they grew fastest and most densely in regions along key waterways: the Mediterranean coasts of Italy, France, and Spain; northern Italy along the Po River; the river system of Rhône-Saône-Meuse; the Rhineland; the English Channel; the shores of the Baltic Sea. During the eleventh and twelfth centuries, these waterways became part of a single, interdependent economy. At the same time, new roads through the countryside linked urban centers to rural districts and stimulated the growth of fairs (regular, short-term, often lively markets). (See Map 5.3.)

Business Arrangements

This revival of urban life and expansion of trade, dubbed the "commercial revolution" by historians, was sustained and invigorated by merchants. They were a varied lot. Some were local traders, like one monk who supervised a manor twenty miles south of his monastery and sold its surplus horses and grain at a local market. Others—mainly Jews and Italians—were long-distance traders, much in demand because they supplied fine wines, spices, and fabrics to the aristocracy. Some Jews had long been involved at least part time in long-distance trade as vintners. In the eleventh century, as lords reorganized the countryside, Jewish landowners were driven out and forced into commerce and urban trades full time. Other long-distance traders came from Italy. The key players were from Genoa, Pisa, and Venice; it is no accident that these cities had trading outposts along the Golden Horn at Constantinople. (See Map 4.1 on p.132.) But Italian traders found the Islamic world nearly as lucrative. Establishing bases at ports such as Tunis, they imported Islamic wares—ceramics, textiles, metalwork—into Europe. Near Pisa, for example, the facade of the cathedral of San Miniato (Plate 5.1) was decorated with shiny bowls (Plate 5.2) imported by Pisan traders

Plate 5.1 (facing page): San Miniato (late 12th cent.). The facade of San Miniato was once decorated with *bacini*, bowls that sparkled in the Italian sun. In this picture you can see the small round cavities where they used to be. The *bacino* in **Plate 5.2** was slightly above and just to the left (from the viewer's point of view) of the oculus (the round window). The *bacini* were, in effect, cheap and attractive substitutes for marble or mosaics.

Plate 5.2: Bowl, North Africa (late 12th cent.). This earthenware bowl (*bacino*), imported from North Africa, and decorated with pseudo-Arabic writing, once adorned the facade of San Miniato. Islamic artisans knew how to make a very white tin-based glaze against which the painted colors of the design stood out. (See **Plate 3.3**, p.104, for a far more sophisticated version from the Abbasid period.) The resulting bowls were in great demand by Italians, not only for the façades of their churches but also for their kitchens.

from North African artisans. In turn, merchants from the west exported wood, iron, and woolen cloth to the east.

Merchants invented new forms of collective enterprises to pool their resources and finance large undertakings. The Italian *commenda*, for example, was a partnership established for ventures by sea. A *compagnia* was created by investing family property in trade. Contracts for sales, exchanges, and loans became common, with the interest on loans hidden in the fiction of a penalty for "late payment" in order to avoid the church's ban on usury.

Pooled resources made large-scale productive enterprises possible. A cloth industry began, powered by water mills. New deep-mining technologies provided Europeans with hitherto untapped sources of metals. Forging techniques improved, and iron was for the first time regularly used for agricultural tools and plows, enhancing food production.

Whether driven by machines or handwork, the new economy was sustained by the artisans, financiers, and merchants of the cities. They formed guilds to regulate and protect themselves. In these social, religious, and economic associations, guild members prayed for and buried one another, agreed on quality standards for their products, and regulated their work hours, materials, and prices. Guilds guaranteed their members—mostly male—a place in the market by controlling production within each city. They represented the social and economic counterpart to urban walls, giving their members protection, shared identity, and recognized status.

The political counterpart to the walls was the "commune"—town self-government. City dwellers—keenly aware of their special identity in a world dominated by knights and peasants—recognized their mutual interest in reliable coinage, laws to facilitate commerce, freedom from servile dues and services, and independence to buy and sell as the market dictated. They petitioned the political powers that ruled them—bishops, kings, counts, castellans, dukes—for the right to govern themselves.

Collective movements for urban self-government were especially prevalent in Italy, France, and Germany. Already Italy's political life was city centered; communes there were attempts to substitute the power of one group (the citizens) for another (the nobles and bishops). At Milan in the second half of the eleventh century, for example, popular discontent with the archbishop, who effectively ruled the city, led to numerous armed clashes that ended, in 1097, with the transfer of power from the archbishop to a government of leading men of the city. Outside of Italy movements for city independence—sometimes violent, as at Milan, at other times peaceful—took place within a larger political framework. For example, William Clito, who claimed the county of Flanders, willingly granted the townspeople of Saint-Omer the rights they asked for in 1127 in return for their support of his claims. He recognized them as legally free, with the right to mint coins, make laws, set up courts, and pay fewer taxes.

CHURCH REFORM AND ITS AFTERMATH

Disillusioned citizens at Milan denounced their archbishop not only for his tyranny but also for his impurity; they wanted their pastors to be untainted by sex and by money. In this they were supported by a new-style papacy, keen on reform in the church and society. The "Gregorian Reform," as this movement came to be called, broke up clerical marriages, unleashed civil war in Germany, modified the procedure for episcopal elections, and transformed the papacy into a monarchy. It began as a way to free the church from the world; but in the end the church was deeply involved in the new world it had helped to create.

The Coming of Reform

Freeing the church from the world: what could it mean? In 910 the duke and duchess of Aquitaine founded the monastery of Cluny with some unusual stipulations. They endowed the monastery with property (normal and essential if it were to survive), but then they gave it and its worldly possessions to Saints Peter and Paul. In this way they put control of the monastery into the hands of the two most powerful heavenly saints. They designated the pope, as the successor of Saint Peter, to be the monastery's worldly protector if anyone should bother or threaten it. The whole notion of "freedom" at this point was very vague. But Cluny's prestige was great because of the influence of its founders, the status of Saint Peter, and the fame of its elaborate round of prayers. The Cluniac monks fulfilled the role of "those who pray" in dazzling manner. Through their prayers, they seemed to guarantee the salvation of all Christians. Rulers, bishops, rich landowners, and even serfs (if they could) gave Cluny donations of land, joining their contributions to the land of Saint Peter. Powerful men and women called on the Cluniac abbots to reform new monasteries along the Cluniac model.

The abbots of Cluny came to see themselves as reformers of the world as well as the cloister. They believed in clerical celibacy, preaching against the prevailing norm in which parish priests and even bishops were married. They also thought that the laity could be reformed, become more virtuous, and cease its oppression of the poor. In the eleventh century, the Cluniacs began to link their program to the papacy. When they disputed with bishops or laypeople about lands and rights, they called on the popes to help them out.

The popes were ready to do so. A parallel movement for reform had entered papal circles via a small group of influential monks and clerics. Mining canon (church) law for their ammunition, these churchmen emphasized two abuses: nicolaitism (clerical marriage) and simony (buying church offices). The new patrilineal family taught them the importance of limiting offspring. (In their eyes, celibate priests should have even higher status than first-born sons.) The new profit economy sensitized them to the crass commercial meanings of gifts; in their eyes, churchmen should not give gifts in return for their offices.

Initially, the reformers got imperial backing. In the view of German king and emperor Henry III (*r.*1039-1056), as the anointed of God he was responsible for the well-being of the church in the empire. (For Henry and his dynasty, see Genealogy 5.2: The Salian Kings and Emperors.) Henry denounced simony and personally refused to accept money or gifts when he appointed bishops to their posts. He presided over the Synod of Sutri which, in 1046, deposed three papal rivals and elected another. When that pope died, Henry appointed Leo IX (1049-1054). But Leo

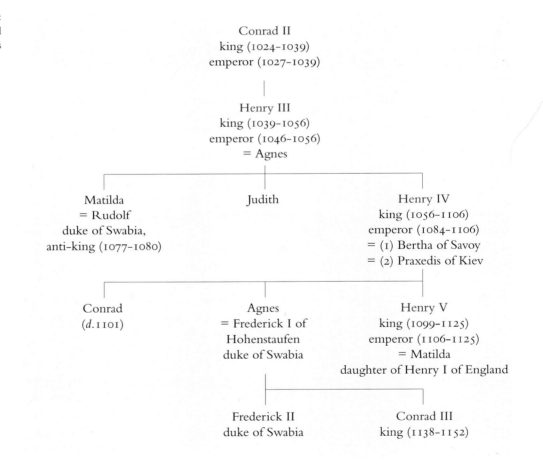

Genealogy 5.2:
The Salian Kings and
Emperors

Conrad II
king (1024-1039)
emperor (1027-1039)

Henry III
king (1039-1056)
emperor (1046-1056)
= Agnes

Matilda
= Rudolf
duke of Swabia,
anti-king (1077-1080)

Judith

Henry IV
king (1056-1106)
emperor (1084-1106)
= (1) Bertha of Savoy
= (2) Praxedis of Kiev

Conrad
(*d.*1101)

Agnes
= Frederick I of
Hohenstaufen
duke of Swabia

Henry V
king (1099-1125)
emperor (1106-1125)
= Matilda
daughter of Henry I of England

Frederick II
duke of Swabia

Conrad III
king (1138-1152)

surprised his patron: he set out to reform the church under papal, not imperial, control.

Leo revolutionized the papacy. He had himself elected by the "clergy and people of Rome" to satisfy the demands of canon law. He left Rome (as popes had rarely done before) to preside over church councils and make the pope's influence felt in France and Germany. He sponsored the creation of a canon lawbook—the *Collection in 74 Titles*—that emphasized the pope's power. To the papal curia Leo brought the most zealous church reformers of his day: Peter Damian, Hildebrand (later Gregory VII), and Humbert of Silva Candida.

With Humbert, the newly aggressive papacy was felt at Byzantium. On diplomatic mission at Constantinople in 1054, Humbert argued against the patriarch of Constantinople on behalf of the new, lofty claims of the pope. When the patriarch resisted, Humbert excommunicated him. In retaliation, the patriarch excommunicated Humbert. Clashes between the two churches had occurred before and had been patched up, but this one, called the Great Schism, proved insurmountable (until 1965). After 1054, the Roman Catholic and Greek Orthodox churches largely went their separate ways.

More generally, the papacy began to wield new forms of power. It waged unsuccessful war against the Normans in southern Italy and then made the best of the situation by granting them parts of the region—and Sicily as well—in fief, turning former enemies into vassals. It supported the Christian push into the *taifa* kingdoms of al-Andalus, transforming the *"reconquista"*—the conquest of Islamic Spain—into a holy war: Pope Alexander II (1061-1073) forgave the sins of the Christians on their way to the battle of Barbastro.

The Investiture Conflict and its Effects

The papal reform movement is associated particularly with Pope Gregory VII (1073-1085), hence the term "Gregorian reform." A passionate advocate of papal primacy (the theory that the pope is the head of the church), Gregory was not afraid to clash directly with the king of Germany, Henry IV (r.1056-1106), over church leadership. In Gregory's view—an astonishing one at the time, given the religious and spiritual roles associated with rulers—kings and emperors were simple laymen who had no right to meddle in church affairs. Henry, on the other hand, brought up in the traditions of his father, Henry III, considered it part of his duty to appoint bishops and even popes to ensure the well-being of church and empire together.

The pope and the emperor first clashed over the appointment of the archbishop of Milan. Gregory disputed Henry's right to "invest" the archbishop (put him into his office). In the investiture ritual, the emperor or his representative symbolically gave the church and the land that went with it to the bishop or archbishop chosen for the job. This was, for example, the role that Henry II played in Thietmar of Merseburg's episcopal installation (see above, p. 157.) In the case of Milan, two rival candidates for archepiscopal office (one supported by the pope, the other by the emperor) had been at loggerheads for several years when, in 1075, Henry invested his own candidate. Gregory immediately called on Henry to "give more respectful attention to the master of the Church," namely Peter and his living representative — Gregory himself.[2] In reply, Henry and the German bishops called on Gregory, that "false monk," to resign. This was the beginning of what historians delicately call the "Investiture Conflict" or "Investiture Controversy." In fact it was war. In February of 1076, Gregory called a synod that both excommunicated Henry and suspended him from office:

> I deprive King Henry [IV], son of the emperor Henry [III], who has rebelled against [God's] Church with unheard-of audacity, of the government over the whole kingdom of Germany and Italy, and I release all Christian men from the allegiance which they have sworn or may swear to him, and I forbid anyone to serve him as king.[3]

The last part of this decree gave it real punch: anyone in Henry's kingdom could rebel against him. The German "princes" — the aristocrats — seized the moment and threatened to elect another king. They were motivated partly by religious sentiments — many had established links with the papacy through their support of reformed monasteries — and partly by political opportunism, as they had chafed under strong German kings who had tried to keep their power in check. Some bishops, too, joined with Gregory's supporters, a major blow to Henry, who needed the troops that they supplied.

Attacked from all sides, Henry traveled in the winter of 1077 to intercept Gregory, barricaded in a fortress at Canossa, high in the Italian alps. It was a refuge provided by the staunchest of papal supporters, Countess Matilda of Tuscany. In an astute and dramatic gesture, the king stood outside the castle (in cold and snow) for three days, barefoot, as a penitent, until Gregory lifted his excommunication and received Henry back into the church. For his part, the pope had the satisfaction of seeing the king humiliate himself before the papal majesty. In any event, the whole episode solved nothing. The princes elected an anti-king, and bloody civil war continued intermittently until 1122.

The Investiture Conflict ended with a compromise. The Concordat of Worms (1122) relied on a conceptual distinction between two parts of investiture — the spiritual (in which the bishop-to-be received the symbols of his office) and the secular (in which he received the symbols of the material goods that would allow him to function). Under the terms of the Concordat, the ring and staff, symbols of church office, would be given by a churchman in the first part of the ceremony. Then the emperor or his representative would touch the bishop with a scepter, signifying the land and other possessions that went with his office. Elections of bishops in Germany would take place "in the presence" of the emperor—that is, under his influence. In Italy, the pope would have a comparable role.

In the end, then, secular rulers continued to influence the appointment of churchmen. But just as the new investiture ceremony broke the ritual into spiritual and secular halves, so too it implied a new notion of kingship separate from the priesthood. The Investiture Conflict did not produce the modern distinction between church and state—that would develop only very slowly—but it set the wheels in motion. At the time, its most important consequence was to shatter the delicate balance among political and ecclesiastical powers in Germany and Italy. In Germany, princes consolidated their lands and powers at the expense of the king. In Italy, the communes came closer to their goals: it was no accident that Milan gained its independence in 1097. And everywhere the papacy took on new authority.

Papal influence was felt at every level. At the abstract level of canon law, papal primacy was enhanced by the publication *c.*1140 of the *Decretum*, written by a teacher of canon law named Gratian. Collecting nearly two thousand passages from the decrees of popes and councils as well as the writings of the Church Fathers, Gratian set out to demonstrate their essential agreement. In fact, the book's original title was *Harmony of Discordant Canons*. If he found any "discord" in his sources, Gratian usually imposed the harmony himself by arguing that the conflicting passages dealt with different situations. A bit later a different legal scholar revised and expanded the *Decretum*, adding Roman law to the mix. At a more local level, papal denunciations of married clergy made inroads on family life. At Verona, for example, "sons of priests" disappeared from the historical record in the twelfth century. At the mundane level of administration, the papal claim to head the church helped turn the curia at Rome into a kind of government, complete with its own bureaucracy, collection agencies, and law courts. It was the teeming port of call for litigious churchmen disputing appointments and for petitioners of every sort.

The First Crusade

On the military level, the papacy's proclamations of holy wars led to bloody slaughter, tragic loss, and tidy profit. We have already seen how Alexander II encouraged the *reconquista* in Spain; it was in the wake of his call that the *taifa* rulers implored the

Almoravids for help. An oddly similar chain of events took place at the other end of the Islamic world. Ostensibly responding to a request from the Byzantine Emperor Alexius for mercenaries to help retake Anatolia from the Seljuks, Pope Urban II (1088-1099) turned the enterprise into something new: a pious pilgrimage to the Holy Land to be undertaken by an armed militia—one commissioned like those of the Peace of God, but thousands of times larger—under the leadership of the papacy. "Enter upon the road to the Holy Sepulcher," Urban exhorted the crowd at Clermont in 1095, "Wrest that land from the wicked race, and subject it to yourselves." On all sides the cry went up: "God wills it!"[4]

The event that historians call the First Crusade (1096-1099) mobilized a force of some 50,000-60,000 combatants, not counting women, children, old men, and hangers-on. The armies were organized not as one military force but rather as separate militias, each authorized by the pope and commanded by a different individual. One band, not authorized by the pope, was made up of commoners. This "Peasants' (or People's) Crusade," which started out before all the others under the leadership of an eloquent but militarily unprepared preacher, Peter the Hermit, took a route through the Rhineland in Germany before going on to Anatolia, where most of its participants were slaughtered.

Peter's indirect route through the Rhineland was no mistake. He was looking for "wicked races" closer to home: the Jews. Under Henry IV many Jews had gained a stable place within the cities of Germany, particularly those along the Rhine. The Jews received protection from the local bishops (imperial appointees, of course) in return for paying a tax. Living in their own neighborhoods—Bishop Rüdiger even built walls around the one at Speyer—the Jews' tightly-knit communities focused on the synagogue, which was a school and community center as well as a place of worship. Nevertheless, Jews also participated in the life of the larger Christian community. Archbishop Anno of Cologne made use of the services of Jewish money-lenders, and other Jews in Cologne were allowed to trade their wares at the fairs there.

Although officials pronounced against the Jews from time to time, and although Jews were at times briefly expelled from some cities (Mainz is one example), they were not persecuted systematically until the First Crusade. Then some peasant crusaders, joined by some local nobles and militias from the region, threatened the Rhineland Jews with forced conversion or death. Some relented when the Jews paid them money; others, however, attacked. The beleaguered Jews occasionally found refuge with bishops or in the houses of Christian friends, but in many cities—Metz, Speyer, Worms, Mainz, and Cologne—they were massacred. Turning from the Rhine to the Moselle, some of the militias forced numerous Jews there to convert. Other armed groups left the Rhineland to seek out the Holy Land via Hungary; at least one stopped off at Prague to massacre more Jews there. Only a small number of these motley armies continued on.

From the point of view of Emperor Alexius at Constantinople, even the "official" crusaders were potentially dangerous. One of the crusade's leaders, the Norman Bohemond, had, a few years before, tried to conquer Byzantium itself. Hastily forcing oaths from Bohemond and the other lords that any previously Byzantine lands conquered would be restored to Byzantium, Alexius shipped the armies off to Nicaea.

The main objective of the First Crusade—to conquer the Holy Land—was accomplished largely because of Muslim disunity. We have already seen how Jerusalem was ruled before the crusaders got there: it had been taken over by Atsiz to the dismay of the Fatimids. As the crusaders made good their conquests (they took Antioch on June 3, 1098, killing every Turk in the city), the Fatimids happily recovered Jerusalem. At that moment, they considered the crusaders potential allies. They were entirely unprepared for the attack which, on July 15, 1099, gave Jerusalem to the Christians.

RULERS WITH CLOUT

While the papacy was turning into a monarchy, other rulers were beginning to turn territories into states. They discovered ideologies to justify their hegemony, hired officials to work for them, found vassals and churchmen to support them. Many of these rulers were women.

The Crusader States

In the Holy Land, the leaders of the crusade set up four tiny states, European colonies in the Levant. Two (Tripoli and Edessa) were counties, Antioch was a principality, Jerusalem a kingdom. (See Map 5.4.) The Europeans held on to them, tenuously, until 1291, though many new crusades had to be called in the interval to shore them up.

Created by conquest, these states were treated as lordships. The new rulers carved out estates to give as fiefs to their vassals, who, in turn, gave portions of their holdings in fief to their own men. The peasants continued to work the land as before, and commerce boomed as the new rulers encouraged lively trade at their coastal ports. Italian merchants—the Genoese, Pisans, and Venetians—were the most active, but others—Byzantines and Muslim traders—participated as well. Enlightened lordship dictated that the mixed population of the states—Muslims, to be sure, but also Jews, Greek Orthodox Christians, Monophysite Christians and others—be tolerated for the sake of production and trade. Most Europeans had gone home after the First

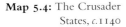

Map 5.4: The Crusader States, *c*.1140

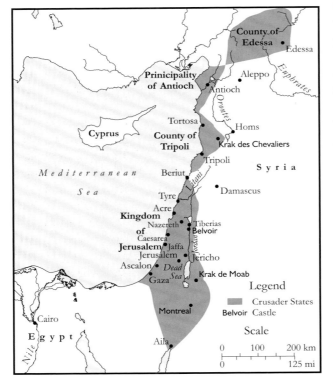

Crusade; those left behind were obliged to preserve the population that remained.

The main concerns of the crusader states' rulers were military, and these could be guaranteed as well by a woman as by a man. Thus Melisende (*r*.1131–1152), oldest daughter of King Baldwin II of Jerusalem, was declared ruler along with her husband, Fulk, formerly count of Anjou, and their infant son. Taking the reins of government into her own hands after Fulk's death, she named a constable to lead her army and made sure that the greatest men in the kingdom sent her their vassals to do military service. Vigorously asserting her position as queen, she found supporters in the church, appointed at least one bishop to his see, and created her own chancery, where her royal acts were drawn up.

But vassals alone, however well commanded, were not sufficient to defend the fragile crusader states, nor were the stone castles and towers that bristled in the countryside. New knights had to be recruited from Europe from time to time, and a new and militant kind of monasticism developed in the Levant: the Knights Templar. Vowed to poverty and chastity, the Templars at the same time devoted themselves to war. They defended the town garrisons of the crusader states and ferried money from Europe to the Holy Land. Even so, they could not prevent a new Seljuk leader, Zengi, from taking Edessa in 1144. The slow but steady shrinking of the crusader states began at that moment. The Second Crusade (1147–1149), called in the wake of Zengi's victory, came to a disastrous end. After only four days of besieging the walls of Damascus, the crusaders, whose leaders could not keep the peace among themselves, gave up and went home.

England under Norman Rule

Anglo-Saxon England was early linked to the Continent by the Vikings, who settled in England's eastern half. In the eleventh century it was further tied to Scandinavia under the rule of Cnut (r.1016-1035), king of a state that extended from England to Denmark, Norway, and part of Sweden. But it was with its conquest by William, duke of Normandy, that England was drawn inextricably into the Continental orbit.

William the Conqueror, duke of Normandy, carried a papal banner with him when he left his duchy in 1066 to dispute the crown of the childless King Edward the Confessor. The one-day battle of Hastings was decisive, and William was crowned the first Norman king of England. (See Genealogy 6.1: The Norman and Angevin Kings of England, on p.213.) Treating his conquest like booty (as the crusaders would do a few decades later in their new states), he kept about 20 per cent of the land for himself and divided the rest, distributing it in large but scattered fiefs to a relatively small number of his barons—his elite followers—and family members, lay and ecclesiastical, as well as to some lesser men, such as personal servants and soldiers. In turn, these men maintained their own vassals; they owed the king military service (and the service of a fixed number of their vassals) along with certain dues, such as reliefs (money paid upon inheriting a fief) and aids (payments made on important occasions).

These were noble obligations; William expected their servile counterpart from the peasantry. In 1086, he ordered a survey of the land and landholders of England. Quickly dubbed "Domesday Book" because, like the records of people judged at doomsday, it provided facts that could not be appealed, it was the most extensive inventory of land, livestock, taxes, and people that had ever been compiled anywhere in medieval Europe. According to a chronicler of the time, William

> sent his men over all England into every shire and had them find out how many hundred hides [a measure of land] there were in the shire, or what land and cattle the king himself had in the country, or what dues he ought to receive every year from the shire.... So very narrowly did he have the survey to be made that there was no single hide nor a yard of land, nor indeed ... one ox or one cow or one pig left out.[5]

The surveys were made by the king's men by consulting Anglo-Saxon tax lists and by taking testimony from local jurors, men sworn to answer a series of formal questions truthfully. Summarized in Domesday, the answers gave William what he needed to know about his kingdom and the revenues—including the Danegeld, which was now in effect a royal tax—that could be expected from it.

Communication with the Continent was constant. The Norman barons spoke a brand of French; they talked more easily with the peasants of Normandy (if they bothered) than with those tilling the land in England. They maintained their estates on the Continent and their ties with its politics, institutions, and culture. English wool was sent to Flanders to be turned into cloth. The most brilliant intellect of his day, Saint Anselm of Bec (1033-1109), was born in Italy, became abbot of a Norman monastery, and was then appointed archbishop in England. English adolescent boys were sent to Paris and Chartres for schooling. The kings of England often spent more time on the Continent than they did on the island. When, on the death of William's son, King Henry I (r.1100-1135), no male descendent survived to take the throne, two counts from the Continent—Geoffrey of Anjou and Stephen of Blois—disputed it as their right through two rival females of the royal line. (See Genealogy 6.1 again.)

Christian Spain

While initially the product of defeat, Christian Spain in the eleventh and twelfth centuries turned tables and became, in effect, the successful western counterpart of the crusader states. The disintegration of al-Andalus into *taifas* opened immense opportunities to the Spanish princes of the north. Wealth flowed into their coffers not only from plundering raids and the confiscation of lands and cities but also (until the Almoravids put an end to it) from tribute, paid in gold by *taifa* rulers to stave off attacks.

It was not just the rulers who were enriched. When Rodrigo Diaz de Vivar, the Cid (from the Arabic *sidi*, lord), fell out of favor with his lord, King Alfonso VI (r.1065-1109) of León-Castile, he and a band of followers found employment with al-Mutamin, ruler of Zaragoza. There the Cid defended the city against Christian and Muslim invaders alike. In 1090, he left employment for good and took his chances at Valencia:

> My Cid knew well   that God was his strength.
> There was great fear   in the city of Valencia
> It grieves those of Valencia.   Know, they are not pleased
> They took counsel   and came to besiege him.[6]

Thus were the two sides depicted in the *Poem of the Cid*, written perhaps a century later: beleaguered inhabitants versus an army of God, even though the Cid had just come from serving a Muslim ruler. In the end, the Cid took Valencia in 1094 and ruled there until his death in 1099. He was a Spaniard, but other opportunistic armies sometimes came from elsewhere. The one that Pope Alexander II authorized to besiege Barbastro in 1064 was made up of Frenchmen.

The French connection was symptomatic of a wider process: the Europeanization of Spain. Initially the Christian kingdoms had been isolated islands of Visigothic culture. But already in the tenth century, pilgrims from France, England, Germany, and Italy were clogging the roads to the shrine of Saint James (Santiago) of Compostela; in the eleventh century, monks from Cluny and other reformed monasteries arrived to colonize Spanish cloisters. Alfonso VI actively reached out beyond the Pyrenees, to Cluny — where he doubled the annual gift of 1000 gold pieces that his father, Fernando I, had given in exchange for prayers for his soul — and to the papacy. He sought recognition from Pope Gregory VII as "king of Spain," and in return he imposed the Roman liturgy throughout his kingdom, stamping out the traditional Visigothic music and texts.

In 1085 Alfonso made good his claim to be more than the king of León-Castille by conquering Toledo. (See Map 5.5.) After his death, his daughter Queen Urraca

Map 5.5: Spain at the Death of Alfonso VI (1109)

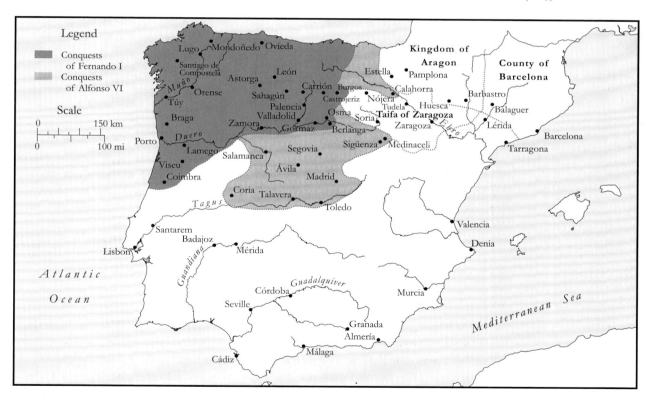

(*r*.1109-1126) ruled in her own right a realm larger than England. Her strength came from many of the usual sources: control over land, which, though granted out to counts and others, was at least in theory revocable; church appointments; an army — everyone was liable to be called up once a year, even arms-bearing slaves — and a court of great men to offer advice and give their consent.

Praising the King of France

Not all rulers had opportunities for grand conquest. How did they maintain themselves? The example of the kings of France reveals the possibilities. Reduced to battling a few castles in the vicinity of the Ile-de-France, the Capetian kings nevertheless wielded many of the same instruments of power as their conquering contemporaries: vassals, taxes, commercial revenues, military and religious reputations. Louis VI the Fat (*r*.1108-1137), so heavy that he had to be hoisted onto his horse by a crane, was nevertheless a tireless defender of royal power. (See Genealogy 5.3: The Capetian Kings of France.)

Louis's virtues were amplified and broadcast by his biographer, Suger (1081-1152), the abbot of Saint-Denis, a monastery just outside Paris. A close associate of the king, Suger was his chronicler and propagandist. When Louis set himself the task of consolidating his rule in the Ile-de-France, Suger portrayed the king as a righteous hero. He was more than a lord with rights over the French nobles as his vassals; he was a peacekeeper with the God-given duty to fight unruly strongmen. Careful not to claim that Louis was head of the church, which would have scandalized the papacy and its supporters, Suger nevertheless emphasized Louis's role as protector of the church and the poor and insisted on the sacred importance of the royal dignity. When a pope happened to arrive in France, Louis, not yet king, and his father, Philip I (*r*.1060-1108), bowed low, but (said Suger) "the lord pope lifted them up and made them sit before him like devout sons of the apostles. In the manner of a wise man acting wisely, he conferred with them privately on the present condition of the church."[7] Here the pope was shown needing royal advice. Meanwhile, Suger stressed Louis's piety and active defense of the faith:

> Helped by his powerful band of armed men, or rather by the hand of God, he abruptly seized the castle [of Crécy] and captured its very strong tower as if it were simply the hut of a peasant. Having startled those criminals [Thomas of Marle, a regional castellan, and his retinue], he piously slaughtered the impious, cutting them down without mercy because he found them to be merciless.[8]

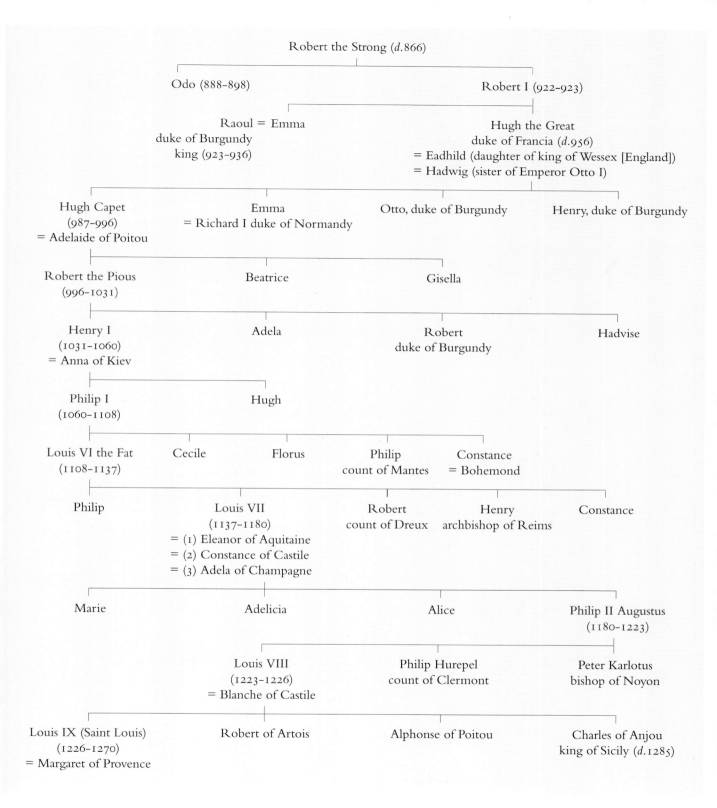

When Louis VI died in 1137, Suger's notion of the might and right of the king of France reflected reality in an extremely small area. Nevertheless, Louis laid the groundwork for the gradual extension of royal power. As the lord of vassals, the king could call upon his men to aid him in times of war (though the great ones could defy him). As king and landlord, he collected dues and taxes with the help of his officials, called *prévôts*. Revenues came from Paris as well, a thriving commercial and cultural center. With money and land, Louis could employ civil servants while dispensing the favors and giving the gifts that added to his prestige and power.

NEW FORMS OF LEARNING AND RELIGIOUS EXPRESSION

The commercial revolution, the newly reorganized church, close contact with the Islamic world, and the revived polities of the early twelfth century paved the way for the growth of schools and new forms of scholarship. Money, learning, and career opportunities attracted many to the new centers. On the other hand, the cities and the schools repelled others, who retreated from the world to seek poverty and solitude. Yet the new learning and the new money had a way of seeping into the cracks and crannies of even the most resolutely separate institutions.

Schools and the Liberal Arts

Connected to monasteries and cathedrals since the Carolingian period, schools had traditionally trained young men to become monks or priests. Some schools were better endowed than others with books and masters (teachers); a few developed reputations for particular expertise. By the end of the eleventh century, the best schools were those connected to cathedrals in the larger cities: Reims, Paris, Bologna, Montpellier.

Eager students sampled nearly all of them. The young monk Gilbert of Liège was typical: "Instilled with an insatiable thirst for learning, whenever he heard of somebody excelling in the arts, he rushed immediately to that place and drank whatever delightful potion he could draw from the master there."[9] For Gilbert and other students, a good lecture had the excitement of the theater. Teachers at some schools were sometimes forced to find larger halls to accommodate the crush of students. Other teachers simply declared themselves "masters" and set up shop by renting a room. If they could prove their mettle as lecturers, they had no trouble finding paying students.

What the students sought, above all, was knowledge of the seven liberal arts. Grammar, rhetoric, and logic (or dialectic) belonged to the "beginning" arts, the so-called trivium. Logic, involving the technical analysis of texts as well as the application and manipulation of arguments, was a transitional subject leading to the second, higher part of the liberal arts, the quadrivium. This comprised four areas of study that might today be called theoretical math and science: arithmetic (number theory), geometry, music (theory rather than practice), and astronomy. Of these arts, logic had pride of place in the schools, while masters and students who studied the quadrivium generally did so outside of the classroom.

The goal of twelfth-century scholars was to gather, order, systematize, and clarify all knowledge. That God existed, nearly everyone believed. But scholars like Anselm of Bec were not satisfied by belief alone. Anselm's faith, as he put it, "sought understanding." He emptied his mind of all concepts except that of God and then, using the tools of logic, proved God's very existence in his *Monologion*. Gilbert of Poitiers (c.1075-1154) systematized Bible commentaries, helping to create the *Glossa Ordinaria*, the standard compendium of all teachings on the Bible. Peter Abelard (1079-1142), who declared that "nothing can be believed unless it is first understood," drew together conflicting authoritative texts on 156 key subjects in his *Sic et Non (Yes and No)*, including "That God is one and the contrary" and "That it is permitted to kill men and the contrary." Leaving the propositions unresolved, Abelard urged his students to discover the reasons behind the disagreements. Soon Peter Lombard (c.1100-1160) adopted Abelard's method of juxtaposing opposing positions, but he supplied his own reasoned resolutions as well. His *Sententiae* was perhaps the most successful textbook of the twelfth century.

One key logical issue for twelfth-century scholars involved the question of "universals": whether a universal—something that can be said of many—is real or simply a linguistic or mental entity. For example, when we look at diverse individuals of one kind, say Fluffy and Mittens, we say of each of them that they are members of the same species: cat. Abelard sneered at one of his teachers, William of Champeaux, who maintained (in Abelard's words) "that ... the whole species was essentially the same in each of its individuals."[10] William was what we call a "realist," for he argued that the species was indeed real. Others, whom we call "nominalists," denied this reality. Abelard was essentially a nominalist, seeing Fluffy and Mittens as radically individual. However, he partly allied himself with the realists by seeking a real basis in individuals for universal terms. This he found in the idea of the status or condition which all individuals of a species share. This was not a "thing," just a mode of being. For Abelard, there was no "thing" common to Fluffy and Mittens; they were not cats by virtue of some extra-linguistic or extra-mental entity. Nevertheless, they *were* really cats by their common status, namely being a cat.

Later in the twelfth century, scholars found precise tools for this and other logical questions in the works of Aristotle. During Abelard's lifetime, very little of Aristotle's work was available in Europe because it had not been translated from Greek into Latin. By the end of the century, however, that lack had been filled by translators who traveled to Islamic or formerly Islamic cities — Toledo in Spain, Palermo in Sicily — where Aristotle had already been translated into Arabic and carefully commented on by Islamic scholars like Ibn Sina (Avicenna) (980-1037) and Ibn Rushd (Averroes) (1126-1198). By the thirteenth century, Aristotle had become the primary philosopher for the scholastics (the scholars of the European medieval universities).

Figure 5.1 (facing page): Hypothetical Plan of the Monastery of Cluny, 1157

The lofty subjects of the schools had down-to-earth, practical consequences in books for preachers, advice for rulers, manuals for priests, textbooks for students, and guides for living addressed to laypeople. Nor was mastery of the liberal arts the end of everyone's education. Many students went on to study medicine (the great school for that was at Montpellier) or theology (Paris was the center). Others studied law; at Bologna, for example, where Gratian worked on canon law, other jurists — such as the so-called Four Doctors — achieved fame by teaching and writing about Roman law. By the mid-twelfth century, scholars had made real progress towards a systematic understanding of Justinian's law codes (see p.52). The lawyers who emerged from the school at Bologna went on to serve popes, bishops, kings, princes, or communes. Thus the learning of the schools was preached in the churches, consulted in the law courts, and used on the operating tables. It came to unify European culture.

Robert Pullen's life may serve to illustrate the career of a moderately successful schoolman while suggesting some of the practical benefits of the new learning. Born in England, Pullen was sent to school at Laon, in France. Good at his studies, he became a master in turn. Back in England, he was (in the 1130s) the first lecturer in theology at Oxford. But Paris beckoned as the center of theological studies, and as soon as he got a church position in England (and the revenues attached to it), he went off to France. From there, he went to Rome, where his academic training helped him get appointed papal chancellor. He served perfectly capably in this post, meanwhile finding good jobs at the papal curia for some of his students, helping his nephew get a church post (the very one that Pullen had abandoned in England), and obtaining papal privileges for the monastery of yet another of his relatives.

Monastic Splendor and Poverty

That monastery, Sherborne Abbey, was an old-fashioned Benedictine house. There were many others, the most famous of them the monastery of Cluny, which, by the early twelfth century, housed some 400 brothers. Physically, it was a palatial complex of buildings, but the monks, following the *Rule* of Saint Benedict, still slept in a com-

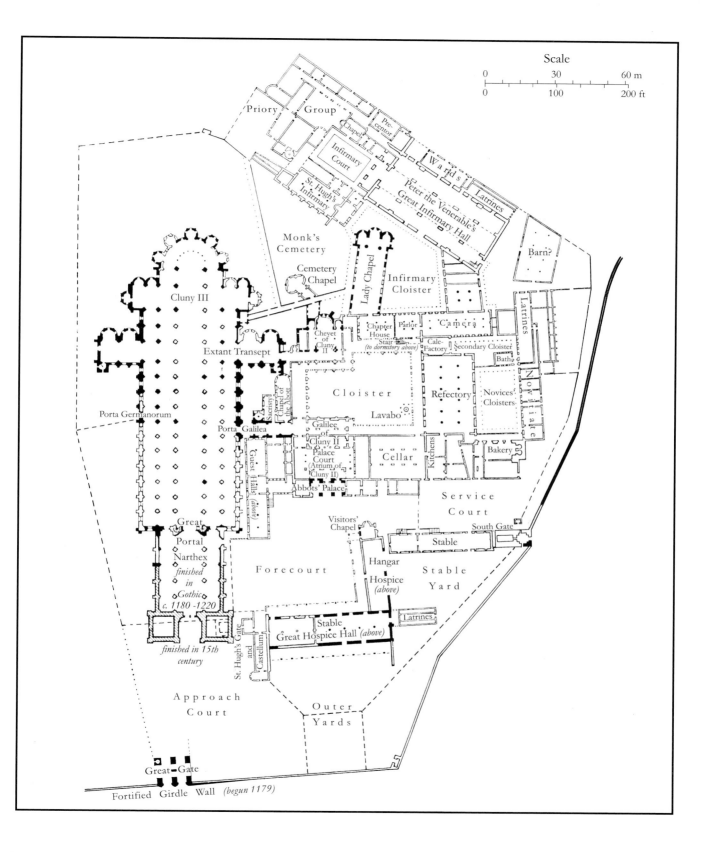

Scale

0   30   60 m
0   100   200 ft

Priory Group

Precentor

Chapel

Infirmary Court

Wards

Latrines

Peter the Venerable's Great Infirmary Hall

St. Hugh's Infirmary

Monk's Cemetery

Barn?

Cemetery Chapel

Lady Chapel

Infirmary Cloister

Cluny III

Chevet of Cluny II

Chapter House Stair (to dormitory above)

Parlor

Camera

Latrines

Extant Transept

Cale-Factory

Secondary Cloister

Bath

Cloister

Refectory

Novices Cloisters

Novitiate

Porta Germanorum

Chapel of the Abbot

Sacristy

Lavabo

Porta Galilea

Galilee of Cluny II

Kitchens

Bakery

Guest Halls (above)

Palace Court (Atrium of Cluny II)

Cellar

Abbots' Palace

Service Court

Visitors' Chapel

South Gate

Great Portal Narthex finished in Gothic c. 1180-1220

Stable

Hangar

Hospice (above)

Stable Yard

Forecourt

finished in 15th century

St. Hugh's Gate and Castellum

Stable Great Hospice Hall (above)

Latrines

Approach Court

Outer Yards

Great Gate

Fortified Girdle Wall (begun 1179)

mon dormitory and ate in a common dining room. (See Figure 5.1.) They were served—in the kitchen, cellar, and hospital—by men who increasingly lived "off campus" with their wives and children, in a town nestled right outside the monastery doors. By the end of the eleventh century, Pope Urban II, on his way to preach the First Crusade, declared a sacrosanct zone around Cluny, making it a sort of miniature Holy Land in the middle of Burgundy. Within their various circles of power and sanctity, the Cluniacs—and other "black monks" (so-called because of the color of their robes) and also nuns following their example—carried out a life of arduous, nearly continuous prayer. Every detail of their lives was ordered, every object splendid, every space adorned to render due honor to the Lord of heaven.

Since the time of Charlemagne, Gregorian chant had expanded enormously. By the twelfth century, a large repertoire of melodies had grown up, and new methods of musical notation had been elaborated to convey them. Scribes drew staves, sometimes multicolored, to show pitch. In Plate 5.3, a manuscript from the monastery of Saint-Evroult in Normandy, the scribe used a four-line staff (one red, one green, and

Plate 5.3: Gloria with Musical Notation, Saint-Evroult (12th cent.). The "Gloria," for which this manuscript page gives both text and music, was a chant of the Mass. Here the usual text of the Gloria has additional tropes (new words and music).

Plate 5.4 (facing page): A Mode of the Chant, Cluny (1088–1095). Each of the eight modes of the Gregorian chant was associated with one of four characteristic notes. Four carvings on the capitals of Cluny's choir represented each of these notes; the one on the left here portrays the "third" note, while the one to its right (slightly out of focus) is the fourth tone.

two others lightly sketched) to indicate the locations of the pitches a–c–e–f. Ever since the Carolingian period, the scalar patterns that these pitches reflected were called "modes." They were so integral to the way that chants were understood and classified that the monks of Cluny personified the modes on some of the columns circling the choir of their church. (See Plate 5.4.)

This sculpture of a chant tone—in high relief yet wedded to the shape and surface of the capital (the top of a column or pier) that it springs from—is in the so-called "Romanesque" style. Another example of this style, this time from the cathedral of Autun (Plate 5.5), is far less tranquil in depicting the suicide of Judas, the apostle who betrayed Christ. Yet even these furious demons and the gagging Judas are contained by the shape of the capital, their cramped postures adding to the emotional frenzy of the composition.

Romanesque, representing the first wave of European monumental architec-

ture, was the style of the building boom—especially of the great Benedictine monasteries—in the early twelfth century. Romanesque churches, built of stone, are massive, weighty, and dignified; but they are enlivened by sculpture, wall paintings, and the texture of patterns. At Durham cathedral (built between 1093 and 1133 in the north of England), the stone itself is a warm yellow/pink color, given added zest by piers incised with diamond or zig-zag patterns. (See Plate 5.6.) At Berzé-la-Ville, a small church near Cluny, wall paintings decorate the interior; Plate 5.7 shows the martyrdom of Saint Vincent, roasting on a grill. At Pisa, the famous leaning tower is in fact a Romanesque bell tower; here (Plate 5.8) the decoration is on the exterior, where the bright Italian sun heightens the play of light and shadow.

Santiago de Compostela (built between 1078 and 1124) may serve as an example of a "typical" Romanesque church, though in fact the most typical aspect of that style is its extreme variety. Most of Santiago's exterior was rebuilt in the Baroque period, but the interior is still much as it must have been when twelfth-century pilgrims entered the shrine of Saint James. (See Plate 5.9.) Striking is the "barrel" or "tunnel" vault whose ribs, springing from thin columns attached to the piers, mark the long church into sections called bays. There are only two levels: the first is for the arches that open onto the side aisles of the church; the second is the gallery. (Many other Romanesque churches have a third story—a clerestory—of windows.) The plan of Santiago (see Figure 5.2) shows its typical basilica shape with a transept crossing and, at the east end, an aisle (called an "ambulatory") that allowed pilgrims to visit the relics housed in the chapels.

Not all medieval people agreed that such opulence

Plate 5.5: Suicide of Judas, Autun (1125-1135). According to Matt. 27:3-6, Judas repented betraying Jesus, tried to return the money he had gained for it, and finally "went and hanged himself with a halter." The sculptor of this capital at Autun Cathedral carved the scene, with winged devils pulling the noose.

Plate 5.6 (facing page): Durham Cathedral, Interior (1093-1133). Huge and imposing, Durham Cathedral is also inviting and welcoming, with its lively piers, warm colors, and harmonious spaces. Built by Norman bishops, it housed the relics of the Anglo-Saxon Saint Cuthbert; in just such ways did the Normans appropriate the power and prestige of English saints' cults.

Plate 5.7: Martyrdom of Saint Vincent, Berzé-la-Ville (late 11th or early 12th cent.). As at many other Romanesque churches, the walls of Berzé-la-Ville are covered with frescoes of religious scenes. Note the contrast between the calm, rounded Saint Vincent (*d.*304) and his frenetic, angular tormentors.

pleased or praised God, how-ever. At the end of the eleventh century, the new commercial economy and the profit motive that fueled it led many to reject wealth and to embrace poverty as a key ele-ment of religious life. The Carthusian order, founded by Bruno, one-time bishop of Cologne, was such a group. La Chartreuse, the chief house of the order, was built in an Alpine valley, lonely and inac-cessible. Each monk took a vow of silence and lived as a hermit in his own small hut. Only occasionally would the monks join the others for prayer in a common oratory. When not engaged in prayer or meditation, the Carthusians copied manuscripts: for them, scribal work was a way to

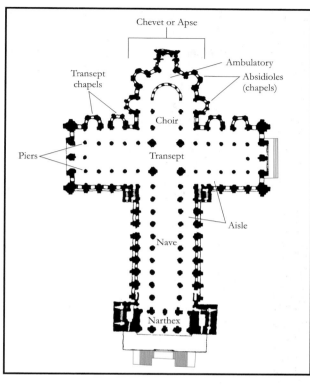

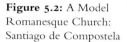

Figure 5.2: A Model Romanesque Church: Santiago de Compostela

preach God's word with the hands rather than the mouth. Slowly the Carthusian order grew, but each monastery was limited to only twelve monks, the number of Christ's Apostles.

By contrast, the Cistercians expanded rapidly, often by reforming and incorporat-ing existing monasteries. The first Cistercian house was Cîteaux (in Latin, *Cisterci-um*), founded in 1098 by Robert of Molesme (*c.*1027-1110) and a few other monks seeking a more austere way of life. Austerity they found—and also success. With the arrival of Saint Bernard (*c.*1090-1153), who came to Cîteaux in 1112 along with about thirty friends and relatives, the original center sprouted a small congregation of houses in Burgundy. (Bernard became abbot of one of them, Clairvaux.) By the mid-twelfth century there were more than 300 monasteries—many in France, but also in Italy, Germany, England, Austria, and Spain—following what they took to be the customs of Cîteaux. By the end of the twelfth century, the Cistercians were an order: their member houses adhered to the decisions of a General Chapter; their liturgical practices and internal organization were standardized. Many nuns, too, as eager as

Plate 5.8: Leaning Tower (Bell Tower) of Pisa (late 12th cent.). The tower is part of a large cathedral and baptistery complex which, in its layout and design, was meant to imitate—and outshine—the Temple Mount complex at Jerusalem.

Plate 5.9 (facing page): Santiago de Compostela, Interior (1078–1124). Santiago (in the far northwest corner of Spain) was known for its relics of Saint James the Great (*d.*44), apostle and martyr. From the twelfth through fifteenth centuries a major pilgrimage center, the cathedral was built to hold crowds and to usher them, via aisles, from chapel to chapel.

monks to live the life of simplicity and poverty that the Apostles had endured and enjoyed, adopted Cîteaux's customs; some convents later became members of the order.

Although the Cistercians claimed the *Rule* of Saint Benedict as the foundation of their customs, they elaborated a style of life and an aesthetic all their own, largely governed by the goal of simplicity. They even rejected the conceit of dying their robes—hence their nickname, the "white monks." White, too, were their houses. Despite regional variations and considerable latitude in interpreting the meaning of "simplicity," Cistercian buildings had a different feel than the great Benedictine monasteries of black monks. Foursquare and regular, Cistercian churches and other buildings conformed to a fairly standard plan. (See Figure 5.3.) The churches tended to be small, made of smooth-cut, undecorated stone. Wall paintings were eschewed, sculpture modest at best. Indeed, Saint Bernard wrote a scathing attack on Romanesque sculpture in which, ironically, he admitted its sensuous allure:

What is the point of ridiculous monstrosities in the cloister where there are brethren reading—I mean those extraordinary deformed beauties and beautiful deformities? What are those lascivious apes doing, those fierce lions, monstrous centaurs, half-men and spotted leopards…. It is more diverting to decipher marble than the text before you, and to spend the whole day in gazing at such singularities in preference to meditating upon God's laws.[11]

The Cistercians had few such diversions, but the simplicity of their buildings and of their clothing also had its beauty. Illuminated by the pure white light that came through clear glass windows, Cistercian churches were luminous, cool, and serene. Plate 5.10 shows the nave of Fontenay Abbey, begun in 1139. There are no wall paintings, no sculpture, no incised pillars. Yet the subtle play of thick piers and thin

columns along with the alternation of curved and linear capitals lend the church a sober charm.

True to their emphasis on purity, the communal liturgy of the Cistercians was simplified and shorn of the many additions that had been tacked on in the houses of the black monks. Only the liturgy as prescribed in the *Rule* of Saint Benedict and one daily Mass were allowed. Even the music for the chant was modified: the Cistercians rigorously suppressed the B flat, even though doing so made the melody discordant, because of their insistence on strict simplicity.

On the other hand, Benedict's *Rule* did not prevent the Cistercians from creating a new class of monks — the lay brothers — who were illiterate and unable to participate in the liturgy. These men did the necessary labor — field work, stock raising — to support the community at large. A closer look at Figure 5.3 shows that the Cistercian monastery was in fact a house divided: the eastern half was for the "choir" monks, the western half for the lay brethren. Each half had its own dining room, latrines, and dormitories. The monks were strictly segregated, even in the church, where a screen kept them apart.

Plate 5.10 (facing page): Fontenay Abbey Church, Interior (1139-1147). Compare the bare walls of this Cistercian church with the frescoed walls of Berzé-la-Ville (**Plate 5.7**). How do these different artistic sensibilities reflect religious ones?

Figure 5.3: Schematic Plan of a Cistercian Monastery

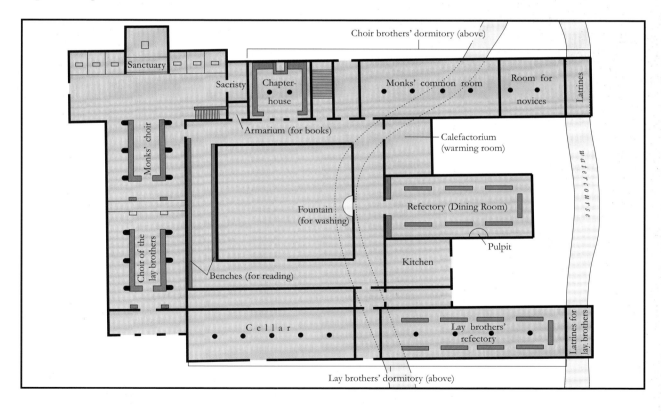

The choir monks dedicated themselves to private prayer and contemplation and to monastic administration. The Cistercian *Charter of Charity* (*c.*1165), in effect a constitution of the order, provided for a closely monitored network of houses, and each year the Cistercian abbots met to hammer out legislation for all of them. All the houses had large and highly organized farms and grazing lands called "granges," and the monks spent much of their time managing their estates and flocks of sheep, both of which yielded handsome profits by the end of the twelfth century. Clearly part of the agricultural and commercial revolutions of the Middle Ages, the Cistercian order made managerial expertise a part of the monastic life.

Yet the Cistercians also elaborated a spirituality of intense personal emotion. As Bernard said,

> Often enough when we approach the altar to pray our hearts are dry and lukewarm. But if we persevere, there comes an unexpected infusion of grace, our breast expands as it were, and our interior is filled with an overflowing love; and if somebody should press upon it then, this milk of sweet fecundity would gush forth in streaming richness.[12]

The Cistercians emphasized not only human feeling but also the humanity of Christ and Mary. While pilgrims continued to stream to the tombs and reliquaries of saints, the Cistercians dedicated all their churches to the Virgin Mary (for whom they had no relics) because for them she signified the model of a loving mother. Indeed, the Cistercians regularly used maternal imagery (as Bernard's metaphor of a flowing breast illustrates) to describe the nurturing care provided to humans by Jesus himself. The Cistercian God was approachable, human, protective, even mothering.

★   ★   ★   ★

In the twelfth century, Europe was coming into its own. Growing population and the profitable organization of the countryside promoted cities, trade, and wealth. Townspeople created new institutions of self-regulation and self-government. Kings and popes found new means to exert their authority and test its limits. Scholars mastered the knowledge of the past and put it to use in classrooms, royal courts, and papal offices. Monks who fled the world ended up in positions of leadership; the great entrepreneurs of the twelfth century were the Cistercians; and Saint Bernard was the most effective preacher of the Second Crusade.

The power of communities was recognized in the twelfth century: the guilds and communes depended on this recognition. So too did the new theology of the time. In his theological treatise, *Why God Became Man*, Saint Anselm put new emphasis on Christ's humanity: Christ's sacrifice was that of one human being for another. The

Cistercians spoke of God's mothering. Historians sometimes speak of the rise of "humanism"—with its emphasis on the dignity of human beings, the splendor of the natural world, and the nobility of reason—in the twelfth century. Yet the new stress on the loving bonds that tied Christians together also led to the persecution of others, like Jews and Muslims, who lived outside the Christian community. In the next century communities would become more ordered, regulated, and incorporated. By the same token, they became even more exclusive.

CHAPTER FIVE KEY EVENTS

1049–1054	Papacy of Leo IX
1066	Norman conquest of England by William of Normandy
1072	Battle of Manzikert
1073–1085	Papacy of Gregory VII
1075–1122	Investiture Conflict
1081–1118	Reign of Alexius I Comnenus
1085	Conquest of Toledo by Alfonso VI
1086	Domesday Book
1094	Al-Andalus under Almoravid (Berber) control
1096–1099	The First Crusade
1097	Establishment of a commune at Milan
1099–1291	Crusader States in the Holy Land
1109	Death of Anselm of Bec, theologian and archbishop of England
1122	Concordat of Worms
c.1140	Publication of Gratian's *Decretum*
1142	Death of Peter Abelard
1147–1149	The Second Crusade
1153	Death of St. Bernard

NOTES

1. *Chronique de Saint-Bertin*, quoted in Histoire de la France urbaine, Vol. 2: La ville médiévale (Paris, 1980), p.71, here translated from the French.
2. Gregory, Letter of December 8, 1075, in *The Correspondence of Pope Gregory VII: Selected Letters from the Registrum*, ed. and trans. Ephriam Emerton (New York, 1969), p.87.
3. Roman Lenten Synod (1076), in *The Correspondence of Pope Gregory VII*, p.91.
4. Donald White, ed., *Medieval History. A Source Book* (Homewood, Illinois, 1965), pp.351–52.

5. From the Anglo-Saxon Chronicle "E", a. 1085, quoted in David C. Douglas, *William the Conqueror: The Norman Impact upon England* (Berkeley, 1967), p.348.

6. *Poem of the Cid*, trans. W.S. Merwin (New York, 1959), p.119-20.

7. Suger, *The Deeds of Louis the Fat*, ed. and trans. Richard C. Cusimano and John Moorhead (Washington, 1992), p.48.

8. Suger, p.107.

9. Helene Wieruszowski, *The Medieval University* (Princeton, 1966), pp.123-24.

10. Abelard, "Historia calamitatum," in *The Letters of Abelard and Heloise*, trans. Betty Radice (Harmondsworth, 1974), p.60.

11. Wolfgang Braunfels, *Monasteries of Western Europe: The Architecture of the Orders* (Princeton, 1972), p.242.

12. Bernard of Clairvaux, *On the Song of Songs*, Vol. 1. trans. Kilian Walsh, Cistercian Fathers Series, 4 (Kalamazoo, 1977), p.58.

FURTHER READING

For searchable maps, genealogies, and other materials for this chapter, please visit the *Short History of the Middle Ages* website at www.broadviewpress.com/shorthistory.

Arnold, Benjamin. *Medieval Germany, 500-1300: A Political Interpretation*. Toronto, 1997.

Benson, Robert L., and Giles Constable, eds. *Renaissance and Renewal in the Twelfth Century*. Cambridge, 1982.

Berman, Constance Hoffman. *The Cistercian Evolution: The Invention of a Religious Order in Twelfth-Century Europe*. Philadelphia, 2000.

Blumenthal, Uta-Renate. *The Investiture Controversy: Church and Monarchy from the Ninth to the Twelfth Century*. Philadelphia, 1988.

Clanchy, Michael T. *Abelard: A Medieval Life*. Oxford, 1997.

Fletcher, Richard. *The Quest for El Cid*. New York, 1989.

Lawson, M.K. *Cnut: The Danes in England in the Early Eleventh Century*. London, 1993.

Little, Lester K. *Religious Poverty and the Profit Economy in Medieval Europe*. Ithaca, NY, 1978.

Miller, Maureen C. *The Formation of a Medieval Church: Ecclesiastical Change in Verona, 950-1150*. Ithaca, NY, 1993.

Phillips, Jonathan. *The Crusades, 1095-1197*. Harlow, 2002.

Reilly, Bernard F. *The Kingdom of León-Castilla under Queen Urraca, 1109-1126*. Princeton, 1982.

Riley-Smith, Jonathan, ed. *The Oxford History of the Crusades*. Oxford, 1999.

Robinson, Ian S. *Henry IV of Germany*. Cambridge, 2000.

Southern, R.W. *Scholastic Humanism and the Unification of Europe*. Vol. 1: *Foundations*. Oxford, 1995.

Weinfurter, Stefan. *The Salian Century: Main Currents in an Age of Transition*. Trans. Barbara M. Bowlus. Philadelphia, 1999.

Winroth, Anders. *The Making of Gratian's* Decretum. Cambridge, 2000.

SIX

INSTITUTIONALIZING ASPIRATIONS
(c.1150-c.1250)

The lively movements of early twelfth-century Europe were institutionalized in the next decades. Fluid associations became corporations. Rulers hired salaried officials to staff their administrations. Churchmen defined the nature and limits of religious practice. While the Islamic world largely went its own way, only minimally affected by European developments, Byzantium was carved up by its Christian neighbors.

TWO NON-EUROPEAN HEIRS OF THE ROMAN EMPIRE: THE SEQUEL

Nothing could be more different than the fates of the Islamic world and of Byzantium at the beginning of the thirteenth century. The Muslims remained strong; the Byzantine empire nearly came to an end.

Islam on the Move

Like grains of sand, irritating but also generative, the Christian states of the Levant and Spain helped spark new Islamic principalities, one based in the Maghreb, the other in Syria and Egypt. In the Maghreb, the Almohads (1147–1266), a Berber group espousing a militant Sunni Islam, combined conquest with a program to "purify" the morals of their fellow Muslims. In al-Andalus their appearance induced some Islamic rulers to seek alliances with the Christian rulers to the north. But other Andalusian rulers joined forces with the Almohads, who replaced the Almoravids as rulers of the whole Islamic far west by 1172. (See Map 6.1.) At war continuously with Christian Spanish rulers, in 1212 they suffered a terrible defeat. For the Christian victors, the battle was known simply by its place name, Las Navas de Tolosa; but for the Almohads, it was known as "The Punishment." It was the beginning of the end of al-Andalus.

Meanwhile, however, in the shadow of the crusader states, Nur al-Din (Nureddin) (r.1146-1174), son of Zengi, forged a united Syria. Soon, in the 1150s, he conquered the county of Edessa and cut the principality of Antioch in half; in the 1160s he brought Egypt under his sway. Like the Almohads, Nur al-Din was inspired by three principal goals: to best competing Muslim rulers, to reform the faith, and to wage *jihad* against the Christian states in his backyard. He was succeeded by his Kurdish general Saladin (r.1171-1193), who made Egypt the base of his power. Finding Cairo

Map 6.1: The Almohads Before the Battle of Las Navas de Tolosa (1212)

still a hotbed of Shi'ite Islam, Saladin ousted its followers and forbade its teachings while setting up Sunni madrasas and instituting Sunni prayers. Meanwhile he attended to military matters. Importing the Buyid institution of the *iqta'* whereby the revenues of state lands were assigned to the army, Saladin was able to support a force of some 14,000 troops in Egypt alone. Master of Syria by the 1180s, he waged a *jihad* against the Kingdom of Jerusalem in 1187. At the battle of Hattin, the Christian army was badly defeated and the crusader states reduced to a few port cities. For about a half-century thereafter, Saladin's descendants held on to power. Then rule over Egypt fell (as we have often seen happen) to military leaders. The chief difference this time was that these leaders were uniformly of Turkic slave and ex-slave origins — they were *mamluks.* The Mamluk sultanate of Egypt, which soon took Syria as well, was exceptionally stable, surviving until 1517.

The Undoing of Byzantium

In 1204 the leaders of the Fourth Crusade made a "detour" and conquered Constantinople instead. We shall later explore some of the reasons why they did so. But in the context of Byzantine history, the question is not why the Europeans attacked but rather how the Byzantines had become weak enough to be taken.

Certainly the Byzantines themselves had no idea they were "in decline." Prior to 1204, they had reconquered some of Anatolia. Meanwhile, at home, the imperial court continued to function; its bureaucracy and machinery of taxation were still in place; and powerful men continued to vie to be emperors — as if there were still power and glory in the position. Yet much had changed from the heyday of the Comneni. Militarily the government was weak. It had almost no navy. Few of its troops were paid wages; they received *pronoiai* (land grants) instead, which diverted their interests to the provinces rather than the capital. Exacerbating this regionalism were the *dynatoi*, themselves greedy for more *pronoiai* and busy building up provincial enclaves ready to defy imperial law. At Philadelphia (today Alaşehir) in Anatolia, for example, one of them declared himself "emperor" in 1188.

At the capital city itself, the population was restive and impoverished. Above all, the citizens of Constantinople resented the "Franks" — as they called all Europeans — because of their special privileges. Along the Golden Horn, like pearls on a string, were the Venetian Quarter, the Amalfitan Quarter, the Pisan Quarter, and the Genoese Quarter: these were the neighborhoods of the Italian merchants, exempt from imperial taxes and uniformly wealthy. (See Map 4.1 on p.132.) It did not take much prodding to get the Constantinopolitans to attack and loot the Italian quarters in 1182 and again in 1203, when they could see the crusaders camped right outside their city.

Map 6.2: The Angevin and Capetian Realms in the Late Twelfth Century

Map 6.3: Central Europe, *c.*1250

Their demoralization arose in part from imperial policy. In the preceding century, the emperors had allowed Byzantium to become inextricably involved with Europeans. The Byzantine army was staffed with many Normans and Franks; its small navy included many Venetians. Italians dominated Byzantium's long-distance trade, and Italian neighborhoods (complete with homes, factories, churches, and monasteries) crowded the major cities of the empire.

None of this meant that Europeans had to take over, of course. Yet in 1204, crusader armies breached the walls of Constantinople, encountered relatively little opposition, plundered the city for three days, and finally declared one of their leaders, Baldwin of Flanders, the new Byzantine emperor. The Venetians gained the city harbor, Crete, and key Greek cities; other crusaders carved out other states. (See Map 6.3.) So did some Byzantines, however, and eventually, in 1261, their successors managed to recapture Constantinople and re-establish their empire until it fell for good in 1453 to the Ottoman Turks.

THE INSTITUTIONALIZATION OF GOVERNMENT IN THE WEST

Some Byzantines thought that the West bested them in 1204 because it had a better "sense of decorum," a better sense of order, than they had.[1] Given the meticulous court protocol and well-oiled bureaucracy at Constantinople, it is hard to see how people there could have viewed the Europeans as better organized. But the Byzantine critics had a point. While their emperors were favoring family members and their *dynatoi* were creating regional dynasties, some Western governments were becoming more impersonal. They were, in effect, in the midst of a new phase of self-definition, codification, and institutionalization.

Law, Authority, and the Written Word in England

One good example is England. The king hardly needed to be present: the government functioned by itself, with its own officials to handle administrative matters and record keeping. The very circumstances of the English king favored the growth of an administrative staff: his frequent travels to and from the Continent meant that officials needed to work in his absence, and his enormous wealth meant that he could afford them.

True, a long period of civil war (1135-1154) between the forces of two female heirs to the Norman throne (Matilda, daughter of Henry I, and Adela, Henry's sister) threatened royal power. As in Germany during the Investiture Conflict, so in England the barons and high churchmen consolidated their own local lordships during the war; private castles, symbols of their independence, punctuated the countryside. But the war ended when Matilda's son, Henry of Anjou, ascended the throne as the first "Angevin" king of England.[2] (See Genealogy 6.1: The Norman and Angevin Kings of England.) Under Henry II (r.1154-1189), the institutions of royal government were extended and strengthened.

THE REFORMS OF HENRY II

Henry was count of Anjou, duke of Normandy, and overlord of about half the other counties of northern France. He was also duke of Aquitaine by his marriage to Eleanor, heiress of that vast southern French duchy. As for his power in the British

Genealogy 6.1:
The Norman and Angevin Kings of England

William I the Conqueror (1066-1087) = Matilda of Flanders

Robert
duke of Normandy

William II Rufus
(1087-1100)

Henry I
(1100-1135)
= Edith Matilda

Adela (d.1137)
= Stephen of Blois

Stephen (1135-1154)

Matilda (d.1167) = Geoffrey Plantagenet (d.1151)
Anjou

William
duke of Normandy

Henry II = Eleanor
(1154-1189)   duchess of Aquitaine (d.1204)

Henry
(d.1183)

Richard I the Lion-Heart
(1189-1199)

Geoffrey
(d.1186)

John Lackland
(1199-1216)

Henry III
(1216-1272)

Edward I
(1272-1307)

Isabella of France = Edward II
(1307-1327)

See Genealogy 8.1

Isles: the princes of Wales swore him homage and fealty; the rulers of Ireland were forced to submit to him; and the king of Scotland was his vassal. Thus Henry exercised sometimes more, sometimes less power over a realm stretching from northern England to the Pyrenees. (See Map 6.2.) For his Continental possessions, he was vassal of the king of France.

Once on the English throne, Henry destroyed or confiscated the private castles built during the civil war and regained the lands that had belonged to the crown. Then he proceeded to extend his power, above all by imposing royal justice. Already the Anglo-Saxon kings had claimed rights in local courts, particularly in capital cases, even though those courts were dominated by powerful men largely independent of royal authority. The Norman kings added to Anglo-Saxon law in the area of land holding. Henry built on these institutions, regularizing, expanding, and systematizing them. "Throughout the realm," wrote one of Henry's admirers, "he appointed judges and legal officials to curb the audacity of wicked men and dispense justice to litigants according to the merits of their case."[3]

"Throughout the realm": this meant *common* law, law applicable throughout England to all free men and women (that is, people of the knightly class or above). The "appointment of judges and legal officials" was nothing new, but under Henry they were many, and they were professional legists for the first time. "Dispensing justice" had long been a tradition of the crown, but under Henry mechanisms were set in place to make royal justice routine. The most important of these was a system of judicial visitations called "eyres" (from the Latin *iter*, "journey"); Henry sent royal justices on regular trips to every locality in England. He required twelve representatives of the knightly class to meet during each eyre and either give the sheriff the names of those suspected of committing crimes in the vicinity or arrest the suspects themselves and hand them over to the royal justices. Penalties for convicted criminals were normally hanging or mutilation. Cases that we would call "civil" were equally embraced by these courts. To bring suit over a property claim, for example, a litigant could bring suit in a non-royal local court; but under Henry, he or she had the alternative of purchasing a royal writ and bringing the matter into a royal court.

The whole system was no doubt originally designed to put things right after the civil war. The earliest civil cases in Henry's courts concerned disputed properties that had "changed hands" during the fighting. Criminal cases came next, with the requirement (set down in the Assize of Clarendon, 1166) for twelve local representatives to name "any man accused or notoriously suspect of being a robber or murderer or thief" before the justices in eyre.[4]

Although these law-and-order measures were initially expensive for the king—he had to build many new jails, for example—they ultimately served to increase royal income and power. Fines came from condemned criminals and also from any knightly representative who might shirk his duties before the eyre; revenues poured in from the purchase of writs. The exchequer, as the financial bureau of England was called, recorded all the fines paid for judgments and the sums collected for writs. The amounts, entered on parchment sewn together and stored as rolls, became the Receipt Rolls and Pipe Rolls, the first of many such records of the English monarchy and an indication that writing had become a tool to institutionalize royal power in England.

Perhaps the most important outcome of this expanded legal system was to enhance royal power and prestige. The king of England touched (not personally but through men acting in his name) nearly every free man and free woman in the realm. On the other hand, the great majority of people in England were not free but rather "villains." If they went to court, it was commonly a local one, under the jurisdiction of a local lord, not justices in eyre. Barons and other lords remained jealous of their prerogatives.

Even more jealous was the church. A separate system of justice had long been available to the clergy and others who enjoyed church protection, and these church courts gave out mild punishments. Churchmen objected to submitting to the jurisdiction of Henry's courts, and the ensuing contest between Henry II and his appointed archbishop, Thomas Becket (1118-1170), became the greatest battle between the church and the state in the twelfth century. The conflict over jurisdiction simmered for six years, until Henry's henchmen murdered Thomas, unintentionally turning him into a martyr. Although Henry's role in the murder remained ambiguous, public outcry forced him to do public penance for the deed. In the end, the struggle made both institutions stronger, as church and royal courts expanded side-by-side to address the concerns of an increasingly litigious society.

DEFINING THE ROLE OF THE ENGLISH KING

Henry II and his sons Richard I the Lion-Heart (r.1189-1199) and John (r.1199-1216) were English kings with an imperial reach. But John must have felt a bit like the Byzantine emperor in 1204, for in that very year, the king of France, Philip II (r.1180-1223), confiscated his northern French territories for defying his overlordship. It was a purely military victory, and John set out to win the territories back by gathering money wherever and however he could in order to pay for an abler army. He forced his barons to pay him "scutage"—a tax—in lieu of military service. He extorted money in the form of "aids"—the fees that his barons ordinarily paid on rare occasions, such as the knighting of the king's eldest son. He compelled the widows of his barons and other vassals to marry men of his choosing or pay him a hefty fee to remain single.

All was to no avail. Philip's forces soundly defeated John's in 1214 at the battle of Bouvines. It was a defining moment, not so much for the Continent (English rule would continue there until the fifteenth century) as for England, where the barons organized, rebelled, and called the king to account. At Runnymede, just south of London, in June 1215, John was forced to agree to the charter of baronial liberties called Magna Carta, or "Great Charter," so named to distinguish it from a smaller charter issued around the same time concerning royal forests.

Magna Carta was intended to be a conservative document defining the "customary" obligations and rights of the nobility and forbidding the king to break from these without consulting his barons. Beyond this, it maintained that all free men in England had certain customs and rights in common that the king was obliged to uphold. In this way, Magna Carta documented the subordination of the king to written provisions; it implied that the king was not above the law. Copies of the charter were sent to sheriffs and other officials, to be read aloud in public places. Everyone knew what it said, and later kings continued to issue it—and have it read out—in one form or another. Though not a "constitution," nevertheless, Magna Carta was an important step in the institutionalization of the English government.

Plate 6.1:
Reliquary Casket for Charlemagne's Arm (*c.*1166-1170). Pairing the cult of Charlemagne with that of the Madonna, this reliquary casket, made to hold Charlemagne's arm, depicts Mary and the Child in the center of an arcade. Mother and child are flanked on either side by archangels. Frederick Barbarossa is depicted within the arch on the far left, while his wife, Beatrice, is on the far right, thus associating the reigning rulers with the sainted emperor.

France in the Making

A glance at Map 6.2 shows that late-twelfth-century France—consisting essentially of the Ile-de-France—was a dwarf surrounded by giants. When Philip II came to the throne at the age of fourteen, he seemed an easy target for the ambitions of Henry II and the counts of Flanders and Champagne. Philip, however, played them off against one another. Through inheritance he gained a fair portion of northeastern France from the county of Flanders in 1190. Soon he showed military skill as well, as he wrenched Normandy, Anjou, Maine, Touraine, and Poitou from the king of England in 1204-1206. A contemporary chronicler dubbed him Philip "Augustus"—the "enlarger"—because he added so much territory to his realm.

But Philip did more than enlarge; he integrated as well. This was particularly true in Normandy. Many of the Norman aristocrats promised him homage and fealty (in the process they broke from England, where their lands were confiscated and redistributed), and Philip's royal officers went about their business—taxing, hearing cases—careful not to tread on local customs and equally careful to enhance the flow of income into Philip's treasury. Gradually the Normans were brought into a new "French" orbit just beginning to take shape, constructed partly out of the common language of French and partly out of a new notion of the king as ruler of all the people in his territory.

Although there was never a French "common law" to supersede local ones, the French king, like the English, succeeded in extending royal power through administration. After 1194, Philip had all his decrees written down, establishing permanent repositories in which to keep them. Like the Angevins, he relied on members of the lesser nobility — knights and clerics, most educated in the schools — to do the work of government. They served as officers of his court; as *prévôts*, officials who oversaw the king's estates and collected his taxes; and as *baillis* (or, in some places, seneschals) who not only supervised the *prévôts* but also functioned as judges, presiding over courts that met monthly, making the king's power felt locally as never before.

Of Empires and City-States

The empire ruled by the German king was an oddity. Elsewhere, smaller states were the norm. But the German king's empire spanned both Germany and Italy. In its embrace of peoples of contrasting traditions, it was more like Hungary than like England and France. The location of the papacy made the empire different as well. Every other state was a safe distance away from the pope; but the empire had the pope in its throat. Tradition, prestige, and political self-respect demanded that the German king be emperor: Conrad III (r.1138-1152), though never actually crowned at Rome, nevertheless delighted in calling himself "August Emperor of the Romans" (while demeaning the Byzantine emperor as "King of the Greeks"!). But being emperor meant controlling Italy and Rome. The difficulty was not only the papacy, defiantly opposed to another major power in Italy, but also the northern Italian communes, independent city-states in their own right.

THE REVIVAL AND DETERIORATION OF THE EMPIRE

Like Henry II of England, Frederick I Barbarossa (r.1152-1190), who ushered in the Staufen dynasty of Germany, came to the throne after a long period of bitter civil war. (See Genealogy 6.2: Rulers of Germany and Sicily.) Like Henry, he held a kingdom and more. But he lacked Henry's wealth. As a result he was forced to rely on personal loyalties, not salaried civil servants. He could not tear down princely castles as Henry had done. Instead, he conceded the German princes their powers, requiring them in turn to recognize him as the source of those powers, and committing them to certain obligations, such as attending him at court and providing him with troops.

But a German king had to deal with more than the princes; he had to confront the papacy. In 1157, at the Diet of Besançon, Adrian IV sent Frederick a letter that coyly referred to the imperial crown as the pope's *beneficium* — "benefit" or, more ominously, "fief." In the wake of this incident, Frederick countered the "holy church" by coin-

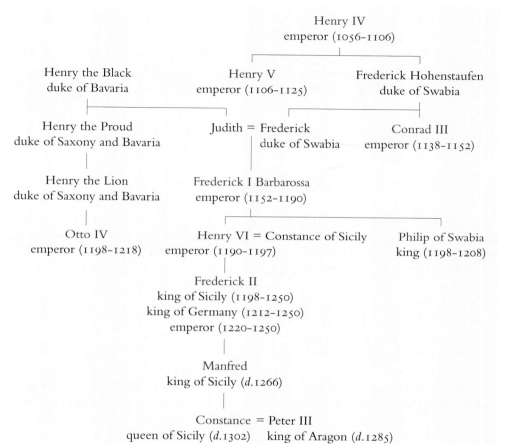

Henry IV
emperor (1056-1106)

Henry the Black
duke of Bavaria

Henry V
emperor (1106-1125)

Frederick Hohenstaufen
duke of Swabia

Henry the Proud
duke of Saxony and Bavaria

Judith = Frederick
duke of Swabia

Conrad III
emperor (1138-1152)

Henry the Lion
duke of Saxony and Bavaria

Frederick I Barbarossa
emperor (1152-1190)

Otto IV
emperor (1198-1218)

Henry VI = Constance of Sicily
emperor (1190-1197)

Philip of Swabia
king (1198-1208)

Frederick II
king of Sicily (1198-1250)
king of Germany (1212-1250)
emperor (1220-1250)

Manfred
king of Sicily (d.1266)

Constance = Peter III
queen of Sicily (d.1302)   king of Aragon (d.1285)

ing an equally charged term for his empire: *sacrum imperium*—the "sacred empire." In 1165 he exhumed the body of Charlemagne, enclosing the dead emperor's arm in an ornate reliquary casket (Plate 6.1) and setting the wheels of canonization in motion. (Charlemagne was named a saint by Frederick's anti-pope, Pascal III. See the list of Popes and Antipopes to 1500 on p.335 to see the many competing popes of Barbarossa's reign.)

Finally, a German king had to deal with Italy. As emperor, Frederick had claims on all of Italy. He had no hope, or even interest, in gaining the south. But, to his own inheritance in Swabia (in southwestern Germany) he needed to add northern Italy if he was to command a power base with the revenues that he needed. (See Map 6.3.)

Taking northern Italy was, however, nothing like, say, conquering Normandy, which was used to ducal rule. The communes of Italy were themselves states (autonomous cities, yes, but each also with a good deal of surrounding land, the *contado*), jealous of their liberties, rivalrous, and fiercely patriotic. Frederick made no concessions to their sensibilities. Emboldened by theories of sovereignty that had been elaborated by the revival of Roman law, he marched into Italy and, at the Diet of Roncaglia (1158), demanded all

> dukedoms, marches, counties, consulates, mints, market tolls, forage taxes, wagon tolls, gate tolls, transit tolls, mills, fisheries, bridges, all the use accruing from running water, and the payment of an annual tax, not only on the land, but also on their own persons.[5]

Meanwhile, he brought the Four Doctors (see p.192) from Bologna to Roncaglia to hear court cases. He insisted that the cities he conquered be governed by his own men, sending in *podestà* (city managers), often German-speaking and heavy handed. No sooner had the *podestà* at Milan taken up his post, for example, than he immediately ordered an inventory of all taxes due the emperor and levied new and demeaning labor duties. He even demanded that the Milanese carry the wood and stones of their plundered city to Pavia, to build new houses there. This was a double humiliation: Milan had been at war with Pavia.

By 1167, most of the cities of northern Italy had joined with Pope Alexander III (1159–1181) to form the Lombard League against Frederick. Defeated at the battle of Legnano in 1176, Frederick made peace with Alexander and withdrew most of his forces from the region. But his failure in the north led him to try a southern strategy. By marrying his son Henry VI (r.1190–1197) to Constance, heiress of the Kingdom of Sicily, Barbarossa linked the fate of his dynasty to a well-organized monarchy that commanded dazzling wealth.

The Sicilian kingdom had been created by Normans. Originally called into southern Italy as mercenaries of Lombards battling the Byzantines, the Normans, led by two brothers, Robert Guiscard (meaning "the wily one") and Roger, carved out a state bit by bit in the course of the 1070s. Guiscard founded a duchy in Apulia and held it as vassal of the pope. Roger conquered Sicily and held it from his brother. Under Roger's son, Roger II, the two parts came together and, in 1130, he was proclaimed "king."

In theory, Roger's kingdom was held as a fief from the pope. Yet it was both multi-lingual and multi-religious, with Jews, Muslims, Greeks, and Italians. Indeed, the Normans saw themselves as heirs to the Byzantines and Muslims, and from time to time they vainly attempted to conquer Byzantium and North Africa. They were more successful in taking over the Byzantine and Islamic administrative apparatuses already in place in their own kingdom. In the early twelfth century, Norman Sicily had a highly centralized government, with royal justices sent in circuit and salaried civil servants drawn from the level of knights and townsmen.

Henry's and Constance's son Frederick II (1194-1250) tried to unite Sicily, Italy, and Germany into an imperial unit, but he failed. The popes, eager to carve out their own well-ordered state in the center of Italy, could not allow a strong monarch to encircle them. Declaring war on Frederick, the papacy not only excommunicated him several times but also (in 1248) declared him a heretic and proclaimed a crusade against him. These were fearsome actions. The king of France urged negotiation and reconciliation, but others saw in Frederick the devil himself. In the words of one chronicler, Frederick was "an evil and accursed man, a schismatic, an heretic, and an epicurean, who 'defiled the whole earth' (Jer.51:25)" because he sowed the seeds of division and discord in the cities of Italy.[6]

This was one potent view. There were others, more admiring. Frederick was a poet, a patron of the arts, and the founder of the first state-supported university, which he built at Naples. His administrative reforms in Sicily were comparable to Henry II's in England: he took what he found and made it routine. In the *Constitutions of Melfi* (1231) he made sure that his salaried officials worked according to uniform procedures, required nearly all litigation to be heard by royal courts, regularized commercial privileges, and set up a system of royal taxation. In 1232 he began minting gold coins, a turning point in European currency.

The struggle with the papacy obliged Frederick to grant enormous concessions to the German princes to give himself a free hand. In effect, he allowed the princes to turn their territories into independent states. Until the nineteenth century, Germany was a mosaic, not of city-states like Italy but of principalities. Between 1254 and 1273 the princes, split into factions, kept the German throne empty by electing two different foreigners who spent their time fighting each other. Oddly enough, it was during this low point of the German monarchy that the term "Holy Roman empire" was coined. In 1273, the princes at last united and elected a German, Rudolf (*r.*1273-1291), whose family, the Habsburgs, was new to imperial power. Rudolf used the imperial title to help him gain Austria for his family. But he did not try to assert his power in Italy. For the first time, the word "emperor" was freed from its association with Rome.

The Kingdom of Sicily was similarly parceled out. The papacy tried to ensure that the Staufen dynasty would never again rule by calling upon Charles of Anjou, brother of the king of France, to take it over in 1263. Undeterred, Frederick's granddaughter, Constance, married to the King of Aragon (Spain), took the proud title "Queen of Sicily." In 1282, the Sicilian communes revolted against the Angevins in the uprising known as the "Sicilian Vespers," begging the Aragonese for aid. Bitter war ensued, ending only in 1302, when the Kingdom of Sicily was split: the island became a Spanish outpost, while its mainland portion (southern Italy) came under Angevin control.

A HUNGARIAN MINI-EMPIRE

Just across the Adriatic Sea from Angevin Italy, the Kingdom of Hungary was reaping the fruits of a period of expansion. In the eleventh century, having solidified their hold along the Danube river (the center of their power), the kings of Hungary moved north and east. In an arc ending at the Carpathian Mountains, they established control over a multi-ethnic population of Germans and Slavs. In the course of the twelfth century, the Hungarian kings turned southward, taking over Croatia and fighting for control over the coastline with the powerful Republic of Venice. They might have dominated the whole eastern Adriatic had not the Kingdom of Serbia re-established itself west of its original site, eager for its own share of seaborne commerce.

THE TRIUMPH OF THE CITY-STATES

That Venice was strong enough to rival Hungary over the eastern Adriatic was in part due to the confrontations between popes and emperors in Italy, which weakened both sides. The winners of those bitter wars were not the papacy, not the Angevins, not even the Aragonese, and certainly not the emperors. The winners were the Italian city-states. Republics in the sense that a high percentage of their adult male population participated in their government, they were also highly controlling. For example, to feed themselves, the communes prohibited the export of grain while commanding the peasants in the *contado* to bring a certain amount of grain to the cities by a certain date each year. City governments told the peasants which crops to grow and how many times per year they should plow the land. The state controlled commerce as well. At Venice, exceptional in lacking a *contado* but controlling a vast maritime empire instead, merchant enterprises were state run, using state ships. When Venetians went off to buy cotton in the Levant, they all had to offer the same price, determined by their government back home.

Italian city-state governments outdid England, Sicily, and France in their bureaucracy and efficiency. While other governments were still taxing by "hearths," the communes devised taxes based on a census (*catasto*) of property. Already at Pisa in 1162 taxes were being raised in this way; by the middle of the thirteenth century, almost all the communes had such a system in place. But even efficient methods of taxation did not bring in enough money to support the two main needs of the commune: paying their officials and, above all, waging war. To meet their high military expenses, the communes created state loans, some voluntary, others forced. They were the first in Europe to do so.

CULTURE AND INSTITUTIONS IN TOWN AND COUNTRYSIDE

Organization and accounting were the concerns of lords outside of Italy as well. But no one adopted the persona of the business tycoon; the prevailing ideal was the chivalrous knight. Courts were aristocratic centers, organized not only to enhance but also to highlight the power of lord and lady. Meanwhile, in the cities, guilds constituted a different kind of enclave, shutting out some laborers and women but giving high status to masters. Universities too were a sort of guild. Artistic creativity, urban pride, and episcopal power were together embodied in Gothic cathedrals.

Inventorying the Countryside

Not only kings and communes but great lords everywhere hired literate agents to administer their estates, calculate their profits, draw up accounts, and make marketing decisions. Money financed luxuries, to be sure, but even more importantly it enhanced aristocratic honor, so dependent on personal generosity, patronage, and displays of wealth. In the late twelfth century, when some townsmen could boast fortunes that rivaled the riches of the landed nobility, noble extravagance tended to exceed income. Most aristocrats went into debt.

The nobles' need for money coincided with the interests of the peasantry, whose numbers (and mouths to feed) were expanding. The solution was the extension of farmland. By the middle of the century, isolated and sporadic attempts to bring new land into cultivation had become regular and coordinated. Great lords offered special privileges to peasants who would do the backbreaking work of plowing marginal land. In 1154, for example, the bishop of Meissen (in Germany) proclaimed a new village and called for peasants from Flanders to settle in it. Experts in drainage, the new settlers received rights to the swampland they reclaimed. They owed only light monetary obligations to the bishop, who nevertheless expected to reap a profit from their tolls and tithes. Similar encouragement came from lords throughout Europe, especially in northern Italy, England, Flanders, and Germany. In Flanders, where land was regularly inundated by seawater, the great monasteries sponsored drainage projects, and canals linking the cities to the agricultural regions let boats ply the waters to virtually every nook and cranny of the region.

Sometimes free peasants acted on their own to clear land and relieve the pressure of overpopulation, as when the small freeholders in England's Fenland region cooperated to build banks and dikes to reclaim the land that led out to the North Sea. Villages were founded on the drained land, and villagers shared responsibility for repairing and maintaining the dikes even as each peasant family farmed its new holding individually.

On old estates, the rise in population strained to its breaking point the manse organization that had developed in Carolingian Europe, where each household was settled on the land that supported it. Now, in the twelfth century, many peasant families might live on what had been, in the ninth century, the manse of one family. Labor services and dues had to be recalculated, and peasants and their lords often turned services and dues into money rents, payable once a year. With this change, peasant men gained more control over their plots — they could sell them, will them to their sons, or even designate a small portion for their daughters. However, for these privileges they had either to pay extra taxes or, like communes, join together to buy their collective liberty for a high price, paid out over many years to their lord. Peasants, like town citizens, gained a new sense of identity and solidarity as they bargained with a lord keen to increase his income at their expense.

The Culture of the Courts

When Henry II and his wife Eleanor came to Aquitaine, they were never alone. Accompanying them were relatives, vassals, officials, priests, knights, probably a doctor or two, and certainly troubadours. These were poets, musicians, and entertainers all in one. They sang love poems in Occitan, the vernacular of southern France. Eleanor's grandfather, Duke William IX of Aquitaine (1071-1126), is counted the first of the troubadours. But there were certainly people singing his kind of poetry in both Arabic and Hebrew in al-Andalus, which, as we have seen, was just at this time first coming into contact (mainly violent, to be sure) with armies from the north. By Eleanor's day, there were many troubadours, welcomed at major courts as essential personnel. Bernart de Ventadorn (*fl.*1150-1180) was among them. Here is one of his verses:

> Ai Deus! car no sui ironda,
> que voles per l'aire
> e vengues de noih prionda
> lai dins so repaire?

> Ah, God! couldn't I be a swallow
> and fly through the air
> and come in the depths of the night
> into her dwelling there.[7]

The rhyme scheme *seems* simple: *ironda* goes with *prionda*, *aire* with *repaire*. But consider that the verse before it (not printed here) has the *-onda* rhyme in the second and fourth lines (rather than the first and third), while the verse after it has *-aire* in the first and third lines (rather than the second and fourth). In fact the scheme is extremely complex and subtle, an essential skill for a poet whose goal was to dazzle his audience with brilliant originality.

In rhyme and meter, troubadour songs resembled Latin liturgical chants of the same region and period. Clearly, lay and religious cultures overlapped. They overlapped in musical terms as well, in the use, for example, of plucking and percussive instruments. Above all, they overlapped in themes: they spoke of love. The monks (we have already seen an example with Saint Bernard) thought about the worshiper's love for God; the troubadours thought about erotic love. Yet the two were deliciously entangled. The verse in which Bernart wishes he could be a swallow continues:

> I fear the heart will melt within me
> if this lasts a little longer.
> Lady, for your love
> I join my hands and worship.
> Beautiful body of the colors of youth,
> what suffering you make me bear.[8]

This is playing with religious imagery. Bernart is ready to pray; he is thinking of a youthful body; he is suffering: he could be a worshiper identifying with Christ on the Cross. At the same time, he subverts the religious: he is thinking of his mistress as (he says) he tosses and turns "on the edge of the bed."[9]

Female troubadours flirted with the same themes. La Comtessa de Dia (*fl.c.*1200?) sang

> I am so aggrieved by the one to whom I am the friend,
> for I love him more than anything that can be.
> Pity does not help me toward him, nor courtliness [*cortezia*],
> nor my beauty, nor my good name, nor my wit.[10]

Here as elsewhere, the key to the lover's worth is *cortezia*, "courtliness" or "courtesy"—the refinement of a person who lives at court and who strives to achieve an ideal of beauty, virtue, and wit.

Historians and literary critics used to use the term "courtly love" to emphasize one of the themes of this literature: the poet expresses overwhelming love for a beautiful married noblewoman who is far above him and utterly unattainable. But this was only one of the many aspects of love that the troubadours sang about: some boasted of sexual conquests; others played with the notion of equality between lovers; still others preached that love was the source of virtue. The real theme of these poems was not courtly love; it was the power of women. No wonder Eleanor of Aquitaine and other aristocratic women patronized the troubadours: they enjoyed the image that it gave them of themselves. Nor was this image a delusion. There were many powerful female lords in southern France. They owned property, had vassals, led battles, decided disputes, and entered into and broke political alliances as their advantage dictated. Both men and women appreciated troubadour poetry, which recognized and praised women's power even as it eroticized it.

From southern France the lyric love song spread to Italy, northern France, England, and Germany. Here Occitan was a foreign language, so other vernaculars were used: the *minnesingers* (literally, "love singers") sang in German; the *trouvères* sang in the Old French of northern France.

Some troubadours wrote about war, not love. But warfare was more truly the subject of another genre of poems, lengthy *chansons de geste*, "songs of heroic deeds." Following a long oral tradition, these vernacular poems appeared at about the same time as love songs. Like troubadour poems, the *chansons de geste* played with aristocratic codes of behavior, in this case on the battlefield.

They were responding to social and military transformations. By the end of the twelfth century, nobles and knights had begun to merge into one class, threatened from below by newly rich merchants and from above by newly powerful kings. At the same time, the knights' ascendancy on the battlefield, where they unhorsed one another with lances and long swords and took prisoners rather than killing their opponents, was waning in the face of mercenary infantrymen who wielded long hooks and knives that ripped easily through chain mail. A knightly ethos and sense of group solidarity emerged within this changed landscape.

Thus the protagonists of heroic poems yearned not for love but for battle:

The armies are in sight of one another. They go forward cautiously and reconnoiter as they go. The cowards tremble as they march, but the brave hearts rejoice for the battle.[11]

Examining the moral issues that made war both tragic and inevitable, poets played on the often contradictory values of their society, such as the conflicting loyalties of friendship and vassalage or a vassal's right to a fief versus a son's right to his father's land.

These poems, later called "epics," focused on battle; other long poems, later called "romances," explored relationships between men and women. Enormously popular in the late twelfth and early thirteenth century, romances took up such themes as the tragic love between Tristan and Isolde and the virtuous knight's search for the Holy Grail. Above all, romances were woven around the many fictional stories of King Arthur and his court. In one of the earliest, Chrétien de Troyes (c.1150-1190) wrote about the noble and valiant Lancelot, in love with Queen Guinevere, wife of Arthur. Coming across a comb bearing some strands of her radiant hair, Lancelot is overcome:

> Never will the eye of man see anything receive such honour as when he begins to adore these tresses. A hundred thousand times he raises them to his eyes and mouth, to his forehead and face… Even for Saint Martin and Saint James he has no need.[12]

By making Guinevere's hair an object of adoration, a sort of secular relic, Chrétien here not only conveys the depths of Lancelot's feeling but also pokes a bit of fun at his hero. When Guinevere tests Lancelot in the middle of a tournament by sending him a message to do his "worst," the poet evokes a similar mix of humor and loftiness:

> When he heard this, he replied: "Very willingly," like one who is altogether hers. Then he rides at another knight as hard as his horse can carry him, and misses his thrust which should have struck him. From that time till evening he continued to do as badly as possible in accordance with the Queen's desire.[13]

It is an odd, funny, and pitiful episode: the greatest of all knights bested at the whim of a lady. Yet this is part of the premise of "chivalry." The word, deriving from the French *cheval* ("horse"), emphasizes above all that the knight was a horseman, a warrior of the most prestigious sort. Perched high in the saddle, his heavy lance couched in his right arm, the knight was an imposing and menacing figure. Chivalry made him gentle, gave his battles a higher meaning, whether for love of a lady or of God. The chivalric hero was constrained by courtesy, fair play, piety, and devotion to an ideal. Did real knights live up to these ideals? They knew perfectly well that they could not and that it would be absurd if they tried to do so in every particular. But they loved playing with the idea. They were the poets' audience, and they liked to think of themselves as fitting into the tales. When William the Marshal, advisor of English kings, died, his biographer wrote of him as a model knight, courteous with the ladies, brave on the battlefield.

Urban Guilds Incorporated

Courtly "codes" were poetic and playful. City codes were drier but no less compelling. In the early thirteenth century, guilds drew up statutes to determine dues, regulate working hours, fix wages, and set standards for materials and products. Sometimes they came into conflict with town government; this happened to some bread-bakers' guilds in Italy, where communes considered bread too important a commodity to be left to its producers. At other times, the communes supported guild efforts to control wages, reinforcing guild regulations with statutes of their own. When great lords rather than communes governed a city, they too tried to control and protect the guilds. King Henry II of England, for example, eagerly gave some guilds in his Norman duchy special privileges so that they would depend on him.

There was nothing democratic about guilds. In the cloth-making business, the merchant guild that imported the raw wool was generally the overseer of the other guilds—the shearers, weavers, fullers (the workers who beat the cloth to shrink it and make it heavier), and dyers. In Florence, professional guilds of notaries and judges ranked in prestige and power above craft guilds. Within each guild was another kind of hierarchy. Apprentices were at the bottom, journeymen and -women in the middle, and masters at the top. Young boys and occasionally girls were the apprentices; they worked for a master for room and board, learning a trade. An apprenticeship in the felt-hat trade in Paris, for example, lasted seven years. After their apprenticeship, men and women often worked many years as day laborers, hired by a master when he needed extra help. Some men, but almost never women, worked their way up to master status. They were the ones who dominated the offices and set guild policies.

Codification of guild practices and membership worked against women, who were slowly being ousted from the world of workers during the late twelfth century. In Flanders, for example, as the manufacture of woolen cloth shifted from rural areas to cities, and from light to heavy looms, women were more rarely involved in cloth production than they had been on traditional manors. Similarly, water- and animal-powered mills took the place of female hand labor grinding grain into flour—and most millers were male. Some women were artisans and traders, and their names occasionally appeared in guild memberships. But they did not become guild officers, and they played no official role in town government. Women of the late twelfth century certainly worked, but they were increasingly dominated by men. Bernarda Cordonaria ("Shoemaker") was not the only woman in Toulouse at the beginning of the thirteenth century who took her last name not from her own trade but from her husband's craft.

Universities were another example of all-male guilds. The word *universitas* is in fact the Latin for "guild." Beginning as organizations of masters and students, the term eventually came to apply to the school itself. At the beginning of the thirteenth century, the universities regulated student discipline, scholastic proficiency, and housing while determining the masters' behavior in equal detail. At the University of Paris, for example, the masters were required to wear long black gowns, follow a particular order in their lectures, and set the standards by which students could become masters themselves. The University of Bologna was unique in having two guilds, one of students and one of masters. At Bologna, the students participated in the appointment, payment, and discipline of the masters.

The University of Bologna was unusual because it was principally a school of law, where the students were often older men, well along in their careers (often in imperial service) and used to wielding power. At the University of Paris, young students predominated, drawn by its renown in the liberal arts and theology. The universities of Salerno (near Naples) and Montpellier (in southern France) specialized in medicine. Oxford, once a sleepy town where students clustered around one or two masters, became a center of royal administration; its university soon developed a reputation for teaching the liberal arts, theology, science, and mathematics.

The curriculum of each university depended on its speciality and its traditions. At Paris in the early thirteenth century students spent at least six years studying the liberal arts before gaining the right to teach. If they wanted to continue their studies with theology, they attended lectures on the subject for at least another five years. With books both expensive and hard to find, lectures were the chief method of communication. These were centered on important texts: the master read an excerpt aloud, delivered his commentary on it, and disputed any contrary commentaries that rival masters might have proposed. Students committed the lectures to memory.

Within the larger association of the university, students found more intimate groups with which to live: "nations," linked to the students' place of origin. At Bologna, for example, students incorporated themselves into two nations, the Italians and the non-Italians. Each nation protected its members, wrote statutes, and elected officers.

Masters and students both were considered part of another group: the clerics. This was an outgrowth of the original purposes of the schools, and it had two important consequences. First, there were no university women. And second, university men were subject to church courts rather than the secular jurisdiction of towns or lords. Many universities could also boast generous privileges from popes and kings, who valued the services of scholars. The combination of clerical status and special privileges made universities virtually self-governing corporations within the towns. This sometimes led to friction. When the townsmen of Oxford tried to punish a student suspected of killing his mistress, the masters protested by refusing to teach and leaving the city. Such disputes are called "town against gown" struggles because students and masters wore gowns (imitated by graduation gowns today). But since university towns depended on scholars to patronize local taverns, shops, and hostels, town and gown normally learned to negotiate with one another to their mutual advantage.

Gothic Style

Certainly town and gown agreed on building style: by *c.*1200, "Gothic" (the term itself comes from the sixteenth century) was the architecture of choice. Beginning as a variant of Romanesque in the Ile-de-France, Gothic style quickly took on an identity of its own. Gothic architects tried to eliminate heavy walls by enlivening them with sculpture or piercing them with glass, creating a soaring feel by using pointed arches. Suger, abbot of Saint-Denis and the promoter of royal power (see p.188), was the style's first sponsor. When he rebuilt portions of his church around 1135, he tried to meld royal and ecclesiastical interests and ideals in stone and glass. At the west end of his church, the point where the faithful entered, Suger decorated the portals with figures of Old Testament kings, queens, and patriarchs, signaling the links between the present king and his illustrious predecessors. Rebuilding the interior of the east end of his church as well, Suger used pointed arches and stained glass to let in light, which Suger believed to be God's own "illumination," capable of transporting the worshiper from the "slime of earth" to the "purity of Heaven."

Gothic was an urban architecture, reflecting — in its grand size, jewel-like windows, and bright ornaments — the aspirations, pride, and confidence of rich and powerful merchants, artisans, and bishops. The Gothic cathedral, which could take centuries to complete, was often the religious, social, and commercial focal point of a city. Funds for these buildings might come from the bishop himself, from the canons (priests) who served his cathedral, or from townsmen. Notre Dame of Paris (Plate 6.2) was begun in 1163 by Bishop Maurice de Sully, whose episcopal income from estates, forests, taxes, and Parisian properties gave him plenty of money to finance the tallest church of its day. Under his successors, the edifice took shape with three stories, the upper one filled with stained glass. Bristling on the outside with flying buttresses — the characteristic "look" of a French Gothic church — it gave no hint of the light and calm within. (See Plate 6.3.) But at Mantes-la-Jolie (about 25 miles west of Paris), it was the merchant guild and the Capetian king together — rather than a bishop — who sponsored the building of the new collegiate church.

However financed, Gothic cathedrals were community projects, enlisting the labor and support of a small army of quarrymen, builders, carpenters, and glass cutters. Houses of relics, they attracted pilgrims as well. At Chartres cathedral, proud home of the Virgin's tunic, crowds thronged the streets, the poor buying small lead figures of the Virgin, the rich purchasing wearable replicas of her tunic.

The technologies that made Gothic churches possible were all known before the twelfth century. The key elements included ribbed vaulting, which could give a sense of precision and order (as at Bourges in France: see Plate 6.4) or of richness and playful inventiveness (as at Lincoln cathedral in England: see Plate 6.5). Flying buttresses took the weight of the vault off the walls, allowing most of the wall to be cut away and the open spaces filled by glass. (See Figure 6.1.) Pointed arches made the church appear to surge heavenward.

By the mid-thirteenth century, Gothic architecture had spread to most of Europe. Yet the style varied by region, most dramatically in Italy. Sant'Andrea in Vercelli is what *Italian* architects meant by a Gothic church. It has a ribbed vault and pointed arches. (See Plate 6.6.) But with only two stories, the second one pierced by very small windows, its focus is not on light and height but on walls and columns. With flying buttresses rare and portal sculpture unobtrusive, Italian Gothic churches convey a spirit of spare and quiet beauty.

Gothic art, both painting and sculpture, echoed and decorated the Gothic cathedral. While Romanesque sculpture played upon a flat surface, Gothic figures were liberated from their background, turning, bending, interacting. At Reims cathedral the figure of Saint Joseph on the west portal, elegant and graceful, reveals a gentle smile. (See Plate 6.7.) Behind him is carved foliage of striking naturalness. Portals like this were meant to be "read" for their meaning. Joseph is not smiling for nothing; in the original arrangement of the portal he was looking at the figure of a servant while, further to his left, his wife, Mary, presented the baby Jesus in the temple. This was the New Testament story brought to life.

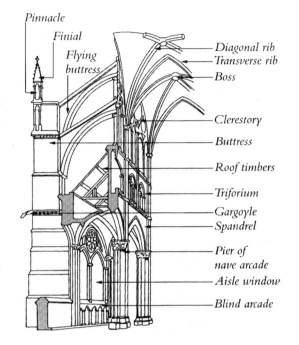

Figure 6.1: Elements of a Gothic Church. Section through the nave at Amiens. The diagram shows the most important feature of a Gothic cathedral.

Plate 6.2: Notre Dame of Paris, Exterior (begun 1163). To take the weight of the vault off the walls and open them to glass and light, the architects of Gothic churches such as Notre Dame used flying buttresses, which sprang from the top of the exterior wall. In this photograph you can see them best over the tops of the trees partly obscuring the apse (here the right side) of the cathedral.

Following Pages:

Plate 6.3: Notre Dame of Paris, Interior (begun 1163). Compare this interior with that of Santiago in **Plate 5.9** (p.201). Santiago is a typical Romanesque church, with a barrel vault, two stories, and little natural light. By contrast, at the Gothic cathedral of Notre Dame (shown here) there is an arched vault, three stories, and light (from the top-most story) suffusing the entire nave.

Plate 6.4: Bourges Cathedral, Interior (begun *c.*1195). The bays of the vault of Bourges cathedral, like that of other Gothic churches, is sectioned and marked off by ribs, visually unifying the church from top to bottom. The exceptionally tall, slender piers of its nave help make this particular cathedral appear to soar.

Plate 6.3

Plate 6.4

Plate 6.5 (facing page): Lincoln Cathedral, Interior (begun *c.*1225). Many English Gothic cathedrals emphasized surface ornament. Here the ribs, which spring from carved moldings on the walls of the nave, are splayed into fans on the vault. Can you find other decorative elements?

Plate 6.6: Sant'Andrea, Vercelli, Interior (begun *c.*1219). Its pointed arches and ribbed vault allow this to be classified as a "Gothic" church, but comparison with French and English Gothic church interiors (see **Plates 6.3, 6.4, and 6.5**) suggests that Italian Gothic was more conservative, emphasizing solidity and proportion, here enlivened by alternating light and dark stone.

THE CHURCH IN THE WORLD

Just as the church was taking new interest in the human dimension of Joseph and his wife, so it concerned itself as never before in the lives of ordinary Christians. Under Innocent III (1198–1216)—the first pope to be trained at the city schools and to study both theology and law—the papacy gained a newly grand sense of itself. Innocent thought of himself as ruling in the place of Christ the King; secular kings and emperors existed simply to help the pope, who was the real lawmaker—the maker of laws that would lead to moral reformation. In the thirteenth century, the church sought to define Christianity, embracing some doctrines, rejecting others, and turning against Jews and Muslims with new vigor.

The Fourth Lateran Council (1215)

A council was the traditional method of declaring church law, and this is what Innocent intended when he convened one at his Lateran Palace at Rome in 1215. Presided over by the pope himself, the Fourth Lateran Council produced a comprehensive set of canons—most of them prepared by the pope's committees beforehand—to reform both clergy and laity. In effect it produced a code, in this case one for Christian society as a whole.

For laymen and -women perhaps the most important canons concerned the sacraments. The Fourth Lateran required Christians to attend Mass and to confess their sins to a priest at least once a year. Marriage was declared a sacrament, and bishops were assigned jurisdiction over marital disputes. Forbidding secret marriages, the council expected priests to uncover evidence that might impede a marriage. There were many impediments: people were not allowed to marry their cousins nor anyone related to them by godparentage nor anyone related to them through a former marriage. Children conceived within clandestine or forbidden marriages were to be considered illegitimate; they could not inherit property from their parents, nor could they become priests.

Like the code of chivalry, the rules of the Fourth Lateran about marriage worked better on parchment than in life. Well-to-do London fathers included their bastard children in their wills. On English manors, sons conceived out of wedlock regularly took over their parents' land. The prohibition against secret marriages was only partially successful. Even churchmen had to admit that the consent of both parties made a marriage valid.

The most important sacrament was the Mass, the ritual in which the bread and wine of the Eucharist was transformed into the flesh and blood of Christ. In the

Plate 6.7 (facing page): Saint Joseph, West Portal, Reims Cathedral (c.1240). Compare Saint Joseph on this Gothic portal with Judas on the Romanesque capital of Autun (**Plate 5.5**, p.196). Forgetting, for the moment, the differences in subject matter, note the change in style: the Judas carving is framed by the shape of the capital; Joseph is free of any frame and is carved fully in the round.

twelfth century a newly rigorous explanation of this transformation was promulgated according to which Christ's body and blood were truly present in the bread and wine on the altar. The Fourth Lateran Council not only declared this to be dogma but also explained it by using a technical term coined by twelfth-century scholars. The bread and wine were "transubstantiated": though the Eucharist continued to *look* like bread and wine, after the consecration during the Mass the bread became the actual flesh and the wine the real blood of Christ. The council's emphasis on this potent event strengthened the role of the priest, for only he could celebrate this mystery (the transformation of ordinary bread and wine into the flesh of Christ) through which God's grace was transmitted to the faithful.

The Ins and the Outs

As the Fourth Lateran provided rules for good Christians, it turned against all others. Some canons singled out Jews and heretics for special punitive treatment; others were directed against Byzantines and Muslims. These laws were of a piece with wider movements. With the development of a papal monarchy that confidently declared a single doctrine, discipline, and dogma, all dissidence was perceived as heresy, all non-Christians seen as treacherous.

New Groups Within the Fold

The Fourth Lateran prohibited the formation of new monastic orders. It recognized that the trickle of new religious groups — the Carthusians is one example — of the early twelfth century had become a torrent by 1215. Only a very few of the more recent movements were accepted into the church, among them the Franciscans, the Beguines, and the Dominicans.

Saint Francis (c.1182–1226) had begun a promising career as a cloth merchant at Assisi when he experienced a complete conversion. Clinging to poverty as if, in his words, "she" were his "lady" (thus borrowing the vocabulary of chivalry), he accepted no money, walked without shoes, wore only one coarse tunic, and refused to be confined even in a monastery. He and his followers (called "friars," from the Latin term for "brothers") spent their time preaching, ministering to lepers, and doing manual labor. In time they dispersed, setting up fraternal groups throughout Italy, France, Spain, the crusader states, and later Germany, England, Scotland, Poland, and elsewhere. Always they were drawn to the cities. Sleeping in "convents" on the outskirts of the towns, the Franciscans became a regular part of urban community life as they preached to crowds and begged their daily bread. Early converts included women; in 1212 Clare, a young noblewoman, formed the Order of the Sisters of Saint Francis.

At first the women worked alongside the friars, but the church disapproved of their worldly activities, and soon the sisters were confined to cloisters under the *Rule* of Saint Benedict. In the course of the thirteenth century a third order, the "Tertiaries," was formed of laypeople, many of them married. They dedicated themselves to works of charity and to daily church attendance.

The Beguines were still more integral to town life. In the cities of northern France, the Low Countries, and Germany, these women plied the trades of launderers, weavers, and spinners. (Their male counterparts, the "Beghards," were far less numerous). Choosing to live together in informal communities, taking no vows, free to marry if they wished, they dedicated themselves to simplicity and piety. If outwardly ordinary, however, inwardly their religious lives were often emotional and ecstatic, infused with the imagery of love. Mary of Oignies (1177-1213), for example, felt herself to be a pious mother entrusted with the Christ-child, who "nestled between her breasts like a baby. Sometimes she kissed him as though He were a little child and sometimes she held Him on her lap as if He were a gentle lamb."[14]

Saint Dominic (1170-1221), founder of the Dominican order, was more hardheaded. Reckoning that most preachers failed to counter the sway of heretics in southern France because they came richly clad, on horseback, and followed by a retinue, he and his followers rejected material riches and instead went about on foot, preaching and begging. They soon came to resemble the Franciscans, both organizationally and spiritually; they too were called friars.

Defining the Other

The heretics that Dominic confronted were the Albigensians, one of a number of dualist groups that sprang up in the twelfth century in Italy, the Rhineland, and Languedoc (southern France). Calling themselves Christ's Poor, they preached a world torn between two great forces, one good and the other evil. As the material world was the creation of the devil, they renounced it, rejecting wealth, sex, and meat, and denying the efficacy of the sacraments. Attracting both men and women, these "friends of God" (as they put it) saw themselves as followers of Christ's original message. But the church called them heretics.

The church condemned other, non-dualist movements as heretical not on doctrinal grounds but because these groups allowed their lay members to preach, assuming for themselves the privilege of bishops. At Lyon (in southeastern France) in the 1170s, for example, a rich merchant named Waldo decided to take literally the Gospel message, "If you wish to be perfect, then go and sell everything you have, and give to the poor" (Matt. 19:21). The same message had inspired countless monks and would worry the church far less several decades later, when Saint Francis established his new order. But when Waldo went into the street and gave away his belongings, announcing, "I am not really insane, as you think," he scandalized not only the bystanders but the church as well.[15] Refusing to retire to a monastery, Waldo and his followers, men and women called Waldensians, lived in poverty and went about preaching, quoting the Gospel in the vernacular so that everyone would understand. But the papacy rejected Waldo's bid to preach freely; and the Waldensians—denounced, excommunicated, and expelled from Lyon—wandered to Languedoc, Italy, northern Spain, and the Moselle valley, just east of France.

EUROPEAN AGGRESSION WITHIN AND WITHOUT

Jews, heretics, Muslims, Greeks, and pagans: all felt the heavy hand of Christian Europeans newly organized, powerful, and self-righteous. Meanwhile, even the undeniable Catholicism of Ireland did not prevent its takeover by England.

The Jews

Prohibited from joining guilds, Jews increasingly were forced to take the one job Christians could not have: lending on credit. Even with Christian moneylenders available (for some existed despite official prohibitions), lords borrowed from Jews. Then, relying on dormant anti-Jewish feeling, they sometimes "righteously" attacked their creditors. This happened in 1190 at York, for example, where local nobles orchestrated a brutal attack on the Jews of the city to rid themselves of their debts and the men to whom they owed money. Kings claimed the Jews as their serfs and Jewish property as their own. In England a special royal exchequer of the Jews was created in 1194 to collect unpaid debts due after the death of Jewish creditors. In France, Philip Augustus expelled the Jews from the Ile-de-France in 1182, confiscating their houses, fields, and vineyards for himself. He allowed them to return—minus their property—in 1198.

Attacks against Jews were inspired by more than resentment against Jewish money or desire for power and control. They grew out of the codification of Christian religious doctrine. The newly rigorous definition of the Eucharist as the true body and blood of Christ meant to some that Christ, wounded and bleeding, lay upon the altar. Miracle tales sometimes reported that the Eucharist bled. Reflecting Christian anxieties about real flesh upon the altar, sensational stories, originating in clerical circles but soon widely circulated, told of Jews who secretly sacrificed Christian children in a morbid revisiting of the crucifixion of Jesus. This charge, called "blood libel" by historians, led to massacres of Jews in cities in England, France, Spain, and Germany.

Jews had no rituals involving blood sacrifice at all, but they were convenient and vulnerable scapegoats for Christian guilt and anxiety about eating Christ's flesh.

After the Fourth Lateran Council, Jews were easy to spot as well. The council required all Jews to advertise their religion by some outward sign, some special dress. Local rulers enforced this canon with zeal, not so much because they were anxious to humiliate Jews as because they saw the chance to sell exemptions to Jews eager to escape the requirement. Nonetheless, sooner or later Jews almost everywhere had to wear a badge as a sign of their second-class status: in southern France and Spain they had to wear a round badge; in Vienna they were forced to wear pointed hats.

Crusades

Attacks against Jews coincided with newly vigorous crusades: in Spain the *reconquista* continued; in the Levant, fresh armies shored up the crusader states and, as we have seen (p.212), took Byzantium as well; along the Baltic, crusaders redrew Germany's eastern border.

Against the Albigensians in southern France, Innocent III demanded that northern princes take up the sword, invade Languedoc, wrest the land from the heretics, and populate it with orthodox Christians. This Albigensian Crusade (1209–1229) marked the first time the pope offered warriors fighting an enemy within Christian Europe all the spiritual and temporal benefits of a crusade to the Holy Land. In the event, the political ramifications were more notable than the religious results. After twenty years of fighting, leadership of the crusade was taken over in 1229 by the Capetian kings. Southern resistance was broken and Languedoc was brought under the control of the French crown. (On Map 6.2, the area taken over by the French crown corresponds more or less with the region of Toulouse.)

Meanwhile, continued military successes in Spain created the three-fold political configuration that would last for centuries: to the east was the kingdom of Aragon-Catalonia; in the middle was León-Castile, whose ruler styled himself emperor; and in the southwest was Portugal, whose ruler took the title of king. (See Map 6.1.) We have already followed the advance of the Christians from the Muslim point of view (see p.208). The army that defeated the Almohads at Las Navas de Tolosa in 1212 was led jointly by the kings of Aragon and Castile. Afterwards the king of Castile exulted:

> On their side 100,000 armed men or more fell in the battle … But of the army of the Lord … incredible though it may be, unless it be a miracle, hardly 25 or 30 Christians of our whole army fell. O what happiness! O what thanksgiving![16]

At Europe's northeastern frontier the story was similar. By the twelfth century, the peoples living along the Baltic coast—partly pagan, mostly Slavic- or Baltic-speaking—had learned to make a living and even a profit from the inhospitable soil and climate. Through fishing and trading, they supplied the rest of Europe and Russia with slaves, furs, amber, wax, and dried fish. Like the earlier Vikings, they combined commercial competition with outright raiding, so that the Danes and the Saxons (that is, the Germans in Saxony) both benefitted and suffered from their presence. It was Saint Bernard who, preaching the Second Crusade in Germany, urged one to the north as well. Thus began the Northern Crusades, which continued intermittently until the early fifteenth century.

In key raids in the 1160s and 1170s, the king of Denmark and Henry the Lion, the duke of Saxony, worked together to bring much of the region between the Elbe and Oder rivers under their control. They took some of the land outright, leaving the rest in the hands of the Baltic princes, who surrendered, converted, and became their vassals. Churchmen arrived: the Cistercians built their monasteries right up to the banks of the Vistula River, while bishops took over newly declared dioceses. In 1204 the

Map 6.4: The German Push to the East

"bishop of Riga"—in fact he had to bring his own Christians with him to his lonely outpost amidst the Livs—founded a military/monastic order called the Swordbrothers. The monks soon became a branch of the Teutonic Knights, a group originally founded in the Crusader States. They organized crusades, defended newly conquered regions, and launched their own holy wars against the "Northern Saracens."[17] By the end of the thirteenth century, they had brought the lands between Estonia and the Vistula under their sway. (See Map 6.4.) Meanwhile knights, peasants, and townsmen streamed in, colonists of the new frontier. Although less well known than the crusades to the Levant, the Northern Crusades had more lasting effects, settling the Baltic region with a German-speaking population that brought its western institutions—cities, laws, guilds, universities, castles, manors, vassalage—with it.

Colonization was the unanticipated consequence of the Fourth Crusade as well. Called by Innocent III, who intended it to re-establish the Christian presence in the Holy Land, the crusade was diverted when the organizers overestimated the numbers joining the expedition. The small army mustered was unable to pay for the large fleet of ships that had been fitted out for it by the Venetians. Making the best of adversity, the Venetians convinced the crusaders to "pay" for the ships by attacking Zara (today Zadar), one of the coastal cities that it disputed with Hungary. Then, taking up the cause of one claimant to the Byzantine throne, the crusaders turned their sights on Constantinople. We already know the political results. The religious results are more subtle. Europeans disdained the Greeks for their independence from the pope; on the other hand, they considered Constantinople a treasure trove of the most precious of relics, including the True Cross. When, in the course of looting the city, one crusader, the abbot of a German Cistercian monastery, came upon a chest of relics, he "swiftly and avidly plunged in both his hands." There was a long tradition of relic theft in the West; it was considered pious, a sort of holy sacrilege. Thus, when the abbot returned to his ship to show off his booty, the crusaders shouted, "Thanks be to God."[18] In this sense Constantinople was taken so that the saints could get better homes.

Ireland

In 1169 one of the lesser Irish kings, Diarmait Mac Murchada (Dermot MacMurrough), enlisted some lords and knights from England to help him battle the stronger Irish kings. The English fighters succeeded all too well; when Diarmait died (1171), some of the English decided to stay, claiming a lordship that spanned the Irish Sea. The king of England, Henry II, reacted swiftly. Gathering an army, he invaded Ireland in 1171. The lords of the 1169 expedition recognized his overlordship almost immediately, keeping their new territories, but now redefined as fiefs from the king. Most of the native Irish kings submitted in similar manner. The whole of one kingdom, Meath, was given to one of Henry's barons.

The English came to stay, and more—they came to put their stamp on the Irish world. It became "English Ireland": England's laws were instituted; its system of counties and courts was put in place; its notions of lordship (in which the great lords parceled out some of their vast lands to lesser lords and knights) prevailed. Small wonder that Gerald of Wales (d.1223) could see nothing good in native Irish culture: "they are uncultivated," he wrote, "not only in the external appearance of their dress, but also in their flowing hair and beards. All their habits are the habits of barbarians."[19]

★   ★   ★   ★

In the fifty years before and after 1200, Europe, aggressive and determined, pushed against its borders. Whether gaining territory from the Muslims in Spain and Sicily, colonizing the Baltic region and Ireland, or creating a Latin empire at Constantinople, conquering Europeans accommodated to the natives only minimally. For the most part, they imposed their institutions and their religion, all defined, formalized, and self-confident.

Self-confidence also led lords and ladies to pay poets to celebrate their achievements and bishops and townsmen to commission architects to erect towering Gothic churches in their midst. Similar certainties lay behind guild statutes, the incorporation of universities, the development of common law, and the Fourth Lateran's written definitions of Christian behavior and belief.

An orderly society would require institutions so fearlessly constructed to be acutely conscious of both their individual and collective goals. But in the next century, while harmony was the ideal and sometimes the reality, discord was an ever-present threat.

1152–1190	Frederick Barbarossa (king of Germany and emperor)
1154–1189	King Henry II of England
1170	Murder of Thomas Becket
1171	Henry II conquers Ireland
1176	Battle of Legnano
1182	Jews expelled from the Ile-de-France
1187	Battle of Hattin
1192–1250	Frederick II
1198–1216	Pope Innocent III
1204	Fall of Constantinople to Crusaders
1204	Philip II of France takes King John of England's northern French possessions
1212	Battle of Las Navas de Tolosa
1214	Battle of Bouvines
1215	Magna Carta
1215	Fourth Lateran Council
1226	Death of St. Francis
1273	Election of Rudolf of Habsburg as Holy Roman Emperor

NOTES

1. *Michael Akominatou tou Choniatou ta sozomena*, ed. Spiro P. Lampros (Athens, 1879–80), 1:183 as quoted in Michael Angold, *The Byzantine Empire: A Political History, 1025-1204*, 2nd ed. (London, 1997), p.314.

2. Henry's father, Geoffrey of Anjou, was nicknamed Plantagenet from the genêt, the name of a shrub that he liked. Historians sometimes use the sobriquet to refer to the entire dynasty, so Henry II was the first "Plantagenet" as well as the first "Angevin" king of England.

3. *English Historical Documents*, ed. David C. Douglas, Vol 2: 1042–1189 (London, 1953), p.323.

4. Assize of Clarendon, quoted in John Hudson, *The Formation of the English Common Law: Law and Society in England from the Norman Conquest to Magna Carta* (London, 1996), p.130.

5. Otto of Freising and his continuator, Rahewin, *The Deeds of Frederick Barbarossa*, trans. Charles Christopher Mierow with the collaboration of Richard Emery (New York, 1966), p.238, slightly modified.

6. *The Chronicle of Salimbene de Adam*, ed. and trans. Joseph L. Baird, Giuseppe Baglivi and John Robert Kane, Medieval & Renaissance Texts & Studies 40 (Binghamton, 1986), p.5.

7. *Lyrics of the Troubadours and Trouvères: An Anthology and a History*, ed. and trans. Frederick Goldin (New York, 1973), pp.132–33.
8. *Lyrics of the Troubadours*, p.133.
9. *Lyrics of the Troubadours*, p.133.
10. *Lyrics of the Troubadours*, p.185, slightly modified.
11. *Raoul de Cambrai: An Old French Feudal Epic*, trans. Jessie Crosland (New York, 1966), p.74, spelling slightly modified.
12. Chrétien de Troyes, *Arthurian Romances*, trans. W.W. Comfort (New York, 1975), pp.288–89, spelling slightly modified.
13. Chrétien, p.341.
14. Jacques de Vitry, "The Life of Marie d'Oignies," trans. Margot King in Elizabeth Alvilda Petroff, *Medieval Women's Visionary Literature* (New York, 1986), p.182.
15. Quoted in Lester K. Little, *Religious Poverty and the Profit Economy in Medieval Europe* (Ithaca, NY, 1978), p.122.
16. Letter of Alfonso VIII, quoted in Joseph F. O'Callaghan, *A History of Medieval Spain* (Ithaca, NY, 1975), p.248.
17. Desmond Seward, *The Monks of War: The Military Religious Orders* (London, 1972), p.99.
18. Gunther of Pairis, quoted in *Christian Society and the Crusades, 1198-1229*, ed. Edward Peters (Philadelphia, 1971), p.19.
19. Gerald of Wales, *The History and Topography of Ireland* (Harmondsworth, 1982), p.102.

FURTHER READING

For searchable maps, genealogies, and other materials for this chapter, please visit the *Short History of the Middle Ages* website at www.broadviewpress.com/shorthistory.

Abulafia, David. *Frederick II: A Medieval Emperor*. London, 1988.

Baldwin, John. *The Government of Philip Augustus: Foundations of French Royal Power in the Middle Ages*. Berkeley, 1986.

Bartlett, Robert. *England under the Norman and Angevin Kings, 1075-1225*. Oxford, 2000.

——. *The Making of Europe: Conquest, Colonization and Cultural Change, 950-1350*. Princeton, 1993.

Bouchard, Constance Brittain. *Strong of Body, Brave and Noble: Chivalry and Society in Medieval France*. Ithaca, NY, 1998.

Cheyette, Fredric L. *Ermengard of Narbonne and the World of the Troubadours*. Ithaca, NY, 2001.

Christiansen, Eric. *The Northern Crusades*. 2nd ed. London, 1997.

Clanchy, Michael T. *From Memory to Written Record: England 1066-1307*. 2nd ed. Oxford, 1993.

Crouch, David. *William Marshal: Court, Career and Chivalry in the Angevin Empire, 1147-1219*. London, 1990.

Evergates, Theodore, ed. *Aristocratic Women in Medieval France*. Philadelphia, 1999.

Farmer, Sharon, and Barbara H. Rosenwein, eds. *Monks and Nuns, Saints and Outcasts: Religion in Medieval Society*. Ithaca, NY, 2000.

Ferruolo, Stephen C. *The Origins of the University: The Schools of Paris and Their Critics, 1100-1215*. Stanford, CA, 1985.

Frame, Robin. *The Political Development of the British Isles, 1100-1400*. Oxford, 1990.

Gaunt, Simon, and Sarah Kay, eds. *The Troubadours: An Introduction*. Cambridge, 1999.

Geary, Patrick J. *Furta Sacra: Thefts of Relics in the Central Middle Ages*. Princeton, 1990.

Haverkamp, Alfred. *Medieval Germany, 1056-1273*. Trans. Helga Braun and Richard Mortimer. Oxford, 1988.

Hudson, John. *The Formation of the English Common Law: Law and Society in England from the Norman Conquest to Magna Carta*. London, 1996.

Lawrence, C.H. *The Friars: The Impact of the Early Mendicant Movement on Western Society*. London, 1994.

Menocal, Maria Rosa. *The Arabic Role in Medieval Literary History: A Forgotten Heritage*. Philadelphia, 1987.

Moore, R.I. *The First European Revolution, c. 970-1215*. Oxford, 2000.

——. *The Formation of a Persecuting Society: Power and Deviance in Western Europe, 950-1250*. Oxford, 1987.

Pegg, Mark Gregory. *The Corruption of Angels: The Great Inquisition of 1245-1246*. Princeton, 2001.

Simons, Walter. *Cities of Ladies: Beguine Communities in the Medieval Low Countries, 1200-1565*. Philadelphia, 2001.

Stoddard, Whitney S. *Art and Architecture in Medieval France*. New York, 1990.

Waley, Daniel. *The Italian City-Republics*. 3rd ed. London, 1988.

SEVEN

DISCORDANT HARMONIES
(*c.*1250-*c.*1350)

IN THE SHADOW OF a great Mongol empire that, for about a century, stretched from the East China Sea to the Black Sea and from Moscow to the Himalayas, Europeans were bit players in a great Eurasian system tied together by a combination of sheer force and open trade routes. Taking advantage of the new opportunities for commerce and evangelization offered by the new mammoth empire, Europeans ventured with equal verve into experiments in their own backyards: in government, thought, and expression. Above all, they sought to harmonize disparate groups, ideas, and artistic modes. At the same time, unable to force everything into unified and harmonious wholes and often confronted instead with discord and strife, they tried to purge their society of deviants of every sort.

THE MONGOL HEGEMONY

The Mongols, like the Huns and Seljuks before them, were pastoralists. Occupying the eastern edge of the great steppes that stretch west to the Hungarian plains, they herded horses and sheep while honing their skills as hunters and warriors. Believing in both high deities and slightly lower spirits, the Mongols were also open to other religious ideas, easily assimilating Buddhism, Islam, and even some forms of Christianity. Their empire, in its heyday stretching about 4000 miles from east to west, was the last to be created by the nomads from the steppes.

Plate 7.1
(facing page): Pietro Lorenzetti, Birth of the Virgin (1342).
This painted altarpiece creates an architectural space of real depth in which figures of convincing solidity act and interact. Compare them with Saint Joseph in **Plate 6.7**, p.238. Note how the ribs and arches of a Gothic church are used here as both decorative and unifying elements.

The Contours of the Mongol Empire

The Mongols formed under the leadership of Chingiz (or Genghis) Khan (*c.*1162–1227). Fusing together various tribes of mixed ethnic origins and traditions, Chingiz created a highly disciplined, orderly, and sophisticated army. Impelled out of Mongolia in part by new climatic conditions that threatened their grasslands, the Mongols were equally inspired by Chingiz's vision of world conquest. All of China came under their rule by 1279; meanwhile, the Mongols were making forays to the west as well. They took Rus in the 1230s, Poland and Hungary in 1241, and might well have continued into the rest of Europe, had not unexpected dynastic disputes and insufficient pasturage for their horses drawn them back east. In the end, the borders of their European dominion rolled back east of the Carpathian Mountains.

Something rather similar happened in the Islamic world, where the Mongols took Seljuk Rum, the major power in the region, by 1243. They then moved to Baghdad, putting a temporary end to the caliphate in 1258. From there they moved into Syria in 1259–1260, threatening the fragile crusader states a few miles away. Even so, a few

Map 7.1: The Mongol Empire, *c.*1260–1350

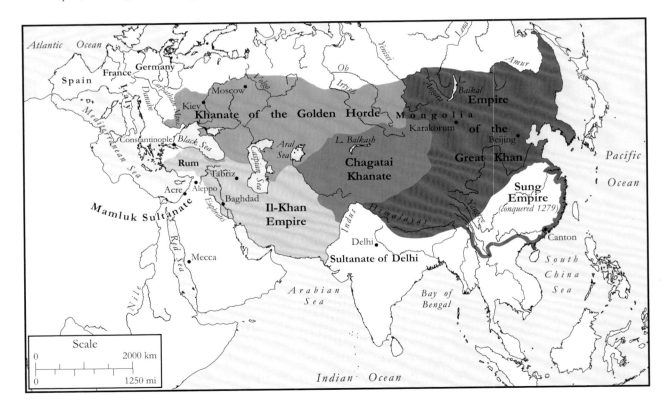

months later they withdrew their troops, probably (again) because of inadequate grasslands and dynastic problems. The Mamluks of Egypt took advantage of the moment to conquer Syria themselves. This effectively ended the Mongol push across the Islamic world. It was the Mamluks, not the Mongols, who took Acre in 1291, snuffing out the last bit of the crusader states.

By the middle of the thirteenth century, the Mongol empire had taken on the contours of a settled state. (See Map 7.1.) It was divided into four regions, under the rule of various progeny of Chingiz. The western-most quadrant was dominated by the rulers of Rus, the so-called Golden Horde ("horde" derived from the Turkish word for "camp"). Settled along the lower Volga River valley, the Mongols of the Golden Horde combined traditional pastoralism with more settled activities. They founded cities, fostered trade, and gradually gave up their polytheism in favor of Islam. While demanding regular and exactly calculated tribute, troops, and recognition of their overlordship from the indigenous Rus rulers, they nevertheless allowed the Rus princes considerable autonomy. Their policy of religious toleration allowed the Orthodox church to flourish, untaxed, and willing in turn to offer up prayers for the soul of the Mongol khan (ruler). Kiev-based Rus, largely displaced by the Mongols, gave way to the hegemony of northern Rus princes, such as those centered in Lithuania (on the Baltic) and Muscovy, the area around Moscow. As Mongol rule fragmented, in the course of the fifteenth century, Moscow-based Russia emerged.

Mongols and Europeans

Once settled, the Mongols wooed Europe. They sent embassies west, welcomed Christian missionaries, and encouraged European trade. For their part, Europeans initially thought that the Mongols must be Christians; news of Mongol onslaughts in the Islamic world gave ballast to the myth of a lost Christian tribe led by a "Prester John" and his son "King David." Even though Europeans soon learned that the Mongols were neither Christian nor friendly, they dreamed of new triumphs: they imagined, for example, that Orthodox Christians under the Golden Horde would now accept papal protection (and primacy); they flirted with the idea of a Mongol-Christian alliance against the Muslims; and they saw the advent of the "new" pagans as an opportunity to evangelize. Thus in the 1250s the Franciscan William of Rubruck traveled across Asia to convert the Mongols in China; on his way back he met some Dominicans determined to do the same. European missions to the east became a regular feature of the West's contact with the Mongol world.

Such contact was further facilitated by trade. European caravans and ships crisscrossed the Mongol world, bringing silks, spices, ceramics, and copper back from China, while exporting slaves, furs, and other commodities. (See Map 7.2.) The

Genoese, who allied with the Byzantines to overthrow the Latin Empire of Constantinople in 1261, received special trading privileges from both the newly installed Byzantine emperor, Michael VIII Paleologus, and the khans of the Golden Horde. Genoa, which set up a permanent trading post at Caffa (today Feodosiya), on the Black Sea, was followed by the Venetians, who established their own trade-station at Tana and soon at Tabriz as well. These were sites well poised to exploit overland routes. Other European traders and missionaries traveled arduous sea routes, setting sail from the Persian Gulf (controlled by the Mongols) and rounding India before arriving in China. Marco Polo (1254–1324) was the most famous of the travelers to the east only because he left a fascinating travel book:

> Taidu [a city in China] is built in the form of a square with all its sides of equal length and a total circumference of twenty-four miles.... I assure you that the streets are so broad and straight that from the top of the wall above one gate you can see along the whole length of the road to the gate opposite. The city is full of fine mansions, inns, and dwelling-houses. All the way down the sides of every main street there are booths and shops of every sort.[1]

Map 7.2: Mongol-European Trade Routes

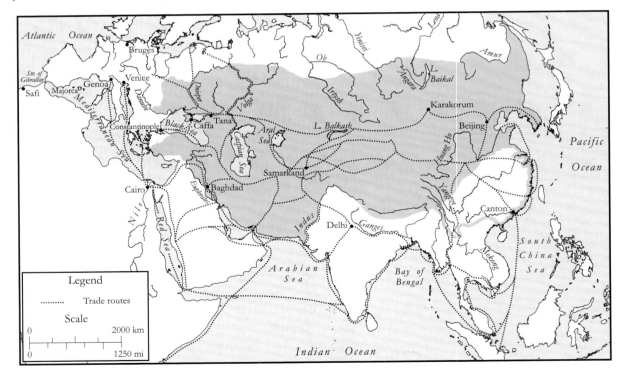

Descriptions such as this fired up new adventurers, eager to seek out the fabulous wealth of the orient. In a sense, the Mongols initiated the search for exotic goods and missionary opportunities that culminated in the European "discovery" of a new world, the Americas.

THE MATURATION OF THE EUROPEAN ECONOMY

The pull of the east on the trade of the great Italian maritime cities was part of a series of shifts in Europe's commercial patterns. Another one, perhaps even more important, was towards the Atlantic. At the same time, new roads and bridges made land trade both possible and profitable. The linkages gave Europeans access to material goods of every sort, but they also heightened social tensions, especially within the cities.

New Routes

The first ships to ply the Atlantic's waters in regular trips were the galleys of Genoese entrepreneurs. By the 1270s they were leaving the Mediterranean via the Straits of Gibraltar, stopping to trade at various ports along the Spanish coast, then making their way north to Bruges (in Flanders) and England. (See Map 7.3.) In the western Mediterranean, Mallorca, recently conquered by the king of Aragon, sent its own ships to join the Atlantic trade at about the same time. Soon the Venetians began state-sponsored Atlantic expeditions using new-style "great galleys" that held more cargo yet required fewer oarsmen. Eventually, as sailing ships — far more efficient than any sort of galley — were developed by the Genoese and others, the Atlantic passage replaced older overland and river routes between the Mediterranean and Europe's north.

Equally important for commerce were new initiatives in North Africa. As the Almohad empire collapsed, weak successor states allowed Europeans new elbow room. Genoa had outposts in the major Mediterranean ports of the Maghreb and new ones down the Atlantic coast, as far south as Safi (today in Morocco). Pisa, Genoa's traditional trade rival, was entrenched at Tunis. Catalonia, whose commercial star was rising fast, had its own settlements in the port cities of the Maghreb. Profits were enormous. Besides acting as middlemen, trading goods or commodities from northern Europe, the Italian cities had their own products to sell (Venice had salt and glass products, Pisa had iron) in exchange for African cotton, linen, spices, and, above

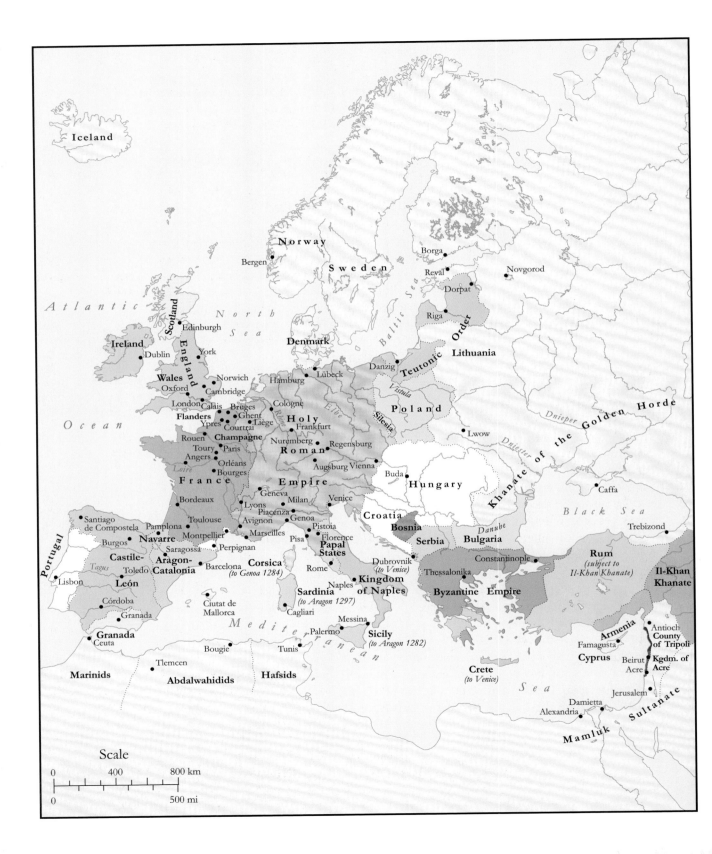

Iceland

Atlantic

North
Sea

Scotland
Edinburgh

Ireland
Dublin
York

Wales
Oxford
Norwich
Cambridge

London Calais Bruges
Flanders Ghent
Ypres Liège
Courtrai

Champagne
Rouen
Toury Paris
Angers
Orléans
Bourges

France

Bordeaux

Geneva
Lyons
Piacenza
Avignon Genoa
Marseilles
Pisa
Florence
Pistoia

Toulouse

Montpellier
Perpignan

Barcelona

Corsica
(to Genoa 1284)

Rome

Sardinia
(to Aragon 1297)

Cagliari

Naples

Kingdom
of Naples

Sicily
(to Aragon 1282)

Messina
Palermo

Mediterranean

Sea

Bergen

Norway

Sweden

Denmark

Hamburg
Lübeck

Cologne
Holy
Frankfurt

Nuremberg
Regensburg

Augsburg Vienna

Empire

Milan
Venice

Croatia

Bosnia

Serbia

Bulgaria

Danube

Thessalonika

Byzantine Empire

Crete
(to Venice)

Baltic
Sea

Borga

Reval
Novgorod
Dorpat

Riga

Danzig Teutonic Order Lithuania

Vistula

Poland

Silesia

Elbe

Rhine

Loire

Tagus

Papal
States

Dubrovnik
(to Venice)

Constantinople

Lwow

Buda

Hungary

Dnieper of the Golden Horde

Dniester

Khanate of the Golden Horde

Caffa

Black Sea

Trebizond

Rum
(subject to
Il-Khan Khanate)

Il-Khan
Khanate

Armenia
Famagusta

Cyprus

Antioch
County
of Tripoli

Beirut
Acre

Jerusalem

Kgdm. of
Acre

Damietta
Alexandria

Mamluk Sultanate

Portugal

Lisbon

Santiago
de Compostela

Burgos

Castile-

Toledo

León

Córdoba

Granada

Granada
Ceuta

Marinids

Tlemcen

Abdalwahidids

Pamplona

Navarre

Saragossa

Aragon-
Catalonia

Ciutat de
Mallorca

Bougie

Tunis

Hafsids

Scale

0   400   800 km

0   500 mi

all, gold. In the mid-thirteenth century, Genoa and Florence were minting coins from gold panned on the upper Niger river, while Venice began minting gold ducats in 1284. The silver standard, which Europe had adhered to since the Carolingian age, was giving way to the gold.

At the same time as Genoa, Pisa, and Catalonia were forging trade networks in the south, some cities in the north of Europe, the future "Hanseatic League," were creating their own marketplace in the Baltic Sea region. Built on the back of the Northern Crusade, the Hansa was created by German merchants following in the wake of Christian knights to prosper in cities like Danzig (today Gdansk, in Poland), Riga, and Reval (today Tallinn, in Estonia). Lübeck, founded by the duke of Saxony, formed the Hansa's center. There were no city rivalries here, unlike the competition between Genoa and Pisa in the south. But there was also little glamor. Pitch, tar, lumber, furs, herring: these were the stuff of northern commerce.

Map 7.3 (facing page): Europe, c.1280

The opening of the Atlantic and the uniting of the Baltic were dramatic developments. Elsewhere the pace of commercial life quickened more subtly. By 1200 almost all the cities of pre-industrial Europe were in existence. By 1300 they were connected by a spider's web of roads that brought even small towns of a few thousand inhabitants into wider networks of trade. To be sure, some old trading centers declined: the towns of Champagne, for example, had been centers of major fairs, periodic but intense commercial activity; by the mid-thirteenth century the fairs' chief functions were as financial markets and clearing houses. On the whole, however, urban centers grew and prospered. As the burgeoning population of the countryside fed the cities with immigrants, the population of many cities reached their medieval maximum: in 1300 Venice and London each had perhaps 100,000 inhabitants, Paris an extraordinary 200,000. Many of these people became part of the urban labor force, working as apprentices or servants; but others could not find jobs or became disabled and could not keep them. The indigent and sick posed new challenges for urban communities. To be sure, rich townspeople and princes alike supported the building of new charitable institutions: hospices for the poor, hospitals for the sick, orphanages, refuges for penitent prostitutes. But in big cities the numbers that these could serve were woefully inadequate. Beggars (there were perhaps 20,000 at a time in Paris alone) became a familiar sight, and not all prostitutes could afford to be penitent.

Conflict in the Cities

Cities that were part of the most complex trade networks were also the most restive. This was certainly true in Flanders, where the urban population had grown enormously since the twelfth century. (See Map 7.4 for the ballooning of the walls at Bruges, a fair measure of its expanding population.) Flemish cities depended on England for wool to supply their looms and on the rest of Europe to buy their finished textiles. But Flemish workers were unhappy with their town governments, run by wealthy merchants, the "patricians," whose families had held their positions for generations. When, in the early 1270s, England slapped a trade embargo on Flanders, discontented laborers, now out of work, struck, demanding a role in town government. While most of these rebellions resulted in few political changes, workers had better luck early in the next century, when the king of France and the count of Flanders went to war. The workers (who supported the count) defeated the French forces at the battle of Courtrai in 1302. Thereafter the patricians, who had sided with the king, were at least partly replaced by artisans in the apparatus of Flemish town governments. In the early fourteenth century, Flemish cities had perhaps the most inclusive governments of Europe.

Map 7.4: The Walls of Bruges, Ninth to Fourteenth Centuries

A similar range of opposition and rebellion beset the northern Italian cities. Here it was the pope and emperor who took the place of king and count. "Outsiders," they nevertheless affected interurban politics. City factions often fought under the party banners of the Guelfs (papal supporters) or the Ghibellines (imperial supporters), even though for the most part they were fighting very local battles. As in the Flemish cities, the late thirteenth century saw a movement by the Italian urban lower classes to participate in city government. The *popolo* ("people") who demanded the changes was in fact made up of many differ-

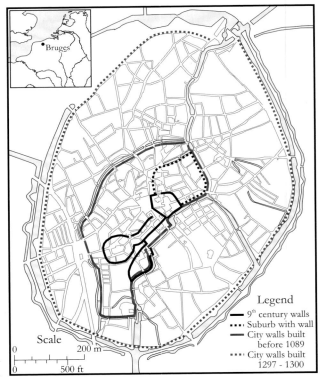

Legend
— 9th century walls
▪▪▪ Suburb with wall
— City walls built before 1089
▪▪▪ City walls built 1297 - 1300

Scale
0   200 m
0   500 ft

ent groups, including crafts and merchant guildsmen, fellow parishioners, and even members of the commune. The *popolo* acted as a sort of alternative commune for these groups, a sworn association dedicated to upholding the interests of its members within the city. Armed and militant, the *popolo* demanded a say in matters of government, particularly taxation. In 1222 at Piacenza, for example, the *popolo*'s members won half the government offices; a year later they and the nobles (the traditional leaders of the city) worked out a plan to share the election of their city's *podestà*, or governing official. Such power sharing was fairly common, but more polarized outcomes were normal as well. At Pistoia, the *popolo* was supposed to prevail over the commune (run by the nobles) if the two came into conflict:

> If there are any clauses in the constitution of the commune of Pistoia [runs one of the clauses in the statutes of the *popolo* there] which are harmful or contrary to any clause of the constitution of the Popolo of Pistoia, then the clauses of the constitution of the Popolo are to be valid and binding and are to be observed and acted upon, and not those clauses in the commune's constitution which are contrary to them.[2]

The commune, of course, did not quietly accede to this stipulation, and ongoing clashes, negotiations, and compromises went on at Pistoia, as elsewhere, as the citizens struggled for power, honor, and peace.

Weakened by constant friction, the communes became tempting prey for great regional nobles who, allying with one or another faction, established themselves as *signori* ("lords"; *sing.: signore*) of the cities, maintaining order at the price of repression. In these circumstances, the commune gave way to the *signoria* (a state ruled by a *signore*), with one family dominating the government. The fate of Piacenza over the course of the thirteenth century was typical: first dominated by nobles, its commune granted the *popolo* a voice in 1222; but by mid-century it was taken over by Oberto Pallavicino and later in the century by another powerful family, the Scotti. In the late fourteenth century, many communes came to an end as Italian cities fell under the control of *signori*.

XENOPHOBIA

Urban discord was fairly successfully defused in Flanders, fairly well silenced in Italy. In neither instance was pluralism valued. Europeans had no interest in hearing multiple voices; rather they were eager to purge and purify themselves of the pollutants in their midst.

Driving the Jews from the Ile-de-France in the twelfth century (see p. 242) was a dress rehearsal for the expulsions of the thirteenth. In England, the Jews were expelled by local lords and municipalities from various cities in the 1230s and 1240s, at the same time as unusually harsh taxes began to be assessed by King Henry III (r. 1216-1272). By the end of Henry's reign, the Jews were impoverished and their numbers depleted. There were perhaps 3000 Jews in all of England when King Edward I (r. 1272-1307) drew up the "Statute of the Jews" in 1275, stipulating that they end the one occupation that had been left open to them: moneylending. They were expected to turn to "productive labor" instead. Fifteen years later Edward expelled them from England entirely. (For the English kings, see Genealogy 8.1 on p. 294.)

The story was similar in France. King Louis IX (r. 1226-1270; see Genealogy 8.1 on p. 294), later canonized as Saint Louis, reportedly could not bear to look at a Jew and worried that their "poison" might infect his kingdom.[3] In 1242, he presided over the burning of two dozen cartloads of the Talmud (ancient rabbinic commentaries on the Bible), judged at a show-trial in Paris to be insulting to Christians. Actively promoting the conversion and baptism of Jews, Louis offered converts pensions, new names, and an end to special restrictions. His grandson, Philip IV ("The Fair") (r. 1285-1314), gave up on conversion and expelled the Jews from France in 1306. By contrast with England, the French Jewish population had been large; after 1306, perhaps 125,000 French men, women, and children became refugees in the Holy Roman empire, Spain, and Italy. The few who were later allowed to return were wiped out in popular uprisings in the early 1320s.

Some anti-Jewish movements linked the Jews with lepers. Occupying a profoundly ambivalent place in medieval society, lepers were both revered and despised. Saint Louis used to feed the lepers who came to him, and he supported *leprosaria*, houses to care for them. Saint Francis was praised for ministering to lepers and admired for kissing them on hand and mouth. On the other hand, lepers were thought tainted by horrible sin; their rights to private property were restricted; they were expected to live apart from others and to carry a bell (if they moved about) to alert everyone to their ominous presence. In the south of France in the 1320s they were accused of horrific crimes: of poisoning the wells and streams and of giving Jews consecrated hosts for their wicked rites. Hauled in by local officials, the lepers were tortured, made to confess, then burned.

Only by comparison with lepers does the revulsion against beggars seem mild. Like leprosy, poverty too was thought to have its social uses. Certainly the mendicants like the Franciscans and Dominicans, who went about begging, were understood to be exercising the highest vocation. And even involuntary beggars were thought (and expected) to pray for the souls of those who gave them alms. Nevertheless the sheer and unprecedented number of idle beggars led to calls for their expulsion:

If there is a man who has nothing [reads the "Customs of Touraine and Anjou"], and who lives in the town without earning anything, and he likes to go to the tavern, the judge should arrest him and ask what he lives on. And if he understands him to be lying, and that he is debauched [*de mauvaise vie*, literally: of a bad way of life], he should throw him out of the town.[4]

But no group suffered social purging more than heretics. Beginning in the thirteenth century, church inquisitors, aided by secular authorities, worked to search out and extirpate heretics from Christendom. Based in the south of France, the mid-Rhineland, and Italy, the inquisitors began their scrutiny in each district by giving a sermon and calling upon heretics to confess. Generally the inquisitors granted a grace period for heretics to come forward. After that they called suspected heretics to meetings, interrogating them. Often imprisonment, along with torture both physical and mental, was used to extract a confession. Then penalties were assigned. Bernard Gui, an inquisitor in Languedoc between 1308–1323, gave out 633 punishments. Nearly half involved imprisonment, usually for life. A few heretics were required to go on penitential pilgrimages. Forty-one people (6.5 per cent of those punished by Bernard) were burned alive. A large number of (former) heretics were forced to wear crosses sewn to their clothing, rather like Jews, but dishonored by a different marker.

STRENGTHENED MONARCHS AND THEIR ACCOMMODATIONS

The impulse behind "purification" was less hatred than the exercise of power. Expelling the Jews meant confiscating their property and calling in their loans while polishing an image of zealous religiosity. Burning lepers was one way to gain access to the assets of *leprosaria* and claim new forms of hegemony. Imprisonment and burning put the heretic's property into the hands of secular authorities. Yet even as kings and other great lords manipulated the institutions and rhetoric of piety and purity for political ends, they learned how to accommodate, mollify, and use—rather than stamp out—new and up-and-coming classes. They came to welcome the broad-based support that representative institutions afforded them.

All across Europe, from Spain to Poland, from England to Hungary, rulers summoned parliaments. Growing out of ad hoc advisory sessions that kings and other rulers held with the most powerful people in their realms, parliaments became solemn and formal assemblies in the thirteenth century, moments when rulers celebrated their power and where the "orders"—clergy, nobles, and commons—assented to their wishes. Eventually parliaments became organs through which groups not ordinarily at court could articulate their interests.

The orders (or "estates") were based on the traditional division of society into those who pray, those who fight, and those who work. Unlike modern classes, defined largely by economic status, medieval orders cut across economic boundaries. The clerics, for example, included humble parish priests as well as archbishops; the commons included wealthy merchants as well as impoverished peasants. That, at least, was the theory. In practice, rulers did not so much command representatives of the orders to come to court as they summoned the most powerful members of their realm, whether clerics, nobles, or important townsmen. Above all they wanted support for their policies and tax demands.

Spanish Cortes

The *cortes* of León–Castile were among the earliest representative assemblies called to the king's court and the first to include townsmen. As the *reconquista* pushed southward across the Iberian peninsula (see p.243), Christian kings called for settlers to occupy new frontiers. Enriched by plunder, fledgling villages soon burgeoned into major commercial centers. Like the cities of Italy, Spanish towns dominated the countryside. Their leaders—called *caballeros villanos*, or "city horsemen," because they were rich enough to fight on horseback—monopolized municipal offices. In 1188, when King Alfonso IX (r.1188–1230) summoned townsmen to the *cortes* for the first time on record, the city *caballeros* served as their representatives, agreeing to Alfonso's plea for military and financial support and for help in consolidating his rule. Once convened at court, these wealthy townsmen joined bishops and noblemen in formally counseling the king and assenting to royal decisions. Beginning with Alfonso X (r.1252–1284), Castilian monarchs regularly called on the *cortes* to participate in major political and military decisions and to assent to new taxes to finance them.

Local Solutions in the Empire

In the Holy Roman empire, the royal and imperial level was less important than the local. Yet every local ruler had to deal with the same two classes on the rise: the townsmen (as in Castile and elsewhere) and a group unique to Germany, the ministerials. The ministerials were legally serfs whose services—collecting taxes, administering justice, and fighting wars—were so honorable as to garner them both high status and wealth. By 1300 they had become "nobles" in every way but one: marriage. In the 1270s at Salzburg, for example, the archbishop required his ministerials to swear that they would marry within his lordship or at least get his permission to marry a woman from elsewhere. Apart from this indignity (which itself was not always imposed), the ministerials, like the other nobles, profited from German colonization to become enormously wealthy landowners. Some held castles, and many controlled towns. They became counter-weights to the territorial princes who, in the wake of the downfall of the Staufen, had expected to rule unopposed. In Lower Bavaria in 1311, for example, when the local duke was strapped for money, the nobles, in tandem with the clergy and the townsmen, granted him his tax but demanded in return recognition of their collective rights. The privilege granted by the duke was a sort of Bavarian Magna Carta. By the middle of the fourteenth century, princes throughout the Holy Roman empire found themselves negotiating periodically with various noble and urban leagues.

English Parliament

In England, the consultative role of the barons at court had been formalized by the guarantees of Magna Carta. When Henry III (*r.*1216-1272) was crowned at the age of nine, England was governed for a time by a council consisting of a few barons, professional administrators, and a papal legate. Although not quite "rule by parliament," this council set a precedent for baronial participation in government. But once grown up and firmly in the royal saddle, Henry so alienated barons and commoners alike by his wars, debts, choice of advisers, favoritism, and lax attitude toward reform that the barons threatened rebellion. At Oxford in 1258, they forced Henry to dismiss his foreign advisers (he had favored the Lusignans, from France). He was henceforth to rule with the advice of a Council of Fifteen chosen jointly by the barons and the king and to limit the terms of his chief officers. Yet even this government was riven by strife, and civil war erupted in 1264. At the battle of Lewes in the same year, the leader of the baronial opposition, Simon de Montfort (*c.*1208-1265), routed the king's forces, captured the king, and became England's de facto ruler.

By Simon's day the distribution of wealth and power in England differed from the time of Magna Carta. Well-to-do merchants in the cities could potentially buy out most knights and even some barons many times over. Meanwhile, in the rural areas, the "knights of the shire" as well as some land-holders below them were rising in wealth and standing, to join the barons as "nobles." This precursor of the "gentry" class was politically active: the knights of the shire attended local courts and served as coroners, sheriffs, and justices of the peace, a new office that gradually replaced the sheriff's. The importance of the knights of the shire was clear to Simon de Montfort, who called a parliament in 1264 that included them; when he summoned another parliament in 1265, he added, for the first time ever, representatives of the towns—

the "commons." Even though Simon's brief rule ended that very year and Henry's son Edward I (*r*.1272–1307) became a rallying point for royalists, the idea of representative government in England had emerged, born out of the interplay between royal initiatives and baronial revolts. Under Edward, parliament met fairly regularly, a by-product of the king's urgent need to finance his wars against France, Wales, and Scotland.

French Monarchs and the "Estates"

Louis IX, unlike Henry III, was a born reformer. He approached his kingdom as he did himself: with zealous discipline. As an individual, he was (by all accounts) pious, dignified, and courageous. He attended church each day, diluted his wine with water, and cared for the poor and sick (we have already seen his devotion to lepers). Hatred of Jews and heretics followed as a matter of course. Twice Louis went on crusade, dying on the second expedition.

Generalized and applied to the kingdom as a whole, Louis's discipline meant doling out proper justice to all. As the upholder of right in his realm, Louis would hear cases directly:

> In the summer, after hearing mass, the king often went to the wood of Vincennes [wrote Louis's biographer Joinville], where he would sit down with his back against an oak, and make us all sit round him. Those who had any suit to present could come to speak to him without hindrance from an usher or any other person. The king would address them directly, and ask: "Is there anyone here who has a case to be settled?" Those who had one would stand up. Then he would say: "Keep silent all of you, and you shall be heard in turn, one after the other."[5]

This personal touch polished Louis's image, but his wide-ranging administrative reforms were even more fundamentally important for his rule. Most cases that came before the king were not, in fact, heard at the oak tree of Vincennes but rather by professional judges in the *parlement*, a newly specialized branch of the royal court.[6] *Enquêteurs* were sent to the provinces to oversee the seneschals and *baillis* and to act as a court of appeals to hear local complaints. Royal ordinances set heavy penalties for government corruption. For the administration of the city of Paris, which had been lax and corrupt, Louis found a solution in the joint rule of royal officials and citizens.

There were discordant voices in France, but they were largely muted and unrecognized. Paris may have been governed by a combination of merchants and royalists, but at the level of the royal court, no regular institution spoke for the different orders.

This began to change only under Louis's grandson, Philip IV The Fair (r.1285-1314). When Philip challenged the reigning pope, Boniface VIII (1294-1303), over rights and jurisdictions, he felt the need to explain, justify, and propagandize his position. Summoning representatives of the clergy, nobles, and townspeople to Paris in 1302, Philip presented his case in a successful bid for support. In 1308 he called another representative assembly, this time at Tours, to ratify his actions against the Templars — the Crusading order that had served as de facto bankers for the Holy Land. Philip had accused the Templars of heresy, arrested their members, and confiscated their wealth. He wanted the estates to applaud him, and he was not disappointed. These assemblies, ancestors of the French Estates General, were convened sporadically until the Revolution of 1789 overturned the monarchy. Yet representative institutions were never fully or regularly integrated into the pre-revolutionary French body politic.

THE CHURCH MILITANT, HUMILIATED, AND REVAMPED

On the surface, the clash between Philip the Fair and Boniface VIII seemed yet one more episode in the ongoing struggle between medieval popes and rulers for power and authority. But at the end of the thirteenth century the tables had turned: the kings had more power than the popes, and the confrontation between Boniface and Philip was one sign of the dawning new principle of national sovereignty.

The Road to Avignon

The issue that first set Philip and Boniface at loggerheads involved the English king Edward I as well: taxation of the clergy. Eager to finance new wars, chiefly against one another but also elsewhere (Edward, for example, conquered Wales and tried, unsuccessfully, to subdue Scotland), both monarchs needed money. When the kings financed their wars by taxing the clergy along with everyone else (as if they were going on crusade), Boniface reacted. In the bull *Clericis Laicos* (1296), he asserted that only the pope could authorize the taxation of clerics. Threatening to excommunicate kings who taxed prelates without papal permission, Boniface called upon clerics to "pay nothing" to "laymen."[7]

Reacting swiftly, the kings soon forced Boniface to back down. But in 1301, testing his jurisdiction in southern France by arresting Bernard Saisset, the bishop of Pamiers, on a charge of treason, Philip precipitated another crisis. Boniface reacted with outrage, but we already know how Philip adroitly rallied public opinion in his favor. In response to Boniface's declaration in the bull *Unam Sanctam* (1302) that "it is altogether necessary to salvation for every human creature to be subject to the Roman Pontiff," Philip's agents invaded Boniface's palace at Anagni (southeast of Rome) to capture the pope, bring him to France, and try him for heresy. Although the citizens of Anagni drove the agents out of town, Philip's power could not be denied. A month later, Boniface died, and the next two popes quickly pardoned Philip and his agents.

The papacy was never quite the same thereafter. In 1309, forced from Rome by civil strife, the popes settled at Avignon, a city technically in the Holy Roman empire but very close to, and influenced by, France. There they remained until 1378. The Avignon popes, many of them French, established a sober and efficient organization that took in regular revenues and gave the papacy more say than ever before in the appointment of churchmen and the distribution of church benefices and revenues. Its authority grew: it became the unchallenged judge of sainthood. And the Dominicans and Franciscans became its foot soldiers in the evangelization of the world and the purification of Christendom. These were tasks that required realistic men. When a group of Franciscans objected to their fellows building convents and churches within the cities, they were condemned. The Spirituals, as they were called, cultivated a piety of poverty and apocalypticism, believing that Saint Francis had ushered in a new Age of the Holy Spirit. But the popes, who were the official keepers of Franciscan wealth, advocated the repression of the Spirituals and even had a few burned at the stake.

Plate 7.2: Virgin and Child (1330–1350). Carved in France, this ivory was once painted in color and gilded with gold. Flanked by wings on both sides (each probably containing scenes from the Virgin's life) that could close over the central portion, this portable "box" was a devotional aid suitable for a lay person.

In some ways, then, the papacy had never been so powerful as it was at Avignon. On the other hand, it was mocked and vilified by contemporaries, especially Italians, whose revenues suffered from the popes' exile from Rome. Francesco Petrarch (1304–1374), one of the great literary figures of the day, dubbed Avignon both "Babylon" and "hell." Pliant and accommodating to the rulers of Europe, especially the kings of France, the popes were slowly abandoning the idea of leading all of Christendom and were coming to recognize the right of secular states to regulate their internal affairs.

Lay Religiosity

They may have been secular states, but they were peopled by subjects who took their religion very seriously. With the doctrine of transubstantiation (see p.240), Christianity became a religion of the body: the body of the wafer in the mass, the body of the communicant who ate it, and equally the body of the believers who celebrated together in the feast of Corpus Christi (The Body of Christ). First established in 1246 at Liège, a city on the northwest fringe of the empire, Corpus Christi turned into gestures and chant a Eucharistic piety already widespread, especially among women, in the most urbanized regions of Europe. Taken up by the papacy and promulgated as a universal feast, its texts written by the young scholastic Thomas Aquinas (1225-1274), Corpus Christi was adopted throughout western Europe. Whole cities created processions for the day. Fraternities dedicated themselves to the Body of Christ, holding their meetings on the feast day, focusing their regular charity on bringing the *viaticum* (or final Eucharist) to the dying. Dramas were elaborated on the theme.

Along with new devotion to the flesh of Christ was devotion to his mother. In the hands of the Sienese painter Pietro Lorenzetti (*c.*1280/90-1348), for example, Mary's life took on lively detail. In Plate 7.1, an altarpiece depicting the Birth of the Virgin, two servants—one probably the midwife—tenderly wash the infant Mary. Her mother, clearly modeled on the mistress of a well-to-do Italian household, sits up in

Plate 7.3: Bronze Effigy of Bishop Evrard de Fouilloi (*d.*1222). Beginning in the eleventh century, bishops, kings, and other great office holders commemorated themselves with bronze effigies on their tombs, celebrating their power on earth and reminding others to pray for their souls in heaven. Evrard's tomb—showing him in full episcopal garb and trampling a demon beneath his feet—lies in the nave of Amiens Cathedral.

bed, gazing at the child with dreamy eyes, while, in another room, a little serving boy whispers news of the birth to the expectant father. Both publicly, in feasts dedicated to the major events in Mary's life, and privately, in small and concentrated images made to be contemplated by individual viewers, the Virgin was the focus of intense religious feeling. The ivory carving in Plate 7.2, tiny enough to be held in one hand, was meant to be an aid to private devotion.

That worship could be a private matter was part of a wider change in the ways that people negotiated the afterlife while here on earth. The doctrine of Purgatory, informally believed long before it was declared dogma in 1274, held that the Masses and prayers of the living could shorten the purgative torments that had to be suffered by the souls of the dead. Soon families were endowing special chapels for themselves, private spaces for offering private Masses on behalf of their own members. High churchmen and wealthy laymen insisted that they be buried within the walls of the church rather than outside of it, reminding the living to pray for them by commissioning effigies of themselves on their tombs. (See Plate 7.3.)

THE SCHOLASTIC SYNTHESIS AND ITS FRAYING

Widespread religiosity went hand-in-hand with widespread literacy. In some rural areas, schools for children were attached to monasteries or established in villages. In the south of France, where the church still feared heresy, preachers made sure that they taught children how to read along with the tenets of the faith. In the cities, all merchants and most artisans had some functional literacy: they had to read and write to keep accounts, and, increasingly, they owned religious books for their private devotions. In France, Books of Hours were most fashionable; Psalters were favored in England.

The broad popularity of the friars fed the institutions of higher education. Franciscans and Dominicans now established convents and churches *within* cities; their members attended the universities as students, and many went on to become masters. By the time the other theologians at the University of Paris saw the danger to their independence, the friars were too entrenched to be budged. Besides, the friars — men like Thomas Aquinas and Bonaventure — were unarguably the greatest of the scholastics. They mastered the use of logic to summarize and reconcile all knowledge, and they used it in the service of contemporary society.

In Thomas Aquinas's *Summa Theologiae* (or *Summa Theologica*), for example, all topics, human and divine, were harmonized in a large, systematic treatise (a *summa*). Using the technique of juxtaposing opposite positions, as Abelard had done in his *Sic et Non*, Aquinas (unlike Abelard) carefully explained away or reconciled contradictions, using Aristotelian logic as his tool for analysis and exposition. Aquinas wanted to reconcile faith with reason, to demonstrate the harmony of belief and understanding even though (in his view) faith ultimately surpassed reason in knowing higher truths. Aquinas's topics ranged over every conceivable issue, from complex matters of theology to the simmering ethical dilemmas of his day. Is it lawful to sell something for more than its worth? Are Jews heretics? Are there evil human acts? In the work of Albertus Magnus (c.1200-1280), Aquinas's teacher, the topics ranged from biology and physics to theology. In the writings of Saint Bonaventure (1217-1274), for whom Augustine replaced Aristotle as the key philosopher, the topics as such were secondary to an overall vision of the human mind as the recipient of God's beneficent illumination. For Bonaventure, minister general of the Franciscan Order, spirituality was the font of theology. Yet it was the Spiritual Franciscan Peter Olivi (1248-1298) who first defined the very practical word "capital": wealth with the potential to generate more wealth.

These ideas were preached to townsmen by the friars as a matter of course. They came as well to permeate the thought of the reclusive contemplatives in the cities of Italy, the Netherlands, and the Rhineland, who absorbed the vocabulary of the schools from their confessors. The Dominican Meister Eckhart (d.1327), who studied at Paris before beginning a career of teaching and preaching in Germany, and who enriched the German language with new words for the abstract ideas of the schools, was himself a contemplative: a mystic who saw union with God as the goal of human life.

These thirteenth-century scholastics united in apparent harmony the secular realm with the sacred. But at the end of the century, fissures began to appear. In the *summae* of the Franciscan John Duns Scotus (c.1266-1308), for example, the world and God were less compatible. As with Bonaventure, so too with John, human reason could know truth only by divine illumination. But John argued that this illumination came not as a matter of course but only when God chose to intervene. John saw God as willful rather than reasonable; the divine will alone determined whether human reason could soar to knowledge. Further unraveling the knot tying reason and faith together was William of Ockham (1270?-1349), another Franciscan who nevertheless disputed Duns Scotus vigorously: "What he cites as support [of an argument about the nature of God's intellect] ... is not relevant to showing the conclusion."[8] In fact, for Ockham, reason was unable to prove the truths of faith; it was apt only for things human and worldly, where, in turn, faith was of no use. Ockham himself turned his attention to the nature of government, arguing the importance of the state for human society. But several of his contemporaries looked at the physical world: Nicole Oresme (c.1320-1382), for example, following Ockham's view that the simplest explanation was the best, proposed that the sun, not earth, was the center of the heavens.

HARMONY AND DISSONANCE IN WRITING, MUSIC, AND GOTHIC ART

On the whole, writers, musicians, architects, and artists, like scholastics, presented complicated ideas and feelings in harmony. Writers explored the relations between this world and the next; musicians found ways to bridge sacred and secular genres of music; artists used fleshy, natural forms to evoke the divine.

Vernacular Literature

In the hands of Dante Alighieri (1265–1321), vernacular poetry expressed the order of the scholastic universe, the ecstatic union of the mystic's quest, and the erotic and emotional life of the troubadour. "Siena made me," says one of his characters in the *Commedia*—later known as the *Divine Comedy*—written between 1313 and 1321.[9] If so, Florence made Dante. An ardent Florentine patriot and member of the "Whites" party, the faction that opposed papal intervention in Tuscany, he was condemned to death and expelled from the city by the "Blacks" after their victory in 1301. The *Commedia* was written in bitter exile, peopled with Dante's friends, lovers, enemies, and the living and dead whom he admired and reviled. Told in the first person, Dante presented himself as a traveler who passes through Hell, Purgatory, and Paradise, a soul seeking and finding God in the blinding light of love. Just as Thomas Aquinas used Aristotle's logic to lead him to important truths, so Dante used the pagan poet Virgil as his guide through Hell and Purgatory. And just as Aquinas believed that faith went beyond reason to even higher truths, so Dante found a new guide, Beatrice, representing earthly love, to lead him through most of Paradise. But only faith in the form of the divine love of the Virgin Mary could bring Dante to the culmination of his journey, the inexpressible and ravishing vision of God.

In other writers, the harmony of heaven and earth were differently expressed. In the anonymous prose *Quest of the Holy Grail* (c.1225), the adventures of the knights of King Arthur's Table are turned into a fable to teach the doctrine of transubstantiation and the wonder of the vision of God. In *The Romance of the Rose*, begun by one author (Guillaume de Lorris, a poet in the romantic tradition) and finished by another (Jean de Meun, a poet in the scholastic tradition), a lover seeks the rose, his true love, but is continually thwarted by personifications of love, shame, reason, abstinence, and so on. They present him with arguments for and against love, but in the end, erotic love is embraced in the divine scheme—and the lover plucks the rose.

The Motet

Already by the tenth century, the chant in unison had been joined by a chant of many voices: polyphony. At first voice met voice in improvised harmony, but in the twelfth century polyphony was increasingly composed as well. In the thirteenth century its most characteristic form was the motet. Created at Paris, probably in the milieux of the university and the royal court, the motet harmonized the sacred with the worldly, the Latin language with the vernacular.

Two to four voices joined together in a motet. The most common sort from the second half of the thirteenth century had three voices. The lowest, often taken from a liturgical chant, generally consisted of one or two words, suggesting that it was normally played on an instrument (such as a vieille or lute) rather than sung. The second and third voices had different texts and melodies, sung simultaneously. The form allowed for the mingling of religious and secular motives. Very likely motets were performed by the clerics who formed the entourages of bishops or abbots—or by university students—for their own entertainment and pleasure. In the motet "S'Amours," whose opening music is pictured in Plate 7.4, the top voice complains (in French): "If Love had any power, I, who have served him all my life with a loyal heart, should surely have noticed." By contrast, the middle voice, also singing in French, rejoices in Love's rewards: "At the rebirth of the joyous season, I must begin a song, for true Love, whom I desire to serve, has given me a reason to sing." Meanwhile the lowest voice sings the Latin word "Ecce" — "Look!"[10]

Complementing the motet's complexity was the development of new schemes to indicate rhythm. The most important, that of Franco of Cologne in his *Art of Measurable Song* (*c.*1260), used different shapes to mark the number of beats each note should be held. (See Figure 7.1; the music in Plate 7.4 uses a similar rhythmic system.)

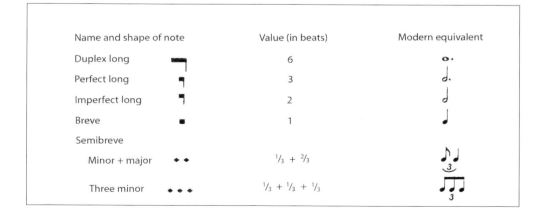

Figure 7.1: Single Notes and Values of Franconian Notation

Amours eust point de

por ie men deusse bien

a pexcuon qui lai seru

e tout mon uiuant de

cuer loiaumit mes ie cor

renouuela

du noli tans

mestpet co

Lee

Allowing for great flexibility and inventiveness in composition, Franco's system became the basis of modern musical notation.

New Currents in Art

Flexibility and inventiveness describe the art of Franco's time as well. It had new patrons to serve: the urban elite. In the Paris of Saint Louis's day, for example, wealthy merchants coveted illuminated law books and romances, rich students prized illustrated Bibles as essential fashion accessories, churchmen wanted beautiful service books, the royal family wanted lavishly illustrated Bibles and Psalters, and the nobility aspired to the same books as their sovereigns. The old-fashioned *scriptoria* that had previously produced books, with scribes and artists working in the same place, gave way to specialized workshops, often staffed by lay people. Some produced the raw materials: the ink, gold leaf, or parchment; others employed scribes to copy the texts; a third kind was set up for the illuminators; and a fourth did nothing but bind the finished books. This was not mass production, however, and the styles of the different artists are clear, if subtle. In Plate 7.5, the artist of one workshop has made the apostle John conform to the shape of an S, his body out of joint, yet utterly elegant. But another Parisian artist working at about the same time in a different shop on a different book painted a thinner John, almost ramrod straight, with a flaming head of hair. (See Plate 7.6.)

Meanwhile, in Italy, especially at Pisa, sculptors, also working in shops, were melding the sort of Gothic naturalism exemplified by the Saint Joseph of Reims in Plate 6.7 (on p.238) with the classical style of Roman sculpture we saw on Trajan's column in Plate 1.3 (on p.33). By 1250 Pisa was a commercial and artistic hub: it was the port of call for Byzantine artists after 1204, and it was in intense competition with Genoa (as we have seen) for Mediterranean trade. But it was also losing ground, its place soon to be taken by Catalonia. In this highly charged atmosphere, artistic development was rapid. For the Duomo of Siena, for example, Nicola Pisano and his assistants created a pulpit (built 1265-1268) composed of eight panels. The Adoration of the Magi, the panel shown in Plate 7.7, has the same dense crowds as Trajan's column, though the figures are less agile and lively. Today all the color is gone, but originally Nicola painted the backgrounds and gilded the hemlines with gold, emphasizing details that brought the event "to life," melding the secular day-to-day of horses and clothing with the mystery of the divine incarnation.

Within a half-century, the weighty, natural forms of the sculptors found a home in painting as well, above all in the paintings of Giotto (1266-1337). In one of his commissions to decorate the private chapel of the richest man in Padua, for example, Giotto filled the walls with frescoes of scenes from Christ's and the Virgin's lives. (See

Plate 7.4 (facing page): The Motet "S'Amours" (*c.*1300). Like the composer of "S'Amours," the artist of this page (painted not long after the music itself was written) weaves together three separate stories. In the "S" of the word "S'Amours," which is sung by the disconsolate lover (the top voice), the artist presents, by contrast with the text, two very contented lovers petting both animals and each other. To the right of this happy scene is the initial A, the first letter of the word "Au," which is sung by the victorious lover of the middle voice. Again ironically, *this* figure is sad and lonely. By reversing the moods of the two voices with his pictures, is the artist commenting on the fickleness of love? Beneath the "Ecce" of the third voice is a hunting scene, complete with stag, hound, and hawk. The hunt was often used as a metaphor for amorous relations.

maligno positus e. Et scimus
qm filius dei uenit et dedit
nob sensu ut cognoscam uer
dm et simul in uero filio eius.
Hic e uerus ds et uita etna. Fi
lioli custodite uos a simula
cris amen. Explic epla iohis i.

Enior incipit
electe due et
natis eius
qs ego diligo
in ueritate et non
ego solus sz et os q cognouerut
ueritate pp ueritate q pmanet
in nob et nobcu erit in etnu
sit nobcu gra mia pax a do
pre et a xpo ihu filio pris in ueri
tate et caritate. Gauisus sum
ualde qm inueni de filus tuis
ambulantes in ueritate sicut ma
datu accepim a pre. Et nc rogo
te dna no tanqm mandatu
nouu scribens tibi sz qd habu
mus ab initio ut diligamus
alter utru. Et hec caritas ut
ambulem scdm mandata eius
hoc e eni mandatu ut quemad
modu audistis ab initio in
eo ambuletis qm multi se
ductores exierut i mundo q
no cofitetur ihm xpm uenisse
i carne hic e seductor et antixps.

uidete nosmetipos ne ptatis
qd opati estis sz ut mcede ple
na accipiatis. Omnis qui rece
dit et non pmanet in doctina xpi
dm no ht. Qui pmanet i doc
tina xpi hic et filiu et pem ht
si quis uenit ad uos et hanc
doctinam no affert nolite eu re
cipe in domu nec aue ei dixi
tis. Qui eni dicit ei aue comu
nicat opibz eius malignis. Et
cepdixi nob ut in die dni nri
ibit xpi no cofutamini plu
ra habui uob scribe noltu p car
tam et atramtu spero eni me
futuri ad uos et os ad os loq
ut gaudiu urm sit plenu
Salutat te filii sororis tue e
lecte amen. Explic epla iohis ii.

Enior seip trita
gaio karmo q
ego diligo in
ueritate karme
de omibz oro
ne facio pspere te ingredi
et ualere sicut pspere agit aia
tua. Gauisus su ualde ue
nientibz fribz et testimoniu
phibentibz ueritati tue sicut
tu in ueritate ambulas. maio
rem hac no habeo letitia qm
ut audiā filios meos in ueri

G omnis
tsgrediens
et n pmanet
i doctina x

G spo n
uenire ad
uos et os
ad os loq.

G tra
G. ka
leuauit
karin
gñm
iorem

Durannui lib Serm

non habeo gratiam que in gratia coclebs uitgium

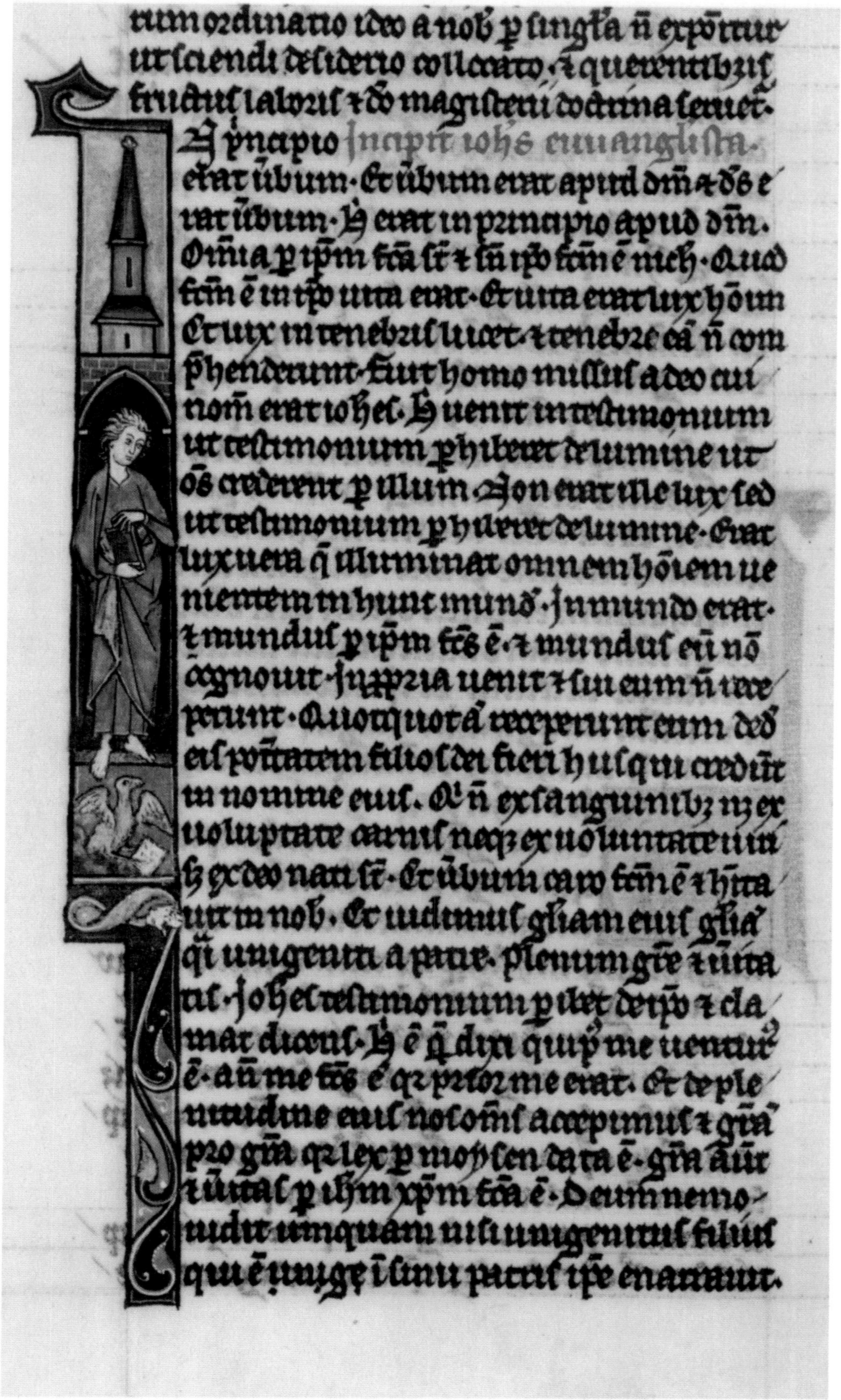

Plate 7.5 (facing page): Saint John, "Dominican" Bible (mid 13th cent.). The graceful and elegant "S" curve of these depictions of Saint John is characteristic of late Gothic figural style. Here the evangelist bisects the first letter of the first word — "senior," "elder" — of two of his own texts, 2 John and 3 John.

Plate 7.6: Saint John, "Aurifaber" Bible (mid 13th cent.). An artist working at another workshop at about the same time as the artist of **Plate 7.5** produced a very different Saint John, hardly curved at all. He stands in a miniature church, while beneath him is his symbol, an eagle holding a book.

Plate 7.7:
Nicola Pisano, Pulpit (1265–1268). The Adoration of the Magi, the scene on this panel of the Siena pulpit, was a very traditional Christian theme (see an early representation on the Franks Casket, **Plate 2.7**), but here the sculptor, Nicola Pisano, has imagined it as a crowd scene and filled it with little details — like the camels — to make it "come to life."

Plate 7.8 (facing page):
Giotto, Arena Chapel, Padua (1304–1313). Giotto brought to painting the sensibilities of a sculptor. Just as Nicola Pisano's figures (see **Plate 7.7**) had depth and roundness, so did Giotto's painted ones. And just as Nicola used telling details to humanize scenes from the bible, so Giotto's paintings, which covered the walls of the Arena Chapel with the narrative of humanity's Redemption and the Final Judgment, were filled with homey particulars.

Plate 7.8.) Throughout, Giotto experimented with the illusion of depth, weight, and volume, his figures expressing unparalleled emotional intensity as they react to events in the world-space created by painted frames. In the Massacre of the Innocents, depicted in Plate 7.9, Herod gives the order; we see his soldiers carrying it out, mothers resisting and weeping, children piled dead and naked on the ground, and one child, legs akimbo, readied for the final blow. The colors, largely soft pastels, were utterly new and revolutionary. But the painting was also traditional, depicting an allegory of spiritual battle, with the bloody powers of the secular state arrayed (on the left) against the moral authority of the church (on the right) represented by pleading mothers, innocent babes, and a baptistery looming above them all.

Just as Italian art was influenced by northern Gothic style, so in turn the new Italian currents went north. In France, for example, illuminators for the royal court made miniature spaces for figures in the round, creating illusions of depth. On the left-hand page in Plate 7.10, thought to be by Jean Pucelle (*d.*1334), the old S-shape figures are still favored, but the soldiers who crowd around Christ are as dense and dramatic as Herod's minions in Giotto. And on the right-hand page, Mary, surprised by the angel of the Annunciation, sits in a space as deep as Herod's tower in Plate 7.9. Influenced perhaps by the look of sculpted figures such as those on Nicola's Siena pulpit, Pucelle painted in *grisaille*, a bare grey highlighted by light tints of color.

CRISIS

The artistic interest in crowd scenes may have been inspired not only by ancient art but by current living conditions. The cities were swollen with immigrants from the overcrowded countryside. By 1300, the only land left uncleared in France and England was marginal or unworkable with the tools of the day. It is true that farms were producing more than ever before, but families also had more hungry mouths to feed. One plot that had originally supported a single family in England was, by the end of the thirteenth century, divided into twenty tiny parcels for the progeny of the original peasant holder. The last known French *villeneuve* ("new town") was founded in 1246; after that, new settlements ceased.

Consider the village of Toury, about 45 miles south of Paris (Map 7.5). It originally consisted of a few peasant habitations (their houses and gardens) clustered around a central enclosure belonging to the lord, in this case the monastery of Saint-Denis (see p.188). Nearby, across the main route that led from Paris to Orléans, was a parish church. In 1110 Abbot Suger constructed a well-fortified castle on the site of the enclosure. In the course of the thirteenth century, encouraged both by Saint-Denis's policy of giving out lots in return for rents and by a market granted by the king, the village grew rapidly, expanding to the east, then to the west, and finally (by the fourteenth century) to the north. Meanwhile the lands cultivated by the villagers — once called upon to support only a small number of householders — were divided into more than 5000 parcels, which appear as tiny rectangles on Map 7.6.

In general, population growth seems to have leveled off by the mid-thirteenth century, but the static supply of farmland meant that from that time onward France and England faced sudden and severe grain shortages.

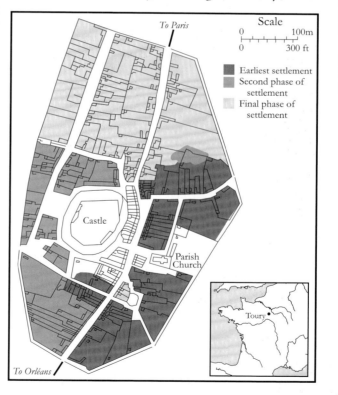

Map 7.5: The Village of Toury, Fourteenth and Fifteenth Centuries

Plate 7.9 (facing page):
Giotto, Massacre of the Innocents, Arena Chapel (1304–1313). Giotto organized the Arena Chapel paintings like scenes in a comic book, to be read from left to right. The Massacre of the Innocents is at the far right on the south wall; the next scene, in the band underneath, is on the far left. Viewers must make a sort of pilgrimage around the church as they follow the scenes from start to finish.

incipiunt hoze bte marie uir
gis scdm vsum pdicatoz.

Plate 7.10:
Jean Pucelle, Hours of Jeanne d'Evreux
(*c.*1325–1328).
Tiny in the original (measuring 3¾ in. x 2½ in.), this book was lavishly illustrated for the queen of France with exquisite *grisaille* paintings.

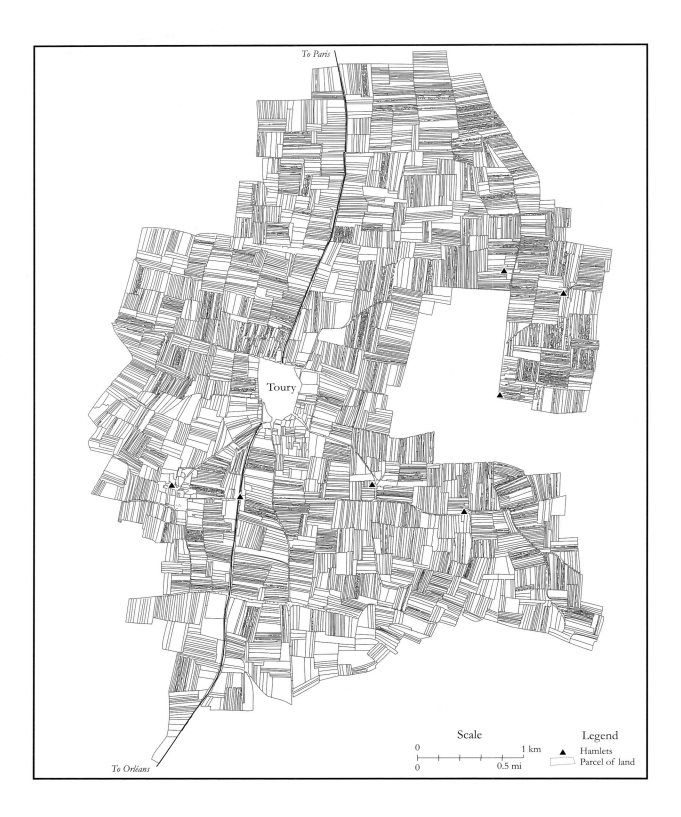

To Paris

Toury

To Orléans

Scale

0   1 km

0   0.5 mi

Legend

▲ Hamlets

▭ Parcel of land

Climatic changes compounded the demographic situation. In 1309 an extremely wet growing season ruined the grain harvest in southern and western Germany; the towns, where food had to be imported, were hit especially hard.

The so-called Great Famine of 1315-1322 was only the longest and most severe of the cycles of food shortage that afflicted northern Europe. The region around Paris was struck then, to be sure, and then again in 1328, 1334, and 1340-1341. No sooner had Florence recovered from one famine then it was hit by another: in 1276, 1282, 1286, 1291, 1299, 1302-1303, 1305. A Flemish chronicler describing the effects of ruined crops in 1315 recalls a scene reminiscent of the piles of babies in Giotto's fresco:

> The people were in such great need that it cannot be expressed. For the cries that were heard from the poor would move a stone, as they lay in the streets with woe and great complaint, swollen with hunger and remaining dead of poverty, so that many were thrown by set numbers, sixty and even more, into a pit.[11]

Map 7.6 (facing page): The Lands of Toury, Fourteenth and Fifteenth Centuries

A whole western European population of vagabonds was created, some of whom may have wandered as far as beyond the Elbe River, to settle in eastern Germany and Poland.

Warfare also took its toll on economic life. To consolidate their rule, princes hired mercenary troops but paid them such poor wages that they plundered the country-side even when they were not fighting. Warring armies had always disrupted farms, ruining the fields as they passed, but in the thirteenth century burning became a bat-tle tactic, used both to devastate the enemy's territory and to teach the inhabitants a lesson. Here too the cities felt the repercussions. A city's own army could defend its walls against roving troops, but it could not easily stop the flow of refugees who streamed in seeking safety. Lille's population, for example, nearly doubled as a result of the wars between Flanders and France during the first two decades of the thir-teenth century. Meanwhile, like other Flemish cities, Lille was obliged to impose new taxes on its population to pay for its huge war debts.

Pressed by war debts, the need for food, and the desire for gain, landlords and town officials alike strove to get more money. Everywhere, customary and other dues were deemed inadequate. In 1315 the king of France offered liberty to all his serfs, mainly to assess a new war tax on all free men. In other parts of France, lords imposed a *taille*, an annual money payment, and many peasants had to go into debt to pay it. Pro-fessional moneylenders set up loan offices in the countryside, or wealthy neighbors served as unofficial creditors. Although richer peasants might profit from these developments, the cycle of loan, debt, and payment left poorer peasants even more impoverished.

In other areas, such as Italy, England, and southern Germany, lords found it useful to give out short-term leases to their peasants. Bypassing the fixed and customary dues whose value decreased as prices rose, these lords simply charged a rent that changed with the market. In Bavaria, for example, the abbot of Baumburg met each year with his peasants to announce new leases and negotiate new rents. In Italy, where peasants had long labored under twenty-five-year leases, landlords and cities introduced a short-term lease; one monastery in Milan doubled its rental income as a result.

To enforce their new taxes and lease arrangements, great lords, both lay and ecclesiastical, installed local agents, eager to collect taxes and to draft young villagers into military service. These officials lived near the villages in fortified houses, well placed to keep an eye on local conditions. They kept account books and computed their profits and their costs. One calculated, for example, that

> You can well have three acres weeded for a penny, and an acre of meadow
> for fourpence, and an acre of waste meadow for threepence-halfpenny....
> And know that five men can well reap and bind two acres a day of each
> kind of [grain], more or less. And where each takes twopence a day then
> you must give five-pence an acre....[12]

The remuneration for rural labor was here as finely calculated as a note in Franco's rhythmic scheme.

★ ★ ★ ★

On the western fringe of the Eurasian landmass, Europeans found ways to mesh their institutions of commerce and religion with those of the mammoth Mongol empire to their east. In many ways medieval Europe reached the zenith of its prosperity, certainly of its population, during the century bisected by 1300. The cities became the centers of culture and wealth. Universities took wing, producing scholasticism, a "scientific revolution" in logical and systematic thought. The friars, ministering to an attentive, prosperous, increasingly literate laity, installed themselves right in the center of towns.

Harmony was often achieved through clashes. The synthesis of a scholastic *summa* was possible only when opposite ideas were faced and sorted out. The growth of representative institutions nearly always entailed accommodating the demands of the discontented with the enlightened self-interest of rulers. The great artistic innovations of the day involved reconciling classical with Gothic styles. Poems and musical compositions worked to assimilate the secular order with the divine.

The harmonies were not always sweet, but sweetness need not be a value, in music or in life. More ominous were the attempts to sound single notes: to suppress the voices of the Jews and the heretics, to silence the bells of the lepers. Cities tried to close their gates to beggars. In the next century terrible calamities would construct new arenas for discord and creativity.

CHAPTER SEVEN KEY EVENTS

1188	King Alfonso IX (r.1188–1230) summons townsmen to the *cortes*
1222	Popolo at Piacenza wins role in government
1225–1274	Thomas Aquinas
1226–1270	King Louis IX (St. Louis) of France
1230s	Mongols conquer Rus
1265	Commons included in English Parliament
1266–1337	Giotto
1279	Mongols conquer China
1284	Gold ducats first minted at Venice
1290	Jews expelled from England
1291	End of the Crusader States
1302	Battle of Courtrai
1302	*Unam Sanctam*
1306	Jews expelled from France
1309–1378	Avignon papacy
1315–1322	Great Famine
1321	Death of Dante

NOTES

1. Marco Polo, *The Travels*, trans. R.E. Latham (Harmondsworth, 1968), p.128.

2. Quoted in Daniel Waley, *The Italian City-Republics* (New York, 1969), p.192.

3. Quoted in *Church, State, and Jew in the Middle Ages*, ed. Robert Chazan (West Orange, NJ, 1980), p.217.

4. *The Etablissements de Saint Louis: Thirteenth-Century Law Texts from Tours, Orléans, and Paris*, trans. F.R.P. Akehurst (Philadelphia, 1996), p.27.

5. Joinville and Villehardouin, *Chronicles of the Crusades*, trans. M.R.B. Shaw (Harmondsworth, 1963), p.177.

6. Despite the similarity between the terms *parlement* and Parliament, both deriving from *parler*, "to talk," the two institutions were different. The first was the central French court of law, the second the English representative institution. It is true that the English parliament did hear legal cases, but

it also discussed foreign affairs, published royal statutes, and (above all) granted taxes to the king.

7. Boniface, "Clericis Laicos," in *The Crisis of Church and State, 1050-1300*, ed. Brian Tierney (rpt. Toronto, 1988), pp.175-76.

8. William of Ockham, excerpts from Quodlibet in *Basic Issues in Medieval Philosophy: Selected Readings*, ed. Richard N. Bosley and Martin M. Tweedale (Peterborough, 1997), p.129.

9. Dante Alighieri, *Purgatorio* v, 134, trans. Charles S. Singleton (Princeton, 1973), 1:53.

10. *The Montpellier Codex*, Part IV: *Text and Translations*, trans. Susan Stakel and Joel C. Relihan in *Recent Researches in the Music of the Middle Ages and Early Renaissance* 8 (Madison, 1985), p.81.

11. Quoted in David Nicholas, *Medieval Flanders* (Harlow, Essex, 1992), p.207.

12. "Walter of Henley's Husbandry," excerpted in Georges Duby, *Rural Economy and Country Life in the Medieval West*, trans. Cynthia Postan (rpt. Philadelphia, 1998), p.388.

FURTHER READING

For searchable maps, genealogies, and other materials for this chapter, please visit the *Short History of the Middle Ages* website at www.broadviewpress.com/shorthistory.

Abu-Lughod, Janet L. *Before European Hegemony: The World System A.D.1250-1350*. New York, 1989.

Binski, Paul. *Medieval Death: Ritual and Representation*. Ithaca, NY, 1996.

Camille, Michael. *The Medieval Art of Love: Objects and Subjects of Desire*. New York, 1998.

Epstein, Steven A. *Genoa and the Genoese, 958-1528*. Chapel Hill, 1996.

Farmer, Sharon. *Surviving Poverty in Medieval Paris: Gender, Ideology, and the Daily Lives of the Poor*. Ithaca, NY, 2002.

Given, James B. *Inquisition and Medieval Society: Power, Discipline, and Resistance in Languedoc*. Ithaca, NY, 1997.

Glick, Leonard B. *Abraham's Heirs: Jews and Christians in Medieval Europe*. Syracuse, 1999.

Jones, P.J. *The Italian City-State: From Commune to Signoria*. Oxford, 1997.

Jordan, William Chester. *The French Monarchy and the Jews: From Philip Augustus to the Last Capetians*. Philadelphia, 1989.

—. *The Great Famine: Northern Europe in the Early Fourteenth Century*. Princeton, 1996.

Martin, Janet. *Medieval Russia, 980-1584*. Cambridge, 1995.

Morgan, David. *The Mongols*. Malden, MA, 1986.

Mundill, Robin R. *England's Jewish Solution: Experiment and Expulsion, 1262-1290*. Cambridge, 1998.

Nirenberg, David. *Communities of Violence: Persecution of Minorities in the Middle Ages*. Princeton, 1996.

O'Callaghan, Joseph F. *The Cortes of Castile-León, 1188-1350*. Philadelphia, 1989.

Pegg, Mark Gregory. *The Corruption of Angels: The Great Inquisition of 1245-1246*. Princeton, 2001.

Rubin, Miri. *Corpus Christi: The Eucharist in Late Medieval Culture*. Cambridge, 1991.

Strayer, Joseph R. *The Reign of Philip the Fair*. Princeton, 1980.

White, John. *Art and Architecture in Italy, 1250-1400*. 3rd ed., New Haven, 1993.

EIGHT

CATASTROPHE AND CREATIVITY
(c.1350-c.1500)

STRUCK BY A PLAGUE that carried off at least a fifth of its population, shaken by Ottoman Turks who conquered Constantinople and moved into the Balkans, buffeted by internal wars that threatened the very foundations of its political life, Europe shuddered for a moment, then shrugged and forged ahead. Those who survived war and disease enjoyed a higher standard of living than before; new-style political entities garnered powers that the old had never had; and new-rigged sailing ships, manned by hopeful adventurers and financed by rich patrons, plied the seas east- and westwards. By 1500, Europe was poised to conquer the globe.

CRISES AND CONSOLIDATIONS

In the 1340s, as the first pandemic since the eighth century began to make its inroads on Europe, France and England were waging a long and debilitating Hundred Years' War. Popular revolts and insurrections rocked both town and countryside, the bitter harvest of war and economic contraction. Meanwhile a schism within the church — setting first two, then three popes against one another — shattered all illusions of harmony within Christendom. At the same time, however, smaller units gained apparent cohesion under new-style princes.

The Black Death

It was probably *Yersinia pestis*, the bacillus of the plague, that struck Hupei Province in China in 1320 and then wended its way slowly westward, carried by the fleas on infected rats along the overland routes that travelers like Marco Polo followed, all the way to Caffa in 1346. From Caffa, the Genoese outpost in the Crimea, it swiftly moved by ship into Europe and the Middle East, hitting Constantinople and Cairo along the way, and soon leaving the port cities for the hinterlands. (Its route closely tracks the trade routes in Map 7.2 on p.254.) In early 1348 the citizens of Pisa and Genoa, fierce rivals on the seas, were being felled without distinction by the plague. Early spring of the same year saw the disease at Florence; two months later it had hit Dorset in England. Dormant during the winter, it revived the next spring to infect French ports and countryside, moving swiftly on to Germany. By 1351 it was at Moscow, where it stopped for a time, only to recur in slightly less virulent cycles throughout the fourteenth century.

The effect on Europe's population was immediate and devastating. Famines had already weakened many people's resistance to disease. At Paris, by no means the city hardest hit, about half the population died, mainly children and poor people. In eastern Normandy, fully 70 to 80 per cent of the population succumbed. At Bologna, even the most robust—men able to bear arms—were reduced by 35 per cent in the course of 1348. In general, somewhere between one-fifth and one-half of the entire European population died in the epidemic that historians call the Black Death. Demographic recovery began only in the second half of the fifteenth century.

Deaths, especially of the poor, led to acute labor shortages in both town and country. Already in 1351, King Edward III of England issued the Statute of Laborers, forbidding workers to take pay higher than pre-plague wages and fining employers who offered more. Similar laws were promulgated—and flouted— elsewhere. In the countryside, landlords needed to keep their profits up even as their workforce was decimated. They were forced to strike bargains with enterprising peasants, furnishing them, for example, with oxen and seed; or they turned their land to new uses, such as pasturage. In the cities, the guilds and other professions recruited new men, survivors of the plague. Able to marry and set up households at younger ages, these *nouveaux riches* helped reconstitute the population. Although many widows were now potentially the heads of households, deeply rooted customs tended to push them either into new marriages (in northern Europe) or (in southern Europe) into the house of some male relative, whether brother, son, or son-in-law.

The plague affected both desires and sentiments. Upward mobility in town and country meant changes in consumption patterns as formerly impoverished groups found new wealth. They chose silk clothing over wool, beer over water. In Italy,

where a certain theoretical equality within the communes had restrained consumer spending, cities passed newly toughened laws to restrict finery. In Florence in 1349, for example, a year after the plague first struck there, the town crier roamed the town shouting out new or renewed prohibitions: clothes could not be adorned with gold or silver; capes could not be lined with fur; the wicks of funeral candles had to be made of cotton; women could wear no more than two rings, only one of which could be set with a precious stone; and so on. As always, such sumptuary legislation affected women more than men.

At around the same time, death became an obsession and a cult. There was newly intense interest in the macabre. The dead were depicted not as in life but as gruesome corpses. Death itself was personified, skeletal and ugly. In the artistic and literary genre known as the Dance of Death, life itself becomes a dance with death, as men and women from all walks of life are escorted—sooner or later—to the grave by ghastly skeletons. Plate 8.1 is one of a series of woodcuts made c.1462 by an anonymous artist for a poem written by Johannes von Saaz at the beginning of the century. Here death is both literally a grim reaper, cutting down his victims with a scythe, and an archer, ready to shoot two careless young men. Blaming their own sins for the disease, penitent pilgrims, occasionally bearing whips to flagellate themselves, crowded the roads. Some fed the rumor that Jews had caused the plague by poisoning the wells, an idea that spread from southern France and northern Spain (where, as we have seen, similar charges had already been leveled in 1320) to Switzerland, Strasbourg, and throughout Germany. At Strasbourg more than 900 Jews were burned in 1349, right in their own cemetery.

Upheavals of War

"And westward, look! Under the Martian Gate," wrote the English poet Geoffrey Chaucer (c.1340-1400) in *The Canterbury Tales*, continuing,

> Arcita and his hundred knights await,
> And now, under a banner of red, march on.
> And at the self-same moment Palamon
> Enters by Venus' Gate and takes his place
> Under a banner of white, with cheerful face.
> You had not found, though you had searched the earth,
> Two companies so equal in their worth.[1]

Chaucer's association of war with "cheer" and "valor" was a central conceit of chivalry, giving a rosy tint to the increasingly "total" wars that engulfed even civilian populations in the fourteenth and fifteenth centuries. In the east, the Ottoman Turks took the Byzantine empire by storm; in the west, England and France fought a bitter Hundred Years' War. Dynastic feuds and princely encroachments marked a tumultuous period in which the map of Europe was remade.

THE OTTOMAN EMPIRE

The establishment of a new Islamic empire—the Ottoman—just south of the Danube river, marked an astonishing transformation of Europe's southeast. (See Map 8.1.) In the interstices between the Mongol empire and Byzantine hegemony, thirteenth-century Turkish tribal leaders in Anatolia increasingly encroached on Byzantine territory, carving out ephemeral principalities for themselves. At the beginning of the fourteenth century, Osman, after whom the Ottomans were named, took the lead. (See list of Ottoman Emirs and Sultans on p.336.) Capturing Nicaea in 1301 as part of his "holy war" against all infidels, Osman became the acknowledged regional leader, attracting other Turkish princes to fight under his banner. Rather than unite

Map 8.1: The Ottoman Empire, *c.*1500

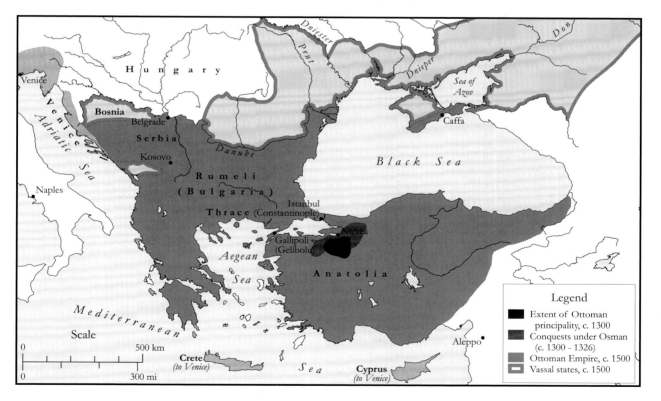

in the face of these developments, rival factions within the Byzantine state tried to take advantage of the Ottomans. It was as ally to one claimant for the Byzantine throne that Ottoman troops arrived in Gallipoli in 1354. They remained long after their welcome had run out. In the 1360s they took Thrace and then, under the energetic leadership of Bayezid I (r.1389-1402), they conquered much of the Balkans, taking Serbia (at the battle of Kosovo) in 1389 and Bulgaria in 1393.

Map 8.2 (facing page):
The First Phase of the
Hundred Years' War

To the east, the Ottoman advance was aided by the disintegration of the Mongol empire, which began in China with the overthrow of the khanate there. To be sure, the Ottomans were halted by Timur the Lame (Tamerlane) (1336-1405), a warrior leader from the region of Samarkand, who saw himself as restoring the Mongol empire. But with Timur's death, the Ottomans slowly regained their hold, in part because of the superiority of their elite troops, the Janissaries, professional soldiers of slave origin. Adopting the new military hardware of the west—cannons and muskets—the Ottomans retook Anatolia and the Balkans. Under Mehmed II the Conqueror (r.1451-1481), their cannons accomplished what former sieges had never done, breaching the thick walls of Constantinople. In 1453 the city was conquered, and the Byzantine empire came to an end.

The new Ottoman state had come to stay. Its rise was due to its military power and the weakness of its neighbors. But its longevity—it did not begin to decline until the late seventeenth century—was due to more complicated factors. Building on a theory of absolutism that echoed similar ideas in the Christian West, the Ottoman rulers acted as the sole guarantors of law and order; they considered even the leaders of the mosques to be their functionaries, soldiers without arms. Prospering from taxes imposed on their relatively well-to-do peasantry, the new rulers spent their money on roads to ease troop transport and a navy powerful enough to oust the Italians from their eastern Mediterranean outposts. Eliminating all signs of rebellion (which meant, for example, brutally putting down Serb and Albanian revolts), the Ottomans created a new world power.

The new state eventually changed Europe's orientation. Europeans could—and did—continue to trade in the Mediterranean, even with the Ottomans. But on the whole they preferred to treat them as a barrier to the Orient. Not long after the fall of Constantinople, as we shall see, the first transatlantic voyages began.

THE HUNDRED YEARS' WAR

Although in the seventeenth century English rulers would set their sights on the Americas and the Indies, between 1350 and 1500, they were still preoccupied with older claims. The Hundred Years' War (in fact fought sporadically over more than a century, from 1337 to 1453) was the English king's bid to become ruler of France.

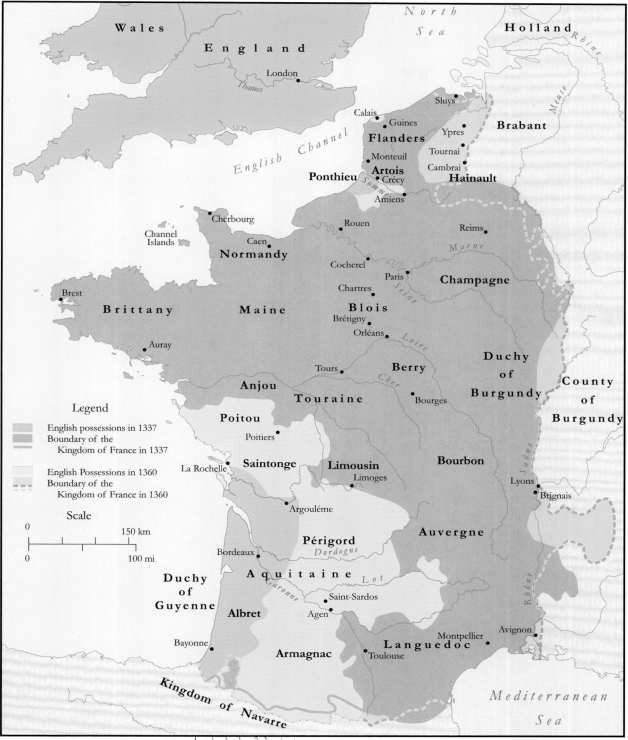

Wales

England

London

Thames

North Sea

Holland

Rhine

Meuse

Brabant

Calais
Guines
Sluys
Ypres
Tournai
Cambrai

Flanders

Monteuil

Artois

Crécy

Hainault

Ponthieu

Somme

Amiens

Reims

English Channel

Channel Islands

Cherbourg

Caen

Normandy

Rouen

Cocherel

Paris

Marne

Champagne

Brest

Brittany

Maine

Chartres

Blois

Brétigny

Orléans

Seine

Duchy of Burgundy

County of Burgundy

Auray

Tours

Berry

Cher

Loire

Saône

Anjou

Touraine

Bourges

Poitou

Legend

English possessions in 1337
Boundary of the
Kingdom of France in 1337

English Possessions in 1360
Boundary of the
Kingdom of France in 1360

Poitiers

Saintonge

La Rochelle

Limousin

Limoges

Bourbon

Lyons

Brignais

Auvergne

Scale

0   150 km

0   100 mi

Argouléme

Périgord

Dordogne

Bordeaux

Aquitaine

Lot

Garonne

Duchy of Guyenne

Albret

Saint-Sardos

Agen

Bayonne

Armagnac

Toulouse

Languedoc

Montpellier

Avignon

Rhône

Mediterranean Sea

Kingdom of Navarre

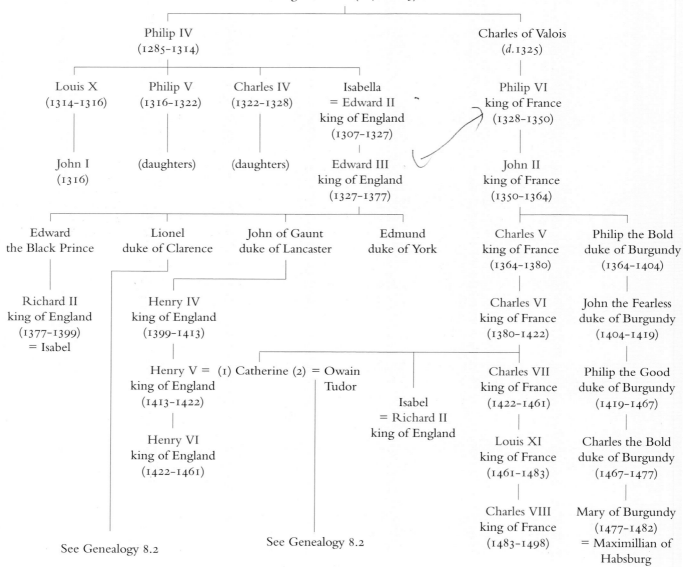

Beyond a dynastic dispute were England's long-standing claims to Continental lands, many of which had been confiscated by Philip II of France and the rest by Philip VI in 1337. Beyond that were Flemish-English economic relations, to which English prosperity and taxes were tied. Ultimately, the war was not so much between England and France as between two conceptions of France: one, a centralized monarchy, the other, an association of territories ruled by counts and dukes.

As son of Isabella, last living child of the French king Philip the Fair, Edward III of England was in line for the French throne when Charles IV died in 1328. The French nobles awarded it, instead, to Philip VI, the first Valois king of France. (See Genealogy 8.1: Kings of France and England and the Dukes of Burgundy during the Hundred Years' War.) Edward's claims led to the first phase of the Hundred Years' War, when adroit raids and use of longbowmen—fighters with a new-style bow and arrows that flew far and penetrated deeply—gave English troops the clear advantage. By 1360, the size of English possessions in southern France was approximately what it had been in the twelfth century. (Compare Map 8.2 with Map 6.2 on p.210.)

English successes were nevertheless short-lived. Harrying the border of Aquitaine, French forces chipped away at it in the course of the 1380s. Meanwhile, sentiments for peace were gaining strength in both England and France; a treaty to put an end to the fighting for a generation was drawn up in 1396. Yet the "generation" was hardly past puberty when Henry V (r.1413-1422) came to the English throne and revived the crown's Continental claims. Demanding nearly all of the land that the Angevins had held in the twelfth century, he struck France in 1415. After capturing the city of Harfleur with cannon fire, he met the French army at Agincourt. There the English (mounted archers) decimated the French knights. Normandy was soon Henry's, and, determined to keep it, he forced all who refused him loyalty into exile, confiscating their lands and handing the property over to his own followers.

Henry's plans were aided by a new regional power: Burgundy. A marvel of shrewd marriage policies, the Burgundian state forged by Philip the Bold (r.1364-1404) was a cluster of principalities with one center at Dijon (the "traditional" Burgundy) and another at Lille, in the north. Unity was forged at the top, by the ducal court and the courtiers who made up its council. Philip, like the kings of France, was of Valois lineage, but his grandson, Philip the Good (r.1419-1467), decided to link his destiny with England, long the major trading partner of Flanders.

With the support of the Burgundians, the English easily marched into Paris, inadvertently helped by the French king, Charles VI (r.1380-1422), whose frequent bouts of insanity created a vacuum at the top of France's leadership. The Treaty of Troyes (1420) made Henry V the heir to the throne of France.

Had Henry lived, he might have made good his claim. But he died in 1422, leaving behind an infant son to take the crown of France, under the regency of the duke

Genealogy 8.1 (facing page): Kings of France and England and the Dukes of Burgundy during the Hundred Years' War

of Bedford. Meanwhile, with Charles VI dead the same year, Charles VII, the French "dauphin," or crown prince, was holed up at Bourges, disheartened by defeats. Only in 1428 did his mood change; Jeanne d'Arc (Joan of Arc), a sixteen-year-old peasant from Domrémy (part of a small enclave in northern France still loyal to the dauphin), convinced Charles and his theologians that she had been divinely sent to defeat the English. In effect, she inherited the moral capital that had been earned by the Beguines and other women mystics. When the English forces laid siege to Orléans (the prelude to their crossing into southern France—see Map 8.3), Jeanne was allowed to join the French army. Its "miraculous" defeat of the English at Orléans (1429) turned the tide. "Oh! What an honor for the feminine sex!" wrote the poet Christine de Pisan (1364-c.1430), continuing,

Map 8.3 (facing page): English and Burgundian Hegemony in France, 1429

It is obvious that God loves it
That all those vile people,
Who had laid the whole kingdom to waste—
By a woman this realm is now made safe and sound,
Something more than five thousand men could not have done—
And those traitors purged forever![2]

Soon thereafter Jeanne led Charles to Reims, where he was anointed king. Captured by the English in 1430 and burned as a heretic the following year, Jeanne later became a symbol of triumphant French resistance. But in fact it took many more years, indeed until 1453, for the French to win the war. And part of the reason that they did so was that the duke of Burgundy abandoned the English and supported the French, at least in lukewarm fashion, after 1435.

The Hundred Years' War devastated France in the short run. During battles, armies destroyed cities. Even when not officially "at war," bands of soldiers—"Free Companies" of mercenaries that hired themselves out to the highest bidder, whether in France, Spain, or Italy—roved the countryside, living off the gains of pillage. Yet soon after 1453, France began a long and steady recovery. Merchants invested in commerce, peasants tilled the soil, and the king exercised more power than ever before. A standing army was created, trained, billeted, and supplied with weapons (including cannons and gunpowder), all under royal command. Burgundy, so brilliantly created a century earlier, was dismantled just as brilliantly by the French kings and, by 1493, was largely absorbed into France. A year later, France was leading an expedition into Italy, claiming the crown of Naples.

In England, the Hundred Years' War brought about a similar political transformation. Initially France's victory affected mainly the topmost rank of the royal house itself. The progeny of Edward III formed two rival camps, York and Lancaster

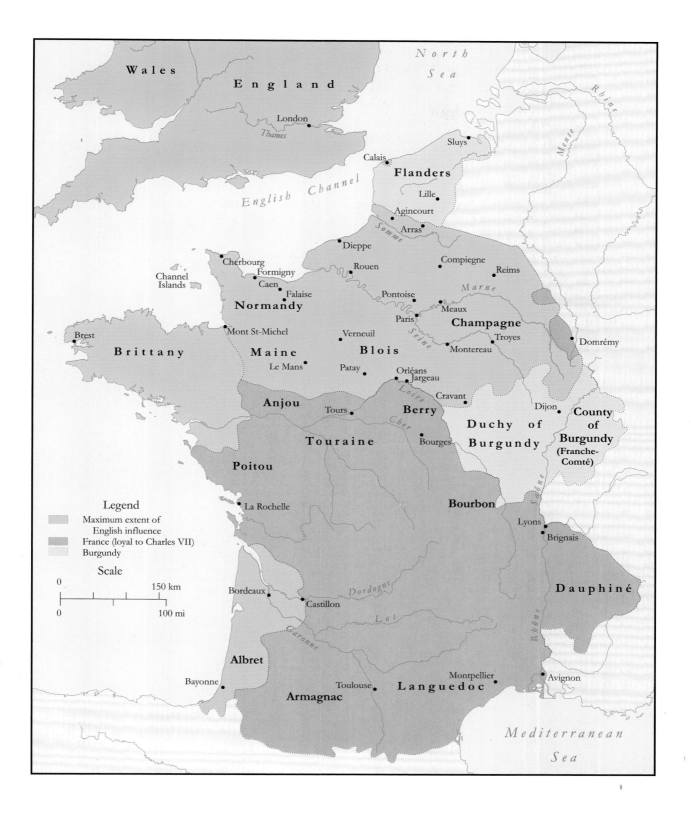

Wales

England

North
Sea

London

Thames

Sluys

Calais

Flanders

English Channel

Lille

Agincourt

Arras

Somme

Dieppe

Compiegne

Reims

Cherbourg
Formigny
Caen

Channel
Islands

Rouen

Marne

Falaise

Normandy

Pontoise

Meaux

Troyes

Domrémy

Brest

Mont St-Michel

Verneuil

Paris

Seine

Champagne

Brittany

Maine

Blois

Montereau

Le Mans

Patay

Orléans
Jargeau

Anjou

Tours

Berry

Cravant

Dijon

County
of
Burgundy
(Franche-
Comté)

Touraine

Cher

Bourges

Duchy of
Burgundy

Poitou

Bourbon

La Rochelle

Lyons

Brignais

Saône

Legend

Maximum extent of
English influence
France (loyal to Charles VII)
Burgundy

Scale

0

150 km

0

100 mi

Bordeaux

Dordogne

Castillon

Lot

Dauphiné

Garonne

Rhône

Albret

Avignon

Bayonne

Toulouse

Montpellier

Languedoc

Armagnac

*Mediterranean
Sea*

Rhine

Meuse

(named after some of their lands in northern England). (See Genealogy 8.2: York and Lancastrian [Tudor] Kings.) Already in 1399, unhappy with Richard II, who had dared to disinherit him, the Lancastrian Henry had engineered the king's deposition and taken the royal scepter himself as Henry IV. But when his grandson Henry VI lost the war to France, the Yorkists quickly took advantage of the fact. A series of dynastic wars—later dubbed the "Wars of the Roses" after the white rose badge of the Yorkists and the red of the Lancastrians—was fought from 1455-1487. In 1461, Edward of York deposed Henry, becoming Edward IV. Upon his death in 1483 there was further intrigue as his brother, Richard III, seized the eleven-year-old Edward V and his brother, packing them off to the Tower of London, where they were soon murdered. Two years later, Richard himself was dead on the fields of Bosworth and Henry VII, the first Tudor king, was on the throne.

Genealogy 8.2:
York and Lancastrian
(Tudor) Kings

YORKIST DYNASTY   LANCASTRIAN (TUDOR) DYNASTY

Edward III
(1327-1377)

Edward   Lionel   John of Gaunt
the Black Prince   duke of Clarence   duke of Lancaster
(d.1376)   (d.1368)   (d.1399)

Richard II   Henry IV
(1377-1399)   (1399-1413)

                                    Henry V = (1) Catherine (2) = Owain
                                    king of England   Tudor
                                    (1413-1422)

Richard III   Edward IV   Henry VI   Henry VII
(1483-1485)   (1461-1483)   (1422-1461)   (1485-1509)

                         Edward V
                         (1483)

| direct descendant
= married to
┊ indirect descendant

All of this would later be grist for Shakespeare's historical dramas, but at the time it was more the stuff of tragedy, as whole noble lines were killed off, Yorkist lands were confiscated for the crown, and people caught in the middle longed for a strong king who would keep the peace. When the dust settled, the Tudors were far more powerful than previous English kings had been.

Princes, Knights, and Citizens

The Hundred Years' War, the Wars of the Roses, and other, more local wars of the fifteenth century, brought to the fore a kind of super-prince: mighty kings (as in England, Scotland, and France), dukes (as in Burgundy), and *signori* (in Italy). All were supported by mercenary troops and their modern weaponry, putting knights and nobles in the shade. Yet the end of chivalry was paradoxically the height of the chivalric fantasy. When Froissart, a French chronicler of the Hundred Years' War, wanted to tell his readers about the qualifications of a helpful informant named Henry Crystede, he did not report on his subject's education or income; he reported on his "arms": "a chevron gules on a field argent, with three besants gules, two above the chevron and one below."[3] This was heraldry, a system of symbols and signs that, by the fourteenth century, had come to distinguish knights from everyone else, giving them visibility and prestige. When the same chronicler observed the siege of Calais, which resulted in a bad defeat for the French, he nevertheless enthused over the "many fine exploits and feats of arms on land and sea."[4] Kings and other great lords founded and promoted chivalric orders with fantastic names — the Order of the Garter, the Order of the Golden Buckle, the Order of the Golden Fleece. All had mainly social and honorific functions, sponsoring knightly tournaments and convivial feasts precisely when knightly jousts and communal occasions were no longer useful for war.

While super-princes were the norm, there were some exceptions. In the mountainous terrain of the alpine passes, the Swiss Confederation, a coalition of urban and rural communes along with some lesser nobles, promised to aid one another against the Habsburg emperors. Taking advantage of rivalries within the Holy Roman empire, the Swiss created *c.*1500 a militant state of their own. It was structured as a league, where power was in the hands of urban citizenry and members of peasant communes. The nobility gradually disappeared as new elites from town and countryside took over territorial governments. Unlike the great European powers in its "republican" organization, Switzerland nevertheless conveniently served as a reservoir of mercenary troops for its princely neighbors.

Venice maintained its own republicanism via a different set of compromises. It was governed by a Great Council, from whose membership were elected the various officers of the state, including the "doge," a life-long position. Between 1297 and 1324 the size of the Council grew dramatically: to its membership of 210 in 1296, more than a thousand new names were added by 1340. At the same time, however, the Council was gradually closed off to all but certain families, which were in this way turned into a hereditary aristocracy. Accepting this fact constituted the compromise of the lower classes. Its counterpart by the ruling families was to suppress (in large measure) their private interests in favor of the general welfare of the city. That welfare depended mainly on the sea for both necessities and wealth. Only at the beginning of the fifteenth century did the Venetians consider dominating inland cities, extending their control to Verona, Friuli, and even all the way to Bergamo. (See Map 8.4.)

Map 8.4 (facing page): Western Europe, *c.* 1450

Revolts in Town and Country

Where the super-princes prevailed, they were often greeted with revolt. Throughout the fourteenth century popular uprisings across Europe gave vent to discontent. The "popular" component of these revolts should not be exaggerated, as many were led by petty knights or wealthy burghers. But they also involved large masses of people, some of whom were indeed very poor. At times articulating universal principles, these new-style revolts were often deeply rooted as well in local grievances.

Long accustomed to a measure of self-government in periodic assemblies that reaffirmed the customs of the region, the peasants of Flanders reacted boldly when comital officials began to try to collect new taxes. Between 1323 and 1328, Flemish peasants drove out the count's officials and their noble allies, redistributing the lands that they confiscated. The peasants set up an army, established courts, collected taxes, and effectively governed themselves. The cities of Flanders, initially small, independent pockets outside of the peasants' jurisdiction, soon followed suit, with the less wealthy citizens taking over city government. It took the combined forces of the rulers of France and Navarre plus a papal declaration of crusade to crush the peasants at the battle of Cassel in 1328.

Anti-French and anti-tax activities soon resumed in Flanders, however, this time at Ghent, where the weavers had been excluded from city government since 1320. As the English prepared for the opening of the Hundred Years' War, they cut off wool exports to Flanders to force it to their side. The Ghent weavers took up the pro-English cry. Led by Jacob van Artevelde, himself a landowner but now spokesman for the rebels' cause, the weavers overturned the city government. By 1339, Artevelde's supporters dominated not only Ghent but also much of northern Flanders. A year

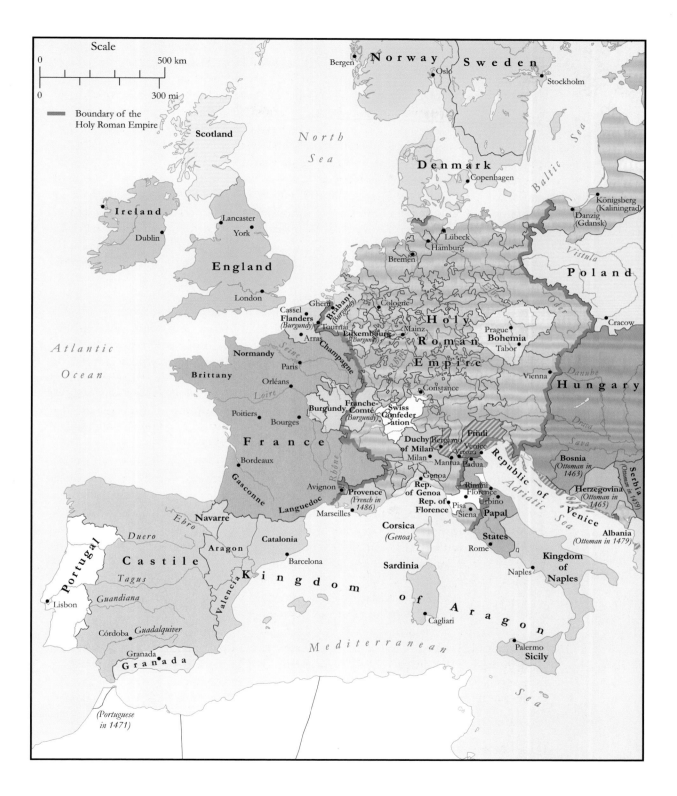

Scale

0 ————— 500 km

0 ————— 300 mi

▬ Boundary of the
Holy Roman Empire

North Sea

Atlantic Ocean

Baltic Sea

NORWAY Bergen Oslo **SWEDEN** Stockholm

Scotland

Ireland Dublin

Lancaster York

England London

Denmark Copenhagen

Königsberg (Kaliningrad)
Danzig (Gdansk)

Lübeck Hamburg
Bremen

Vistula

POLAND

Cracow

Oder

Ghent **Brabant** *(Burgundy)* Cologne
Cassel Tournai
Flanders *(Burgundy)*
Arras **Luxembourg** *(Burgundy)* Mainz

Holy Roman Empire

Prague **Bohemia**
Tabor

Rhine

Champagne

Normandy
Paris
Seine

Brittany
Orléans
Loire

Vienna

Hungary

Danube

Drava

Sava

Poitiers
Bourges

Burgundy **Franche-Comté** *(Burgundy)*
Swiss Confederation
Constance

France

Bordeaux

Gasconne

Avignon
Rhône
Provence *(French in 1486)*
Marseilles
Languedoc

Duchy of Milan Bergamo
Milan Verona Venice
Mantua Padua

Friuli

Rep. of Genoa Genoa

Republic of Venice

Adriatic Sea

Bosnia *(Ottoman in 1463)*

Serbia *(Ottoman in 1459)*

Herzegovina *(Ottoman in 1465)*

Rep. of Florence Rimini
Florence
Pisa Urbino
Siena

Papal States

Rome

Albania *(Ottoman in 1479)*

Ebro

Navarre

Aragon **Catalonia**
Barcelona

Valencia **Kingdom of Aragon**

Corsica *(Genoa)*

Sardinia

Kingdom of Naples
Naples

Portugal Lisbon

Duero

Castile

Tagus

Córdoba *Guadalquiver*
Granada **Granada**

Guandiana

Cagliari

Palermo **Sicily**

Mediterranean Sea

(Portuguese in 1471)

later, he was welcoming the English king Edward III to Flanders as king of France. Although Artevelde was assassinated in 1345 by weavers who thought he had betrayed their cause, the tensions that brought him to the fore continued. The local issues that pitted weavers against the other classes in the city were exacerbated by being tied to the ongoing hostility between England and France. Like a world war, the Hundred Years' War engulfed its bystanders.

In France, uprisings in the mid-fourteenth century signaled further strains of the war. At the disastrous battle of Poitiers (1356), King John II of France was captured and taken prisoner. The Estates General, which prior to the battle had agreed to heavy taxes to counter the English, met in the wake of Poitiers to allot blame and to reform the government. When the new regent (the ruler in John's absence) stalled in instituting the reforms, Étienne Marcel, leader of the merchants of Paris, led a plot to murder some royal councillors and take control of Paris. But the presence of some Free Company troops in Paris led to disorder there, and some of Marcel's erstwhile supporters blamed him for the riots, assassinating him in 1358.

Meanwhile, outside Paris, the Free Companies harried the countryside. In 1358 a peasant movement formed to resist them. Called the Jacquerie by dismissive chroniclers, probably after their derisive name for its leader, Jacques Bonhomme (Jack Goodfellow), it soon turned into an uprising against the nobility, who were seen as failures both in fighting at Poitiers and in defending the rural peace. The revolt was depicted in sensationally gory detail: "Those evil men," wrote Froissart, "pillaged and burned everything and violated and killed all the ladies and girls without mercy, like mad dogs."[5] Perhaps. But the repression of the Jacquerie was at least equally brutal and even quicker.

More permanent in its consequences was the English Peasants' Revolt of 1381, in which groups of peasants converged on London demanding an end to serfdom. Most immediately, the revolt was a response to a new poll tax—a tax on all adults—passed by Parliament to recoup the expenses of war. More profoundly, it was a clash between new expectations of freedom (in the wake of the Black Death, labor was worth much more) and old obligations of servitude. The egalitarian chant of the peasants signaled a growing sense of their own power:

> When Adam delved and Eve span,
> Who then was the gentleman?

Although the leader of the revolt, Wat Tyler, was soon killed and the rest of the peasants dispersed, the death knell of serfdom in England had in fact been sounded, as peasants went home to bargain with their landlords for new-style leases.

In the decades just before this in a number of Italian cities, cloth workers chafed under regimes that normally barred them from guilds and gave them no say in government. At Florence in 1378, matters came to a head as a coalition of wool workers, small businessmen, and some disaffected guild members challenged the ruling elites. The "ciompi" (wool-carders) rebellion, as the movement was called, succeeded briefly in taking over the Florentine government and permitting three new guilds there. But the movement soon splintered, and, strapped for money, it resorted to forced loans, an expedient that backfired. By 1382, the old elite was back in power determined not to let the lower classes rise again; in the next century, the Florentine republic would give way to rule by a powerful family of bankers, the Medici.

Economic Contraction

While the Black Death was good for the silk trade, and the Hundred Years' War stimulated the manufacture of arms and armor, in other spheres economic contraction was the norm. After 1340, with the fragmentation of the Mongol empire, easy trade relations between Europe and the Far East were destroyed. Within Europe, rulers' war machines were fueled by new taxes and forced loans. Some of the loans were paid back, but others were not; even the wealthy could not withstand the losses. Other loans to heads of state were not forced, but they were nevertheless hard to refuse; the great import-export houses, which loaned money as part of their banking activities, found themselves advancing too much to rulers all too willing to default. In the 1340s the four largest firms went bankrupt, producing, in domino effect, the bankruptcies of hundreds more.

War did more than gobble up capital. Where armies raged, production stopped. Even in intervals of peace, Free Companies harried not only the countryside but also merchants on the roads. To ensure its grain supply, Florence was obliged to supply guards all along the route from Bologna. Merchants began investing in insurance policies, not only against losses due to weather but also against robbers and pirates.

Meanwhile, the plague dislocated normal economic patterns. Urban rents fell as houses went begging for tenants, while wages rose as employers sought to attract scarce labor. In the countryside, whole swaths of land lay uncultivated. The monastery of Saint-Denis, so rich and powerful under Abbot Suger in the twelfth century, lost more than half its income from land between 1340 and 1403. As the population fell and the demand for grain decreased, the Baltic region—chief supplier of rye to the rest of Europe—suffered badly; by the fifteenth century, some villages had disappeared.

Yet, as always, the bad luck of some meant the prosperity of others. While Tuscany lost its economic edge, cities in northern Italy and southern Germany gained new muscle, manufacturing armor and fustian (a popular textile made of cotton and flax) themselves and then distributing their products across Europe. The whole center of economic growth was in fact shifting northwards, from the Mediterranean to the European heartlands. There was one unfortunate exception: the fourteenth century saw the burgeoning of the slave trade in southern Europe. Girls, mainly from the Mongol world but also sometimes Greeks or Slavs (and therefore Christians), were herded onto ships; those who survived the harrowing trip across the Mediterranean were sold on the open market in cities such as Genoa, Florence, and Pisa. They were high-prestige purchases, domestic "servants" with the allure of the Orient.

THE CHURCH DIVIDED

The fourteenth and fifteenth centuries saw deep divisions within the church. Popes fought over who had the right to the papacy, and ordinary Catholics disputed about that as well as the very nature of the church itself.

The Great Schism

Between 1378 and 1409, two rival popes claimed to rule as vicar of Christ; from 1409 to 1417, a third one joined them. Each excommunicated the others, each surrounded himself with a college of cardinals, each commanded loyal followers. The Great Schism (1378-1417)—as this period of popes and antipopes is called—was both a spiritual and a political crisis.

Exacerbating political tensions, the schism fed the Hundred Years' War: France supported the pope at Avignon, England the pope at Rome. In some regions the schism polarized individual communities: for example, around 1400 at Tournai, on the border of France and Flanders, two rival bishops, each representing a different pope, fought over the diocese. Portugal, more adaptable and further away, simply changed its allegiance four times.

The papal monarchy painstakingly built up at Avignon was now split, the half at Avignon largely dependent on French resources to support it, the half at Rome transformed into a *signoria*, complete with mercenary troops (*condottieri*) to collect its taxes and fight its wars. To establish himself at Rome, Boniface IX (1389-1404) reconquered the papal states and set up governors (many of them his family members) to rule over them. Desperate for more revenues, the popes turned all their prerogatives into sources of income. Boniface, for example, put church benefices on the open market and commercialized "indulgences"—acts of piety (such as viewing a relic or attending a special church feast) for which people were promised release from Purgatory for a specified number of days—by making their purchase equivalent to the act. Many willingly made such purchases; many others were outraged that Heaven was for sale.

Solutions to end the schism eventually coalesced around the idea of a council. The "conciliarists"—those who advocated the convening of a council that would have authority over even the pope—included both university men and princes anxious to flex their muscles over the church. Satirizing those who opposed the council, the conciliarist Pierre d'Ailly gave the Devil the last word:

> Never ask what may bring peace to Jerusalem [says the Devil, mocking those who wanted a council], but act in such wise that its kingdom, divided against itself, be desolated by a whirlwind of wars.[6]

Even the Council of Constance (1414–1417), which deposed the rivals and elected Martin V as pope, did not end the conciliar movement, which in the course of the fifteenth century developed an influential theory holding that church authority in the final instance resided in a corporate body (whether representing prelates or more broadly the community of the faithful) rather than the pope. Nor did Constance end the fragmentation of the church. National, even nationalist, churches were beginning to form, independent of and sometimes in opposition to papal leadership.

POPULAR RELIGIOUS MOVEMENTS IN ENGLAND AND BOHEMIA

In England, the radical Oxford-trained theologian John Wyclif (c.1330–1384), influenced in part by William of Ockham (see p.269), argued for a very small sphere of action for the church. In his view, the state alone should concern itself with temporal things, the pope's decrees should be limited to what was already in the Gospels, the laity should be allowed to read and interpret the Bible for itself, and the church should stop promulgating the absurd notion of transubstantiation. At first the darling of the king and other powerful men in England (who were glad to hear arguments on behalf of an expanded place for secular rule), Wyclif appealed as well (and more enduringly) to the gentry and literate urban classes. Derisively called "Lollards" (idlers) by the church and persecuted as heretics, the followers of Wyclif were largely, though not completely, suppressed in the course of the fifteenth century.

Considerably more successful were the Bohemian disciples of Wyclif. In Bohemia, part of the Holy Roman empire but long used to its own monarchy (see Map 8.4), religion and philosophy mixed easily with national feeling. At the University of

Prague, founded in 1348 by Emperor Charles IV (*r*.1346-1378), the German-speaking masters were nominalists, the Czech-speakers realists. In the hands of Jan Hus (*c*.1370-1415), one of the Czech masters, the writings of Wyclif were molded to local needs. The church owned about half the land in Bohemia, most of it in the hands of the bishops rather than the parish priests, and it taxed the peasants heavily. In calling for a reformed church based on a moral community of believers, Hus appealed not only to the poorer groups in Bohemia but also to some of the well-to-do, equally disenchanted with clerical wealth and power. Hus envisaged a laity actively reading the Bible and correcting the priests. His friend Jerome of Prague called Czech-speakers who adhered to a church reformed on Hus's model a *natio*, "nation."

Burned as a heretic at the Council of Constance, Hus nevertheless inspired a movement that transformed the Bohemian church. His followers, called Hussites, soon disagreed about demands and methods (the most radical, the Taborites, set up a sort of government in exile in southern Bohemia, pooling their resources while awaiting the Second Coming), but most found willing protectors in the Bohemian nobility. In the struggle between these groups and imperial troops—backed by a papal declaration of crusade in Bohemia—a peculiarly Bohemian church was created, with its own special liturgy for the Mass.

CHURCHES UNDER ROYAL LEADERSHIP: FRANCE AND SPAIN

"National" churches did not need popular revolts to spark them. Indeed, in France and Spain they were forged in the crucible of growing royal power. In the Pragmatic Sanction of Bourges (1438), Charles VII surveyed the various failings of the church in France and declared himself the guarantor of its reform. Popes were no longer to appoint French prelates nor grant benefices to churchmen; these matters now came under the jurisdiction of the king.

Similar rights were claimed by the crown in Spain about a half-century later, when the marriage of Ferdinand (*r*.1479-1516) and Isabella (*r*.1474-1504)—dubbed the "Catholic Monarchs" by the pope—united Aragon and Castile. In their hands, Catholicism became an instrument of militant royal sovereignty. King and queen launched an offensive against the Muslims in Granada (conquering the last bit in 1492) and determined to purge the *conversos* (Christians of Jewish heritage) in their midst.

Like the war against the Muslims, the persecution of the "New Christians" in Spain had deep roots. The relatively peaceful co-existence of Christians and Jews in most of Spain during the twelfth and thirteenth centuries had ended in the fourteenth. Virulent anti-Jewish pogroms in 1391 led many Spanish Jews to convert to Christianity. But the subsequent successes of the *conversos*—some of whom obtained civil and church offices or married into the nobility — stirred resentment among the "Old Christians." Harnessing popular resentments, the Catholic Monarchs set up their own version of the Inquisition in 1478. Under the friar-inquisitor Tomás Torquemada (1420-1498), wholesale torture and public executions became the norm for disposing of "crypto-Jews." When, in 1492, the monarchs demanded that all remaining Jews convert or leave the country, many chose exile over *conversos* status. Soon the newly "purified" church of Spain was extended to the New World as well, where papal concessions gave the kings control over church benefices and appointments.

DEFINING STYLES

Everywhere, in fact, kings were intervening in church affairs, wresting military force from the nobility, harnessing it to the crown, and imposing lucrative taxes to be gathered by their zealous and efficient salaried agents. All of this was largely masked, however, behind brilliant courts that employed every possible means to burnish the image of the prince.

Italy

> For it is in speech that men excel beasts. What is so uncultivated, so unpolished, so unintelligible, so base, that it cannot be set aglow and, so to speak, ennobled by a carefully wrought oration? … And how much more humane, praiseworthy and noble do those states and princes become who support and cultivate these studies! Certainly for this reason this part of philosophy has laid claim for itself to the sweet name of "humanity," since those who are rough by nature become by these studies more civil and mild-mannered.[7]

So spoke Cassandra Fedele in an oration that she gave at the University of Padua in 1487. Pointedly, she praised not scholasticism but eloquence. Scholasticism, largely housed in the faculties of theology and philosophy of northern Europe, never caught fire in Italy, where rhetoric and legal studies held sway. In the course of the fourteenth century Italian intellectuals had begun turning away from scholasticism, from its clear but inelegant phrases, its specialized and often newly created vocabulary ("transubstantiation" is a good example), to ancient models of style. Already in 1333 the young Francesco Petrarch (1304-1374), traveling through the Low Countries looking for manuscripts of the ancient authors, discovered Cicero's *Pro Archia*, a paean to poetry, and carefully copied it out.

Petrarch's taste for ancient eloquence and his ability to write in a new, elegant, "classical" style (whether in Latin or in the vernacular) made him a star. But he was not alone, as Fedele's "Oration" proves; he was simply one of the more famous exemplars of a new group calling themselves "humanists." There had been humanists before: we have seen Saint Anselm's emphasis on Christ's saving humanity, Saint Bernard's evocation of human religious emotion, and Thomas Aquinas's confidence in human reason to scale the heights of truth (see pp.204 and 268). But the new humanists were more self-conscious about their calling, and they tied it to the cultivation of classical literature.

As Fedele's pointed reference to "states and princes" shows, if the humanists' passion was antiquity, their services were demanded with equal ardor by ecclesiastical and secular princes. Poggio Bracciolini (1390-1459), zealous collector of antiquities, was, for example, secretary to several popes. At the Council of Constance, officially entirely focused on resolving the schism, *he* spent his free time scouring the nearby monasteries for classical texts. Petrarch was similarly employed by princes: the splendid palace frescoes commissioned by the Carrara family of Padua, for example, were inspired by Petrarchan themes. (Unfortunately, only fragments remain today.) As Italian artists associated themselves with humanists, working in tandem with them, they too became part of the movement.

Historians have come to give the name Renaissance to this era of artists and humanists. But the Renaissance was not so much a period as a program. It made the language and art of the ancient past the model for the present; it privileged classical books as "must" reading for an eager and literate elite; and it promoted old, sometimes crumbling, and formerly little-appreciated classical art, sculpture, and architecture as inspiring models for Italian artists and builders. Meanwhile, it downgraded the immediate past—the last thousand years!—as a barbarous "Middle" Age. Above all, the Renaissance gave city communes and wealthy princes alike a new repertory of symbols and styles, drawn from a resonant and heroic past, with which to associate their present power.

At Florence, for example, where the Medici family held sway in the fifteenth century behind a facade of communal republicanism, the sculptor Donatello (*c.*1386-1466) cast a bronze figure of David (see Plate 8.2) to stand before the Medici palace. It was accompanied by a Latin inscription, "Behold, a boy overcame the great tyrant. Conquer, O citizens."[8] The appeal to the Florentines to overcome the enemy (very likely Milan) subtly associated the Medici family with the liberty of the citizenry while disparaging the dukes of Milan as tyrants. Donatello's David is strikingly young, self-absorbed—and utterly nude apart from his hat and boots. The first bronze nude cast since antiquity, it combines Christian iconography (David here evokes Christ trampling the serpent) with classical ease (compare David's easy pose with that of the equally triumphant Theseus the Minotaur-slayer in Plate 1.2 on p.32).

Plate 8.2 (facing page): Donatello, David Standing on the Head of Goliath (*c.*1420s). David is here portrayed neither as an Old Testament king nor as the author of the Psalms but as a beautiful boy.

Plate 8.3: Brunelleschi, Foundling Hospital (begun 1419). Compare this exterior with the exterior of Notre Dame Cathedral in **Plate 6.2** on p.232-33 to appreciate the utterly new ideals expressed in Brunelleschi's public architecture.

Florence, whose numerous wealthy corporations patronized artists as generously as did the Medici, was in many ways the heart of the Renaissance. The Foundling Hospital (see Plate 8.3), built by Brunelleschi around the same time as Donatello was casting his David, was commissioned by the Florentine guild of silk merchants. Its calm regularity and low horizontal steadiness signal a radical break from the soaring Gothic architectural style. Still around the same time, Ghiberti (1378–1455) was finishing his panels for the doors of the Florentine baptistery, a project sponsored by the guild of cloth merchants. In the scene of the Flagellation (see Plate 8.4), the figure of Christ is inspired by a classical nude, though his tormentors would be comfortable on the facade of any Gothic cathedral.

The Renaissance flourished in many cities besides Florence, among them Rome, Urbino, Mantua, Venice, and Milan. Under Milan's Duke Ludovico il Moro (r.1480–1499), Leonardo da Vinci (1452–1519) had a number of commissions, including painting the Last Supper (see Plate 8.5) on one of the walls of the dining hall of a Dominican convent c.1497. On the opposite wall, now nearly obliterated, Leonardo added a fresco of Ludovico, his wife, and their two children kneeling before an image of the Crucifixion.

These were religious themes, but Ludovico sponsored classical ones as well, sometimes woven into the very fabric of courtly life. At one of his banquets in 1491, for example, boiled fish were presented under covers consisting "of a model of the Colosseum lavishly decorated with gold and mottoes," while a dessert arrived under

Plate 8.4 (facing page): Ghiberti, Flagellation (1401–1402). The harmony of sculpture and architecture that Renaissance artists strove to achieve is made clear in this panel in which the figures are framed by a quasi-classical structure. Compare Ghiberti's method of filling (and suggesting) space with that of the Romanesque sculptor of **Plate 5.5** on p.196.

Plate 8.5: Leonardo da Vinci, Last Supper (c.1497). Leonardo first made his reputation with the "Last Supper," which evokes the precise moment when Christ said to his feasting apostles, "One of you is about to betray me" (Matt. 26:21). All the apostles react with horror and surprise, but the guilty Judas recoils, his face in shadows.

"ornate lids in gold, in the Royal manner, depicting Rome triumphant with an ox, who together vow never to part, and this represents justice, temperance and great friendship, and many verses testifying to this are recited."[9] No doubt some humanists in Ludovico's employ were kept busy writing the verses.

The Ottoman Court

Some of Ludovico's dinner presentations acted out a different preoccupation—the power of the new Ottoman state. When a whole roasted capon was brought in for each guest, it was accompanied by a little drama:

> A bull is presented by Indians and brought in by slaves of the Sultan in a most elaborately decorated procession of gold and silver with two little moors who sing very elaborately and an ambassador with an interpreter, who translates the words of the embassy.[10]

Here the Ottoman sultan was depicted as the lackey of Duke Ludovico, in a pageant that was meant to be very exotic and in need of "translation" (even though Ludovico himself was dubbed "il Moro," the Moor, because of his swarthy complexion). But imagine that the real sultan—the Ottoman ruler—were holding his own banquet at the same time: at *his* dinner, the lackey would be an *Italian*, and the sultan would have understood his language. For to the Ottomans, the Renaissance court was their court as well. They had taken Byzantium, purified it of its infidel past (turning its churches into mosques), and reordered it along fittingly traditional lines. Although in popular speech Constantinople became Istanbul (meaning "the city"), its official name remained "Qustantiniyya"—the City of Constantine. The Ottoman sultans claimed the glory of Byzantium for themselves.

Thus Mehmed II continued to negotiate with Genoese traders, while he "borrowed" Gentile Bellini (*c.*1429-1507) from Venice to be his own court artist. In 1479, he posed for his portrait (see Plate 8.6), only a few decades after the genre of portrait painting itself had been "invented" in Europe. On the walls of his splendid Topkapi palace, he displayed tapestries from Burgundy portraying the deeds of Alexander the Great. Just as a statue of David gave glory to the Medici family, so Alexander associated the sultan with a great conqueror. The tapestries were themselves trophies of war: a failed Burgundian crusade against the Ottomans in 1396 had ended in the capture of Duke John the Fearless; his ransom was the Alexander tapestry.

Learning as well as art was key to the sultans' notions of power. Mehmed and his successors staffed the administration of their cities with men well schooled in Islamic

Plate 8.6: Gentile Bellini, Portrait of Mehmed II (1479). Mehmed, like other Renaissance princes, hired Renaissance artists to give him luster. In the 1460s he tried to obtain the services of the Rimini artist and architect Matteo de' Pasti, but his plans were foiled by Venice, which wanted no rivals at Constantinople. The Venetians sent their own Gentile Bellini instead, who celebrated the sultan's power with this portrait.

administration and culture and set up madrasas to teach the young. For himself, Mehmed commissioned a copy of Homer's *Iliad* in Greek, epic poetry in Italian, and other literary works by Turkish, Persian, and European writers. His zeal for scholarship was on a lesser scale but not very different in kind from that of Cosimo de' Medici (1389-1464), who in the mid-fifteenth century took over the nearly one thousand volumes of ancient Greek and Latin texts that had been collected with painstaking care by the humanist Niccolò Niccoli (1364-1437). Open to all, the Medici library became the model for princely bibliophiles throughout Italy and elsewhere. Calls for further crusades against the infidel Turks (in 1455 and 1459, for example) were in this sense "family disputes," attempts to contest the East's right to common notions of power and legitimacy.

Northern Europe

Northern Europe shared the same notions, but here the symbols of authority could be more eclectic. Scholasticism still flourished in the universities, although humanists and Renaissance artists were certainly patronized by the courts. In Plate 8.7, the frontispiece for a manuscript entitled *Book of the Secrets of the Philosophers*, two ancient Greek philosophers are depicted in debate, like good contemporary scholastics, while below them the results of their argument are presented to Philip the Good, duke of Burgundy and the patron of the manuscript. That the duke would want to know "philosophical secrets" should be no surprise; everywhere the new sovereigns were espousing interest in "good government" and "public good" and looking to humanists, lawyers, and philosophers to justify their acts in the light of high principles.

Burgundy's court was typical of the northern type, though more brilliant than most. Here Gothic style, modified by influences from Italy, persisted (particularly in architecture), but new styles were emerging as well. Jan van Eyck (*c*.1390-1441), a Flemish painter in service to Philip the Good as both diplomat and artist, is a good example of some of the new trends. In his "Man in a Red Turban" (see Plate 8.8), van Eyck used oil paints, capable of the finest detail and subtlest shading and thus perfectly suited to the artist's desire to render nature as the eye observes it: we even see the stubble of the man's beard. Yet the entirely secular subject of a man in stylish red headgear (evidence of the Turkish allure) is infused with a quiet inner light that endows it with a kind of otherworldliness. Small wonder that Italians called Flemish painting *pietissimo* and *devoto*—very pious and devout.

The authority and power of the fifteenth-century prince in fact depended on an aura of religion. In Burgundy the duke had a fine private chapel and musicians, singers, and composers to staff it. In England wealthy patrons founded colleges—Eton (founded by King Henry VI in 1440-1441) was one—where choruses offered

Plate 8.7: Frontispiece of the *Livre des secrets aux philosophes* (*c.*1450). Compare this plate with **Plate 8.8** to appreciate the many painting styles patronized by the duke of Burgundy Philip the Good. In this manuscript illustration, Philip, the man in imposing head-gear receiving the book, is clearly distinguished from his courtiers by his dress, not by his face.

up prayers in honor of the Virgin. Motets continued to be composed and sung, but now polyphonic music for larger groups became common as well. In the hands of a composer like John Dunstable (c.1385-1453), who probably worked for the duke of Bedford, regent for Henry VI in France during the Hundred Years' War, dissonance was smoothed out. In the compositions of Dunstable and his followers, old juxtapositions of independent lines were replaced by harmonious chords that moved together even as they changed. As Martin le Franc put it in *Le Champion des dames* (1441-1442), "marvelous pleasantness makes their song joyous and notable."[11] Working within the old modal categories, composers made their mark with music newly sonorous and smooth.

NEW HORIZONS

Experiment and play within old traditions were thus the major trends of the period. They can be seen in explorations of interiority, in creative inventions, even in the conquest of the globe. Yet their consequences may fairly be said to have ushered in a new era.

Interiority

Donatello's David, dependent on no one for his quiet satisfaction, and Van Eyck's red-turbaned man, glowing from within, are similar in their self-involved interiority. David's self-centeredness is that of the hero; Van Eyck's man's is that of any ordinary creature of God, the artist's statement about the holiness of nature.

These two styles of interiority were mirrored in religious life and expression. Saint Catherine of Siena (1347-1380) was a woman in the heroic mold. A reformer with a message, she was one of the first in a long line of women (Jeanne d'Arc is another example) to intervene on the public stage because of her private agonies. Chosen by God in distinct words to be his intermediary in the Great Schism, she wrote (or rather dictated) nearly 400 letters to the great leaders of the day, working ceaselessly to bring the pope back to Rome and urging crusade as the best way to purge and revivify the church.

In the Low Countries, northern Germany, and the Rhineland, the *devotio moderna* (the "new devotion") movement, to the contrary, found purgation and renewal in individual reading and contemplation rather than on the public stage. Founded c.1380 by Gerhard Groote (1340-1384), the Brethren of the Common Life lived in male or

Plate 8.8 (facing page): Jan van Eyck, Man in a Red Turban (1433). Compare this head with that of the idealized Theseus (**Plate 1.2** on p.32), the somber Saint Mark (**Plate 3.8** on p.125), the jovial Saint Joseph, (**Plate 6.7** on p.238) and the insouciant David (**Plate 8.2** on p.308). Only Van Eyck paints his anonymous subject without idealizing or beautifying him; the man's worth and dignity derive only (but importantly) from his individuality.

female communities. Emphasizing education, the copying of manuscripts, material simplicity, and individual faith, they were not quite humanists and not quite mystics, but they drew from both for a religious program that depended very little on the hierarchy or ceremonies of the church. Their style of piety would later be associated with Protestant groups.

Inventions

The enormous demand for books—whether by ordinary lay people, adherents of the *devotio moderna*, or humanists eager for the classics—meant that a market was ready-made for the printing press. The invention, however obvious in thought, marked a great practical breakthrough: it depended on a new technique to mold metal type. This was first achieved by Johann Gutenberg at Mainz (in Germany) in the 1450s. The next trick was to get the raw materials that were needed to ensure ongoing production. Paper required water mills and a steady supply of rag (pulp made of cloth); the metal for the type had to be mined and shaped; an ink had to be found that would adhere to metal letters as well as spread evenly on paper.

Yet by 1500 many European cities had publishing houses, with access to the materials that they needed and sufficient clientele to earn a profit. Highly competitive, the presses advertised their wares. They turned out not only religious and classical books but whatever the public demanded. Martin Luther (*c.*1483-1546) may not in fact have nailed his 95 Theses to the door of the church at Wittenberg in 1517, but he certainly allowed them to be printed and distributed in both Latin and German. Challenging prevailing church teachings and practice, the Theses ushered in the Protestant Reformation. The printing press was the first instrument of mass communication.

Less widely useful yet no less decisive for the future were new developments in navigation. Portolan maps, which charted the shape of the Mediterranean coast through accurate measurements from point to point, were used as practical tools by sailors plying the waters. When, at the end of the fifteenth century, Portuguese adventurers made their way down the coast of Africa, they used the same system. But navigating the Atlantic depended on more than maps; it required methods for exploiting the powerful ocean wind systems. New ship designs—the light caravel, the heavy galleon—featured the rigging and sails needed to harness the wind.

Voyages

The initial impetus for the voyages that would take Europeans around the Cape of Good Hope in one direction and to the Americas in the other came from the Portuguese royal house. The enticements were gold and slaves as well as honor and glory. Under King João I (r.1385–1433) and his successors, Portugal extended its rule to the Muslim port of Ceuta and a few other nearby cities. (See Map 8.5.) More importantly, João's son Prince Henry "the Navigator" (1394-1460) sponsored expeditions — mainly by Genoese sailors — to explore the African coast: in the mid-1450s they reached the Cape Verde Islands and penetrated inland via the Senegal and Gambia rivers. A generation later, Portuguese explorers were working their way far past the equator; in 1487 Bartholomeu Dias (c.1450-1500) sighted the Cape of Good Hope, and at the end of the century Vasco da Gama (c.1460-1524) went around Africa and sailed all the way to Calicut (today Kozhikode) in India. In his account of the voyage he made no secret of his methods: when he needed water, he landed on an island and bombarded the inhabitants, taking "as much water as we wanted."[12]

Map 8.5: Long-distance Sea Voyages of the Fifteenth Century

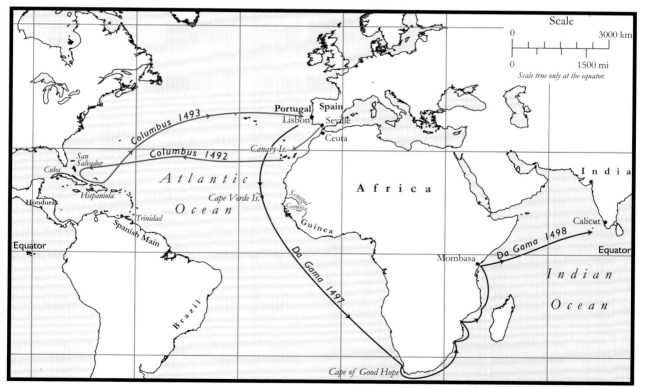

Da Gama's cavalier treatment of the natives was symptomatic of a more profound development: European colonialism. Already in the 1440s, Henry was portioning out the uninhabited islands of Madeira and the Azores to those of his followers who promised to find peasants to settle them. The Azores remained a grain producer, but, with financing by the Genoese, Madeira began to grow cane sugar. The product took Europe by storm. Demand was so high that a few decades later, when few European settlers could be found to work sugar plantations on the Cape Verde Islands, the Genoese Antonio da Noli, discoverer and governor of the islands, brought in African slaves instead. Cape Verde was a microcosm of later European colonialism, which depended on just such slave labor.

Portugal's successes and pretensions roused the hostility and rivalry of Castile. Ferdinand and Isabella's determination to conquer the Canary Islands was in part their "answer" to Portugal's Cape Verde. When, in 1492, they half-heartedly sponsored the Genoese Christopher Columbus (1451–1506) on a westward voyage across the Atlantic, they knew that they were playing Portugal's game. But they also thought they were doing more than that: they imagined that they were continuing the *reconquista*. Their conquest of Granada was not meant to spell the end of their Christian mission but rather to announce the glorious prelude to new conquests by Saint James. When the *conquistadores* found temples in the New World, they called them mosques. The old battles lived on.

★　　★　　★　　★

Between the years 1350 and 1500, a series of catastrophes struck Europe. The Black Death felled at least a fifth of the population of Europe. The Hundred Years' War wreaked havoc when archers shot and cannons roared; it loosed armies of freebooters in both town and country during its interstices of peace. The Ottomans destroyed Byzantium, took over the Balkans, and threatened Austria and Hungary. The church splintered as first the Great Schism and then national churches tore at the loyalties of churchmen and laity alike.

Yet these catastrophes were confronted, if not always overcome, with both energy and inventiveness. In England, peasants loosed the bonds of serfdom; in Italy and elsewhere, bibliophiles and artists discovered wisdom and beauty in the classical past; in Portugal and Spain, adventurers discovered gold and land via the high seas; and everywhere princes flexed the muscles of sovereignty. History books normally divide this period into two parts, the crises going into a chapter on the Middle Ages, the creativity saved for a chapter on the Renaissance. But the two happened together, witness to Europe's aggressive resilience. Indeed, in the next century it would parcel out the globe.

NOTES

1. Geoffrey Chaucer, *The Canterbury Tales*, trans. Nevill Coghill (Harmondsworth, 1977), p.88.

2. Christine de Pisan, *The Tale of Joan of Arc*, quoted in Nadia Margolis, "The Mission of Joan of Arc," in *Medieval Hagiography: An Anthology*, ed. Thomas Head (New York, 2000), p.822.

3. Froissart, *Chronicles*, ed. and trans. Geoffrey Brereton (Harmondsworth, 1968), p.417.

4. Froissart, p.98.

5. Froissart, p.151.

6. Pierre d'Ailly, "Epistola Diaboli Leviathan (1381)," in *Unity, Heresy and Reform, 1378-1460: The Conciliar Response to the Great Schism*, ed. C.M.C. Crowder (New York, 1977), p.44.

7. Cassandra Fedele, "Oration to the University of Padua (1487)," in *The Renaissance in Europe: An Anthology*, ed. Peter Elmer, Nick Webb, and Roberta Wood (New Haven, 2000), pp.54-55.

8. Quoted in Evelyn Welch, *Art and Society in Italy, 1350-1500* (Oxford, 1997), p.211.

9. "A Sforza banquet menu (1491)," in *The Renaissance in Europe: An Anthology*, pp.172-75.

10. "A Sforza banquet menu," p.173.

11. Quoted in Gustave Reese, *Music in the Renaissance*, rev. ed. (New York, 1959), p.13; translated by Charles Brauner.

12. *A Journal of the First Voyage of Vasco da Gama, 1497-1499*, ed. and trans. E.G. Ravenstein (rpt. New York, 1963), p.30.

FURTHER READING

For searchable maps, genealogies, and other materials for this chapter, please visit the *Short History of the Middle Ages* website at www.broadviewpress.com/shorthistory.

Allmand, Christopher. *The Hundred Years War: England and France at War, c.1300-c.1450*. Cambridge, 1988.

Blair, Sheila S., and Jonathan M. Bloom. *The Art and Architecture of Islam, 1250-1800*. New Haven, 1994.

Blockmans, Wim, and Walter Prevenier. *The Promised Lands: The Low Countries under Burgundian Rule, 1369-1530*. Trans. Elizabeth Fackelman. Ed. Edward Peters. Philadelphia, 1999.

Eisenstein, Elizabeth L. *The Printing Press as an Agent of Change: Communications and Cultural Transformations in Early-Modern Europe*. 2 vols in 1. Cambridge, 1980.

Epstein, Steven A. *Speaking of Slavery: Color, Ethnicity, and Human Bondage in Italy*. Ithaca, NY, 2001.

Fernández-Armesto, Felipe. *Before Columbus: Exploration and Colonization from the Mediterranean to the Atlantic, 1229-1492*. Philadelphia, 1987.

Fleet, Kate. *European and Islamic Trade in the Early Ottoman State: The Merchants of Genoa and Turkey*. Cambridge, 1999.

Fresh Verdicts on Joan of Arc. Ed. Bonnie Wheeler and Charles Wood. New York, 1996.

Herlihy, David. *The Black Death and the Transformation of the West*. Ed. Samuel K. Cohn, Jr. Cambridge, MA, 1997.

Hudson, Anne. *The Premature Reformation: Wycliffite Texts and Lollard History*. Oxford, 1988.

Inalcik, Halil. *The Ottoman Empire: The Classical Age, 1300-1600*. Trans. Norman Itzkowitz and Colin Imber. London, 1973.

Jardine, Lisa, and Jerry Brotton. *Global Interests: Renaissance Art between East and West*. Ithaca, NY, 2000.

Keen, Maurice. *Chivalry*. New Haven, 1984.

Kent, F.W., and Patricia Simons. *Patronage, Art, and Society in Renaissance Italy*. Canberra and Oxford, 1987.

Klassen, John Martin. *The Nobility and the Making of the Hussite Revolution*. New York, 1978.

Mack, Rosamond E. *Bazaar to Piazza: Islamic Trade and Italian Art, 1300-1600*. Berkeley, 2002.

Remensnyder, Amy G. "The Colonization of Sacred Architecture: The Virgin Mary, Mosques, and Temples in Medieval Spain and Early Sixteenth-Century Mexico." In *Monks and Nuns, Saints and Outcasts: Religion in Medieval Society*. Ed. Sharon Farmer and Barbara H. Rosenwein. Ithaca, NY, 2000.

Shaw, S.J. *History of the Ottoman Empire and Modern Turkey*, vol. 1: Empire of the Gazis. Cambridge, 1976.

TeBrake, William H. *A Plague of Insurrection. Popular Politics and Peasant Revolt in Flanders, 1323-1328*. Philadelphia, 1993.

Tierney, Brian. *The Idea of Natural Rights: Studies on Natural Rights, Natural Law and Church Law, 1150-1625*. Atlanta, 1997.

EPILOGUE

Spanish *conquistadores* may have fought in the New World as if they were still engaged in the *reconquista*, but clearly the *reality* was so changed that we are right to see the years around 1500 as the turning point between the Middle Ages and a new phase of history. The Middle Ages began when the Roman provinces came into their own. They ended as those provinces—now vastly expanded, rich, and powerful: now "Europe," in fact—became in turn a new empire, its tentacles in the New World, Asia, and Africa. In the next centuries, as Europeans conquered most of the world, they (as the Romans had once done) exported themselves, their values, cultures, diseases, inventions, and institutions, while importing, usually without meaning to, many of the people, ideas, and institutions of those whom they conquered. In another phase, one not yet ended, those colonies—at least some of them—became, in their turn, the center of a new-style empire involving economic and cultural hegemony. It remains to be seen if this empire will eventually be overtaken by its peripheries.

Does anything now remain of the Middle Ages? Without doubt. Bits and pieces of the past are clearly embedded in the present: universities, parliaments, ideas about God and the cosmos, colonialism. We cling to some of these bits with ferocious passion, while repudiating others and allowing still more to float in and out of our unquestioned assumptions. Many things that originated in the Middle Ages are now so transformed that only their names are still medieval. And beyond that? Beyond that, "persistence" is the wrong question. The past need not be replayed because it is "us" but rather because it is "not us," and therefore endlessly fascinating.

GLOSSARY

aids In England, this refers to payments made by vassals to their lords on important occasions.

antiking A king elected illegally.

antipope A pope elected illegally.

Book of Hours A book for lay devotion containing readings in honor of the Virgin Mary (see below) based on simplified versions of the Divine Office (see Office below). Often, but not always, lavishly illustrated.

bull An official document issued by the papacy. The word derives from *bulla*, the lead impression of the pope's seal that was affixed to the document to validate it.

canon law The laws of the church. These were at first hammered out as need arose at various regional church councils and in rules issued by great bishops, particularly the pope. Early collections of canon law were incomplete and sometimes contradictory. Beginning in the ninth century, commentators began to organize and systematize them. The most famous of these treatises was the mid-twelfth-century *Decretum* of Gratian, which, although not an official code, became the basis of canon law training in the schools.

cathedral The principal church of a bishop or archbishop.

church To the Roman Catholics of the Middle Ages, this had two related meanings. It signified in the first place the eternal institution created by Christ, composed of the whole body of Christian believers, and served on earth by Christ's ministers—priests, bishops, the pope. Related to the eternal church were individual, local churches (parish churches, cathedrals, collegiate churches, chapels) where the daily liturgy was carried out and the faithful received the sacraments.

cleric A man in church orders.

collegiate church A church for priests living in common according to a rule.

Crucifixion The execution of Jesus by hanging on a cross (*crux* in Latin). The scene, described in some detail in the Gospels, was often depicted in art; and free-standing crucifixes (crosses with the figure of Jesus on them) were often placed upon church altars.

dogma The authoritative truth of the church.

empire Refers in the first instance to the Roman empire. Byzantium thought of itself as a continuation of that empire. In the West, there were several successor empires all ruled by men who took the title "emperor": there was the empire of Charlemagne, which included more or less what later became France, Italy, and Germany; it was followed in the tenth century (from the time of Otto I on) by the empire held (after a crowning at Rome) by the German kings. This could be complicated: a ruler like Henry IV was king of Germany in 1056, at the age of five; he took the real reins of power in 1066; but he was not crowned emperor until 1084. Nevertheless, he *acted* as an emperor long before that. That empire, which lasted until the thirteenth century, included Germany and (at least in theory) Italy. Some historians call all of these successor empires the "Holy Roman Empire," but in fact that term was not used until 1254. The Holy Roman Empire, which had nothing to do with Rome, ended in 1806. By extension, the term empire can refer to other large realms, often gained through conquest, as the Mongol empire or the Ottoman empire.

episcopal As used for the Middle Ages, this is the equivalent of "bishop's." An "episcopal church" is the bishop's church; an "episcopal appointment" is the appointment of a bishop; "episcopal power" is the power wielded by a bishop.

excommunication An act or pronouncement that cuts someone off from participation in the sacraments of the church and thus from the means of salvation.

Flagellation The scene in the Gospels (Matt 27:26, Mk 15:15) where Christ is scourged by his executioners prior to his Crucifixion (see above). The scene was frequently depicted by artists.

fresco A form of painting using pigments on wet plaster, frequently employed on the walls of churches.

grisaille Painting in monochrome greys highlighted with color tints.

Guelfs and Ghibellines Guelf was the Italian for Welf (the dynasty that competed for the German throne against the Staufen), while Ghibelline referred to Waiblingen (the name of an important Staufen castle). In the various conflicts between the popes and the Staufen emperors, the "Guelfs" were the factions within the Italian city-states that supported the papacy, while the "Ghibellines" supported the emperor. More generally, however, the names became epithets for various inter- and intra-city political factions that had little or no connection to papal/imperial issues.

illumination   The term used for paintings in medieval manuscripts. These might range from simple decorations of capital letters to full-page compositions. An "illuminated" manuscript is one containing illuminations.

layman/ laywoman/laity   Men and women not in church orders, not ordained. In the early Middle Ages it was possible to be a monk and a layperson at the same time. But by the Carolingian period, most monks were priests, and, although nuns were not, they were not considered part of the laity because they had taken vows to the church.

Levant   The lands that border the eastern shore of the Mediterranean; the Holy Land.

liturgy   The formal worship of the church, which included prayers, readings, and significant gestures at fixed times appropriate to the season. While often referring to the Mass (see below), it may equally be used to describe the Offices (see below).

Maghreb   A region of northwest Africa embracing the Atlas Mountains and the coastline of Morocco, Algeria, and Tunisia.

Mass   The central ceremony of Christian worship; it includes prayers and readings from the Bible and culminates in the consecration of bread and wine as the body and blood of Christ, offered to believers in the sacrament of the "Eucharist," or "Holy Communion."

New Testament   This work, a compilation of the second century, contains the four Gospels (accounts of the life of Christ) by Matthew, Mark, Luke, and John; the Acts of the Apostles; various letters, mainly from Saints Paul, Peter, and John to fledgling Christian communities; and the Apocalypse. It is distinguished from the "Old Testament" (see below).

Office   In the context of monastic life, the day and night were punctuated by eight periods in which the monks gathered to recite a precise set of prayers. Each set was called an "Office," and the cycle as a whole was called the "Divine Office." Special rites and ceremonies might also be called offices, such as the "Office of the Dead."

Old Testament   The writings of the Jewish Bible that were accepted as authentic by Christians, though reinterpreted by them as prefiguring the coming of Christ; they were thus seen as the precursor of the "New Testament" (see above), which fulfilled and perfected them.

referendary A high Merovingian administrative official responsible for overseeing the issuing of royal documents.

relief This has two separate meanings. In connection with medieval English government, the "relief" refers to money paid upon inheriting a fief. In the history of sculpture, however, "relief" refers to figures or other forms that project from a flat background. "Low relief" means that the forms project rather little, while "high relief" refers to forms that may be so three-dimensional as to threaten to break away from the flat surface.

sacraments The rites of the church that (in its view) Jesus instituted to confer sanctifying grace. With the sacraments, one achieved salvation. Cut off from the sacraments (by anathema, excommunication, or interdict), one was damned.

scriptorium (pl. scriptoria) The room of the monastery where parchment was prepared and texts copied, illuminated, and bound.

summa (pl. summae) A compendium or summary. A term favored by scholastics to title their comprehensive syntheses.

The Virgin/ The Gospels of Matthew (1:18-23) and Luke (1:27-35) assert that
The Virgin Mary/ Christ was conceived by the Holy Spirit (rather than by a man)
The Blessed and born of Mary, a virgin. Already in the fourth century the
Virgin Church Fathers stressed the virginity of Mary because it guaranteed the holiness of Christ. In the fifth century, at the Council of Chalcedon (451), Mary's perpetual (eternal) virginity was made a matter of dogma. In the medieval church, Mary was celebrated with four feasts — her Nativity, Purification, the Annunciation (of the birth of Jesus), and her Assumption (into heaven). She was understood as the exact opposite of (and antidote to) Eve. Devotion to her cult increased in the later Middle Ages as her role as intercessor with her son in Heaven was increasingly stressed.

APPENDIX: LISTS

LATE ROMAN EMPERORS

(Usurpers in italics)

Maximinus (235-238)
Gordian I (238)
Gordian II (238)
Balbinus and Pupienus (238)
Gordian III (238-244)
Philip the Arab (244-249)
Decius (249-251)
Trebonianus Gallus (251-253)
Aemilian (253)
Valerian (253-260)
Gallienus (253-268)
Postumus (260-268)
Claudius II Gothicus (268-270)
Quintillus (270)
Aurelian (270-275)
Tacitus (275-276)
Florian (276)
Probus (276-282)
Carus (282-283)
Carinus and Numerian (283-284)

In the West	In the East
Maximian (Augustus) (285-305)	Diocletian (Augustus) (284-305)
Constantius (Caesar) (293-305)	Galerius (Caesar) (293-305)
Constantius (Augustus) (305-306)	Galerius (Augustus) (305-311)
Severus (Caesar) (305-306)	Maximin (Caesar) (305-309)
Severus (Augustus) (306-307)	Galerius (Augustus) (305-311)
Constantine I (Caesar) (306-308)	Maximin (Caesar and Augustus) (305-313)

Maxentius (in Italy) (306-312)

Constantine I (Augustus) (308-337)   Licinius (Augustus) (308-324)

Domitius Alexander (in Africa) (308-311)
Constantine I and Licinius (313-324)
Constantine I (324-337)

Constantine II (337-340)
Constans (340-350)   Constantius II (337-361)
Magnentius (350-353)
Julian Caesar (355-361)   Gallus Caesar (361-364)
Julian Augustus (360-363)

Julian (361-363)
Jovian (363-364)

Valentinian (364-375)   Valens (364-378)
Gratian (375-383)   Theodosius I (379-395)
Valentinian II (375-392)
Maximus (383-388)
Eugenius (392-394)

Theodosius I (394-395)

Honorius (394-423)   Arcadius (395-408)
(Stilicho regent) (395-408)

                                             Theodosius II (408-450)
Constantius III (421)
John (423-425)
Valentian III (425-455)
Petronius Maximus (455)   Marcian (450-457)
Avitus (455-456)
Majorian (457-461)   Leo I (457-474)
Libius Severus (461-465)
Anthemius (467-472)
Olybrius (472)
Glycerius (473)

Julius Nepos (473-475)
Romulus Augustulus (475-476)

Zeno (474-491)
Anastasius I (491-518)
Justin I (518-527)
Justinian I (527-565)
Justin II (565-578)
Tiberius II Constantine (578-582)
Maurice Tiberius (582-602)

BYZANTINE EMPERORS AND EMPRESSES

Justinian I (527-565)
Justin II (565-578)
        Tiberius, Caesar and regent (574-578)
Tiberius II Constantine (578-582)
Maurice Tiberius (582-602)
Phocas the Tyrant (602-610)
Heraclius (610-641)
Constantine III Heraclius (641)
Heraclonas (Heraclius) Constantine (641)
        Martina, regent
Constans II (Constantine) Heraclius the Bearded (641-668)
Constantine IV (668-685)
Justinian II the Slit-Nosed (685-695, 705-711)
Leontius (Leo) (695-698)
Tiberius III Apsimar (698-705)
Philippicus Bardanes (711-713)
Anastasius II Artemius (713-715)
Theodosius III (715-717)
Leo III the Isaurian (717-741)
Constantine V Name of Dung (741-775)
        Artavasdus, rival emperor at Constantinople (741-743)
Leo IV the Khazar (775-780)
Constantine VI the Blinded (780-797)
        Irene the Athenian, regent
Irene the Athenian (797-802)
Nicephorus I the General Logothete (802-811)
Stauracius (811)
Michael I Rhangabe (811-813)

Leo V the Armenian (813–820)
Michael II the Amorian (820–829)
Theophilus (829–842)
Michael III the Drunkard (842–867)
      Theodora, regent (842–856)
Basil I the Macedonian (867–886)
Leo VI the Wise (886–912)
Alexander (912–913)
Constantine VII Porphyrogenitus (913–959)
      Nicholas Mysticus, regent (913–914)
      Zoë Carbonopsina, regent (914–920)
      Romanus I Lecapenus, coemperor (920–944)
Romanus II Porphyrogenitus (959–963)
Basil II the Bulgar-Slayer (963–1025)
      Theophano, regent (963)
      Nicephorus II Phocas, coemperor (963–969)
      John I Tzimisces, coemperor (969–976)
Constantine VIII Porphyrogenitus (1025–1028)
Romanus III Argyrus (1028–1034)
Michael IV the Paphlagonian (1034–1041)
Michael V the Caulker (1041–1042)
Zoë Porphyrogenita (1042)
Constantine IX Monomachus (1042–1055)
Theodora Porphyrogenita (1055–1056)
Michael VI Bringas (1056–1057)
Isaac I Comnenus (1057–1059)
Constantine X Ducas (1059–1067)
Michael VII Ducas (1067–1078)
      Eudocia Macrembolitissa, regent (1067–1068)
      Romanus IV Diogenes, coemperor (1068–1071)
Nicephorus III Botantiates (1078–1081)
Alexius I Comnenus (1081–1118)
John II Comnenus (1118–1143)
Manuel I Comnenus (1143–1180)
Alexius II Comnenus (1180–1183)
      Andronicus Comnenus, regent (1182–1183)
Andronicus I Comnenus (1183–1185)
Isaac II Angelus (1185–1195)
Alexius III Angelus (1195–1203)
Isaac II Angelus (again) (1203–1204)

Alexius IV Angelus, coemperor
Alexius III Angelus, rival emperor
Alexius V Ducas Murtzuphlus (1204)
Alexius III Angelus, rival emperor
Alexius III Angelus (in Thrace) (1204)
Theodore I Lascaris (at Nicaea) (1205-1221)
John III Ducas Vatatzes (at Nicaea) (1221-1254)
Theodore Ducas, emperor at Thessalonica (1224-1230)
John Ducas, emperor at Thessalonica (1237-1242)
Theodore II Lascaris (at Nicaea) (1254-1258)
John IV Lascaris (at Nicaea) (1258-1261)
Michael VIII Palaeologus, coemperor at Nicaea (1259-1261)
Michael VIII Palaeologus (at Constantinople) (1261-1282)
Andronicus II Palaeologus (1282-1328)
Andronicus III Palaeologus, coemperor (1321-1328)
Andronicus III Palaeologus (1328-1341)
John V Palaeologus (1341-1376; 1379-1391)
Anna of Savoy, regent (1341-1347)
John VI Cantacuzenus, coemperor (1347-1354)
Andronicus IV Palaeologus (1376-1379)
Manuel II Palaeologus (1391-1425)
John VIII Palaeologus (1425-1448)
Constantine XI Palaeologus (1449-1453)

POPES AND ANTIPOPES TO 1500* (Antipopes in Italics)

Peter (?-c.64)
Linus (c.67-76/79)
Anacletus (76-88 or 79-91)
Clement I (88-97 or 92-101)
Evaristus (c.97-c.107)
Alexander I (105-115 or 109-119)
Sixtus I (c.115-c.125)
Telesphorus (c.125-c.136)
Hyginus (c.136-c.140)
Pius I (c.140-155)

Anicetus (c.155-c.166)
Soter (c.166-c.175)
Eleutherius (c.175-189)
Victor I (c.189-199)
Zephyrinus (c.199-217)
Calixtus I (Callistus) (217?-222)
Hippolytus (217, 218-235)
Urban I (222-230)
Pontian (230-235)
Anterus (235-236)

* Only since the ninth century has the title of "pope" come to be associated exclusively with the bishop of Rome.

Fabian (236-250)

Cornelius (251-253)

Novatian (251)

Lucius I (253-254)

Stephen I (254-257)

Sixtus II (257-258)

Dionysius (259-268)

Felix I (269-274)

Eutychian (275-283)

Galus (283-296)

Marcellinus (291/296-304)

Marcellus I (308-309)

Eusebius (309/310)

Miltiades (Melchiades) (311–314)

Sylvester I (314-335)

Mark (336)

Julius I (337-352)

Liberius (352-366)

Felix II (355-358)

Damasus I (366-384)

Ursinus (366-367)

Siricius (384-399)

Anastasius I (399-401)

Innocent I (401-417)

Zosimus (417-418)

Boniface I (418-422)

Eulalius (418-419)

Celestine I (422-432)

Sixtus III (432-440)

Leo I (440-461)

Hilary (461-468)

Simplicius (468-483)

Felix III (or II) (483-492)

Gelasius I (492-496)

Anastasius II (496-498)

Symmachus (498-514)

Laurentius (498, 501-c.505/507)

Hormisdas (514-523)

John I (523-526)

Felix IV (or III) (526-530)

Dioscorus (530)

Boniface II (530-532)

John II (533-535)

Agapetus I (535-536)

Silverius (536-537)

Vigilius (537-555)

Pelagius I (556-561)

John III (561-574)

Benedict I (575-579)

Pelagius II (579-590)

Gregory I (590-604)

Sabinian (604-606)

Boniface III (604)

Boniface IV (608-615)

Deusdedit (also called Adeodatus I) (615-618)

Boniface V (619-625)

Honorius I (625-638)

Severinus (640)

John IV (640-642)

Theodore I (642-649)

Martin I (649-655)

Eugenius I (654-657)

Vitalian (657-672)

Adeodatus II (672-676)

Donus (676-678)

Agatho (679-681)

Leo II (682-683)

Benedict II (684-685)

John V (685-686)

Conon (686-687)

Sergius I (687-701)

Theodore (687)

Paschal (687)

John VI (701-705)

John VII (705-707)

Sisinnius (708)

Constantine (708-715)

Gregory II (715-731)

Gregory III (731-741)

Zacharias (Zachary) (741–752)
Stephen II (752–757)
Paul I (757–767)
Constantine (II) (767–768)
Philip (768)
Stephen III (768–772)
Adrian I (772–795)
Leo III (795–816)
Stephen IV (816–817)
Paschal I (817–824)
Eugenius II (824–827)
Valentine (827)
Gregory IV (827–844)
John (844)
Sergius II (844–847)
Leo IV (847–855)
Benedict III (855–858)
Anastasius (Anastasius the Librarian) (855)
Nicholas I (858–867)
Adrian II (867–872)
John VIII (872–882)
Marinus I (882–884)
Adrian III (884–885)
Stephen V (885–891)
Formosus (891–896)
Boniface VI (896)
Stephen VI (896)
Romanus (897)
Theodore II (897)
John IX (898–900)
Benedict IV (900)
Leo V (903)
Christopher (903–904)
Sergius III (904–911)
Anastasius III (911–913)
Lando (913–914)
John X (914–928)
Leo VI (928)
Stephen VII (929–931)

John XI (931–935)
Leo VII (936–939)
Stephen VIII (939–942)
Marinus II (942–946)
Agapetus II (946–955)
John XII (955–964)
Leo VIII (963–965)
Benedict V (964–966?)
John XIII (965–972)
Benedict VI (973–974)
Boniface VII (1st time) (974)
Benedict VII (974–983)
John XIV (983–984)
Boniface VII (2nd time) (984–985)
John XV (or XVI) (985–996)
Gregory V (996–999)
John XVI (or XVII) (997–998)
Sylvester II (999–1003)
John XVII (or XVIII) (1003)
John XVIII (or XIX) (1004–1009)
Sergius IV (1009–1012)
Gregory (VI) (1012)
Benedict VIII (1012–1024)
John XIX (or XX) (1024–1032)
Benedict IX (1st time) (1032–1044)
Sylvester III (1045)
Benedict IX (2nd time) (1045)
Gregory VI (1045–1046)
Clement II (1046–1047)
Benedict IX (3rd time) (1047–1048)
Damasus II (1048)
Leo IX (1049–1054)
Victor II (1055–1057)
Stephen IX (1057–1058)
Benedict (X)(1058–1059)
Nicholas II (1059–1061)
Alexander II (1061–1073)
Honorius (II) (1061–1072)
Gregory VII (1073–1085)

Clement (III) (1080-1100)
Victor III (1086-1087)
Urban II (1088-1099)
Paschal II (1099-1118)
Theodoric (1100-1102)
Albert (also called Aleric) (1102)
Sylvester (IV) (1105-1111)
Gelasius II (1118-1119)
Gregory (VIII) (1118-1121)
Calixtus II (Callistus) (1119-1124)
Honorius II (1124-1130)
Celestine (II) (1124)
Innocent II (1130-1143)
Anacletus (II) (1130-1138)
Victor (IV) (1138)
Celestine II (1143-1144)
Lucius II (1144-1145)
Eugenius III (1145-1153)
Anastasius IV (1153-1154)
Adrian IV (1154-1159)
Alexander III (1159-1181)
Victor (IV) (1159-1164)
Paschal (III) (1164-1168)
Calixtus (III) (1168-1178)
Innocent (III) (1179-1180)
Lucius III (1181-1185)
Urban III (1185-1187)
Gregory VIII (1187)
Clement III (1187-1191)
Celestine III (1191-1198)
Innocent III (1198-1216)
Honorius III (1216-1227)
Gregory IX (1227-1241)
Celestine IV (1241)
Innocent IV (1243-1254)
Alexander IV (1254-1261)
Urban IV (1261-1264)
Clement IV (1265-1268)
Gregory X (1271-1276)
Innocent V (1276)

Adrian V (1276)
John XXI (1276-1277)
Nicholas III (1277-1280)
Martin IV (1281-1285)
Honorius IV (1285-1287)
Nicholas IV (1288-1292)
Celestine V (1294)
Boniface VIII (1294-1303)
Benedict IX (1303-1304)
Clement V (at Avignon, from 1309)
(1305-1314)
John XXII (at Avignon) (1316-1334)
Nicholas (V) (at Rome) (1328-1330)
Benedict XII (at Avignon) (1334-1342)
Clement VI (at Avignon) (1342-1352)
Innocent VI (at Avignon) (1352-1362)
Urban V (at Avignon) (1362-1370)
Gregory XI (at Avignon, then Rome
from 1377) (1370-1378)
Urban VI (1378-1389)
Clement (VII) (at Avignon) (1378-1394)
Boniface IX (1389-1404)
Benedict (XIII) (at Avignon) (1394-1423)
Innocent VII (1404-1406)
Gregory XII (1406-1415)
Alexander (V) (at Bologna) (1409-1410)
John (XXIII) (at Bologna) (1410-1415).
Martin V (1417-1431)
Clement (VIII) (1423-1429)
Eugenius IV (1431-1447)
Felix (V) (also called Amadeus VIII of
Savoy) (1439-1449)
Nicholas V (1447-1455)
Calixtus III (Callistus) (1455-1458)
Pius II (1458-1464)
Paul II (1464-1471)
Sixtus IV (1471-1484)
Innocent VIII (1484-1492)
Alexander VI (1492-1503)

ISLAMIC RULERS

Early Caliphs

Abu-Bakr (632-634)
Umar I (634-644)
Uthman (644-656)
Ali (656-661)

Umayyads

Mu`awiyah I (661-680)
Yazid I (680-683)
Mu`awiyah II (683-684)
Marwan I (684-685)
Abd al-Malik (685-705)
al-Walid I (705-715)
Sulayman (715-717)
Umar II (717-720)
Yazid II (720-724)
Hisham (724-743)
al-Walid II (743-744)
Yazid III (744)
Marwan II (744-750)

Abbasids★

al-Saffah (750-754)
al-Mansur (754-775)
al-Mahdi (775-785)
al-Hadi (785-786)
Harun al-Rashid (786-809)
al-Amin (809-813)
al-Ma`mun (813-833)
al-Mu`tasim (833-842)
al-Wathiq (842-847)
al-Mutawakkil (847-861)
al-Muntasir (861-862)
al-Musta`in (862-866)
al-Mu`tazz (866-869)
al-Muhtadi (869-870)
al-Mu`tamid (870-892)
al-Mu`tadid (892-902)
al-Muqtafi (902-908)
al-Muqtadir (908-932)
al-Qahir (932-934)
al-Radi (934-940)

★Abbasid caliphs continued until 1517.

OTTOMAN EMIRS AND SULTANS

Osman (1281-1326)
Orhan (1326-1362)
Murad I (1362-1389)
Bayezid I (1389-1402)
Sulayman (1402-1411)

Musa (1411-1413)
Mehmed I (1413-1421)
Murad II (1421-1451)
Mehmed II the Conqueror (1451-1481)
Bayezid II (1481-1512)

SOURCES

MAPS

1.4 Tours, *c.*600. Credit: Henri Galinié.

3.1 The Byzantine Empire, *c.*917. Credit: From Mark Whittow, *The Making of Orthodox Byzantium* 600-1025 (University of California Press, 1996), p.166, Copyright © 1996 Mark Whittow. Reprinted by permission of the University of California Press.

4.1 Constantinople before *c.*1100. Credit: From Linda Safran, ed., *Heaven on Earth: Art and the Church in Byzantium* (University Park, PA: The Pennsylvania State University Press, 1998), figs 1.7, 1.9.

5.1 Byzantium and the Islamic World, *c.*1090. Credit: From Christophe Picard, *Le monde musulman du XIe au XVe siècle* © SEDES / HER, 2000. Reprinted by permission of Éditions SEDES, Paris.

7.4 The Walls of Bruges, Ninth to Fourteenth Centuries. Credit: From Großer Historischer Weltatlas, p. 2: Mittelalter (2nd ed.) © Munich, Bayerischer Schulbuch Verlag 1979, p. 83, map n.

7.5 The Village of Toury. Credit: Samuel Leturcq.

7.6 The Lands of Toury, Fourteenth and Fifteenth Centuries. Credit: Samuel Leturcq.

PLATES

1.1 Landscape from Pompeii (A.D.*c.*79). Credit: Museo Archaeologico Nazionale di Napoli.

1.2 Theseus the Minotaur Slayer, Pompeii (A.D.*c.*79). Credit: Museo Archaeologico Nazionale di Napoli.

1.3 Trajan's Column, detail (A.D.113). Credit: Scala / Art Resource, NY.

1.4 Head from Palmyra (A.D.1-50). Credit: Studio Zouhabi, Palmira-Syria.

1.5 Decorated Coffer from Jerusalem (1st cent.?). Credit: © Copyright The British Museum.

1.6 Tombstone from near Carthage (2nd cent.?). Credit: © Copyright The British Museum.

1.7 Base of the Hippodrome Obelisk (*c.*390). Credit: Hirmer Fotoarchiv.

1.8 Ivory Pyx (5th cent.). Credit: Hirmer Fotoarchiv.

1.9 Mosaic from San Vitale, Ravenna (c.540-548). Credit: Archivi Alinari Firenze.

1.10 *Icon of the Virgin*. Egypt, Byzantine period, 6th century. Slit and dove tailed-tapestry weave; wool, 178 x 110 cm. Credit: © The Cleveland Museum of Art, 203. Leonard C. Hanna, Jr., Bequest, 1967.144.

2.1 The Embolos, Ephesus. From Clive Foss, *Ephesus After Antiquity* (Cambridge University Press, 1979), p.66, fig. 20. Credit: Reprinted with the permission of Cambridge University Press and Clive Foss.

2.2 The Great Mosque at Damascus (8th cent.). From the Clive Foss Architectural Photographs Collection at Cambridge. Credit: Reprinted with the permission of Clive Foss.

2.3 Belt Buckle from Sutton Hoo (early 7th cent.). Credit: © Copyright The British Museum.

2.4 Saint Luke, Lindisfarne Gospels (late 7th cent.), Cott.Nero.D.IV., fol. 137v. Credit: By permission of the British Library.

2.5 Carpet Page, Lindisfarne Gospels (late 7th cent.), Cott.Nero.D.IV., fol. 138v. Credit: By permission of the British Library.

2.6 First Text Page, Gospel of Saint Luke, Lindisfarne Gospels (late 7th cent.), Cott.Nero.D.IV., fol. 139. Credit: By permission of the British Library.

2.7 Franks Casket (1st half of 8th cent.). Credit: © Copyright The British Museum.

3.1 Byzantine Book Cover (886-912), cod.Marc.Lat I, 101 (2260). Credit: © Biblioteca Nazionale Marciana.

3.2 Ezechiel in the Valley of Dry Bones, Homilies of Gregory Nazianzen (880-886), MS Graeca 510, fol. 438v. Credit: Cliché Bibliothèque nationale de France, Paris.

3.3 Mesopotamian, Samarra, Bowl, 9th Century, Abbasid Period, Earthenware, lustred. H. 2⅜ in. Diam. 9¾ in. Credit: The Metropolitan Museum of Art, H.O. Havemeyer Collection, Gift of Horace Havemeyer, 1941. (41.165.1) Photograph © 1985 The Metropolitan Museum of Art.

3.4 Córdoba, Great Mosque (late 10th cent.). Credit: Alinari / Art Resource, NY.

3.5 Sacramentary of Saint-Germain-des-Prés (early 9th cent.), MS lat. 2291, fol. 14v. Credit: Cliché Bibliothèque nationale de France, Paris.

3.6 Saint Mark, Soissons Gospels (800-810), MS lat. 8850, fol. 81v. Credit: Cliché Bibliothèque nationale de France, Paris.

3.7 First Text Page, Soissons Gospels (800-810), MS lat. 8850, fol. 82r. Credit: Cliché Bibliothèque nationale de France, Paris.

3.8 Saint Mark, Coronation Gospels (c.800). Credit: Kröngungsevangeliar Fol. 76v, Kunsthistorisches Museum, Wien oder KHM, Wien.

3.9 Utrecht Psalter (c.820-835). Credit: University Library Utrecht, Ms. 32, fol. 4v, Universiteitsbibliotheek Utrecht.

4.1 Christ and the Centurion, Egbert Codex (977-993). Credit: Codex Egberti, Stadtbibliothek Trier MS 24, fol. 22.

4.2 Christ Asleep in the Seastorm, Hitda Gospels (c.1000-1020), MS 1640, fol. 117r. Credit: Hessische Landes- und Hochschulbibliothek Darmstadt.

4.3 Saint Luke, Gospel Book of Otto III (998-1001), Clm 4453, fol. 139v. Credit: Bayerische Staatsbibliothek München.

5.1 View of the Façade, San Miniato Cathedral. Credit: La Scala / Art Resource, NY.

5.2 Bowl, North Africa, late 12th cent. Credit: Musei Nazionali di Pisa.

5.3 Gloria with Musical Notation, Saint-Evroult (12th cent.), Latin 10097, fol. 32v. Credit: Cliché Bibliothèque nationale de France, Paris © BnF.

5.4 A Mode of the Chant, Cluny (1088-1095). Credit: Musée d'art et d'archéologie de Cluny.

5.5 Suicide of Judas, Autun (1125-1135). Credit: Chanoine Denis Grivot, Maître de Chapelle Honoraire de la Cathédrale Conservateur Honoraire des Antiquités et Objets d'Art de Saône-et-Loire, Autun.

5.6 Durham Cathedral (1093-1133), Interior, Nave Looking East. Credit: Anthony Scibilia / Art Resource, NY.

5.7 Martydom of Saint Lawrence. Chapel of the Monks. Early 12th cent. Chapelles des Moines, Berzé-la-Ville, France. Credit: Bridgeman-Giraudon / Art Resource, NY.

5.8 Leaning Tower (Bell Tower) of Pisa (late 12th cent.). Credit: Alinari / Art Resource, NY.

5.9 Santiago de Compostela (1078-1124), Interior. Credit: Instituto Amatller De Arte Hispánico / Institut Amatller D'Art Hispànic.

5.8 Fontenay Abbey Church (1139-1147), Interior, Nave looking East. Credit: Anthony Scibilia / Art Resource, NY.

6.1 Reliquary Casket for Charlemagne's Arm (1166-1170). Credit: Musée du Louvre / Art Resource, NY.

6.2 Notre Dame of Paris (begun 1163), Exterior. Credit: Erich Lessing / Art Resource, NY.

FIGURES

0 7141 0555 4, © Trustees of the British Museum.

5.1 Hypothetical Plan of the Monastery of Cluny (1157). Credit: From Kenneth John Conant, *The Pelican History of Art: Carolingian and Romanesque Architecture 800-1200* (New Haven, CT: Yale University Press, 1974), fig. 5-1. Reprinted by permission of Yale University Press.

5.2 A Model Romanesque Church. Plan of the church of Santiago de Compostela. Credit: From John Beckwith, *Early Medieval Art* (New York: Thames & Hudson, 1964), p.163 ill.155. Reprinted by permission of Thames & Hudson Ltd.

5.3 Schematic Plan of a Cistercian Monastery. *Making of the West.* Lynn Hunt et al. Bedford / St. Martin's, 2001. Adapted from Wolfgang Braunfels *Monasteries of Western Europe*. Princeton, NJ: Princeton University Press, 1972, p.75. Credit: © Dumont Buchverlag GmbH.

7.1 Single Notes and Values of Franconian Notation. Credit: From *Anthology of Medieval Music*, edited by Richard Hoppin. Copyright © 1978. W.W. Norton & Company, Inc.

INDEX

Italicized page numbers refer to Plates

Aachen, 114

Abbasids, 95, 102-6, 118, 138-40, 142

abbess,
    definition of, 48

abbot,
    definition of, 48

Abd al-Rahman I, emir (r.756-788), 108, 110

Abd al-Rahman III, caliph (r.912-961), 108, 140

Abelard, Peter (1079-1142), 191

Abu-Bakr, caliph (r.632-634), 72

Der Ackermann aus Böhmen (c.1462), 288, *289*

Acre, 253

adab literature, 108, 141

Adela, sister of Henry I of England, 212

Adrian IV, pope (1154-1159), 218

Adrianople, battle of (378), 42

Africa, 318-19. *See also* North Africa

agriculture, 76-77, 119, 168. *See also* economy;
        pastoralism
    Byzantine, 65
    Iraq, 139
    12th century, 223-24
    three-field system, 118, 148, 171
    Toury, lands at, 148, 279

aids, 185, 215
    definition of, 324

Alans (barbarian group), 42

Alaric II (r.484-507), 44

Alaric (Visigoth leader), 42

Alba. See Scotland

Albertus Magnus (c.1200-1280), 269

Albigensian crusade (1209-1229), 243

Albigensians, 241, 243

Alcuin (c.732-804), 113, 121

Alexander II, pope (1061-1073), 179, 187

Alexander III, pope (1159-1181), 220

Alexander tapestry, 312

Alexandria, 69

Alexius I Comnenus (r.1081-1118), 170, 183

Alfonso II (r.791-842), 110

Alfonso IX, king (r.1188-1230), 262

Alfonso VI, king (Léon-Castle) (r.1065-1109), 186

Alfonso X, king (r.1252-1284), 187, 262

Alfred the Great, king (r.871-899), 144, 152-54

Ali, caliph (r.656-661), 72, 142

Almohads, 169, 207-8, 243

Almoravids, 169, 182, 186, 208

Alp Arslan, sultan (r.1063-1072), 168-69

alphabets, 98

Ambrose, Saint (339-397), 29-30

Americas, 255, 319-20, 323

Anagni, 266

Anatolia, 40, 65, 97, 135, 168-70, 182, 209, 291-92

al-Andalus, 90, 108-10, 113, 139-40, 169, 179, 186,
        208, 228

Angevin England, 212-16, 295
    genealogy, 213

Angevin Italy, 221-22

Anglo-Saxon culture, 87, 89
    influence on continent, 112, 126

Anglo-Saxon England, 43, 76-77, 81-82, 152-56

Anglo-Saxon vernacular, 87, 152

Anjou, 213, 216, 221

Anno, bishop, 182

anointment, 90, 112, 155, 161

Anselm of Bec, Saint (1033-1109), 186, 191, 204,
        308
    Monologion, 191

Anthony, Saint (250-356), 28-29, 48

antiking
    definition of, 324

Antioch, 69, 134-35
    principality of, 183, 208

antipope
    definition of, 324

apprenticeships (guild), 228

Apulia, 220

Aquinas, Thomas, Saint (1225-1274), 267-70, 308

Aquitaine, 78, 213, 224

Arabia, 66, 105, 139

Arabian Peninsula, 140

Arabic, 59, 75, 142, 192, 228

Arabic numerals, 106

Arabs, 62, 72, 90, 98, 103. *See also* Bedouins;
    Islamic world
Aragon, 221, 306. *See also* Catalonia
Aragon-Catalonia
    kingdom of, 243 (*See also* Spain)
Arena Chapel. *See under* Padua
Arians, 27, 43-44. *See also* Arius; Christianity
aristocrats, 48, 80-81, 83, 113, 118, 150, 223, 226,
    299-300. *See also* courts (political)
    dynatoi, 135-36, 161, 170, 209
    Frankish, 112
    German, 180-81
    lords, 48, 76-77, 118, 147-50
    Norman, 216
Aristotle, 106, 141, 192, 269-70
arithmetic (liberal art), 191
Arius (250-336), 26-27. *See also* Arians
Armenia, 27, 97, 135, 168, 170
armour. *See* weaponry
army
    al-Andalus, 108
    al-khurs, 108
    al-Rahman's, 140
    Alfred's, 144
    Anglo-Saxon (Edgar's), 155
    Byzantine, 60, 96, 135, 170, 212
    Carolingian, 113
    crusade, 182-83, 243, 245
    French standing, 296
    Islamic, 103, 105, 138
    Janissaries, 292
    Mongol, 252
    Ottonian, 156
    Roman empire, 22-23, 41
    Seljuk, 168
    strategoi, 60-61, 66, 97
    themes, 61, 96-98, 135
Arnulf, king of the East Franks (877-899), 146
art. *See entries for individual artists, styles and works;*
    intellectual culture; renaissance
Art of Measurable Song, 271
Arthur, king (literature), 227, 270
Assize of Clarendon (1166), 214
astronomy (liberal art), 191
Athanasius, Saint (*c.*295-373), 26-27, 29, 110
Atlantic Ocean, 143, 255, 257, 318, 320
Atsiz ibn Uwaq, 169

Attila (*d.*453), 42
Augustine, missionary to England, 82
Augustine, Saint (354-430), 26-28, 91, 152, 269
Austria, 78, 221
    Cistercians in, 199
Autun, *196*
    sculpture, 194
Avars, 61, 113
Avicenna. *See* Ibn Sina (980-1037)
Avignon, 266, 304

bacini (bowls), 175
Badr, battle of (624), 69
Baghdad, 104-5, 140, 142, 252
baillis, 218, 264
Baldwin II, king (Jerusalem), 184
Balkans, 40, 61, 96, 98, 170, 292. *See also* Bulgaria;
    entries for individual Balkan states; Pech-
    enegs
Balthild, queen (*d.*680), 78, 80
Baltic Sea region, 244, 257, 303
Bamburg, 284
ban (*bannum*), 113, 149, 157
barbarians, 19, 22, 39-43. *See also* Germans; *indi-*
    vidual barbarian tribes
    law, 52
Barbastro battle of, 179, 187
Barcelona, 151
barons, English, 185-86, 213, 215-16, 263
Basil I (*r.*867-886), 102
Basil II, emp. (*r.*963-1025), 133-36, 161
Basil the Nothos, 133
Bavaria, 263, 284. *See also* Germany
Bayezid I (*r.*1389-1402), 292
Becket, Thomas (1118-1170), 215
Bede (673?-735), 82
Bedford, duke of, 296, 317
Bedouins, 66. *See also* Arabs
beggars. *See* poverty
Beghards, 241
Beguines, 240-41, 296. *See also* laity, piety of
bellatores, 147. *See also* knights; vassals
Bellini, Gentile (*c.*1429-1507), 312
    "Portrait of Mehmed II," *313*
Benedict, Saint (*d.*547), 48
    Rule of, 48-49, 112, 115, 192, 200, 203, 241
Benedict of Aniane, 115

doctrines of, 26, 242, 268
Eucharist in, 28, 52, 239-40, 242, 267
missionaries of, 81-82, 98, 101, 112-13, 253
transubstantiation in, 267
Christine de Pisan (1364-*c*.1430), 296
church
definition of, 324
church courts, 215, 229
Church Fathers, 26, 91, 101, 181
church reform. *See* Gregorian Reform
churches, 102, 110, 118
as centers of town growth, 172
churches (national), 305-6
Cicero, 160
Pro Archia, 308
Cid, 186
Cináed mac Ailpín (Kenneth I MacAlpin)
(*d*.858), 143
ciompi rebellion, 303
Cistercians, 199-200, 203, 205, 244
cities, 19, 76, 91, 114, 168, 204, 262, 269. *See also*
communes
crisis of in late Middle Ages, 279, 283
decline of ancient, 44, 62-65
development of Western, 151, 257-58
Franciscans in, 240
growth of, 171-75
Islamic, 72, 104
City of God (Augustine), 27-28
city-states (Italian), 218, 220, 222
Clairvaux, 199
Clare, disciple of Francis, 240
clergy
definition of, 25
cleric
definition of, 324
clerical marriage, 45, 66, 91, 177, 181. *See also*
Gregorian Reform
Clericis Laicos (1296), 265
Clermont, 182
Clito, William, 176
Clovis, king (*r*.481-511), 43, 78. *See also* Merovin-
gians
Frankish law code, 44
Clovis II, king (639-657), 78
Cluny, monastery of, 177, 192, *193*, 194
Abbot Majolus of, 146

"Mode of the Chant" at, 194, *195*
Cnut (Canute) king (*r*.1017-1035), 155-56
Codex Justinianus (529), 52
coinage, 77, 91, 221
debasement, 22
gold, 77, 257
silver, 77
Ummayad, 75
Collection in 74 Titles (canon lawbook), 179
collegiate church
definition of, 324
Cologne, 160, 182
colonialism (European), 320
Columbanus, Saint (543-615), 80
Columbus, Christopher (1451-1506), 320
Commedia (*Divine Commedy*) (Dante), 270
commenda, 176
commerce. *See* economy
commercial economy, 199
commercial revolution, 171-76
common law (English). *See under* law
commons (in parliament), 264
communes, 176, 181, 204, 218, 220-21, 259, 299.
See also cities
relations with guilds, 228
Comnenus dynasty, 209
Alexius I Comnenus (*r*.1081-1118), 170, 183
compagnia, 176
La Comtessa de Dia (*fl.c*.1200?), 225
Concordance of Discordant Canons (Gratian), 181
Concordat of Worms (1122), 180-81
condottieri, 304
conquistadores, 320, 323
Conrad III (*r*.1138-1152), 218
Consolation of Philosophy (Boethius), 44
Constance of Sicily (wife of Henry VI), 220
Constance of Sicily (wife of Peter of Aragon), 221
Constantine-Cyril, 101
Constantine I, emp. (*r*.306-337), 23, 26
Constantine IX, emp. (*r*.1042-1055), 133
Constantine IX Monomachos, emp. (*r*.1042-
1055), 170
Constantine (later called Cyril), 98
Constantine V, emp. (*r*.741-775), 96
Constantinople, 22, 26, 59-61, 64, 91, 96, 101-2,
245, 254
Black Death at, 288

elections, 177
Estates General, 265, 302
Estonia, 245
Ethelbert, king (*d.*616), 82
ethnogenesis, 40
Eton, 314
Eucharist, 28, 52, 239-40, 242, 267. *See also* Corpus Christi; Mass; transubstantiation
Euclid, 106
Eulogius, 110
eunuchs, 133
Evrarde de Fouilloi
    effigy (tomb), *267*
exchequer, 215
    of the Jews, 242
excommunication, 180, 221, 304
    definition of, 325
eyres, 214
"Ezechiel in the Valley of Dry Bones," *100*, 101-2

fairs, 175, 182, 257. *See also* trade (long distance)
family feuds, 115
family structure (or relations), 116, 142, 178. *See also* marriage
    Byzantine, 65
    inheritance practices, 149, 156
    nuclear, 68
    patrilineal, 177
    Vikings, 143
Farmers' Law, 65
Fatimah, 68, 140
Fatimids, 139-42, 169
fealty, 148, 151, 161
Fedele, Cassandra (1465-1558), 307
    "Oration," 308
federates, 41
Ferdinand, king (Spain) (*r.*1479-1516), 306, 320
Fernando I, king, 187
feudalism, 147-49. *See also* fiefs; lords; peasants; vassals
fideles, 113
fiefs, 147, 183, 185
fighting man or warrior
    in art, 150
Fiqh, 108
Firdawsi (*c.*935-*c.*1020), 141
flagellants, 290

Flagellation
    definition of, 325
"Flagellation" (Ghiberti), *310*, 311
Flanders, 186, 217, 223, 228, 258-59, 295, 302
    peasants' revolt in, 300
Florence, 228, 257, 304, 309, 311
    Black Death at, 288
    ciompi rebellion at, 303
    famines in, 283
    sumptuary legislation of, 290
flying butresses, 231
Fontenay Abbey, 200, *202*, 203
Foundling Hospital (Brunelleschi), 309, 311
Four Doctors, 192, 220
Fourth Lateran Council (1215), 239-40, 242-43
France, 115, 161, 179, 188-89, 216-18, 226, 258, 264-66, 268, 279. *See also* Francia; Gaul; Ile-de-France; Languedoc
    Beguines in, 241
    Black Death in, 288
    Capetian kings of, 188-89, 243
    Cistercians in, 199
    communes in, 176
    expulsion of Jews from, 260
    Franciscans in, 240
    heretics in, 241-42
    Hundred Years' War in, 287, 292-98
    Hungarian raids into, 146
    Jews in, 242-43, 290
    Muslim raiders of, 144
    popular revolts in, 300
    royal leadership of church in, 306
    Valois kings of, 295
    Vikings in, 143
Francia, 75-76, 78, 80-81, 95, 111
    allies with pope, 112
Francis, Saint (*c.*1182-1226), 240-41, 266
Franciscans, 240, 253, 266, 268
    Order of the Sisters of Saint Francis, 240
    tertiaries, 241
Franco of Cologne, 271-72
    Art of Measurable Song, 271
Frankish law code, 44
Frankish/papal alliance, 92
Franks, 39, 41, 43, 92. *See also* Carolingians; Francia; Merovingians
"Franks Casket," 87, *88-89*

Iceland, 143
iconoclasm, 65-66, 72, 92, 96, 101
iconography, 309
    definition of, 30
Ifriqiya, 104
Ile-de-France, 188, 216, 242
    expulsion of Jews from, 260
Iliad (Homer), 314
illumination, 101, 124
    definition of, 326
    God's, 269
    manuscript, 83, 126
    stained glass as, 230
illuminators, 273, 276
imam, 72, 103-4, 140
India, 105-6, 142, 254, 319
indulgences, 305
infanticide, 68
inheritance practices, 149, 156, 239. *See also* family
        structure; marriage (customs and laws)
Innocent III, pope (1198-1216), 243, 245
inquisition, 261, 307
Institutes (534), 52
Institutes of Christian Culture (Cassiodorus), 44
intellectual culture, 95. *See also* humanism; music;
        scholasticism
    at al-Andalus, 108-10
    Anglo-Saxon, 83, 87
    Bedouin storytelling as, 67
    in British Isles, 83-87
    Byzantine, 65, 98, 101, 133
    Carolingian, 114, 119-28
    in courts, 224-28
    English, 186
    in European schools and universities, 190-92,
        268-69, 307
    Islamic, 75, 105-8, 141, 169
    in Macedonian Renaissance, 101
    military ethos and, 150
    Ottoman, 312-13
    Ottonian, 157, 160
    in poetry, 108, 124, 224-28
    Renaissance, 308-11
    in Roman empire, 30-39
interiority, 317
Investiture Conflict, 156-57, 179-81

iqta', 209
Iran, 140, 167
    agriculture, 168
Iraq, 103-5, 139. *See also* Baghdad; Samarra
Ireland, 81, 152, 214
    conquest by England, 245-46
    Vikings in, 143
Irene, empress, 96, 113
Irish monasticism, 81
Isabella, queen (England), 295
Isabella, queen (Spain) (*r.* 1474-1504), 306, 320
Islam, 68, 138
    conversion of Mongols to, 253
    five pillars of, 69
    Hijra, 68-69
    origins of, 66
    Qur'an, 68-69, 75, 169
    ummah, 68-69
Islamic empire. *See* Ottoman empire
Islamic world, 72, 75, 95, 102-10, 138-41, 169, 182,
        207-9, 252
Istanbul, 312
Italy, 42, 76, 151, 226, 259, 269, 273, 303
    Albigensians in, 241
    Angevin, 221-22
    Byzantines in, 75
    Carolingians in, 113
    Cistercians in, 199
    city-states of, 218, 220, 222
    communes in, 176, 181, 218, 228
    Frederick I in, 219-20
    heretics in, 242
    Hungarian raids into, 146
    Jews in, 260
    Justinian's conquest of, 52
    Lombards in, 75, 90-91
    Muslim raids into, 146
    Ostrogoths in, 43, 52
    sumptuary legislation in, 290

Jacob van Artevelde, 300, 302
Jacquerie, 302
James, Saint. *See* Santiago (Saint James) de Com-
        postela
Janissaries, 292
Jarrow, 83